Additional praise for
Flagrant Conduct: The Story of Lawrence v. Texas

"*Flagrant Conduct* is a real-life detective story that reveals the drama behind the scenes of a great Supreme Court victory for human rights. It upends much of what I thought I knew about the case that became *Lawrence v. Texas*. Dale Carpenter shows us that lawyers with guts, resolve, and a bit of good luck don't necessarily need a perfect case—or a perfect client."   —Linda Greenhouse, Yale Law School,
author of *Becoming Justice Blackmun*

"A beautifully told classic Supreme Court drama that reminded me of *Gideon's Trumpet*. The decision changed for the better the rules under which human beings relate."   —William S. McFeely,
author of *Proximity to Death*

"*Flagrant Conduct* is such an important statement on gay rights. But it is much more about human rights, and it reminds us we need to think, act, and live with open minds and caring souls."   —Billie Jean King,
sports icon and social justice pioneer

Flagrant Conduct

W. W. NORTON & COMPANY

NEW YORK LONDON

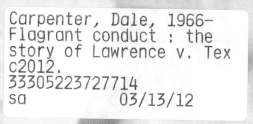

Flagrant Conduct

THE STORY OF *LAWRENCE V. TEXAS*

How a Bedroom Arrest
Decriminalized Gay Americans

DALE CARPENTER

FRONTISPIECE: June 26, 2003: Tyrone Garner (left) and John Lawrence get a hug from Houston resident Michelle Rinehart (center) after a rally at Houston City Hall celebrating the United States Supreme Court decision declaring the Texas sodomy law unconstitutional. At right is Lambda Legal attorney Brian Chase. (© Erich Schlegel / Dallas Morning News / Corbis)

FIRST EDITION

For information about permission to reproduce selections from this book, write to Permissions, W. W. Norton & Company, Inc., 500 Fifth Avenue, New York, NY 10110

For information about special discounts for bulk purchases, please contact W. W. Norton Special Sales at specialsales@wwnorton.com or 800-233-4830

Manufacturing by Courier Westford
Book design by Barbara M. Bachman
Production manager: Devon Zahn

LIBRARY OF CONGRESS
CATALOGING-IN-PUBLICATION DATA

Carpenter, Dale, 1966–
Flagrant conduct : the story of Lawrence v. Texas : how a bedroom arrest decriminalized gay Americans / Dale Carpenter. — 1st ed.
p. cm.
Includes bibliographical references and index.
ISBN 978-0-393-06208-3 (hardcover)
1. Lawrence, John Geddes—Trials, litigation, etc. 2. Texas—Trials, litigation, etc. 3. Trials (Sodomy)—Texas. 4. Homosexuality—Law and legislation—Texas—Criminal provisions. 5. Gays—Legal status, laws, etc.—United States. I. Title.
KF224.L39C37 2012
342.7308'7—dc23
2011047245

W. W. Norton & Company, Inc.,
500 Fifth Avenue, New York, N.Y. 10110
www.wwnorton.com

W. W. Norton & Company Ltd., Castle House,
75/76 Wells Street, London W1T 3QT

1 2 3 4 5 6 7 8 9 0

For my family,
all of it

"YOU DON'T HAVE ANY RIGHT TO BE HERE."[1]

Contents

Introduction

NO ONE COULD HAVE PREDICTED THAT THE NIGHT OF SEPTEMBER 17, 1998, would be anything but routine in Houston, the city of skyscrapers and strip malls and bayous sprawling across the southeastern corner of Texas. A languid, petroleum-sweet air, typical for late summer, hung over the city's east side. Certainly nobody expected that an arrest that night of two gay men for a minor criminal offense would reverberate in American constitutional law, challenging not only the traditional understanding of what makes a family but also the proper role of government in maintaining that understanding. Nobody foresaw the cultural storm that would gather from the events that transpired in a modest second-floor apartment. Nor could anyone have foreseen how a single arrest might expose the deep malignity in a law that was superficially directed at certain conduct, but that in practice was used to brand an entire group of people as strangers to moral tradition.

Even a call to the police that someone was "going crazy with a gun" in an apartment complex known for late-night shenanigans, while dramatic, was hardly out of the ordinary. When Harris County sheriff's deputies arrived minutes later, they did not find a crazed gunman, but they did report that they caught John Lawrence and Tyron Garner *in flagrante delicto* having anal sex inside Lawrence's bedroom. While that act would hardly have been shocking sexual conduct for gay men, it was extraordinary for police officers actually to witness it in the privacy of a home. And the act was still considered extraordinary—criminal, "deviate" sexual activity—under Texas's Homosexual Conduct law.[1] The deputies hauled the offending men to jail for the night. Gay-rights lawyers took their case, *Lawrence v. Texas*,[2] to the Supreme Court, which struck down the Texas sodomy law[3] and similar laws in twelve other states. More than that, though, the Court delivered a potentially lethal blow to the constitutional legitimacy of homosexuals' second-class status, including their exclusion from marriage.

However, that is getting ahead of the story, which opens a door into not only a bedroom but what already may seem like a buried past. The bare-bones version of *Lawrence* told in arid (some would say airy) judicial opinions is in almost every important respect incomplete and questionable. It flattens a complex web of emotions, motivations, and deceptions. It omits the accidents and serendipity without which the case would have been lost to history. It neglects the civil disobedience, heroism, and deep prejudices that animated those involved at every level of the case. It ignores the presence of gender, race, age, and class pulsing in the background.[4] It naïvely accepts the word of law enforcement authorities who harshly, and perhaps deceitfully, enforced a law that remained on the criminal statute books like an unused whip. It neglects the role the closet played in bringing the arrest of Lawrence and Garner to light, given the fortuitous presence of a closeted sheriff's sergeant and his partner, who was himself a closeted clerk for the judge in whose jurisdiction the arrest happened to occur. It disregards the bartender *cum* activist who had already come out as gay, recognized the moment, seized it, and helped broaden the sweep of civil rights history.

The pancaked conventional tale remains—years after the landmark Supreme Court decision in *Lawrence v. Texas*—a stubborn myth. This book attempts to correct and enrich our understanding of the case, by ferreting out what happened that September night in Houston and by explaining the way gay civil rights lawyers rewrote a snarled human story as part of a pristine legal argument acceptable to a basically conservative Supreme Court.

Based on my research, including interviews with most of the important participants in the events and their immediate aftermath, I come to a surprising, but only probabilistic, conclusion: it is unlikely that sheriff's deputies actually witnessed Lawrence and Garner having sex. As we shall see, John Lawrence himself now flatly denies that Garner and he were having sex. Even assuming they were having sex when sheriff's deputies entered Lawrence's apartment, they had probably disengaged by the time the deputies saw the men. If the police did not observe any sex, the whole case is built on law enforcement misconduct that makes it an even more egregious abuse of liberty than the Supreme Court knew.

Flagrant Conduct proceeds chronologically through three main parts. Part I ("Before the Arrests") examines the historical context for the arrests, including a discussion of the background of each of the major participants. Part II ("The Arrests") revisits the night of the arrests, presenting the versions offered by the police and by the defendants and addressing claims of a conspiracy or setup to challenge the state sodomy law. Part III ("After the Arrests") looks at what happened after the arrests, as the case went from a simple charge of petty crime to the highest court in the land. It also affirms that the case had broad national implications that have continued to richochet well beyond the state lines of Texas.

The book then concludes with a description of the historic scene as Justice Anthony Kennedy announced the Court's decision to a courtroom packed with people who had devoted much of their lives to ending discrimination against gay men and lesbians. It tells of the spontaneous joy that then erupted from one coast to the other on the eve of what happened to be gay-pride weekend in June 2003.

In the course of telling the story of *Lawrence v. Texas*, the book exposes both the peculiar corrupting quality of laws that target a class of persons for moral opprobrium and the distance such laws place between the targeted class and the rule of law. If John Lawrence and Tyron Garner were indeed arrested based on a fabrication by sheriff's deputies, their arrests are redolent with the long and noxious history of a bad law maliciously enforced. But even the uncontested facts of the case—including the discretionary decisions to cite the men and to send them to jail for the legal equivalent of a speeding ticket—expose how police power can be used capriciously and invidiously against the class targeted by such a law. Under such conditions, police could, and often did, misuse their authority to make arrests based on nothing more than the personal revulsion they felt at seeing things that disgusted them. Or they could, and did, misuse their authority whenever it was challenged by a person whose very existence disgusted them.[5]

If anyone set up the events that led to *Lawrence*, as some have claimed, it was surely not gay activists. It was inadvertently the authorities who arrested the men. Since sodomy laws, like the one in Texas, were never really about stopping sodomy, it is fitting that they got their comeuppance in a case in which there was probably no sodomy. A law rarely enforced was upended in a case of phantom enforcement. The laws that encouraged gays to lie about their identity were buried in an avalanche of untruths and half-truths triggered by the authorities enforcing them. Sodomy laws were ultimately the victim of overzealous police who had been taught their antigay zealotry in part by sodomy laws themselves.

There was plenty of flagrant conduct in *Lawrence v. Texas*. But this epithet, so often directed at gays and lesbians, does not describe the behavior of Garner and Lawrence on the night they were arrested, even if the police really did intrude upon them *in flagrante*. The flagrant conduct in the case was, in the first instance, the behavior of the police themselves, from the moment they handcuffed the two men to the moment they dragged John Lawrence out of his own apartment. The flagrant conduct was the use of precious prosecutorial time and money to pursue two men for sex in a private home rather than to pursue truly public and genuinely harmful acts. The flagrant conduct was the cowardice of elected state court judges who refused even to listen to the men's legal claims, shifted responsibility to other courts, and likely capitulated to political pressure. The flagrant conduct was the blatant effort by a political party to make judges enforce their policy preferences. The flagrant conduct was the passage of a law selectively burdening one small group of people on the pretext of preserving a moral heritage applicable to all. And the flagrant conduct was the refusal of those stalwart legislators, year after year, session after legislative session, decade after decade, to repeal that law, even when it became obvious that it served no public purpose other than to justify discrimination and to dignify animus in every realm against a tiny minority.

Sodomy laws taught lessons—well learned in Houston—to both homosexuals and heterosexuals. Generations of homosexuals learned silence and shame. Heterosexuals learned privilege and power. The laws conditioned gay men and lesbians to pay their fines and meekly move on. The same laws taught officers of the Harris County Sheriff's Office to write whatever they wanted on an arrest report about flagrant homosexuals without fear of contradiction or repercussion.

By 1998, gay men and lesbians, even those living in the bayous of life, had begun to bridle that silence and shame. Twenty-nine years after the eruption by gays against police abuse at the Stonewall Inn in Greenwich Village, they were no longer following the old script. Silence had yielded to organization; shame, to resistance.

Lawrence v. Texas is connected umbilically to a storied gay past, in all of its legal, sexual, socioeconomic, racial, and gendered complexity. The case was conceived in bars, cloaked in closetedness, nourished by political liberation, and fired by encounters with police repression and corruption. It was born into a rebellion against discrimination and stigma. In *Lawrence*, we have the closet as metaphor and the closet as reality, with its uses both as shield and sword against oppression. We have as well the related metaphor of coming out, including its essential personal and political dimensions, its fear, and its power. We have the bar as a site for political organizing, just as it was in the early days of the gay civil rights movement. We have the law, deformed by ignorance, pressing itself into the lives of marginalized people. We have resistance, generated not by abstractions but by experience. Here, in one case, we have a microcosm of the fight for equality under a regime of inequality. *Lawrence* challenged not only the American legal order but ultimately the cultural assumptions that undergirded it.

Part One

...

BEFORE THE
ARRESTS

I.

A Crime of Deep Malignity

WHEN POLICE ENTERED THE HOME OF JOHN LAWRENCE IN SEPtember 1998, four hundred years of history had preceded them. Even before their ancestors arrived in America, men like Lawrence and his codefendant in *Lawrence v. Texas*, Tyron Garner, were reviled. The diary of one immigrant, the Reverend Francis Higgeson, recorded what happened to five males caught in sexual "wickedness" with one another during a voyage from England in 1629: "This day we examined 5 beastly Sodomiticall boyes, which confessed their wickedness not to bee named. The fact was so fowl we reserved them to bee punished by the governor when we came to new England, who afterward sent them backe to the company to be punished in ould England, as the crime deserved." Sodomy, as the governor well knew, was punishable in England by hanging.[1]

Sir William Blackstone, in his *Commentaries on the Laws of England*, fulminated against sodomy as "the infamous crime against nature, committed either with man or beast ... the very mention of which is a disgrace to human nature." A crime of such "deep malignity" was "not fit to be named." Blackstone alluded to the biblical origins of the word "sodomy," derived from God's destruction of Sodom and Gomorrah for, according to a common interpretation, the cities' sexual perversion.[2] Historically, he noted, sodomites had been publicly burned at the stake or buried alive.[3]

The English revulsion to "unnatural" sexual intercourse—understood to include anal sex and sometimes oral sex as well, no matter whether the offending couple was two men or a man and a woman—was passed on to the colonies, just as many other English legal principles were.[4] The earliest known colonial antisodomy law was enacted in Virginia just three years after the first permanent English settlement was established at Jamestown. In the 1610 code establishing martial law in the colony, the ninth provision, which also made adultery a capital crime, declared, "No man shall commit the horrible, detestable sins of Sodomie upon pain of death."[5] Antisodomy statutes were not limited to Virginia. The Plymouth colony listed eight capital offenses in 1636. In addition to murder, treason, and arson, the colony also punished by death the "solemn compaction or conversing with the devil by way of witchcraft," adultery, and "sodomy, rapes, [and] buggery."[6] Drawing directly on the prohibition, language, and penalty prescribed in Leviticus, the 1671 version of the Plymouth law offered only slightly more detail: "If any Man lyeth with Mankind, as he lyeth with a Woman, both of them have committed Abomination; they both shall surely be put to Death, unless the one party were forced, or be under fourteen years of Age: And all other Sodomitical filthiness, shall be surely punished according to the nature of it."[7]

Colonial Maryland's law likewise prohibited "buggery."[8] A 1641 Massachusetts law punished by death "any man" who worshipped any god "but the Lord God," "any man or woman" who "be a Witch," "any person" who shall "blaspheme the Name of God," "any man or woman" who shall "lie with any beast, or brute creature, by carnal copulation," "any person" who committed adultery, and "a man who lyeth with mankind, as he lyeth with a woman."[9] Similar laws against idolatry, witchcraft, blasphemy, adultery, bestiality, and sodomy were written into the early codes of all the colonies.[10]

Through the nineteenth century and well into the twentieth, every state in the United States had laws prohibiting anal sex, often called in state statutes "crimes against nature," "sodomy," or "buggery."[11] During the same period, states also began specifically prohibiting oral sex. Prior to the late 1960s, such laws applied regardless of the sex of the participants in the act and regardless of whether the couple was married. A husband and wife who engaged in oral sex were potentially as guilty as two men who had anal sex. This reflected the moral view that all sex outside of marriage, and all nonprocreative sex within marriage, were improper expressions of human sexuality. However, there was little enforcement of the laws against private sex between consenting adults;[12] and what occasional enforcement there was fell most harshly on homosexuals.

Pre–Civil War sodomy laws were especially vague, in keeping with the Blackstonian idea that it was a crime "not fit to be named."[13] Many states simply banned the "crime against nature" without specifying what this meant—although there was little confusion about the assumed meaning. Whatever their particular phrasing, the laws and the acts they prohibited generated little public concern before the Civil War. New York City, for example, prosecuted a mere twenty-two sodomy cases between 1796 and 1873.[14]

After the Civil War, the country became increasingly industrialized and, with that, rapidly urbanized. Abandoning small towns and farms, throngs of Americans were joined by millions of immigrants in growing cities. In addition to economic opportunity, these cities offered anonymity and separation from extended families. Large cities brought together people with a variety of sexual desires and afforded more opportunity to satisfy these varied tastes. By 1881, homosexual subcultures existed in New York, San Francisco, St. Louis, Philadelphia, Chicago, Boston, New Orleans, and Washington, D.C.[15]

Reacting to the exponential growth of these subcultures and a feared loosening of moral constraints, cities and states began more aggressively regulating sexuality.[16] Although state sodomy laws played a role in the repression of homosexuality, they had not yet become the main tool of enforcement. Yale law professor William Eskridge has identified four primary categories of early state and municipal laws intended to constrain deviance: laws against cross-dressing; laws against public indecency and sexual solicitation, including those against "disorderly conduct" and "lewd vagrancy"; laws against child molestation; and laws against obscenity.[17]

Some of the laws enacted during this period seem especially draconian by today's more liberal standards. A 1911 Massachusetts statute allowed the state to incarcerate "degenerates," including homosexuals, and other "mental defectives" for indefinite periods of time in state mental institutions. More commonly, state laws called for the sterilization or castration of moral degenerates and sexual perverts, usually for homosexual behavior. In an effort to "treat" homosexuals, hospitals performed prefrontal lobotomies, injected massive doses of male hormones, and administered electric shock and other aversion therapy.[18]

Federal authorities also suppressed homosexuality. They seized and destroyed publications deemed obscene, excluded immigrants convicted of sexual crimes, and barred military service by "degenerates."[19] U.S. Customs censored or seized novels depicting homosexual acts as acceptable or desirable, including the 1886 edition of *The Arabian Nights*. Authorities censored homosexual content from films, since under Supreme Court precedent at the time movies were not entitled to First Amendment protection.[20]

Immediately following World War II, American society and government became increasingly alarmed by the spread of communism, which was linked in the public mind to deviant sexuality. Between 1946 and 1961 alone, when arrests for violation of sodomy laws reached historic highs, government at all levels "imposed criminal punishments on as many as a million lesbians and gay men engaged in consensual adult intercourse, dancing, kissing, or holding hands."[21] Officials worried that homosexuals, like Communists, were infiltrating and undermining government agencies.[22] Senator Joseph McCarthy, whose closest aide, Roy Cohn, was a closeted homosexual, was on the lookout for government officials who tolerated "flagrant homosexual[s]."[23] The "sexual perverts," warned one politico, were "just as dangerous as the actual Communists." In the space of seven months in 1950, the Truman administration investigated the alleged sexual perversion of 382 civil servants, most of whom subsequently resigned. A government report warned that "[o]ne homosexual can pollute an entire office." In fact, more State Department employees were fired for homosexuality than for alleged Communist sympathies in 1951 and 1952, the height of McCarthy-era red-hunting.[24]

At the same time, the individual states also persecuted homosexuals. State and municipal laws were enforced to suppress homosexual association, including groups formed to advocate liberalization of sex regulations. An especially aggressive intrusion on freedom of association came in 1925 against the Society for Human Rights, the first gay organization ever founded in the United States, which supported the repeal of the Illinois sodomy law. After the wife of a member complained to police, they arrested the leaders of the Chicago-based group on disorderly conduct charges, confiscated the group's records, and seized one leader's personal diary.[25] States also used professional licensing laws to prevent homosexuals from becoming doctors, dentists, pharmacists, guardians, lawyers, teachers, and even embalmers.[26]

Law enforcement authorities used both direct and indirect methods to shut down gay bars. As detailed in George Chauncey's masterly history, *Gay New York*, twentieth-century gay history is replete with such abuses.[27] States and municipalities became adroit at closing gay bars through assorted business- and liquor-license schemes. A 1954 Miami ordinance, for example, made it illegal for a bar owner "to knowingly allow two or more persons who are homosexuals, lesbians or perverts to congregate or remain in his place of business." This "one homo per bar" rule resulted in the closing of all of Miami's gay bars by the end of the decade.[28] New York's State Liquor Authority, among others, prohibited bars from serving prostitutes and homosexuals, not an infrequent coupling of vices in public policy of the era.

Law enforcement authorities also aggressively used police stakeouts at suspected gay bars, decoy operations, and police raids to arrest large numbers of socializing homosexuals. For example, a 1960 raid on a San Francisco bar resulted in the disorderly conduct arrests of 103 people for same-sex dancing. Remarkably, when a serial killer targeted homosexuals in Santa Monica in 1956, police used details of the killer's confession to start an antigay cleanup of the city.[29]

Gays reacted to these crusades by organizing politically. Two fledgling gay-rights groups, the Mattachine Society and the Daughters of Bilitis (DOB), formed in the 1950s. The male-dominated Mattachine emerged in Los Angeles in 1950; DOB, organized by lesbians, began in San Francisco in 1955. The Federal Bureau of Investigation closely monitored their activities, beginning an internal security investigation of Mattachine in 1953 and of DOB in 1959. Neither group, of course, represented a credible national security threat.

The FBI, headed by the possibly closeted homosexual J. Edgar Hoover from 1924 until his death in 1972, relentlessly spied on Mattachine and DOB. As Eskridge writes, its agents "infiltrated both organizations, archived their declarations and publications, reported their meetings and activities, recruited informants, compiled lists of members whom they could identify, and speculated on the organizations' influence and future activities." Mattachine members met in secret and resorted to using pseudonyms to protect their identity. At the same time, agents interviewed the staff of the Los Angeles–based magazine for homophiles (as homosexuals were then sometimes called) *One* and notified their employers. Similar monitoring and harassment of gay groups by state and federal authorities occurred throughout the country. Despite the gay civil rights movement's gathering momentum by the time of the Stonewall Riots in June 1969, police harassment and surveillance of gay organizations continued into the 1970s.[30] In some places police raids on gay bars and other forms of harassment of homosexuals continued well into the 1990s, including in the state of Texas.

IN THE LONE STAR STATE, the existence, development, and partial enforcement of the state sodomy law mirrored the pattern seen elsewhere in the country. Although the law as written applied equally to acts committed in broad daylight and to acts committed in the home, it was almost never enforced against the latter. That is, it was almost never enforced against the most prevalent instances of sodomy—those that occur, like the alleged sex between John Lawrence and Tyron Garner, in the privacy of the home. The law's concern was not really with preventing sodomy per se. It worked instead as a symbolic message of disdain directed toward the people thought to commonly engage in sodomy— homosexuals—even though, for much of Texas history, all adults who engaged in any nonprocreative sex, heterosexual or homosexual, were technically sodomites.[31]

The criminal code of the Republic of Texas, in force from 1836 to 1845 while Texas was an independent country, contained, as it turned out, no prohibition on sodomy. However, common-law crimes were punished, and it seems likely the "crime against nature" would have been among them. The fledgling nation of Texas had much more immediate problems—like protecting its very existence—in the immediate aftermath of gaining independence from Mexico.

Texas joined the United States in 1845, nine years after the surrender at the Alamo. In its first fifteen years as a state, it had no statutory sodomy law. In the year before the Civil War began, the state adopted its first such prohibition, using the common-law definition for the crime. Like the laws of other states, it provided: "If any person shall commit with mankind or beast the abominable and detestable crime against nature . . . he shall be punished by confinement in the penitentiary for not less than five nor more than fifteen years."[32] Commentators and courts of the era in other states interpreted this language to prohibit anal sex between a man and a woman as well as between two men. As interpreted in other states, the law did not prohibit oral sex, and it did not prohibit any sexual acts between women.[33] The idea of "homosexual conduct" would have been incomprehensible to Texas legislators of the era since there was no word for "homosexual" in the English language at the time.[34] The Texas law was part of a larger framework outlawing all nonmarital and nonprocreative sex. As such, the sodomy prohibition was applicable to male-female and male-male sex. It applied equally to married and unmarried people.

The Texas law was initially unenforceable. State courts repeatedly refused to affirm convictions under the statute because of a separate law requiring that criminal offenses be "expressly defined."[35] For early Texas courts, outlawing the "crime against nature" was simply too vague. Once the state legislature eliminated the requirement that criminal offenses be clearly defined, in 1879, the Texas sodomy law became enforceable.[36] Thereafter, Texas courts repeatedly held that the law applied to anal sex but not to oral sex,[37] all the while expressing their disgust at this omission. State courts urged "that some legislation should be enacted covering these unnatural crimes [of oral sex]."[38] Moreover, Texas courts held that the sodomy law as enacted applied equally to heterosexual activity.[39]

The statute remained unchanged until 1925, when several parts of the Texas criminal code, including the state's 1860 sodomy law, were inadvertently omitted from the actual bill containing the revised penal code. In 1936, a Texas court held that the omitted sexual acts nevertheless remained crimes. The court's reasoning was significant: "To impute to the Legislature the intent to repeal the statutes defining incest, bigamy, seduction, adultery, and fornication is to lay at its door the charge of ignoring the moral sense of the people of this state and striking down some of the strongest safeguards of the home."[40] Sodomy in Texas, as this court's reasoning made clear, had been criminalized only as part of a larger framework codifying traditional sexual morality, not focused on homosexual intercourse.[41]

The Texas legislature revised the state sodomy law a second time in 1943.[42] The new version, which passed by unanimous votes in both the state house and senate,[43] made oral sex a crime for the first time:

> Whoever has carnal copulation with a beast, or in an opening of the body, except sexual parts, with another human being, or whoever shall use his mouth on the sexual parts of another human being for the purpose of having carnal copulation, or who shall voluntarily permit the use of his own sexual parts in a lewd or lascivious manner by any minor, shall be guilty of sodomy, and upon conviction thereof shall be deemed guilty of a felony, and shall be confined in the penitentiary not less than two (2) nor more than fifteen (15) years.[44]

Bizarre in several ways, the 1943 statute suggested that while oral sex for the purpose of "carnal copulation"[45] was illegal, oral sex for some other purpose was acceptable. It also suggested that while *sexual intercourse* with an animal was illegal, *oral sex* performed on an animal was not a problem since only oral sex performed on "another human being" was prohibited. Still, the law on its face applied equally to heterosexual and homosexual sex.

THE UNITED STATES emerged from the 1960s with a somewhat liberalized view of human sexuality, a broader conception of privacy and constitutional rights, and a more defendant-friendly vision of criminal law. The Supreme Court, under the guidance of Chief Justice Earl Warren, led the way with expansive rulings favoring individual rights, most notably its declaration in *Griswold v. Connecticut* (1965)[46] that the "right to privacy" protects the marital bedroom from police intrusion. This right to privacy was extended to unmarried persons in *Eisenstadt v. Baird* (1972).[47] Texas was subject to these decisions and to the larger cultural changes they reflected. While the Stonewall Riots in New York City seemed far away, the event spawned mini-gay-rights efforts in large cities in Texas itself.

Meanwhile, the legal revolution in the protection of privacy rights was not limited to courts. The Model Penal Code, essentially an expert-drafted list of suggestions for state criminal law reform, had been issued in 1955. It urged states to eliminate or modify archaic sex laws dealing with subjects like adultery, fornication, bestiality, seduction, and sodomy. Beginning in Illinois in 1961, the states began to do just that.

Following this modernizing trend, the Texas legislature comprehensively revised the state's criminal laws. As part of this revision, it liberalized many of the state's long-standing sex laws, decriminalizing adultery, fornication, seduction, and even bestiality.[48] These changes reflected to some extent the legislature's understanding that the Supreme Court had placed new limits on the government's power to control human sexuality. In *Buchanan v. Batchelor*, decided in 1970, a federal judge in Dallas declared the state sodomy law unconstitutional as applied to married couples.[49]

Even if forced by court decision and cultural shift to recognize the privacy rights of married heterosexuals, the Texas legislature was not prepared to stay out of the bedrooms of homosexuals. On the contrary, the very visibility of the gay-rights movement produced a pointed backlash in Austin. Thus, while it liberalized its laws governing the sexuality of heterosexuals, married or unmarried, procreative or nonprocreative, the state legislature tightened the focus of its vestigial sodomy law in a way that codified this antigay backlash.[50] A new law defined "deviate sexual intercourse" as "any contact between any part of the genitals of one person and the mouth or anus of another person."[51] However, under a separate "Homosexual Conduct" provision, it made these acts a crime only if performed "with another individual of the same sex."[52] This made heterosexual sodomy—oral or anal sex between opposite-sex partners— legal in the state. In addition to singling out gay men for punishment, it also made lesbian sex criminal for the first time.[53] "Homosexual conduct" alone became a misdemeanor punishable by a fine of up to $200.[54] The lack of any jail time for conviction of the crime did not reflect sympathy for gay people, but instead the suspicion that gay men would relish the opportunity to spend time in an all-male prison.[55]

In sum, the 1973 Texas Homosexual Conduct law represented an *expansion* of the types of acts historically prohibited under sodomy laws. Both anal and oral sex were now covered. At the same time, it also represented a *narrowing* of the class of people historically covered, since now the law applied only to same-sex couples. This was unprecedented in Texas history. After 1973, in Texas, it was legal to have sex with an animal, but not with another person of the same sex.

This development obviously did not sit well with the few activists willing to be publicly identified with the gay-rights cause in the state at the time. They made several attempts to repeal the law in the biennial sessions of the state legislature over the next twenty-eight years. Most such attempts were only halfhearted, consisting of little more than pro forma bills filed by state legislators representing liberal urban districts.

When the subject came up, proposals for eliminating the homosexual sodomy law drew catcalls and snickers rather than serious debate. There were no openly gay members of the Texas legislature and very few heterosexual legislators who cared at all about the issue. In 1975, a repeal effort led by Houston-area representative Craig Washington lost by a vote of 117–14 in the state house.[56] Again in 1977 and 1979, repeal attempts were made, but the proposals failed to move beyond the committee to which they were assigned.[57] Similar proposals met similar fates in the 1980s. In 1993, during another comprehensive overhaul of the state's criminal code, the Texas senate supported repeal, but the more politically conservative house defeated the effort.[58] Bills to repeal the sodomy law were filed in both the 1997 and 1999 sessions, but each time they failed to make it out of the state house criminal-jurisprudence committee.[59] The next attempt to repeal the sodomy law, during the 2001 session, while *Lawrence* was working its way through the Texas state courts, fell one Republican vote short of getting the bill out of committee.[60]

In addition to legislative efforts, gay-rights supporters made repeated attempts to challenge the Texas law as unconstitutional under the U.S. and Texas constitutions. They failed each time, either for technical reasons or because a court concluded the law was not unconstitutional.[61] In 1985, the Fifth Circuit Court of Appeals reversed a lower court's ruling that the Texas sodomy law violated the constitutional guarantee of "equal protection of the laws."[62]

In state courts, gay-rights advocates fared no better. While they won two state appeals court decisions in the early 1990s involving persons discriminated against on the job for being gay, the state supreme court held that any challenge to the state sodomy law would have to be made through the state's criminal courts.[63] This effectively barred any challenge to the state's sodomy law until the state arrested and prosecuted consensual adults for having sex in the privacy of a home—something that the state itself said it almost never did.

IN THE ENTIRE 143-year history of the Texas sodomy law, from its enactment until struck down in *Lawrence*, there are no publicly reported court decisions involving the enforcement of the law against consensual sex between adult persons in a private space.[64] Admittedly, in some reported decisions, the facts given by the court are too sketchy to determine whether the prosecution was for private, adult, consensual activity. Especially in early cases, the decisions are very short, often no more than a paragraph or two in length. In sodomy cases, courts around the country have often been reluctant even to present the facts. In a typical example, affirming a sodomy conviction, one Kentucky court said simply, "It is not necessary to set out the revolting facts."[65] Any physical description of the act itself seemed more heinous to the court than, say, a detailed description of a murder. Texas courts shared this squeamishness.

All of the published Texas court decisions involving sodomy prosecutions contain some element that makes them meaningfully distinct from *Lawrence*. Many involve a public or quasi-public place, such as a parked car or a jail.[66] Some cases involve force or coercion.[67] Others involve sex with minors.[68] Indeed, in litigation challenging the state sodomy law, the state contended that it enforced the law only in circumstances where force was used, a minor was involved, or the sex occurred in public.[69] This makes the arrest and prosecution of Lawrence and Garner, adults in a private residence, anomalous.

However, the absence of published decisions does not mean that the

Texas sodomy law was never enforced against private activity. We do not have a formal record of such prosecutions because the only publicly recorded cases are those that were, for some reason, appealed and then resulted in a published decision from the appeals court. This is a very small portion of arrests and prosecutions for the violation of any criminal law on any subject, from a sex crime to simple assault. Perhaps because of the shame long associated with homosexuality and homosexual acts, defendants arrested and charged with violating the sodomy law routinely pleaded guilty to the offense, paid whatever fine was imposed, and hushed up about their convictions.[70] There were few appeals and no published decisions concerning private conduct. As a result, almost all of the uses and misuses of the Texas sodomy law (and of sodomy laws in other states) will never be known. They are lost to history because of the shame and fear of the defendants.

This under-the-radar enforcement has been common in the history of sodomy and other laws used to harass homosexuals, including laws against public lewdness. William Eskridge has noted the relative ineffectiveness of legal safeguards as tools to combat antigay harassment. Writing about the enforcement of sex laws against gays from the 1940s through the 1960s, Eskridge notes that "out of fear of further exposure, almost everybody pleaded guilty to charges of lewd vagrancy, degeneracy, and sodomy, and they pleaded guilty at higher rates than defendants did for similar crimes such as vagrancy, disorderly conduct, and rape."[71] Thus, constitutional safeguards did not really raise the costs of enforcement. Police could arrest people, charge them with violating antihomosexual sex laws, and expect that their word would not be challenged. As we shall see, the sheriff's deputies who arrested Lawrence and Garner probably shared the expectation that their version of events would not be disputed by the gay men they were arresting.

One example of unreported sodomy-law enforcement occurred in 1980 in Houston, when police were called to the scene of a loud party in a private home. When they arrived, the officers saw men dancing together, hugging, and kissing. Some of the men were reportedly dressed as women. Ira Jones, an assistant district attorney for Harris County, was on duty when the police brought in "a paddy wagon full of 'em [homosexuals]" on charges of violating the Homosexual Conduct law.

Jones declined to authorize the charges, since police had not observed them violating the letter of the law—that is, the partygoers were not having oral or anal sex. "It was fun for them," said Jones, speaking of the gay men arrested at the party and brought to jail. "They laughed and went away."[72] It is doubtful that the incident was "fun" for the arrested men, but if Jones had been as unscrupulous or as ill informed as the arresting officers, this so-called amusement might have extended into court appearances and fines.

Another instance of sodomy-law enforcement that never made it into a published legal decision occurred a couple of years later. Texas Department of Public Safety deputies in Harris County arrested two men for having sex in a trailer on state park campgrounds near the San Jacinto Monument, a 570-foot stone shaft topped by a 34-foot-high star that sits just outside of Houston and commemorates Texan heroism in the war for independence from Mexico.[73] Inside the camper, the men were shielded from public view and had a reasonable expectation of privacy, sufficient to warrant constitutional protection under the Fourth Amendment, which generally requires that police have probable cause to believe that criminal activity is occurring before entering an otherwise private place.[74] The arresting officer reported that he was walking by the camper when a breeze blew aside the closed curtain, exposing the two men as they had sex. Ray Hill, a longtime gay civil rights and prisoners' rights activist in Houston, learned of the arrest from the presiding justice of the peace (JP) and tried to persuade the defendants' lawyer to use the case as an opportunity to challenge the constitutionality of Section 21.06, the Homosexual Conduct law. The men's lawyer refused to do so, saying that his clients simply wanted to plead guilty and be done with the matter and that he (the lawyer) just wanted to collect his fee.[75] The matter was never appealed and died where it began, in the JP court.

Without doubt, there were numerous occasions in Texas history when sodomy arrests and prosecutions ended with a quiet guilty or no-contest plea, a small fine, no publicity, and continued anonymity for the defendants. Hill, who knew many of the Harris County judges and their staffs handling criminal cases, recalled five such incidents, including the Lawrence and Garner arrests, in Harris County alone since Section

21.06 was adopted in 1973.[76] But for a fortuitous set of coincidences, and the determination of a handful of people, the arrests of John Lawrence and Tyron Garner could very easily have been just another forgotten episode in the history of the Texas sodomy law.

This law's development illustrates an important point: like other sodomy laws around the country, it initially applied to certain *acts*, regardless of the sex of the people involved. It was only through a process of specification[77] (narrowing and targeting) that it came to be aimed at certain *people*—homosexuals—engaged in certain acts. And this development is a very modern, not ancient, one.

While the Texas sodomy law and similar state laws around the country were not usually enforced against private activity, this did not mean they had no effect on the lives of gays. The state of Texas even agreed in one of the court challenges to the law that it "brands lesbians and gay men as criminals and thereby legally sanctions discrimination against them in a variety of ways unrelated to the criminal law."[78] Homosexuals, unprotected from job discrimination in Texas and most other states in the 1990s, could be fired simply for being gay. Divorced gay parents could lose custody or face onerous restrictions on visitation with their children on the ground that they were presumptively criminals. Legislators used the existence of the sodomy law as a reason not to grant any civil rights protections to homosexuals. They used it to oppose hate-crimes laws on the grounds that criminals should enjoy no special protection. Being branded a criminal class was also an invitation to discrimination and even violence against gays by other citizens. While they did not stop gays from having sex, the harmful effects of sodomy laws on their lives were extensive and deep.[79] The Supreme Court finally recognized a few of these burdens in *Lawrence*.

The Texas law, like many such laws, codified a particular cultural assumption about homosexuals as hypersexualized and dangerous. In Texas legal history, that view is perhaps best represented by the remarks allegedly made in 1898 by a district attorney to a jury about a man charged with sodomy. The defendant, "Shorty" Darling, was said to be "a raving, vicious bull, running at large upon the highways, seeking whom he should devour; was dangerous, and should be penned up where he would have no more such opportunities to commit such abominable and detestable crimes."[80]

As we shall see, the view of gays as dangerously hypersexualized crept into the arrests of Lawrence and Garner, leading sheriff's deputies to set aside doubts—and to use their power—against the two men at every step.

2.

The City and the Cause

FOUNDED IN 1836 AND NAMED AFTER SAM HOUSTON, THE FIRST
president of the Republic of Texas, the port city of Houston
stretches over 579 square miles of flat land fifty miles from the Gulf of
Mexico. The fourth largest city in the nation, its metropolitan area
includes almost 6 million people.

The city has what one may call a libertarian look and ethic. It is
business-friendly, home to a huge portion of the country's oil and gas
industry, a large medical complex, and more than a dozen Fortune 500
companies. Taxes are low and regressive. There are no zoning laws,
meaning anything can be built almost anywhere, with the result that
development is almost wholly unplanned. The cost of living, including
the cost of renting a home, is the lowest of any large city in the country.
There are essentially two downtowns, one in the heart of the city, where
a downtown is usually found, and another, known as the "Southwest
skyline," miles away. The jammed freeways are meant to do the work of
public transit, which is almost nonexistent. The pollution is among the
worst in the country; the restaurants, museums, opera, and theater,
among the best. Such is its schizophrenic existence.

It was in or near this city that all of the major players in the background facts of *Lawrence v. Texas*—the defendants, the activists, and the
sheriff's deputies—were raised. Understanding why they acted as they
did in September of 1998 requires some understanding of what brought

the police, guns drawn, to a bedroom door. How Houston's gay-rights activists came to challenge the arrest requires some familiarity with the city's treatment of gay men and lesbians in the years before 1998. This history illuminates the mutual distrust and antagonism between the city's gay population and police.

THE CITY THAT would not zone its buildings had long zoned its homosexuals, keeping them out of sight as much as possible. The live-and-let-live, less-government-is-more libertarianism that defined Houston has not always extended to its gay inhabitants. As early as the 1920s, there were already bars in the city serving a predominantly homosexual clientele.[1] They were not, of course, advertised as such. Knowledge of their existence and their whereabouts spread by word of mouth, as was common in the sub-rosa gay life of American cities at the time.

The Pink Elephant, perhaps the oldest (and for long periods the only) gay bar in the city, remained open into the 1960s. An habitué described the atmosphere of the Houston gay bars through the sixties like this: "They were dark and they were dingy. The people there were kind of grotesque. You rarely would see a really attractive person. And if you saw a really attractive person, he became drunk and haggard pretty quick. We were pretty self-destructive."[2]

Unappealing as the bars might have been, they were practically the only place where homosexuals could gather. Hanging out there was often the sole way for closeted gays to learn about gay life, about the experiences of others who shared their orientation, about the harassment they suffered at the hands of police, and about the ways one might deal with prying family members and friends. They were precursors to the political organizing that would occur in later decades.

Yet fear pervaded the bars. There was fear, if not paranoia, about going to such a place at all, since it constituted a public confession of one's homosexuality to others and to oneself. There was fear of being seen by someone entering or leaving. There was also fear of being harmed by someone you met in the bar: in the 1940s and '50s, men known in the gay subculture as "dirt" would rob and blackmail gay men.[3] A similar phenomenon, sometimes called "dropping a nickel on a sister," involved telephoning a gay acquaintance's employer, informing the employer of the person's homosexuality, getting him fired, and then applying for the vacant job.[4]

And there was the ever-present fear that the bar might be raided by police. This fear was entirely justified, as police raided Houston's gay bars on a regular basis from the 1950s through the mid-1980s, just as they did in cities around the country.[5] "It was a joke to them," asserted Ray Hill, the local gay-rights pioneer, referring to the police. "It wasn't so much meanness as it was entertainment. The cops would come in. 'Up against the wall, motherfucker!' And they'd take everybody's identification and see if you had any outstanding warrants and arrest two or three people for being publicly intoxicated, whether you were drunk or not."[6]

Even private homes where gay people gathered for parties were subject to police raids.[7] In the summer of 1959, police raided an after-hours party where dozens of gay men were socializing and dancing. The men were arrested, loaded into paddy wagons, and taken downtown for processing. "We immediately started destroying any information as to our places of employment," remembered one of the arrested men. "Eating them if necessary since the police always called the employers of the people caught in raids."[8]

The police repeatedly insulted the men. "They hated us and they showed it. We were treated lower than any rapist or murderer in the jailhouse."[9] One of the arrested men asked an officer if he could use the restroom. The officer responded, "Piss in your pants and smell like a man and excite yourself."[10] Yet gay men had learned to deal with harassment and repression by making light of it:

After a while the shock of being in this situation faded and our sense of humor, which had saved many of us from going over the hill, came into play. We were all fingerprinted and photographed. Mug shots with numbers and all for the same price. One of the first to be photographed said, "Officer, could you please take my left profile? It's much better." Soon another person being photographed looked the officer in the eye and asked, "When will the proofs be ready?"[11]

Despite such campy humor, the consequences of an arrest could be life altering. The arrest report noted that the men were charged with "consuming after hours at an alleged homosexual gathering."[12] Most simply paid their fines. "Everybody was afraid of the cops," observed Hill. "They weren't afraid of going to jail because it was nothing to go to jail and get out the next day. But your name was in the paper." Public exposure meant humiliation and alienation from family and friends. It could also mean losing your job. "The 1950s made all of us realize that the only security you have in life is what you build yourself. Education and financial planning coupled with a lasting relationship was paramount."[13]

In the 1960s, gay bars and social life flourished in Houston, at least as compared with the previous decades.[14] By 1967, there were already a dozen gay bars in a city increasingly known as the homosexual playground of the South.[15] But police raids and harassment of the bars continued and life remained uneasy. In the late 1960s, a powerful Houston businessman who controlled a large bank and had founded a prominent law firm in the city decided to purge his gay employees. He hired a private detective to visit known gay bars and record the license plates of cars parked near the establishments. The numbers were then checked against employees' license plates. Dozens of people with matching plates were fired.[16]

In lesbian bars vice cops would enter and arrest women for wearing fly-front jeans (a violation of a local anti-cross-dressing ordinance). According to one account, police raids of lesbian bars were often especially ferocious. "The hatred shown us during a raid, I was told, was minuscule [compared] to what happened when they raided a lesbian bar," one gay man of the era recalled. "The stories were that masculine lesbians were actually beaten."[17]

Gay political organizations were sprouting in the 1950s and '60s in cities like New York, Washington, D.C., San Francisco, and Los Angeles, but not until the late sixties did gay men and lesbians in Houston attempt to organize politically against police harassment. Stimulated by the countercultural and protest movements nationally, Ray Hill, David Patterson, and Rita Wanstrom began organizing Houston gays in 1967.[18] A lesbian group called the Tumblebugs and a male group called the Promethean Society briefly emerged.[19] Since advertising was out of the question, the only means of spreading information about the groups was leafleting cars parked around gay bars. This succeeded in getting some people to meetings but meant there was no continuity; the people who came to the next meeting had not been to the previous one.[20] "We had the same meeting half a dozen times," said Hill.

In 1969, the Promethean Society's vice president was arrested for having sex in the men's room of a local hotel. Hill himself was convicted of a series of commercial jewel, antique, and art thefts, and spent the next six years in prison.[21] The Tumblebugs and Promethean Society did not stand a chance. Their leadership was decimated and their membership was small and unstable. The groups disappeared, victims of the very shame and stigma they were trying to combat. Houston, like much of the country, was not yet ready for gay political organizing.

THEN CAME A defining moment in the modern history of the gay civil rights movement. On Friday, June 27, 1969, police mounted a routine raid of a New York City gay bar known as the Stonewall Inn. There is much dispute about exactly what happened after the raid began, but there is no doubt the people in the bar and out on the street "behaved unlike any homosexual patrons had ever behaved before."[22] They rioted, chanting defiant slogans, hurling rocks, bottles, and other objects at police, setting fires in trash cans, and generally raising hell.[23] The next night, when there was further unrest, the writer Allen Ginsberg observed a change that was already evident. "The guys there were so beautiful," he remarked. "They've lost that wounded look that fags all had ten years ago."[24] The riots inspired homosexuals around the country to begin organizing more aggressively and openly.[25]

But the spirit of Stonewall did not immediately infuse Houston. A leftist group calling itself the Houston Gay Liberation Front formed briefly in 1970, but proved too radical for Houston's relatively conservative gay community.[26] Of more lasting significance was the formation the next year of a local chapter of Integrity, a gay religious group, which was allowed by a local priest to meet at Holy Rosary Church. Its founders were a group of gay men, including Bill Buie, Mark Barron, Hugh Crell, and Keith McGee, who described the group as a "fellowship for homophiles."[27] Membership soon expanded. Integrity/Houston became, in the words of lesbian activist Linda "Pokey" Anderson, "probably the only general purpose organization" for Houston's homosexuals at the time.[28] It formed the first gay speakers bureau and opened the first gay clinic to diagnose and treat venereal diseases. It also supported political candidates, helping to elect Fred Hofheinz as mayor by a narrow margin in 1973.[29] Its leaders were the first to appear before the city council in support of gay causes and were the nucleus of the group that later formed the Gay Political Caucus.[30]

In 1972, the Montrose Gaze Community Center was organized by a group of younger and more militant gay people.[31] It hosted meetings for gay groups and generally acted as a gathering place for activists. A motorcycle club, lesbian softball teams, a gay radio program, and community newspapers sprang up.[32] Late that year, the short-lived Houston Gay Political Coalition emerged, in part as a response to ongoing harassment of gays by the police. The group pushed to end police abuse, to repeal the state sodomy law, to end job discrimination in city employment, and to establish a citizens' police review board to monitor complaints. These requests were shouted down by city council member Frank Mann, who screamed, "You're abnormal. You need to see a psychiatrist instead of city council."[33]

Despite these organizational efforts, several events in the early 1970s held back gay civil rights progress in the city. First, a shelter established to help homeless youths in the city's heavily gay Montrose neighborhood became embroiled in a scandal over alleged sexual exploitation of minors.[34] The summer of 1971 brought a series of notorious raids on local gay bars. Police armed with clubs and shotguns demolished the businesses, breaking glass and overturning furniture. "We will continue to raid places like this until every goddamn queer has been run out of the city," warned one police officer.[35]

Beginning in 1970 and continuing for three years, Dean Corll, who ran his mother's candy business, abducted, raped, and murdered twenty-seven young men in the Houston area. It became a sensational case, one widely followed in the national press and dubbed the Candy Man murders. Corll and his crimes came to light only when one of Corll's accomplices killed him. The authorities then learned that Corll had a grisly modus operandus. He incapacitated his targets with alcohol or tricked them into putting on handcuffs. Once they were helpless, the victims were stripped naked, tied to a plywood board, tortured, sexually assaulted, and then either strangled or shot with a .22 caliber pistol. Corll wrapped the bodies in plastic sheets and deposited them around the Houston area.

The details of these crimes horrified and transfixed the city, as they did the nation at large. At the time, it was the largest toll taken by any serial killer in American history. Because all of Corll's victims were young men and boys who had been sexually tortured before being murdered, the episode contributed to the stereotype of gay men as mentally ill, predatory, perverted, and especially dangerous to children.[36]

Also retarding gay progress for a time was the aforementioned passage of the state's new homosexuals-only sodomy law, which became effective on January 1, 1974. If continued police harassment and being linked in the public eye with pedophilia and serial killing were not bad enough, gays were now confirmed criminals in the eyes of the state of Texas—a fact that could be used against them in every aspect of life.

BY THE SUMMER of 1975, Houston's gay community, beginning to mobilize in a significant way, was ready to fight back. June saw the area's first gay pride parade, as Houston joined New York and other American cities in marking the anniversary of the Stonewall Riots. At the same time, a small group of local activists, including Ray Hill (newly released from prison), Pokey Anderson, Gary Van Ooteghem, Bob Falls, and Jerry Miller, founded the Gay Political Caucus (GPC).[37] Recalling the sneering legislative reaction to the recent unsuccessful effort to repeal the state sodomy law, Anderson told reporters, "To be laughed at is something that's not very pleasant. So we have decided, in Houston, to form the Gay Political Caucus" and to convene "large meetings" to screen candidates for public office.[38]

Van Ooteghem, one of the GPC's founders, had moved south from Chicago when he was recruited as Harris County's comptroller. In July 1975, he began soliciting donations to support the legal efforts of Leonard Matlovich, whose recent discharge from the military for being homosexual was given national coverage. On August 1, Van Ooteghem gave an unprecedented speech to the county commissioners demanding that they end discrimination against gay people and announcing, just as Matlovich had on the cover of *Time* magazine, "I am a homosexual." Van Ooteghem was quickly fired by the county treasurer, allegedly for "politickin' on county time"[39] (he sued the county for wrongful dismissal and eventually won). Van Ooteghem, who would go on to establish the city's chapter of the Log Cabin Republicans in the mid-1990s, was made the first president of the GPC in September 1975.[40]

The GPC organized a small gay-rights parade of about 300 people in the summer of 1976. But the real catalyst for growth came in June 1977, when Anita Bryant was asked to sing at the annual convention of the Texas Bar Association. Bryant, a spokesperson for Florida's orange juice industry, had led a successful effort in that state to repeal Dade County's ordinance prohibiting job discrimination against gay men and lesbians. She had argued that "homosexual acts are illegal" under sodomy laws, and that gay people were trying to recruit children in order to molest them and to "freshen their ranks."[41] With her pink lipstick and beauty-queen looks, Bryant (in fact, a second runner-up to the Miss America crown) had made national headlines and her cause soon spread to other cities that had previously passed ordinances protecting gay men and lesbians from discrimination.

Riled by her presence, Houston gay activists called for a protest march that would begin near the city's gay neighborhood and end one mile away at the downtown Hyatt Regency Hotel, where the bar association conference was being held. Organizers, chief among them Van Ooteghem, expected perhaps 500 people to show up but were astonished when by some estimates the number of marchers swelled to 10,000.[42] There had never been anything like it: Houston was not a city with a history of public protest, much less public protest by homosexuals.

Before the march began, Ray Hill revved up the marchers with a speech that expressed decades of frustration and captured the optimism of the moment. After quieting the crowd, he began:

There's certainly a lot of folks here today. A lot of folks. And I want you to look at one another. You know, if we had come here today like we went to work this morning, dressed for work, then they would be able to tell who were the doctors and who were the lawyers and who were the teachers and who were all these other things. We just look like a crowd of people; but we have always been so much more. And they don't see us as we see ourselves. They don't see us as people with political potential or the people that make the cultural contributions that we make. They see us as perverts and criminals. But we know who we are. And tonight, for the first time in most of our lives, we know that we're not some small group. But we're a big bunch of people, and there's a whole bunch of us that are not here. We are a community, not an interest group.[43]

The throng then walked peacefully to the hotel. Once there, organizers made speeches and read telegrams of support from heterosexual celebrities, among them Jane Fonda, Alan Alda, Rob Reiner, and Ed Asner.[44] "We went down there a bunch of angry, up-to-here, we're-not-going-to-take-this-anymore, pissed-off individuals," said Hill, one of the city's few living gay civil rights organizers from that era. "And we surrounded that hotel and we made so much noise they could not hear Anita Bryant."[45]

Among the marchers that night was a college student named Annise Parker, who would go on to become the first openly gay elected official in Houston's history, first as a member of the city council in 1997 and then as city controller in 2003.[46] In 2009 she won the mayoralty, becoming the first openly gay mayor of any large city in the United States. Both she and Hill, after committing their lives and careers to advancing gay rights, would be called on for advice soon after John Lawrence and Tyron Garner were arrested.

The Anita Bryant march became Houston's Stonewall, a defining moment that launched an era of activism. "We came back from that event believing we were a community," remembered Hill.[47] The march and the communal feeling it created led to a gathering of perhaps 3,500 gay men and lesbians in Houston in late June 1978.[48] Known as the "Town Meeting," it transformed energy into organization. Out of the Town Meeting came a host of community groups dealing with various aspects of gay life in the city: the Montrose Counseling Center (addressing mental health), the Montrose Clinic (addressing physical health, including STDs), the Montrose Patrol (dedicated to fighting hate crimes), the Gay and Lesbian Switchboard (a crisis center that also fielded general questions), the Montrose Sports Association, and the Montrose Activity Center. Membership in the GPC soared.[49]

IN 1979, THE GPC backed its first candidate, Eleanor Tinsley, a liberal reformer running for an at-large seat on the city council. No woman had ever served on the city council and none had ever sought the endorsement of a gay-rights group. Her opponent was Frank Mann, the longtime incumbent who had shouted down gay activists earlier in the decade. Mann labeled her supporters "oddwads and homosexuals," so the GPC created T-shirts proclaiming "Oddwads and Homosexuals for Tinsley." When Tinsley defeated Mann, the city's political establishment awakened to the potential power of the gay vote.[50] In the next citywide election, in 1981, a GPC-endorsed progressive named Kathy Whitmire was elected mayor.

Suddenly gays had gone from the extreme margins of Houston politics to the center of a coalition of progressives and racial minorities that was dislodging the city's so-called good-ol'-boy white male establishment. The GPC delivered volunteers who stuffed envelopes and worked phone banks for endorsed candidates. More importantly, gay people were now seen as a disciplined and reliable bloc of voters who could make an appreciable difference, certainly in any close city contest. A GPC-backed candidate could usually count on 80 percent of the vote in the ten precincts of the heavily gay and eclectic Montrose neighborhood. Even the national media took note of this development, with *Newsweek* running an article in 1981 entitled "Gay Power in Macho Houston."[51]

By the fall of 1983, politicians were lining up for the GPC's endorsement. A progressive majority was elected to city offices for the first time. After the election, a jubilant Whitmire and three council members went on a much publicized tour of the city's gay bars to thank supporters.[52] A conservative political columnist for one of the city's major dailies observed that "gays are being recognized as a legitimate constituency no elected Houston city official can afford to alienate. . . . Houston politi-

cians who want to get elected will no longer campaign on anti-gay platforms. The last three choosing that tactic lost city campaigns by wide
margins."[53] It was without question the high point in the early phase of
the city's gay civil rights movement.

None of this political success meant, however, that gays felt comfortable coming out or that they had now engendered the respect of the
wider population. Beneath the surface of the newfound political respect
there remained a deep reservoir of antigay sentiment. Gay-bashing was
common, especially around bars in Montrose, police raids on gay bars
continued, and police brutality against gays was endemic.[54] When students at Houston's prestigious Rice University formed the first gay student group there in 1979, meetings were held in secret. When the time
came to take an official portrait for the student yearbook, most of the
members felt the need to wear paper bags over their heads.[55] Nevertheless, the remarkable triumphs in municipal politics suggested the future
would see further improvements.

A CHAIN OF EVENTS soon shattered any illusion, however, that gay men
and lesbians might have become a political powerhouse. It would bring
to the surface all the enduring stereotypes that homosexuals were perverted and dangerous—in the end, child-molesting criminals.

On June 19, 1984, the city council passed two ordinances prohibiting
discrimination against gay people in city employment by adding "sexual
orientation" to sections of the city's civil service code that already
banned discrimination on the basis of race, color, religion, age, disability, sex, and national origin. Despite what opponents later said about
them, these ordinances did not establish quotas for the hiring of homosexuals, change any job-related performance criteria for employment,
require that city contracts be awarded to gay-owned businesses, or
require special recruitment efforts for gay employees. A poll showed that
Houstonians supported efforts to end discrimination against homosexuals by a nine-point margin.[56] While the GPC did not initially push for
passage of the ordinances (some leaders feared a political backlash), the
group eventually had no choice but to support it. The vote in the council
was 9–6 on the nondiscrimination ordinance and 8–7 on the second
statute, which dealt with affirmative action, with Mayor Whitmire in the

majority on both votes. The closeness of the votes foreshadowed the political controversy that would ensue. As the council debated the measures, a group of Ku Klux Klansmen stood outside the chambers and chanted, "Death to homosexuals."[57]

The ordinances enraged religious conservatives, who were beginning to coalesce into a local and national movement of their own as a response to what they regarded as attacks on traditional moral values. They were already alarmed by the rise of gay political power in the city and these antidiscrimination measures confirmed their fears. Within a month, they had gathered more than 60,000 signatures from voters for a referendum to repeal the ordinances.

The winter of 1984–85 in Houston saw one of the most viciously antigay political campaigns ever conducted in the nation. It immediately followed Ronald Regan's reelection campaign, during which some of his supporters derided "San Francisco Democrats," which was an explicit reference to the location of the 1984 Democratic National Convention and an implicit reference to the Democrats' comparative liberalism on social issues—especially homosexuality. The "San Francisco values" theme would, in fact, be a major part of the repeal campaign. City ordinances that protected, at most, a few hundred city workers from discrimination on the job became a symbol of the larger culture war being fought across the country. Although the vote officially concerned protecting city workers from antigay discrimination, it actually became a referendum on homosexuality itself.

Gay leaders knew immediately they faced a serious challenge. A meeting of community activists on July 11, 1984, mapped strategy for the coming six months. The group agreed that gay men and lesbians should remain largely invisible during the campaign. "It is essential that all spokespersons be from the non-gay community," read the minutes of the meeting. A fifteen-member steering committee would "work in the background with a city-wide group of non-gays." The main, public face of the campaign committee would "exclud[e] gay activists."[58]

At a time when they had supposedly reached new heights of political power, the city's gay leadership, in other words, opted for a closeted strategy. They would try to hide during the campaign and let others take the public lead. Unfortunately, straight support never materialized in anywhere near the numbers, significance, or dedication the gay community hoped for. With few exceptions, civic, religious, and business leaders were spooked by gay-rights opponents and remained on the sidelines or even joined the repeal drive.

John Goodner, a council member who had previously sought and obtained GPC endorsement but was opposed to the antidiscrimination ordinances, formed a group called the Committee for Public Awareness (CPA) to promote a yes vote on the referendum. It immediately focused attention on the supposed danger of homosexuality itself, rather than on the question of whether city workers should be protected from job discrimination.

The CPA brought Nebraska psychologist Paul Cameron to Houston to speak. Cameron's efforts to "convert" homosexuals into heterosexuals and his shoddy and distorted research on the allegedly harmful effects of homosexuality had caused him to be expelled from the American Psychological Association the year before. "Homosexuals pose a threat to public health," Cameron told the city council in public session. "They carry fungal, amoebal, and viral infections. What gays do in public is disgusting; what they do in private is deadly."[59] These alleged public-health concerns about homosexuality would still dominate the legal briefs supporting the state of Texas in *Lawrence* almost two decades later.

Cameron exploited the public's fears of AIDS, which was then entering the national consciousness as a major health threat. Speaking at a prayer breakfast of the predominantly black Concerned Pastors and Ministers of Houston, Cameron advocated a quarantine of all gay people in cities across the nation to prevent the spread of AIDS. Unless homosexuals were removed from society, Cameron told the ministers, mankind's very existence would be imperiled. "By this time next year very close to all of them [homosexuals] are going to be infected. It's bad enough our boys are being raped" by homosexuals, he said, "but to have them die because of the rape is worse." Cameron noted that homosexual acts had once drawn the death penalty, and that Thomas Jefferson had once called for sodomites to be castrated.[60] Even though Goodner later distanced himself from Cameron, the invidious tone was set.

CPA campaign coordinator Judi Wilson, a veteran of Anita Bryant's successful Dade County repeal effort in 1977, said that the goal of homosexuals was not equality, "but to have control."[61] In a letter to voters, the CPA warned of a gay master plan, a latter-day reincarnation of the Manchurian candidate conspiracy, that would seize control of the city. Houston was in danger of becoming "another San Francisco or New York City—a haven for the ever increasing number of avowed homosexuals that will move to our City." Houston "has been selected [by national gay rights organizations] as the site of what amounts to the critical battleground in the national war on traditional family values." The letter closed with a quote from Annise Parker, who was by then a GPC leader, saying that "a victory [in the referendum] would be a signal that it is time to press ahead for other goals," like nondiscrimination in housing, in teaching, and in "teaching policies regarding alternative lifestyles."[62]

Another pro-repeal group, Campaign for Houston, invited voters to a screening of a sensationalistic 1980 CBS News documentary called *Gay Power, Gay Politics* just eleven days before the referendum. The documentary was widely criticized for reinforcing antigay stereotypes, but it proved to be a useful publicity tool for religious groups trying to repeal gay civil rights ordinances around the country. In its letter, Campaign for Houston said the documentary revealed that in San Francisco "*children may not safely play in the parks without being exposed to* [sic] *by men who are meeting men for 'anonymous' sex in full public view*; sadomasochistic parlors have proliferated; the city's mayor is a pawn of the radical homosexuals; the public schools are mandated to teach homosexuality as an acceptable lifestyle to the children; and more."[63]

Meanwhile, numerous speakers had appeared before the city council in public comment sessions to denounce its action. One described homosexuality as "a disease that destroys the individual and society."[64] The editor of a conservative newsletter told the council that because "homosexuals don't reproduce" they must recruit people, especially the young, into their "sexual perversion cult." He claimed that the "true intention" of gay-rights activists was "the legalization of sex with children and babies." Protecting homosexuals from job discrimination would also lead to domestic violence, including injury and death, he claimed. "Here we have a sexual group that advocates and practices the physical torture of other human beings with the use of chains, leather straps, bondage, prods and so forth."[65]

The city's business establishment, represented by the Houston Chamber of Commerce, also supported repeal. Led by former mayor Louie Welch, business leaders said they feared that protecting gay people from discrimination could hurt the city economically, driving away commerce and tarnishing the city's image.[66]

Lawyers at prominent Houston law firms and the president of the Houston Bar Association also announced support for repeal.[67] Harvard-educated Scott Brister, a partner at the respected Houston-based law firm Andrews and Kurth, said that the ordinance would "protect persons whose sexual practices might be unhealthy, perhaps violent, or sometimes abhorrent to the particular citizens whom they are to serve."[68]

In the midst of an epidemic that threatened the public with a deadly, sexually transmissible virus, medical opinion played a major role in the campaign to repeal the ordinance. Campaign for Houston sponsored advertisements in which local allergist and religious-right activist Steven Hotze warned that homosexual men were the "primary carriers" of AIDS and that Houston would "become a homosexual mecca if we permit laws that encourage *more* homosexuals to settle here, increasing the threat to *your* health. . . . Enough is enough."[69] Another doctor, Edgar M. Thomason, formed a group called Doctors for Houston to support repeal. He warned that the ordinance would lead to rampant homosexual activity in the city and endanger public health. Echoing Cameron's calls for a quarantine of gay men, he suggested that everybody with AIDS "should be put away in a sanitarium or someplace else" to protect the public.[70]

Religious leaders also played an important part in the repeal. Roman Catholic bishop John Morkovsky said those who supported the ordinances were "perverts."[71] Edwin Young, pastor of the Second Baptist Church, predicted that the ordinances would mean protection for "pedophilia, necrophilia, and other sexual perversions." He argued that the ordinances were really designed to stamp social approval on "an immoral practice."[72] These "slippery slope" and morality concerns would be used years later as well to defend the Texas sodomy law in *Lawrence*.

The Harris County GOP strongly backed repeal.[73] The county party's chairman, Russ Mather, played a major role in the campaign. He cited fears that the ordinances were the first step to a quota system, that homosexuals recruit children, and that AIDS was already rampant in the city. Mather further warned that if the ordinances stood, homosexuals would become police officers as a way to have sex with children. "I've heard that the first thing homosexuals do when they join the force is try to infiltrate the juvenile division," he said, evoking age-old fears of gay conspiracies to molest and recruit children. "When you have a homosexual patrolling Montrose, is he a cop first or a homosexual first?" asked Mather. Not surprisingly, the Houston Police Patrolmen's Union also backed the repeal.[74]

Anti-ordinance forces saw the referendum as an opportunity to split the local coalition of gay people, racial minorities, and white progressive voters. Before the ordinances had passed, Councilman Goodner warned they would weaken affirmative action for blacks and other racial minorities because they would be "pitting born minorities against minorities by choice." He predicted gay men and lesbians would win that contest, leading to more discrimination against blacks and Hispanics.[75]

Reverend Floyd Williams spoke for many of the city's blacks when he put the issue of legal protection for gays in explicitly racial terms. "I ain't ready to make no more minorities till my people get a fair share of promotions [in city jobs]," he told other ministers. "We don't need no more [minorities] and the minority they are creating is practically all white." Reverend C. Anderson Davis declared that homosexuals needed "treatment" and that protecting them from discrimination was like outlawing discrimination against drug addicts.[76] Not all black leaders agreed, of course. Former U. S. representative Barbara Jordan, the first black person to be elected to the Texas Senate since Reconstruction and the first black woman to be elected to the U. S. House of Representatives from the South, publicly opposed the repeal of the ordinances.[77]

On the day of the referendum, January 19, 1985, which coincided with celebrations of Martin Luther King Jr.'s birthday, the Committee for Public Awareness ran a large ad in the city's black newspaper, *The Informer and Texas Freeman*. The ad, endorsed by the black Baptist Ministers Association of Houston, warned that the ordinance was "the FIRST STEP in a calculated scheme by homosexuals to gain political power and to force their dangerous lifestyle on our city and nation." It also warned that the next step might be to give prostitutes "special privileges." It closed with this admonition: "We must not create an artificial minority, one that will steal the hard won rights from our born minorities; Females, Blacks, Hispanics, Asians, the disabled and aged. We don't want to make homosexuality something to be proud of!!"[78]

Another CPA-sponsored ad, this one in the *Houston Chronicle*, featured pictures of six prominent black Baptist ministers urging repeal. "Let's not forfeit our hard won rights to an artificial minority!" the ad warned. "This is a moral issue . . . not a discrimination issue. This is a gay power issue . . . not a civil rights issue."[79]

Repeal advocates distributed slick brochures with photographs of schoolchildren exiting buses that warned, "No matter what anyone says, no matter what they promise or deny or cross their hearts about, you know what the next step is: protecting the rights of homosexuals to teach their lifestyle in the classroom." If gay workers were protected, the brochure claimed, "we may face the problem of waiters and waitresses or hairdressers or others having AIDS, and their employers being unable to dismiss them." Stoking resentment among other groups with grievances, the brochure concluded that the ordinances were unfair to union workers because "work rules will favor gays over everybody else," unfair to "true" minorities who had "*earned* their place in the new Houston," and unfair to the 98 percent of Houstonians who weren't gay but had to foot the bill for the election to benefit "practically nobody."[80] Another brochure called homosexuality an "infectious appetite" and, relying on the work of Paul Cameron, associated homosexuals with STDs, prostitution, bestiality, sadism, masochism, suicide, and homicide.[81]

But perhaps the most inflammatory material of all was a brochure distributed during the campaign by Cameron's own Institute for the Scientific Investigation of Sexuality. The front cover of "Murder, Violence and Homosexuality" depicted a young girl cowering and screaming in a corner, her hands attempting to shield her body, as a man wielded a hatchet over her head. The brochure claimed that "you are 15 times more apt to be killed by a gay than a heterosexual during a sexual murder spree, homosexuals have committed most of the sexual conspiracy murders, most of the victims of sex murderers died at the hands of gays," and "half of all sex murderers are homosexuals." Homosexuals, it went on to assert, "are unusually prone to violence. Among police departments, this belief is so pervasive that particularly gory murders are assumed to be homosexual until proven otherwise." The pamphlet described in graphic detail the atrocities committed by what it called "homosexual murderers." The psychopathological spirit of Dean Corll remained alive and well.

The brochure further suggested that problems associated with homosexuality had risen in states where sodomy had been decriminalized. And it offered this observation about the supposed narcissism and selfishness of homosexuals: "Unable, because of their vice, to live genuinely constructive lives, they offer aesthetics instead of moral rectitude, dancing instead of building, 'sensitivity' rather than purposeful contribution." After reciting what it claimed were statistics showing more suicide, smoking, alcohol abuse, and even automobile accidents among gays, the brochure closed with this:

> Homosexuals are not merely parasites—they are more apt to be predatory. They run their lives closer to the ragged edge and they endanger everyone as a consequence. . . . In these and countless other ways homosexuals increase the collective risk of living. And to what advantage? What do homosexuals do *for* us that makes up for the damage they do *to* us? *Nothing*, nothing at all. There are no benefits associated with homosexuality, only liabilities—for them and for us. . . . Do we need this grief? Do our children need to play in a more dangerous world to satisfy the quirks of those given to kinky sex? No. Enough. Homosexuality ought to be suppressed with all deliberate speed, lets [sic] get on with it.[82]

Supporters of the repeal effort staffed a 200-person phone bank on the eve of the election to remind like-minded people to vote, compared with only 45 phones for the pro-ordinance group. And the repeal campaign raised and spent tens of thousands of dollars more than its opponents.[83] All of this activity overwhelmed gay-rights supporters and would have a deleterious effect on the public's perception of gay men and lesbians.

The results of the January 1985 referendum were devastating. Voters rejected the antidiscrimination ordinances by a stunning margin, 80 percent to 20 percent. The repeal won handily in every section of the

city except Montrose. A pall hung over the gay community and its organizations. Just a year before, local gay leaders thought they were the new
power brokers in the city; now nobody would return their phone calls.

On the day of the referendum, John Lawrence was forty-one years
old and Tyron Garner was seventeen. The police officers who would
arrest them thirteen years later were in their late teens or twenties. All
these men were old enough to understand what had happened. To Lawrence, the repeal showed "how stupid people can be."[84] The tone and
ferocity of the repeal campaign proved that homosexuals were still pari-
ahs after all. The campaign had given full voice to a deep-seated bigotry,
and voters had overwhelmingly validated that hatred and disgust. One
local political scientist described public opinion of gay men and lesbians
after the referendum: "They rank with atheists and communists."[85] A
columnist in the local gay newspaper noted that even otherwise progressive voters could not be counted on to stand up for gays. "We deluded
ourselves. We believed our 'progressive coalition' we thought we
belonged to would pull in behind us. . . . It didn't." Homophobia, not job
discrimination, was "the real issue in this campaign." Just a month after
the referendum, 59 percent of Houstonians told pollsters that they
opposed equal rights for gays.[86]

In the next election, not a single candidate for municipal office—not
even Mayor Whitmire—sought the GPC's endorsement. The group was
now, as Annise Parker recalled, "radioactive." Whitmire was running
against her predecessor, Louie Welch, who campaigned primarily on
opposition to gay rights and fear of AIDS. Actor Rock Hudson's death
from the disease on October 2 dominated tabloid news and had even
flooded major news outlets in the weeks before the mayoral election. Ten
days before the vote, Welch responded to a question about how to deal
with the disease by saying the solution was to "shoot the queers." He
later apologized for what he said was an unguarded remark made in a
moment of "levity."[87] Such moments of levity were common in the para-
noid days of 1985 when the fear of AIDS elicited a visceral response from
the public.

"The fallout from that [referendum] was that the community bubble
had been burst," remembered Parker. "We weren't all-powerful and
were shown to be mostly smoke and mirrors." The GPC was $10,000 in

debt, its membership fell, and AIDS itself started to take a serious toll, both by killing leaders in the community and by diverting talent and energy toward dealing with the immense health crisis.[88] While things gradually improved for the GPC and for gays in general, as a bloc, they would not soon regain the perceived influence on city politics they enjoyed in the golden years between 1979 and 1984.

AFTER THE REFERENDUM, Houston's gay activists began a long, slow process of rebuilding. Parker served two consecutive terms as president of the GPC, soon renamed the Houston Gay and Lesbian Political Caucus. "We retrenched," she observed. "I mean, 'tone down the rhetoric and let's pay off the bills, and do the basics and keep our heads down for a little while.'"[89] It helped that Welch and the rest of a self-designated "straight slate" of candidates running on antigay platforms, were defeated in the 1985 municipal election.

Over the next few years candidates gradually returned to seek the caucus's endorsement, although Republican candidates almost always stayed away as the party's religious conservatives exerted increasing influence in each succeeding GOP primary. This turn to social and religious conservatism was transforming the Republican Party around the country, and its effects were particularly evident in Harris County.

Annise Parker herself ran for city council as an openly gay candidate in 1991. Even though her opponent used gay-baiting tactics throughout the campaign and the press continually referred to her as a "lesbian" running for office, she got 20 percent of the vote against an incumbent in a multicandidate field. Four years later, running for an open at-large council seat, she finished a respectable third among nineteen candidates.[90]

In 1997, sensing that she might actually win, Parker ran for another at-large seat. She consciously downplayed her homosexuality and her history of gay-rights activism, knowing that these would be liabilities. As the campaign got started she sat down with representatives of the major press outlets in Houston and explained why she should be considered a mainstream candidate, not merely a lesbian activist. It had been ten years since she was president of the GPC, and Parker insisted to the media that such activity was the same as any other candidate's participation in various aspects of civic affairs. She was an oil and gas analyst, she stressed, a small business owner. If one of her opponents was being identified in a newspaper story as a "minister" or another as a "businessman," she deserved equal treatment, expecting to see "businessperson Annise Parker" or "oil and gas analyst Annise Parker"—not "lesbian Annise Parker." Her years as a gay activist were part of her résumé, but she wasn't going to let that define her campaign. Parker recalled that, remarkably, the local press agreed: "The only times I saw the gay stuff" was in longer articles, and even then it wouldn't be at the start of the piece with her name but somewhere "like the sixth paragraph."[91]

Her strategy worked. In the first round, she finished second and made it into the runoff. Her opponent was a moderate Republican backed by the city's business community and powerful downtown law firms. He occasionally reminded audiences of Parker's homosexuality by using an old trick, saying that he would not make an issue of the fact that his opponent was homosexual.

As before, Parker was backed by a progressive coalition of community groups and activists. This time, however, her backers also included the Baptist Ministers Association, which had strongly supported the 1985 repeal effort. Parker had worked with the association on other issues over the years and courted them in her prior two campaigns for city council. By 1997, she knew the leaders in the black community and they knew—and respected—her.

Winning the runoff by a 16-point margin, Parker became Houston's first openly gay elected official. Holding an at-large council seat in a city of almost two million people, she represented more constituents than any other gay officeholder in the country.

Parker's victory partially healed the scar left by the 1985 referendum, but the decision to downplay her homosexuality, which she and her advisers knew could prove detrimental, exposed the underlying reality: however much progress homosexuals in Houston had made, there remained in the general population a profound feeling of unease, if not outright disgust, toward them.

The unalterable fact was that homophobia was not simply a relic of the AIDS-conscious 1980s, as a brutal gay bashing a few years later showed. Gays in the Montrose area were repeatedly subjected to taunts, teasing, epithets, rock- and bottle-throwing, and physical assault. On the night of July 4, 1991, twenty-seven-year-old banker Paul Broussard and two friends were attacked not far from a local gay bar.

A group of ten young men from a Houston suburb called the Woodlands, all between seventeen and twenty-two, drove to Montrose that evening in two cars and began throwing rocks at men they presumed were gay. According to one account, they had "smashed the windshield of a car and hit a passing man in the mouth" by the time they asked Broussard and his friends for directions to a nearby gay club. As the trio answered, the boys leaped out of their cars and assaulted Broussard and the others "with fists, steel-toed boots, two-by-fours studded with nails, and at least one knife." While his friends escaped, the attack on Broussard continued, with the gang "cheering and yelling wildly, roaring like the crowd in a football game." He suffered numerous abrasions and cuts, a broken rib, bruised testicles, and three stab wounds.[92]

As Broussard "lay almost unconscious on the ground with his hand raised as if pleading for mercy or for help, . . . two of the assailants rifled his pockets and took his comb as a 'souvenir.'" He was treated by EMS at the scene but died eight hours later. Meanwhile, the boys drove home, as if celebrating victory in some sporting event. Their two cars were seen side by side on the highway, with some of the boys "leaning out of the windows and slapping palms together in noisy 'high-fives.'" Later, while they were having breakfast at a local Denny's, one of them "showed a knife to some of the others, and bragged that with it he had 'stuck the queer.'"[93]

For these ten youths, gay-bashing was nothing new. They had done it before, traveling from their homes in the northern suburbs to Montrose for the purpose of harassing and assaulting gay men. They reported that classmates, friends, and even teachers and coaches at their school had known about what they were doing. All of the "Woodlands Ten," as they became known, were convicted. Five received probation and were released. Four others were sentenced to jail but released on parole within a few years. The remaining defendant, who confessed to inflicting the fatal stab wound, was sentenced to forty-five years in prison.[94]

After the Broussard murder, the Houston Police Department, acting on reports of widespread and continual incidents of this type, finally sent undercover cops into Montrose to catch gay-bashers. The decoy police officers were yelled at, derided, and pelted with rocks and other objects by homophobic passersby who assumed they were gay. The assaults were so dangerous, in fact, that the undercover operation was halted to protect the safety of the officers.[95]

This was the world of homophobia and heterosexual anxiety in which John Lawrence and Tyron Garner, and the sheriff's deputies who arrested them, had been born and raised. It remained in large part a world of homosexual shame and defiance, where many gays simply chose to stay in the closet, a world where mutual suspicion between gays and the police was prevalent. The attitudes about gay people that we have seen were a preamble for the events of September 1998 in John Lawrence's apartment. The existence of an organized resistance to those attitudes—a cadre of knowledgeable and committed activists and lawyers both inside and outside of Houston—made possible everything that occurred afterward.

3.

The Defendants and the Troublemaker

*L*ITTLE IS STILL KNOWN PUBLICLY ABOUT THE MEN WHOSE ARRESTS led to the most important gay civil rights decision so far in American history. The Houston attorney who handled their case in the initial phase said, "They're not out to be any more famous than they accidentally came to be. They're private people."[1] Even less has been known about Robert Royce Eubanks, the man whose drunken and hysterical telephone call to the Harris County Sheriff's Office warning of an armed and crazy black man precipitated the chain of events that led to the arrests.

Public ignorance about these three men was the product of a very deliberate effort. Keeping a curious media—and especially partisans opposed to gay rights—away from the defendants and Eubanks while the case wended its way through the courts was a priority for the defense team. Lane Lewis, the first person who talked to John Lawrence about the arrest after he was released from jail, served initially as the men's informal public-relations manager. "My job the first couple of years was keeping the media away from these boys," said Lewis, a gay civil rights activist and former bartender in a Houston gay dance club.[2] Lawyers instructed the men not to discuss the case with any media and to refer all questions back to the legal team.[3] As we shall see, gay-rights attorneys and local activists had good reason to be concerned about how the public might respond to details about the pair if revealed by the media.

John Geddes Lawrence, from whom the Supreme Court case derives its name, was born in Beaumont, Texas, in 1943, to a family of devout white Southern Baptists.[4] His parents divorced when he was six and his father died when he was eleven. Lawrence's mother married a rancher who also had a house-moving business, and Lawrence was mostly raised by his grandmother.

Lawrence knew from "the day [he] was born" that he was attracted to other males, but like many others of the era he had no idea that there was an identity or label associated with that attraction. Thus, in 1960, at the age of seventeen, Lawrence decided to enlist in the U.S. Navy. As he and a friend were filling out the application, they came to a question asking whether they were homosexual. Lawrence turned to his buddy and asked, "What in the heck's a homosexual?" Neither had any idea what the term meant, even though both were gay. So Lawrence concluded, "Well, we're certainly not that." The men checked *no*, turned in their applications, and were accepted to serve in the Navy.

As it turned out, Lawrence served in the Navy for five years, reaching the rank of second-class corpsman. He married a woman he met in the Navy, but they divorced after six months when it turned out there was no "physical attraction." While in the military, he also had sexual relationships with several other men. Even though homosexuals were formally banned from the military, Lawrence's homosexuality had no effect on his service at a base hospital and was, in fact, quietly tolerated by his superiors. Lawrence was so comfortable in this life that he anticipated a full twenty-year military career, with retirement benefits to follow. But when his younger brother was sent to Vietnam, Lawrence's anxiety-filled mother and stepfather persuaded him to quit the military and return home to Texas.

Lawrence was low-key about his homosexuality, or as might be remarked in earlier times, he did not flaunt it. His parents, two sisters and brother knew he was gay and, he avers, accepted it. Beaumont, however, was not an ideal place for young gay men discovering themselves and their sexuality in the late 1960s and early 1970s. By comparison, nearby Houston, with its profusion of gay bars and relative tolerance, was a mecca for gay men of the region, much as it still is today. Lawrence quite naturally gravitated there.

In 1978, Lawrence moved into the Colorado Club Apartments, a complex in working-class far east Houston. Apartment managers appreciated him as a responsible and quiet tenant who always paid his rent on time.[5] A set of private stairs led directly up to Lawrence's small two-bedroom unit. The apartments were less than two miles from the building that housed both the Wallisville substation of the Harris County Sheriff's Office and the Justice of the Peace court where the *Lawrence* case made its first judicial stop. The apartment complex had a reputation as a "party" center for young adults and strippers, and as a result police were regularly called there to break up late-night parties, quell domestic disturbances, and deal with other such problems.[6] The area up and down Normandy Avenue, on which the apartments sat, was considered a high-crime area, with regular reports of shootings, stabbings, rapes, and thefts.[7]

Lawrence met his long-term partner, Jose Garcia, in 1992. Jose, born in 1963 in Durango, Mexico, lived with Lawrence for about two years prior to the arrest but moved out to care for an ailing brother. Jose was not out to his family in Mexico.[8] Starting in the late 1980s, Lawrence worked as a medical technologist analyzing "blood, urine, and pus" at a nearby hospital.[9] Those who knew him described him as quiet, "more like a small-town banker than a social activist."[10] But this tranquil demeanor belied another side. Back in 1967, he had been found guilty of murder-by-automobile in Galveston County and sentenced to five years' probation. Twice since then, in 1978 and 1988, he'd been arrested for driving while intoxicated.[11] The night of his arrest for sodomy in 1998, as we shall see, Lawrence had been drinking and was anything but quiet in reaction to the presence of police in his home.

Then there's the question of Lawrence's conception of himself as a gay man. To David Jones, a criminal defense lawyer who helped with the case in its early stages, Lawrence seemed to be "deep in the closet, behind the dresses,"[12] the very opposite of an activist eager to offer himself as a representative of gay-rights causes. To Lambda Legal Defense Fund attorney Suzanne Goldberg, however, it seemed less that he was closeted than that being gay did not dominate his identity. By the time of his namesake Supreme Court decision in 2003, Lawrence certainly had no problem identifying himself as gay. It seems likely that in 1998 Lawrence thought of himself as gay, socialized with other gay people, and was out to family and selected coworkers. But like many other gay Americans at the time, he was wary of revealing his sexual orientation to strangers or casual acquaintances.

Among Lawrence's earliest gay friends in Houston was a young white gay man, Robert Eubanks, whom he met in the mid-1970s. Born on July 22, 1958, Eubanks had brown hair and eyes, missing and crooked teeth, and a scar-laden face. One person close to the case described him as a "gun-totin', beer-swillin', Gilley's kickin' bubba from Pasadena,"[13] a working-class suburb of Houston. Unlike Lawrence, Eubanks never had a very stable life. He used Houston's skeletal bus system to get around because he did not own a car. Throughout the 1980s and '90s, he worked odd jobs—as a cook, an assistant at a boardinghouse, a clerk at several hotels, and so on—and slept wherever they would take him in. By all accounts, he was loud and temperamental and drank heavily.[14]

Lawrence and Eubanks briefly shared an apartment but, as Lawrence told it, "he kept getting into so much trouble that I finally had to get rid of him." Nevertheless, they remained friends until Eubanks, according to Lawrence, "pulled this shit"—making his infamous call to the Harris County Sherriff's Office, leading to the sodomy arrests. Lawrence came to think of Eubanks as "devious," "under-the-carpet cruel," and more like a two-year-old child than a grown man.[15]

In 1990, Eubanks met a black gay man in his early twenties named Tyron Garner. The youngest of ten children of traditional Baptists, Garner grew up in Houston in poverty. After high school, he took a course in word processing but that did not yield stable employment. Like Eubanks, he worked in a variety of short-term jobs: a cook, a waiter, a dishwasher, a house cleaner. He did not own a car or a home, and never even rented his own apartment. Instead, he moved among the homes and apartments of family members or friends for a few days, weeks, or months at a time. He was unemployed at the time of his sodomy arrest in 1998.[16]

Garner realized he was gay around the age of sixteen. He said that his family knew but he never discussed it with them. "I never had to tell them," he said. "I think they been knowing as long as I've been knowing. I think they just picked up on things." Like Lawrence, he had no involvement in the gay civil rights movement or in any gay-rights groups.[17]

Also like Lawrence, he had no idea homosexual sodomy was against the law in Texas.[18]

Garner had a quiet demeanor, at least around authority figures like police, judges, and attorneys. Goldberg, who met him a few times early in the case, described him as "sweet."[19] He was shy, passive, and according to those who knew him, effeminate. He had a slightly bent, hand-on-hips way of standing. When he smiled, he tended to cover his teeth with his lips, as if embarrassed by their appearance.[20]

In short time, Garner and Eubanks became boyfriends and started living together, sharing a bedroom at the home of Garner's parents for a few months. After that, the two men shared apartments and transient hotel rooms. Garner believed that Eubanks's family did not like the fact that Eubanks was gay and did not approve of their relationship.[21]

After Eubanks introduced them in the mid-1990s, Lawrence and Garner never became much more than acquaintances. They were never in a romantic or sexual relationship with each other, either before or after the sodomy arrests. About once a month, Eubanks and Garner took a bus to Lawrence's apartment twenty miles away to clean and run errands for Lawrence, for which they were paid a small wage. The three men occasionally went to dinner and gay bars together.[22]

Meanwhile, the relationship between Garner and Eubanks was tempestuous, to say the least. Eubanks was prone to calling Garner a "nigger" when he was drunk or angry.[23] Garner was twice charged with assaulting Eubanks, in 1995 and again after the sodomy arrest, in 2000.[24] In addition to these two assault cases, Garner was arrested for possession of marijuana, for aggravated assault on a peace officer in 1986, and for driving while intoxicated in 1990.[25] Garner's encounters with the police prior to 1998, as we shall see, may well have played a role in the events leading up to his arrest for sodomy.

On the evening of September 17, 1998, these three men—John Lawrence, Tyron Garner, and Robert Eubanks—came face-to-face with four deputies of the Harris County Sheriff's Office. It was an encounter, alas all too common in the annals of gay American history, that would change the lives of all involved.

The Department and the Deputies

JOHN LAWRENCE'S APARTMENT WAS NOT EVEN LEGALLY IN HOUS-
ton, but in an unincorporated area outside the city limits. These out-
lying regions fell under the jurisdiction not of the Houston Police
Department but of the Harris County Sheriff's Office (HCSO). Encom-
passing a sprawling area, the HCSO is broken up into five districts, each
with its own subdistricts: John Lawrence's home was in District 3, which
covered 269 square miles and was inhabited by about 170,000 people in
eastern and southern Harris County. Deputies patrolled an assigned
subdistrict in one-person police cars for eight-hour shifts, responding to
incidents they observed or to radio calls from the district dispatcher. In a
recent year, sheriff's deputies in District 3 responded to some 105,000
service calls and made 5,448 arrests, of which more than 1,100 were for
felonies.[1] There is, in the words of one of the officers who made the
arrests in the *Lawrence* case, "hardly ever downtime."[2]

HCSO had long earned a cowboy reputation: macho, trigger-happy,
and prone to excessive force. A review by the *Houston Chronicle* in 2004
showed that deputies fired on unarmed people far more often than similar urban law enforcement agencies during the period 1999–2004.
For example, Cook County (which includes Chicago), with 500 patrol
deputies, had no such incidents during the period. HCSO, with 750
patrol deputies, had fifty such shootings. The HCSO rate was three or
four times that of the New York City Police Department.[3] The gap is at
least partly attributable to the fact that many police departments

around the country have had much stricter use-of-force policies than does Harris County.[4]

Another factor explaining the department's record of excessive force was an ethos celebrating and encouraging machismo. In the same 1999–2004 period, for example, Harris County sheriff's deputies fired into a passing vehicle on at least fourteen occasions, sometimes even putting themselves in the path of the car, in violation of their training. In most of these cases, only minor offenses were at issue. Yet in only two of those fourteen cases were officers disciplined for reckless conduct.[5]

In its treatment of racial, sexual, and other minorities, the record of the HCSO was equally troubling—and far worse than that of the Houston Police Department, which was more responsive to citizen complaints and whose officers were carefully trained to deal with diverse populations. The sheriff's department was "a good-'ol-boys club, a place where Bubbas sporting buzz cuts were more comfortable" than blacks, women, and gays.[6]

The department has historically had an unusually high rate of complaints of racial bias, with the complainants themselves often facing retribution. In 1998, the year of the *Lawrence* arrests, black officers constituted 23 percent of the force. But blacks struggled to find a way into the upper echelons of the department, often filing lawsuits. At the beginning of the twenty-first century, just 13 percent of supervisors were black, and the percentage was lower at every level of promotion. As late as 2004, only one captain and one major in the whole department were black. Yet during the same period, black employees were fired at a much higher rate; they constituted 38 percent of all terminations in the department.[7]

During the years immediately before and after the *Lawrence* arrests, bigoted comments were common among deputies. According to affidavits by two deputies, a major in the department made "racial and/or derogatory remarks toward blacks, women, and homosexuals" on numerous occasions. The officer used the words "nigger" and "queer" in conversation. He told "war stories" about bashing homosexuals when he was young. Yet he did not even receive a reprimand.[8]

In recent decades, almost every leader of the black officers' league in the department has been fired, demoted, or forced to resign.[9] A press account summed up HCSO's record on racial relations:

The last decade [1994–2004] was a particularly ugly time for race relations in the sheriff's office. White employees were punished for using racial slurs and bragging of KKK membership. Twice, white officers supposedly commented that black co-workers resembled monkeys. When the [black officers'] league made an issue of the problems, some white deputies briefly formed a "Caucasian-American Police Association" in the spirit of obstruction.[10]

Needless to say, the sheriff's department was also not a hospitable place for gay and lesbian employees. According to one closeted lesbian in the department who asked not to be identified for fear of the consequences, antigay jokes and remarks were common. Any employee who came out of the closet would be subject to ridicule and ostracism. The environment was especially hostile, she reported, toward gay men.[11] Court personnel involved in *Lawrence v. Texas* confirmed this observation.[12]

Not surprisingly, as late as 2007, there were no openly gay male employees in the department.[13] (As we shall learn, however, there were gay men in the department.) The department's equal employment policy prohibited discrimination on the basis of race, religion, sex, age, national origin, or disability—but not on the basis of sexual orientation.[14]

The head of the department, the sheriff, was elected from a very socially conservative constituency. While deputies got training to make them aware of racial issues, no such training was given to them regarding homosexuals. Perhaps bowing to the antihomosexual views of its constituents, the department refused to include such training.[15]

In its own way, the refusal of the Harris County Sheriff's Office to recognize and train its officers for the realities of modern life made the arrests in *Lawrence* both inevitable and unusually abusive.[16] Their inevitability created a case; the undue force and rudeness made Lawrence so angry that it ensured the case would go well beyond a Justice of the Peace court and a simple fine. In this, as in many other ways, antigay attitudes and discourse indirectly caused the end of sodomy laws in America.

FOUR DEPUTIES IMMEDIATELY responded to the call from a dispatcher about possible gun violence and entered John Lawrence's apartment the night of the arrests: Joseph Quinn, William Lilly, Donald Tipps, and Ken Landry. All of them began their service in the HCSO around 1990. What follows is based on interviews with three of the four. Only Landry did not respond to requests for an interview.

As the first to arrive on the scene at Lawrence's apartment, by department practice Quinn was the lead officer in charge of making arrests and filing reports. More than any other single sheriff's deputy, he was responsible for the case that became known as *Lawrence v. Texas*. He composed and filed the sixty-nine-word report that would provide the only "facts" about the case that the appeals courts, including the Supreme Court, ever saw. Standing six foot two, and weighing 245 pounds, Quinn kept his head shaved in the fashion common among sheriff's department deputies. Born in Des Moines, Iowa, in 1958, he was the youngest of five boys.[17] His family moved to Houston when he was three years old. Although raised a Catholic, Quinn later became a Southern Baptist. He married and had two children.

After high school, Quinn joined the Army, becoming a helicopter pilot. Released from the Army after six years in 1985, Quinn worked odd jobs, flying helicopters for private companies, but the money was not very good and Quinn was restless. As it happened, the sheriff's department was then undertaking a massive hiring program under a court order to improve conditions in the county jails it ran. Quinn's brother, a deputy, suggested that he sign up.

Like all new recruits, Quinn started out working in the county jail as a so-called noncertified detentions officer, which meant he was not yet a true deputy. He wore a white shirt and pants, with no badge, which did not suit his concept of a police officer. Quinn passed a test to become a certified peace officer and in 1989 was promoted to patrol, with the badge and a real uniform, a position that carries much more prestige.

Quinn quickly developed a reputation as a tough cop. "He's the worst nightmare I think anybody would ever come across," said Nathan Broussard, a court clerk who worked in Quinn's district and handled many of the cases Quinn brought in. "When someone thinks about getting arrested and you have this worst-case scenario of an officer, Quinn is the poster child for worst case."[18] Broussard believed Quinn had a notoriously "bad attitude" toward citizens. "He just does not care about [people], the human side of him didn't exist. It's just rough. Rough talk. He's a 'I don't care what you have to say, just get in the car and shut up,' kind of an officer." Quinn continually brought in people for minor offenses like public intoxication and other Class C misdemeanors, which most officers would not bother filing.[19]

The justice of the peace whose precinct covered Quinn's patrol territory in 1998 had similar views of Quinn. Quinn wrote tickets "pretty heavy" in his court, Judge Mike Parrott recalled.

> He's just overzealous. He was "zero tolerance." A lot of times there's pushing and shoving [among kids in a school]—boom!— he'd write the kids a ticket. I'm not so sure they should have got a ticket. These kids have never had a ticket. Joe would have written a ticket, thrown them on the ground, handcuffed them, strip-searched them, cavity-searched them. I mean, that's just Joe.[20]

In fact, Judge Parrott specifically remembered two incidents involving Quinn. In one case, Quinn arrested two mothers whose kids attended the same middle school as Parrot's. Quinn told them to move their cars from a no-parking zone in front of the middle school. When they protested that they were waiting for their children to get out of school, Quinn ordered them to step out, slammed them against their cars, slapped handcuffs on them, and hauled them to jail in front of shocked parents and schoolchildren. The women ended up in Parrott's court, sobbing.

In a second case, Quinn was hired as a private security guard at a kids' soccer game that Parrott attended. The coach for one of the teams arrived and parked her car in a zone for people with disabilities so that she could unload the team's equipment. Quinn ordered her to move her car immediately. She responded that she would be there only for a few minutes. She also pointed to a disability tag on her car, which authorized her to park in the zone. Quinn told her that she didn't look like she had a disability and had better leave immediately. "Oh, what are you, a rent-a-cop?" she retorted. Parrott watched as Quinn then pushed her against her car, arrested her, and took her to jail. "I don't think that would have happened with any other deputy," Parrott remarked.[21]

A review of Quinn's service in the sheriff's department supports the concerns expressed by court personnel. When asked in an interview whether he had ever been subject to discipline by the sheriff's department, Quinn's first reaction was to laugh. He then boasted: "Actually, I have the largest Internal Affairs [complaint] file in the department." He had been placed on administrative suspension. He had been blamed in four or five instances of "fleet accidents" involving damage to a patrol car. On one occasion he was passed over for promotion to sergeant based on incidents in his file. Quinn's record was so troubling to the department that it began a special process under which all citizen complaints against him would automatically be reported to the Internal Affairs division. In 2002, four years after the sodomy arrests, Quinn was reprimanded and sent to work again in the jail, an action he blamed on retaliation because, he said, he arrested a person with "political connections" in the sheriff's department. For a demoted patrol officer, assignment to the jail is a "punishment area." Officers in the department describe it as "like having your dick cut off"—emasculation for a proud patrol deputy.[22] Quinn was later promoted to sergeant, but was still assigned to the jail and not returned to patrol duty.

An incident from Quinn's complaint file, relayed by Quinn himself, gives some flavor of his style of policing. A woman called the sheriff's office because her estranged husband would not return her child. When Quinn arrived, she was talking to the husband on the phone. "You called me here, hang up the phone," Quinn instructed her. She replied, "Well, you need to talk to him."

"No, I'm not here to talk to somebody on the phone. I'm here to talk to you. So hang up the phone or I'm going to leave."

"Fuck you," she responded, "Leave."

"Okay," Quinn said, walking out. When the woman called for him to return, he shouted back, "Okay, well, I think right now you might be a little bit intoxicated and it might not be in the best interest for me to tell your husband to bring your child over here and you to have control over him."

As Quinn got into his patrol car, the woman came out of her apartment and called him a "fat motherfucker." When Quinn threatened to arrest her for disturbing the peace and for public intoxication, the woman did the worst possible thing: she challenged his manhood. "You ain't man enough to arrest me," she shouted.

"Wrong answer," retorted Quinn. "If you tell me I can't do something, I'm going to show you what I can do."

Quinn started toward the woman's apartment. Seeing that, she ran back inside, attempting to close the door. After a struggle, Quinn handcuffed the woman and, as he himself described it, pushed her down the stairs. Quinn said the woman resisted being put into the patrol car and made the throat-clearing sound of someone about to spit. "So I just have a reaction: if she can't exhale, she can't spit," he remembered. "So I grabbed her by the throat."

The woman filed a written complaint about the incident, charging that Quinn used excessive force against her. The complaint included photographs of her neck, which showed in detail bruises where she said each of Quinn's fingers had been. Quinn disputed the woman's charge and even disputed that the photographs depicted bruises caused by him. Both he and the woman passed a polygraph test in the subsequent investigation, he asserted. But the department concluded that her complaint was valid and issued a letter of reprimand. He was also sent to anger-management school, where he got counseling alongside people convicted of assault and domestic violence.

Any police officer, under the pressures of the job, can lose his cool, and false and exaggerated complaints can be filed. Law enforcement is a dangerous job, one often rewarded with ingratitude, suspicion, and even contempt by some members of the public. It would require a superhuman degree of equanimity not to lose one's temper and patience on occasion. Calibrating one's actions perfectly in every situation, no matter how fraught with danger, is impossible. That's especially true when an officer's actions are evaluated in the cool air of hindsight, which is when they are always analyzed. Nevertheless, the sheer volume of complaints against Quinn, larger than any other officer's in the department, suggests that something besides the ordinary pressures and misjudgments of policing is at work.

Consider Quinn's approach to his job. In interviews, he conveyed a deeply ingrained sense of hierarchy and authority. He is the law; the citizen is subject. More important, to Quinn, citizens were unruly subjects, even enemies, and were always potentially dangerous. Quinn likened patrolling to a "war zone." He described his attitude toward his job in this way: "I get on at ten o'clock, I'm going home at six o'clock. Survival mentality. I don't care what I have to do. They're not going to get me. I'm going to . . . you know, if it comes down to it—if I have to run over them with a car, with a baseball bat, shoot them, grab a knife and stab them—whatever it takes, I'm going to win." It is, said Quinn, reciting a common refrain among deputies, "better to be judged by twelve [jurors] than carried by six [pallbearers]."

Quinn also had a disdain for the particular class of people in his patrol area. Quinn himself acknowledged that "something about my personality" did not mix well with the rough language and disrespectful behavior of the poor people and minority groups who live on the east side of Harris County. Here is how he described a prototypical encounter with someone in his patrol area. "I walk up and you know, I'll be talking to somebody and somebody else will start [to interrupt]. 'Whoa, whoa, whoa,'" Quinn might tell the interloper. "You know, and they'll keep talking. 'Shut up.' 'You can't talk to me that way.' 'I just did. Shut up.' 'Well, I'm going to complain on you,'" this typical resident would tell Quinn.

By contrast, Quinn described a similar encounter with a citizen on the wealthier west side of the county: "If I was on the west side in the more affluent area, you know, 'Excuse me, sir, I need to talk to you. Can you come over please?'" But on the east side, Quinn explained, people are different. "Over there [on the east side], it's 'Hey, you. Fucker. Come here.' They don't respond to 'sir.'" Quinn did not function well in a world where people did not use respectful language toward him. In September 1998, Quinn stepped into a working-class stew of homosexuality, alcohol, and disrespectful language. John Lawrence would not address Quinn as "sir."

Additionally, Quinn's tough-cop demeanor was infused with a defensive sense of his own masculinity. It's revealing that in the incident involving the woman recounted above, Quinn did not make the arrest until she shouted that he was not "man enough"—even though there had been verbal provocations before then. Similarly, Quinn's sense of masculinity may have influenced his reaction upon encountering obviously gay men in Lawrence's apartment.

That raises the related question of Quinn's attitudes toward gays. Quinn did not know any openly gay people as he grew up. Until the Lawrence arrests, his encounters with people he knew to be gay were rare. Most of what he knew about gays came from things he heard from friends, family, church, and the various media in a socially conservative area.

Citing the biblical story of Sodom and Gomorrah, Quinn believed that homosexual acts were immoral and thought they should "probably be against the law." Society should "go by God's law, not by man's law." He described homosexuality as a sin. Homosexuals should repent, he said, as should all sinners. "The only unforgivable sin is not to accept the offering of Jesus Christ." He opposed gay marriage because "God said it's not right." While he believed that gays should not be categorically excluded from the military, even on this issue he was palpably uncomfortable. "The thing is, I don't have any part of that," he answered when asked if he would serve in close confines with a homosexual in the military. "Don't come around me with that, you know."

Almost any other officer in the department would probably have released Lawrence and Garner under the circumstances in which they were found, whether they were actually having sex (and thus had violated Texas law) or not. "I just do not think there is another police officer here in this county that would have done it," said Sheryl Roppolo, the office manager for Judge Parrott.[23] With Quinn, however, the barest hint of resistance or disrespect was enough to find a reason to take someone to jail.

Had William Lilly arrived on the scene before Quinn, instead of seconds after him, he would have been the lead officer and would have been responsible for deciding whether to file charges. Lilly was, in fact, the only black man among the arresting deputies and, with Quinn, one of only two who claimed to have witnessed any sex in Lawrence's apartment. Born on March 7, 1962, in Houston, Lilly, like Garner, was raised in the socially conservative black Baptist faith.[24] Unlike Garner, he was one of only three children, regularly attended church, and had both a stable family life and career. He married and had children of his own.

It is significant that Lilly did not stumble haphazardly onto a career in law enforcement because he lacked other options. After high school, he worked for the Texas Department of Corrections, the state's jail system, and briefly for the Galveston County Sheriff's Office. In 1991, he joined the Harris County Sheriff's Office.

Like all deputies, Lilly started out working in the jail. After that, he was moved to the prisoner-transport division, shuttling prisoners to court, to the hospital, and so on. In 1995, he became a patrol deputy assigned to the Wallisville substation of District 3, covering the area where Lawrence lived.

As was true for Quinn and indeed for any deputy, citizen complaints had been filed against Lilly. There were, however, far fewer such complaints against Lilly and only one—for hitting an inmate—that resulted in any disciplinary action, a short probation. After the Lawrence arrest, he rose in the department to sergeant and detective, reflecting his clean record and reliable service.

Of the three deputies interviewed for this book, Lilly was the most forthright, and his views on homosexuality were the most nuanced. In fact, his views appeared to be a microcosm of the shifting and conflicted opinions on homosexuality held by many Americans. He admitted that for a long time he "had a phobia against homosexuals," but believed he had "grown out of that." He thought people were born gay "because I have seen little bitty kids [who were gay], and I know they don't know one way or the other."

In an interview, he was clear that he opposed the criminalization of private sex in the home, the very crime for which Lawrence and Garner were arrested. "I couldn't care less what they do as long as they don't come on to me," he said, echoing an aversion expressed by Quinn and Tipps. Like the other deputies, he opposed gay marriage because "marriage is between a man and a woman according to the Man above." He didn't think homosexuals should serve in the military, at least partly because of a genuine concern for the safety of gay men. "What if you have one guy, a homosexual guy, come on to a straight guy and the straight guy was carrying a firearm? I mean, it could be dangerous," he speculated.

For Lilly, as for many Americans, there was a profound difference between lesbians and gay men. Lesbianism, he believed, was trendy and broadly accepted. In fact, he suspected his two daughters' softball coach was a lesbian, a possibility that did not seem to bother him at all. "But at the same time, I have a four-year-old son and if I knew a Boy Scout leader was homosexual, would I let him be in that group? No." He thought it would be bad for society if male homosexuality were as broadly accepted as lesbianism.

What accounted for his difference in tolerance of gay men, on the one hand, and lesbians, on the other? With gay men, there was a danger of AIDS, Lilly suggested. However, "as far as spreading diseases, they spreading them on themselves so . . ." His voice trailed off.

But Lilly's unease with gay men was much more personal and deeply rooted than a fear of infectious disease. "The thing that bothers me most about gay men is the fact that they try to be so feminine," he said. "And that part bothers me. I mean, I don't dislike them. And like I said, I've had many conversations with gay men. But why do they have to flaunt that part, you know?" Lilly especially remembered one boy he knew while growing. "I couldn't stand this boy because he was gay and just . . . all his feminine twists in it, and trying to . . . I couldn't stand that," he commented. Lilly thought he could spot a gay man or even a "little bitty kid" who might become gay because of this gender nonconformity.

The most effeminate man in the apartment the night of the arrests was, like Lilly, a black man. Lilly's discomfort with gay men's effeminacy may have been intensified by the sight of another black man "flaunt[ing] that part."

Two other deputies, Donnie Tipps and Ken Landry, were also present in Lawrence's apartment that night. During an interview for this book, the six-foot-tall 165-pound Donnie Tipps spoke in a serious, clipped way, and with a heavy Texas drawl. Born on November 14, 1965, in Warsburg, Germany, he was the son of an American soldier who abandoned the family.[25] When Tipps's biological mother decided she was unable to care for him and his three brothers, she gave the children to Boys Country, a Houston organization that describes itself as "a Christian Home, providing children from families in crisis with love, security, a sense of self-worth, and opportunities to prepare them for a successful life."[26] There, a staff member and his wife formally adopted Tipps and his brothers.

Tipps moved to the city of Houston itself in 1983, two years before the referendum on the city's gay-rights ordinances. After high school, he worked for a variety of auto supply and construction companies. He married and had a son. Following the lead of a brother and his adoptive father, who were police officers, Tipps joined the Harris County Sheriff's Office in 1991. He worked in the jail until 1997 and then began uniformed patrol duty, assigned to the Wallisville substation.

During his service in the department, Tipps was investigated several times by the Internal Affairs division. He described such investigations as "part of being a cop." While he said the public complaints were unfounded, several resulted in suspension without pay and he was placed on probation. Not long after the *Lawrence* arrest, he was sent back to work in the jail for a year.

Unlike Lilly, he thought homosexual activity should be illegal, even in the privacy of the home. "The Bible tells you that, the Bible will tell you that's wrong," he asserted. To him, it was like drug use and deadly assault. "If you smoke weed in your home, it's against the law. If you smoke crack, it's against the law. You shoot somebody in your home, it's against the law. I mean, laws in my opinion should be cut-and-dried." Like Quinn, he did think gays should be allowed to serve in the military, explaining that "they can probably do just as good a job as anybody else." Like Quinn and Lilly, he opposed gay marriage.

There were a few known lesbians in the sheriff's department, he reported, but no openly gay males. He said he would not have a problem with a gay man serving on the force "as long as they did their job and kept their homosexual tendencies to their self." Tipps worried that the presence of known male homosexuals in the department might create "a manifest hazard."

In general, Tipps attributed his attitudes about homosexuality to his Southern Baptist upbringing. "I'm from the South," he explained. "I guess we just got grown up that way. It's the way I was raised. I mean, the Bible don't support it—same sex—and I don't either."

Althoughs Tipps did not have any gay friends or family members, he said he had no problem personally with homosexuals as long as, echoing the other deputies, "they don't come bother me with it." The deputies all claimed not to mind homosexuals, but did not like flagrant homosexuals and did not really want male homosexuals around them.

The fourth deputy on the scene in Lawrence's apartment was Ken Landry, who was in his midthirties at the time. Born in Lake Charles,

Louisiana, he graduated from a Houston-area high school in 1981; then served in the Army, reaching the rank of staff sergeant.[27] In 1992, he joined the Harris County Sheriff's Office, where he was assigned to street patrol for the first time in April 1998, just five months before the arrests. He had a mustache and, like Quinn and many other deputies, shaved his head. Quinn reported that Landry liked to "joke and cut up." Tipps described him as hardworking, professional, smart, and disciplined. The role that he and Tipps played in the arrests was, as we shall see, distinctly smaller than the one played by Quinn and Lilly.

These four officers were the first to enter John Lawrence's apartment the night of the arrests looking for what they thought was a dangerous, armed black man. Their anxiety, given those circumstances, was understandable. The arrests that resulted were anything but commonplace in Texas legal history.

Part Two

...

THE ARRESTS

5.

The Intrusion

WHAT HAPPENED THAT NIGHT IN JOHN LAWRENCE'S APART-
ment? In interviews, police claimed that they walked in looking
for a man with a gun and instead found two men having sex in a bedroom in violation of a specific Texas law forbidding oral and anal sex
between persons of the same sex. As might be expected, the accounts of
the deputies and defendants, in their own separate interviews, differ in
significant ways. Perhaps less predictably, and more important, the deputies also differ among themselves about what happened.

In September 1998, the on-again, off-again relationship between
Tyron Garner and Robert Eubanks was back on. By September 17, the
men had arranged to get an apartment together. The timing worked well
for John Lawrence, who offered to give them an old queen-size bed, two
chairs, and some tables he wanted to replace with new furniture. That
afternoon, the three men busied themselves cleaning Lawrence's apartment and moving the old furniture into the guest bedroom. Movers
came at 5:30 p.m. to take the heavy items, like the bed.[1] The next day
Eubanks and Garner planned to rent a truck so they could haul the rest
of the old furniture to their new apartment.[2]

Their work for the day completed, the men treated themselves to
dinner and drinks at Pappasito's, a local Tex-Mex restaurant. They
returned to Lawrence's apartment about nine o'clock. Lawrence and
Garner chatted and watched television in the kitchen. Eubanks, a
heavy drinker, turned on the TV in the living room, plunked himself

into an easy chair, and began downing vodka straight from a bottle. Lawrence had another drink or two back at the apartment but Garner abstained; he was not a heavy drinker and was probably not intoxicated that night. Garner remembered that at some point in the evening a Hispanic male—possibly a friend of Eubanks—arrived. Lawrence had no memory of any other person being in the apartment.

As the evening wore on, Eubanks became increasingly drunk, a state in which he was easily angered. On this particular night, he may have been jealous that Lawrence and Garner were talking to each other; however, recalling the events in interviews, neither Lawrence nor Garner were certain of this. Whatever the cause, Eubanks got louder and more belligerent. Lawrence asked him to leave but offered to let Garner stay, a show of hospitality that must have further enraged Eubanks. Eubanks had a different idea: he offered to spend the night in Lawrence's apartment, but wanted Garner to leave. Garner refused. In any event, the men had arrived by bus, since they had no car, and by now they figured the buses had stopped running. They were stuck for the night. Lawrence, by his own account fairly intoxicated, took the bottle away from Eubanks because he did not want Eubanks "drinking all the damn vodka, which he was extremely good at." Deprived of his liquid solace, Eubanks stared at the living room TV.

About 10:30 p.m., Eubanks got up from the chair, walked into the kitchen and grabbed some change from a drawer. He announced he was going downstairs to get a soda and stormed out. Lawrence, who was anxious about completing the furniture move the next day, began thinking about going to bed. Eubanks negotiated the two dozen stairs down to the first floor and walked fifty feet to a small covered breezeway next to the apartment manager's office. Adjacent to some vending machines was a public telephone lit by overhead fluorescent bulbs. Eubanks may have stood there a few minutes, disconsolate, wondering what he should do. Eventually, he put some change into the telephone and made his soon-to-be infamous call to the Harris County Sheriff's Office.

Precisely what he said to the sheriff's office is unknown, though based on Eubanks's call, the dispatcher informed area patrol cars that there was a report of "a black male going crazy with a gun" inside the apartment. Friends and acquaintances of Eubanks, however, including Garner and Lane Lewis,[3] the first gay activist who learned of the arrests, believed that he may have referred to Garner as a "nigger" when he called the sheriff's office. Eubanks often used the word when referring to black people, even when addressing his own boyfriend, Garner. He was even more likely to use it when drunk and upset, as he was when he made the call. On the other hand, even in his inebriated condition, Eubanks may have had enough sense to know that such words should not be used when reporting an incident to law enforcement authorities.

Another mystery is why Eubanks falsely reported that Garner was threatening people in the apartment with a gun. What did he hope to accomplish? Lawrence speculated that Eubanks wanted to get Garner out of the apartment and must have concluded that the sheriff's department would accomplish this by arresting him. Eubanks was angry at Garner for some reason or reasons, including jealousy over what he probably saw as flirting between Garner and Lawrence. He probably believed that his report would somehow get Garner into trouble with the police. Knowing the neighborhood and the police in the area well, he may also have believed that the danger presented by a black man with a weapon would be taken especially seriously. This may partly explain why he chose to designate Garner rather than Lawrence as the fictitious gunman.

It would have been obvious to a sober person that since Garner did not actually have a gun there would have been no reason for the police to arrest him once they arrived. Indeed, a clearheaded person would surely have realized that he placed himself in jeopardy by lying to the police about a serious matter. But by all accounts, including those of the deputies, Eubanks had parted ways with his faculties that night. Lawrence, for example, recalled that Eubanks's health was rapidly declining and that he was "becoming more and more crazy."[4]

With Eubanks's call, the machinery of law enforcement began churning. At about 10:49 p.m., the sheriff's office dispatcher for east Harris County sent out a high-pitched tone to the radio receivers in all District 3 patrol cars. That tone is well-known to deputies because it indicates serious trouble needing immediate response. Then the dispatcher announced, "Clear units, Beat 20. We have a weapons disturbance at 794 Normandy, the Colorado Club Apartments, apartment 833."[5]

At that moment, Joe Quinn was on his way to get gas. He had just passed the apartment complex. William Lilly was nearing the end of an eight-hour shift and was headed home in his patrol car, but was only four blocks away. Donnie Tipps, also nearing the end of his shift, and Ken Landry were patrolling a bit farther away. For the deputies, it had so far been an uneventful night on patrol.[6]

Quinn immediately radioed the dispatcher, who informed him they'd received a report that there was an armed black man inside apartment 833. Quinn turned his car around and headed into the apartment complex, arriving at 10:52 p.m. He knew that building 800 was toward the back of the complex. He called the dispatcher to say he had arrived, turned off his headlights so as not to alert the offender, and drove cautiously toward the building. He was the first officer to get there, arriving within minutes of receiving the call.

Quinn unholstered his gun and stepped slowly out of his patrol car, all the while looking around to see if he could spot the man with the gun. He was especially keen on watching the balconies of the two-story building in case the gunman might be hiding on one of those. It was dead quiet. There was nobody around. He walked up to a breezeway leading through the middle of building 800 and began looking around for apartment 833. Nearby was the "party pool" and hot tub, where Quinn and the other officers had broken up more than a few late-night bacchanals. But the pool was placid; no one was there. When Quinn reached the other side of the breezeway he turned right. There, standing on the grass at the far end of the building, about fifty feet away, under moderate lighting, he saw a man.

That man, he learned later, was the person who had in fact made the call, Robert Eubanks. Quinn noticed that Eubanks, wearing a white striped shirt and long dark pants, was crying and seemed very upset. As Quinn recalled the moment, Eubanks motioned toward him and in a loud whisper, said, "Over here! Over here!"

"There's a man with a gun?" Quinn asked warily.

"Yeah, he's up there in that apartment," Eubanks responded, pointing to a second-floor apartment on the side of the building.

"Come here," Quinn instructed Eubanks. "Get away from over there." Eubanks, who was paralyzed by fear, emotion, and alcohol, wouldn't budge. For all Quinn knew, it could have been Eubanks who wielded the reported gun. Although Eubanks was white, mistakes can be made in reporting a call and dispatching deputies. He had no reason, however, to believe at this point that Eubanks was gay, much less romantically involved with the black suspect. As Quinn put it, on a potential weapons scene like this, "you're ready for battle."

"Don't put your hands in your pockets," he ordered Eubanks. "Keep your hands out where I can see them."

There the two men stood, as if in a standoff, until first Lilly, then Tipps, and finally Landry arrived (Lilly and Tipps claimed not to have drawn their guns yet at this point). As the first officer on the scene, Quinn was the "priority unit" on the call. The other deputies followed his lead.

After conferring quickly about what to do, the four deputies approached Eubanks and patted him down to make sure he was unarmed. He was still crying and had begun shaking, although the deputies did not know why. They again asked the whereabouts of the reported gunman. Eubanks pointed up to Lawrence's apartment. "There's a black guy up there. And he's got a gun." The deputies instructed Eubanks to back away from the area.

Quinn, Lilly, Tipps, and Landry headed up the stairwell leading directly to apartment 833, guns drawn with their trigger fingers "indexed," which in law enforcement parlance means the fingers were along the side of their weapons, ready to fire. As they climbed the stairwell they formed what is known as a "tactical stack," one deputy right behind the other. Quinn was in the lead position.

When the deputies reached the small landing at the front of the apartment, Quinn saw that the door was mostly closed but not pulled completely shut. It was resting against the doorjamb, slightly ajar, but offered no view into the apartment. The deputies listened for a sound, such as people arguing or moving around, but they heard nothing.

Quinn checked the doorknob. It was unlocked. He knocked on the door, which had the effect of pushing it open slightly. The light in the room was on. Quinn then pushed the door completely open. The deputies were quiet up to this point, not announcing their presence. Standing at the threshold to the apartment, they performed a quick visual scan. They were at the entrance to an unremarkable living room, thirteen by sixteen feet, with a couch, chairs, tables, and television. According to the deputies, nobody was in the room. There was no television, radio, or other sound to be heard. Ahead, at the other end of the living room, the deputies could see an open dining area and, off to the left, a kitchen. Also ahead, past the dining area, there was what turned out to be an unlit bedroom about twenty-five feet away with the door open. Immediately to the left there was another bedroom with the door open and the light on inside. (See the apartment floor plan in the photograph insert.)

"Sheriff's department! Sheriff's department!" Quinn shouted in a voice loud enough for anyone inside the apartment to hear. The purpose of such an announcement is to warn the offender and any potential victim that police are on the scene. This might allow a victim or captive to escape. It also gives the offender the opportunity to surrender peacefully, or at least not to shoot as a reflex upon suddenly and unexpectedly seeing a stranger. Only fifteen to twenty minutes had now passed from the time Eubanks walked out of the apartment, Lawrence and Garner later estimated.[7]

According to the deputies, there was no reaction to Quinn's shout inside the apartment. Nobody appeared and nobody answered. Quinn turned to the other deputies and asked, "You ready? We're going in."

As the deputies entered the living room, they began a "peel off" maneuver in which deputies go in different directions to secure the area. Tipps and Landry peeled off toward the left to investigate one bedroom.[8] The door to that bedroom was open and the light was on. Tipps and Landry did a quick sweep of this bedroom, looking under the bed and in the closet, but there was nobody to be found.

Meanwhile, Quinn and Lilly moved through the living room toward the kitchen area. There the deputies saw a man ("Man #4") wearing a shirt and tan long pants standing beside the refrigerator with his hands in the air, one holding a telephone receiver. He had evidently been talking to someone on the phone when the deputies entered the apartment. Quinn recalled that the man was Hispanic and in his thirties while Lilly thought he might have been white. Tipps did not recall that any fourth man was present in the apartment. At any rate, Man #4 was later identified in Quinn's Offense Report as Ramon Pelayo-Velez.[9] According to Quinn, Man #4 stood about five-foot-ten-inches to six-foot-tall, was in his early thirties, and had a thin build with a dark complexion. He spoke English with a heavy Spanish accent.[10] In an interview, Lawrence denied that Man #4 could have been his partner, Jose Garcia, who matched the description of Pelayo-Velez, insisting that Jose was in Mexico at the time, visiting family.[11]

Quinn shouted at the man, "Do not move! Let me see your hands." Man #4 dropped the receiver. Hearing the commotion, Tipps and Landry came out of the side bedroom to assist. The deputies instructed the man to come into the living room and lay flat on his stomach, where they frisked and handcuffed him. They then sat him down on the couch. According to Quinn, Tipps and Landry stayed with him.[12]

The deputies had still heard no noises in the apartment. The door to the unexamined bedroom was wide open but the light was off inside the room, so its contents were not completely visible. "We've still got that one to check," Quinn told Lilly, pointing toward the back bedroom. Slowly, according to Quinn and Lilly, they approached the bedroom, with Lilly in front and Quinn right behind him, guns pointed straight ahead.[13]

As Lilly entered the room, he could make out Lawrence and Garner with the help of the lights from the living room and dining areas. They were, he said, having sex. "I couldn't believe I was seeing what I was seeing," said Lilly, who had never seen two men having sex right in front of him. "It actually startled him [Lilly], what they were doing," remembered Quinn, who had not yet seen them, "and he lurched back."[14]

Seeing Lilly startled, Quinn guessed that he must have been surprised by seeing the reported gunman. He came around low on Lilly's right side and entered the bedroom in a crouched position. His finger was now fully on the trigger of his gun, ready to fire. That's when Quinn said he saw Lawrence and Garner for the first time.[15]

AT THIS POINT, the stories that Quinn and Lilly told in their separate interviews for this book about what happened and what they saw in John Lawrence's apartment diverge in significant ways. And both deputies' versions differ radically from what Lawrence and Garner themselves, in their separate interviews about the case, indicated was happening when the police arrived.

Quinn claimed that when he and Lilly entered the bedroom, Garner was on the bed on all fours receiving anal sex from Lawrence, who was standing behind Garner at the side of the bed. Both men, he said, were completely naked.[16]

Lilly claimed that, with the passage of time, he was not so sure about what the men were doing. He remembered seeing Lawrence and Garner both on the floor, not on the bed, with their sides toward the deputies. While Lawrence was "butt naked," he said, Garner was not. More important, Lilly was uncertain about whether they were having anal or oral sex—sexual acts that seem hard to confuse, even years after the fact, if the witness actually saw them. (Both acts were illegal under the Homosexual Conduct law in Texas.) Lilly told an interviewer in 2004 that he thought they were having oral sex when the deputies discovered them; but when the interviewer showed him the police report indicating that the men were charged with anal sex, Lilly conceded that "it could have been anal."[17]

By the time he was interviewed for this book in April 2005, Lilly was leaning again toward thinking it was oral sex. "I want to say he [Garner] was having oral sex on the guy; I actually saw penis in mouth, way up." Lilly was certain only that, whichever it was, Lawrence was the dominant, insertive partner. "The black guy was giving him head or they was [sic] doing each other from behind," he said. "I don't remember. Honestly can't recall."[18]

With the deputies' guns pointed straight at the two men, Quinn asked, "What are you doing?"[19] There was no response to this rhetorical question (although in hindsight, the question is less rhetorical, given the officers' contradictory accounts of what the defendants were doing). Lilly flipped on the light switch and said that Lawrence and Garner stopped having sex almost immediately after the deputies entered the room.[20]

Quinn told a more sensationalistic story about the encounter with Lawrence and Garner. According to Quinn, he yelled, "Stop!" and "Step back!" to Lawrence. Despite these orders, according to Quinn, the men continued to have sex. While "Lawrence looked eye to eye" at Quinn, he continued his sexual ministrations. "He saw the gun pointed at him," Quinn remembered, but wasn't even startled. "No expression." Garner, he claimed, responded "Oh!" but did not disengage from Lawrence.[21]

Seeing no firearm, Quinn put his gun back in his holster and repeated his instructions to the men to stop having sex. Despite at least three such instructions, the men, in flagrant violation of Quinn's orders, continued to have sex for what he says was "well in excess of a minute."[22] If true, this was a prodigious sexual feat. The most brazen exhibitionist, using the latest pharmaceutical aids, would be hard put to maintain an erection, much less continue penetration, upon a surprise visit by police. There is no evidence that Lawrence and Garner were such exhibitionists.

Finally, exasperated, Quinn claimed Lawrence had to be pushed away from Garner.[23] Otherwise, he believed, they would not have stopped.

Whoever saw what, and whatever they saw, the deputies agreed that Lawrence and Garner must have heard Quinn announce "Sheriff's department!" twice as the deputies entered the apartment. The door to the bedroom was wide open, there was no other sound in the apartment, and the distance between the spot where Quinn made the announcement and the bedroom door was only about twenty-five feet. Furthermore, Lawrence and Garner should have heard the deputies interact with Man #4, including their instructions to him to put up his hands, since the distance between where they stood at that point and the bedroom door was only a few feet. Quinn estimated that the time between his initial announcement at the front door and the moment Lilly and he entered Lawrence's bedroom was just under a minute, more than enough time for the men to stop having sex.[24]

Quinn also could not fathom why Lawrence and Garner did not stop having sex when it was obvious the deputies were in the bedroom, had turned on the light, aimed their weapons directly at them, and were repeatedly ordering them to cease their fevered activities. "Most people who have any self-dignity would stop," remarked Quinn. "Have some courtesy for me and stop doing that."[25] Courtesy, however, was in short supply that evening.

One explanation Quinn offered for this bizarre alleged behavior was that the men were drunk. The Offense Report Quinn filed that night indicated that Lawrence, Garner, and Eubanks were "extremely intoxicated."[26] "I think they were just intoxicated to the point that they didn't really hear what was going on," he suggested, adding that perhaps "they were caught up in the heat of the moment." Lilly agreed that Lawrence was drunk but did not think Garner was. Tipps didn't think either man was drunk.[27]

To Quinn, the other possibility, in retrospect, was that they were involved in a scheme to launch a legal challenge to the state law. "I thought afterward it was a setup" when all the lawyers became involved, said Quinn, meaning that Lawrence and Garner wanted to be caught in the act in order to be arrested and then to challenge the sodomy law (the improbability of this setup or "cooked case" theory will be discussed in chapter 7).[28]

THE VERY HEART of the officers' case against Lawrence and Garner is disputed. Through their words and actions starting immediately after the arrests, both defendants denied that they were having sex with each other. The police, they asserted, were lying.

Both men were interviewed for this book in 2005, and Lawrence was interviewed a second time in 2011. From these interviews emerged an account starkly different from the one given by the sheriff's deputies. Initially, in each of their interviews in 2005, Garner and Lawrence were advised by their attorneys not to talk about whether they were having sex. Attorneys, in their own interviews, cited a desire to protect the men's "privacy," a rationale that was hard to credit given the invasion of their privacy at the hands of law enforcement.[29] It seemed more likely that the men's lawyers were preventing the disclosure of information— the likelihood that sex had not occurred—that they believed would be unhelpful to the case and larger cause.[30] By 2011, the attorneys relented, in large part because John Lawrence wanted to make sure that his side of the story was finally told and that police were not allowed to get away with their tall tale of seeing uncontrollable gay sex.[31] Unfortunately, the lawyers' change of heart about revealing the defendants' versions came too late for an uncensored interview of Garner, who died in 2006. As we shall see, however, it was evident even in the monitored interview of Garner that he thought the officers' allegations were ludicrous.

After Eubanks had gone outside, Lawrence maintained, he and Garner continued casually talking and watching television, hardly expecting a police raid. Lawrence was lying on the couch, dressed only in his underwear and a T-shirt, watching the late-evening news and about to go to bed. The couch directly faced the front door, so Lawrence would have been the first person the police saw. The television was to the right of the front door, in the corner of the room. The stuffed chair from which Eubanks had emerged "to get a soda" was, from the perspective of a person standing at the threshold, just to the left of the couch. Lawrence claimed that Garner, clad only in slacks, was sitting beyond the couch in the attached and unobstructed dining area, at the far end of the dining room table. He was facing the door, according to Lawrence, fully visible to anyone entering the apartment.[32]

According to Lawrence, the police did not knock before entering. Garner apparently heard someone on the landing at the top of the stairs, got up from the chair, and started toward the front door. At that moment, with Eubanks's assistance, the police "burst through the door" and began demanding to know where the gun was.

"There was no sex," insisted Lawrence in 2011. In fact, he said, Garner and he were not physically touching one another, and were seated as much as fifteen apart. "We always flirted with each other," Lawrence said, acknowledging that this good-natured playfulness had probably enraged Eubanks, prompting his mischief-making exit. "We were always camping and carrying on. It was just second nature." But the men had never before or since had sex. The police invented the story, he declared. "They told bald-faced lies."[33]

Even during the 2005 interviews both Lawrence and Garner intimated that they were not having sex when the police arrived. For example, Garner and Lawrence were certain that no more than fifteen or twenty minutes elapsed between the time Eubanks left the apartment and the time the police entered.[34] There is no reason to question this time frame, since the police themselves said that they arrived at the apartment complex within minutes of getting the dispatch at about 10:49 p.m. Since Lawrence and Garner were not having sex with each other when Eubanks left the apartment, that leaves very little time to get into the bedroom, get undressed, and be in the full throes of anal sex by the time the police arrived. It's not impossible of course—sex acts have been initiated and even completed in far less time—but it does make it more unlikely.

Add to that the fact that Lawrence and Garner would have had to initiate sex with each other while Garner's jealous and angry boyfriend had left the apartment for at most a few minutes to get a soda from a vending machine just feet away. Eubanks could have returned at any moment to find his friend and boyfriend having sex in a bedroom to which the door, according to police, was open. People are often reckless about sex, especially when drunk (as at least Lawrence was), but this degree of audacity is stupefying.

Besides the compressed timeline and the high risk of discovery by a jealous boyfriend, several things Garner said during his interview, at which his attorney, Mitchell Katine, acted almost as opposing counsel, were clearly inconsistent with sexual contact between the men. For example, asked whether he was drunk when the police arrived, Garner responded: "I wasn't drunk." Then, unprompted, he added, "John [Lawrence] was in the bed. . . . He went to bed. I was about to go to bed."[35] That assertion is consistent with Lawrence's statement that he was getting ready for bed when Eubanks left the apartment to get a soda but inconsistent with Lawrence's lying on the living room sofa. Either way, it's obviously inconsistent with the claim that the men were having sex when the police arrived. Sensing this inference might be drawn, Katine interjected, "Okay. Tyron, we don't want to talk about specific details about what was going on or not going on." Garner laughed knowingly at that instruction and said, "Okay."[36]

When asked whether he was allowed to put his pants on after the police arrived, he replied, "I don't think I had my shirt on when they walked in but . . . I had my pants on."[37] That statement was consistent with Lawrence's recollection in 2011 but was inconsistent with Quinn's claim that the men were completely naked and if true, makes more implausible the idea that Garner was receiving anal sex from Lawrence.

Explaining his motivation for letting the national gay group Lambda Legal challenge his conviction, Garner said that he believed "the police had done something wrong." He was asked what they had done wrong. "I didn't even know if I had been arrested. I didn't do anything. But I went to jail. . . . I never even got a chance to explain my part."[38] In context, it seemed that Garner was conveying his view, insofar as he was allowed to convey it, that his real grievance was that the police falsely charged him with having sex when, in fact, he "didn't do anything." The legal system, as he experienced it, never allowed him to tell his side of the story. There was never a factual hearing, never a sworn statement, never a trial.

After our 2005 interview, I drove Garner home from the law office where the interview had been conducted. Katine was not present, and although I was very tempted to ask Garner whether the police had lied, I honored my prior commitment not to ask him questions about what Lawrence and he had been doing. Still, Garner asked me about Quinn's elaborate account of what the police observed, an account I had summarized in our interview, including Quinn's assertions that the men had continued to have sex after Quinn and Lilly entered the bedroom. "Did he really say that?" Garner asked incredulously. "Yes." He started laughing.

Nor was John Lawrence's contradiction of the police version an invention timed for my 2011 interview with him. Specific things Lawrence said during my 2005 interview also indicated that he wanted to convey that the men were not having sex. For example, Lawrence explained that when the police arrived he was in his underwear (not naked, as the police alleged), "ready to go to bed." Furthermore, Lawrence claimed that police became agitated and called him a "fuckin' fag" only after they saw pornographic pencil sketches of an aroused James Dean on his bedroom wall. According to Lawrence, the first thing one would see upon entering the bedroom was the bed itself, which is where they were purportedly having sex. Only after coming into the room could one see to the left the wall facing the bed, which is where the images of James Dean were hanging. It hardly seems plausible that the police, having by hypothesis just witnessed Lawrence engaged in anal sex with another man on or near the bed, would need to examine a sketch on his wall to confirm he was homosexual.

At another point in the 2005 interview, Lawrence wondered what Quinn had said the police had seen. "Where were we supposedly having sex?" he asked, apparently inserting the word "supposedly" to suggest that the police were lying. When he was told on the bed, he responded, "Okay . . . ," in a tone that suggested he wanted to know more about what Quinn had told me. "Let's not get into that," his lawyer quickly interrupted as Lawrence was about to say more. Nevertheless, Lawrence used the word again later in the interview, explaining that the police had arrested "two guys from Texas that supposedly broke a law that was stupid to be on the books in the first place."[39]

There are yet more reasons to believe Lawrence and Garner contradicted the police version of events from the very beginning of the case. The day after their arrests, at a time when they had no legal counsel, both Lawrence and Garner pleaded not guilty to the homosexual conduct charge against them. Only after gay-rights attorneys got involved did their pleas change to no contest. The only other account of September 17, 1998, from a person close to the events comes from Lane Lewis, the first person to contact Lawrence after the arrests. When Lewis learned about the arrest through court personnel (a revelation discussed in detail in part III), he called Lawrence.[40] In this first telephone conversation, and in subsequent conversations between the two, Lawrence explained that he and Garner were *not* having sex when the deputies entered the apartment. In fact, Lawrence told Lewis that he and Garner were in separate rooms when the deputies arrived. Lewis reported that Lawrence also repeated this version of events to him in September 2003. Lewis's account is backed up by handwritten notes he said he scribbled while on the phone with Lawrence during their initial conversation in 1998. The notes indeed indicate the men were "not having sex."[41]

According to Ray Hill, the longtime Houston gay activist, Garner told him that when the police entered the apartment, he and Lawrence were not having sex. As Garner allegedly described it to Hill, "'We weren't doing anything. I was in the living room and he [Lawrence] was in the bedroom.'"[42]

The police and the defendants thus disagree about the central allegation in the case—that they were having sex in violation of the Texas Homosexual Conduct law. Moreover, the officers themselves disagree about significant details of what they saw.

6.

Uncivil Disobedience

WHATEVER SEXUAL ACTIVITY LAWRENCE AND GARNER MIGHT have been engaged in had stopped by the time that Quinn and Lilly's fellow officers, Deputy Tipps and Deputy Landry, entered the bedroom to see what was happening. Neither of them claimed to have seen any sex. Tipps asked Quinn, "What we got?" "Hey, these two guys were in here having sex," Quinn responded. Lilly was silent. Having expected to find a man with a gun, the deputies were surprised that they had walked in on what Quinn told them was live sex.[1]

By all accounts, Lawrence was angry and belligerent. "What the fuck are y'all doing?" he shouted at the deputies. Demanding to see a search warrant, he objected, "You don't have any right to be here."[2] He warned that he would get them fired. He repeatedly demanded to call his lawyer (in fact, he had no attorney at the time).[3] That's the point at which, according to Garner, the police started "roughing up" Lawrence. "They didn't really like him saying that," Garner remembered.[4]

Quinn's version was different. Quinn said he refused to let Lawrence call the attorney he claimed to have, instead ordering him to put his underwear on. But Lawrence continued to argue with Quinn. "Look, I'm not going to tell you again," he warned Lawrence, using the sort of parental phrases that were reminiscent of those he had previously used on recalcitrant citizens. "Put some clothes on or I'm going to handcuff you and sit you out there naked." With the assistance of the deputies, according to Lilly, Lawrence put on his underwear and was handcuffed.[5] Lawrence said he was already wearing his underwear.[6]

The deputies looked around the bedroom and noticed what Quinn described as "two pencil sketchings of James Dean, naked, with an extremely oversized penis on him." Lawrence said that the etchings had been given to him by a "Polynesian guy" he met at a gay bar in about 1990.[7] The explicit renderings of Dean's supposed anatomy "were hung up like regular pictures" in Lawrence's bedroom facing the bed, recalled Quinn. "Like if you were laying [sic] in the bed you could see it," Quinn explained, unwittingly envisioning himself in the position of an aroused homosexual. "It was like his fixture, his art manifesto up there on the wall." There were also other posters with sexual content, Quinn said "but the main thing that stuck out was that big drawing of James Dean." Quinn remembered that the deputies later laughed about the sketches. "Did you see that sketching in there?" asked Landry, according to Quinn. "Yeah, I saw it," replied Quinn. They lingered over the image of Dean, appraising its likeness to the legendary actor. "Well it did look like James Dean," Landry began to remark, then added, "well, *facially* it looked—it was a pretty good sketch of his facial." Quinn noted that they remarked sarcastically, "This is the kind of thing I would have in my house!" As for the gay men he met that night, Quinn later concluded that "it's obvious what their focal point was."[8]

The mood in the apartment changed as the deputies' anxiety about weapons quickly diminished. It soon became one of derision of the gay men who were now in their custody. Garner recalled the police using the words "queers," "fags," and "faggots" while in the apartment. When the police noticed Eubanks's seizure medication, Garner said, they began looking for drugs by scraping the ashtrays, laughing and apparently joking about a big drug bust. "I felt violated," Garner remembered, "and scared."[9]

According to Lawrence, after the police made disparaging and homophobic remarks about his bedroom pictures of James Dean, they handcuffed him.[10] Garner said that the police patted him down (since by his account he had his pants on when they arrived), looking for the gun Eubanks had reported.[11] As the entourage entered the living room, Lawrence stumbled, according to the police, or was pushed, according to

Lawrence, into the coffee table, breaking a ceramic bird his mother had given him.[12]

The deputies sat Lawrence, Garner, and Man #4 on the couch.[13] By now, more deputies had begun to arrive, including a veteran of the force, Sergeant Kenneth O. Adams.[14] The deputies questioned the men about the reported gun, but they said they knew nothing about it. Quinn told Tipps, "Go get our reportee and bring him up here."

They were soon joined by Eubanks, who confessed that he had invented the story about an armed black man in order to retaliate against Lawrence and Garner. According to the deputies, Eubanks volunteered that he was jealous because his lover, Garner, was cheating on him with Lawrence. Eubanks was "mouthing off" to the police throughout the interrogation.[15]

When Garner and Lawrence learned that it was Eubanks who called the police, the three men began arguing among themselves. At one point Eubanks became so agitated that he stood up, shouted at Garner, and had to be forced to sit back down.[16] (Garner said that the deputies punched Eubanks to force him down.) Eubanks became especially upset when he learned that he was going to be charged for making a false report; he had apparently thought he would get Garner in trouble but never imagined that he might be on the hook himself.

While seated on the couch, Lawrence remained angry and, as Tipps described it, "kept running his mouth." His furor was not only vented at Eubanks, who had precipitated the initial confrontation in the first place. He called the deputies "Gestapo," "storm troopers," and "jack-booted thugs."[17] He said the deputies were "harassing" the men simply because they were gay. Quinn remembered telling Lawrence, "I don't know you. And I don't know your sexual orientation. So how can I be harassing you because you're homosexual—other than that I caught you in the act?"[18]

Lawrence justified his defiant words and actions by asserting that the deputies improperly intruded in his home and then, once there, mishandled him. "Would you be cooperative with the police when they had someone walk into your apartment and start dragging you around and throwing you around like you're some kind of common criminal in your home?" he said.[19]

Garner was cooperative and quiet, letting Lawrence do all the talking. He complied with all instructions from the deputies. The deputies remembered Garner as slim, passive, and "extremely effeminate." In his interview, Quinn derided Garner as a "naggy little bitch, kind of, you know, 'nyah, nyah, nyah.'"[20]

While on the scene, the deputies conducted a search of the apartment for a gun, but never found one. There were also no illegal drugs in the house. They did, however, notice numerous pornographic gay magazines and videotapes inside the apartment. The magazines and videotape boxes exposed the deputies to very explicit images of men engaged in sexual acts with one another. "The apartment was loaded with pornography," remembered Quinn. "Everywhere you looked there was some kind." Lilly recalled a magazine rack full of gay pornography in the bedroom. The deputies perused the material, Lilly recalled, "to make sure there wasn't no child porn, or anything of that nature." They found none.[21]

Lilly remembered "a bad odor" permeating the apartment, like "people were having a lot of sex in it." "That whole apartment smelled of gay," he told one interviewer. "An anal odor. Very unpleasant."[22] Tipps, however, remembered no such odor.[23]

Now the deputies had to decide what to do with the men they had arrayed on the couch before them.

THERE WAS NO DOUBT Eubanks was going to be cited for making a false report and that Man #4 would go free, since he had neither participated in the false report nor engaged in illegal sexual conduct. But the decision about whether to charge Lawrence and Garner with a crime, and about whether to take them to jail, was more complex. One thing was clear: it was Quinn's decision to make. Even beyond that standard protocol, the other deputies deferred to his judgment. "He knew the penal code and the law upside down, sideways, and backward," Lilly explained. "It was his call," Tipps agreed, since Quinn was the "priority unit" at the scene.[24]

The priority unit was initially uncertain whether he could cite the men for having anal sex. He was sure it must be illegal in Texas. But he was unsure whether people could be arrested for having sex in their own home. To get approval for a citation and possible arrest, he decided to call the assistant district attorney on duty—an attorney with the county prosecutor's office who is available twenty-four hours a day to approve arrests and offer rudimentary legal advice to deputies in the field.[25] The assistant D.A. on duty that night was Ira Jones, a thirty-year veteran of the prosecutor's office.[26] Although Jones could not remember the details of his conversation with Quinn, typically the assistant D.A. on intake duty listens to the officer's account of events and makes a determination whether there is probable cause for an arrest. Sometimes the assistant D.A. will look up the text of a statute to determine whether the alleged facts fall within the letter of the law, but he or she does not conduct further legal research. The volume of calls is so heavy—every felony and misdemeanor arrest must be approved by the assistant D.A.—that there is little time available for each individual call. It is also not the assistant D.A.'s role to determine the credibility of the officer's account. "In Texas," declared Jones, "police officers are presumed to be credible."[27]

According to Quinn, he asked Jones whether it mattered, under Texas law, that the homosexual sex occurred in a home rather than in a public place. Jones looked up the text of the statute: "§ 21.06. HOMO-SEXUAL CONDUCT. (a) A person commits an offense if he engages in deviate sexual intercourse with another individual of the same sex. . . ." State law defined "deviate sexual intercourse" as follows:

> § 21.01. DEFINITIONS. In this chapter: (1) "Deviate sexual intercourse" means: (A) any contact between any part of the genitals of one person and the mouth or anus of another person; or (B) the penetration of the genitals or the anus of another person with an object.

The statute said nothing about the location of the offense. Based on this language, Jones concluded that it did not matter where the offense occurred. It was illegal in public or in private. That was all Quinn needed to hear.

Quinn now had two important choices to make. First, he had the discretion to let the men go free, charging them with nothing, just as police officers sometimes issue warnings, rather than actual citations, for speeding. Second, if he did charge the men, he had to decide whether to arrest them. Homosexual conduct was punishable by fine but not prison, so Quinn could simply issue a citation without taking them to jail.

Quinn decided to charge them with violating the Homosexual Conduct law *and* to take them to jail for it. It was a pivotal moment in the case. If Quinn had decided not to cite Lawrence and Garner, they would have had no grounds to challenge the state sodomy law and there never would have been a *Lawrence v. Texas*. Even if Quinn had only issued a citation without taking the pair to jail, they probably would have simply paid their fines and let the matter go.[28] Quinn explained his decision thus:

> I think the totality of the circumstances, where I think there's a guy with a gun and I almost have to shoot, that it warranted me giving them a citation. It was a lovers' triangle that could have got somebody hurt. I could have killed these guys over having sex. They were stupid enough to let it go that far.[29]

This rationale may explain why Eubanks was cited and jailed—it was his telephone call to the sheriff's department that created mortal danger for all involved—but Lawrence and Garner had not made the false report of a weapons disturbance. They were, however, mixed up in a "lovers' triangle" with the man who had made the false report. And while there was no state law against jealousy or infidelity to a lover, the shocking nature (to Quinn) of the relationship among the defendants, and the circumstances in which he encountered them, undoubtedly influenced his decision. Quinn said that he was personally offended that Lawrence and Garner, lacking "self-dignity," had not stopped having sex when the deputies entered the apartment and announced their presence. "Do you realize that not once but twice we called out?" Quinn remembered telling them. "You were close to being shot."

Quinn considered their behavior "childish" and, in an interview, even suggested that they may have known Eubanks was calling the police yet were heedlessly determined to have sex anyway. "You know, this is a private matter," he said of the sex he saw. "Keep it amongst yourselves and keep it out of where somebody else can see you."[30] Of course, if Lawrence and Garner were having sex in Lawrence's bedroom, they *were* keeping it private. But, for Quinn, Eubanks's histrionic telephone call spilled their private matter into the public domain.

Lawrence's foul-mouthed disrespect of the deputies also played a role in getting the men arrested, according to all the deputies. "His whole attitude toward the police was very, very poor," observed Tipps in an interview. "I'll be honest with you, ninety percent of the time people talk themselves into jail, or a traffic ticket, just by running their mouth."[31]

There is yet another important factor to explain why Quinn might have decided to cite and arrest Lawrence and Garner: the case involved male homosexuals. On patrol, the deputies had often encountered men and women having sex in parked cars. Under state criminal law, that would be an act of public lewdness punishable by fine and jail. However, unless one of the participants is a minor or there is evidence of rape, the deputies said they had never cited or taken people to jail in these circumstances.[32]

Tipps bluntly explained the difference in treatment. "It was a male and a male," he said.[33] Lilly speculated that "if this had been two women it probably wouldn't have went anywhere" because lesbians were more accepted. Like Tipps, his reaction to two men having sex was one of visceral disgust. If it had been two women (or a man and a woman), Lilly thought he might not even have "lurched back" upon seeing them.[34] On paper at least, the Texas sodomy law equally applied to lesbian and gay male sex, but, as enforced, it was aimed mainly at gay men.

Lilly was also disturbed by the age and physical differences between the men. Garner was slender; Lawrence was much heavier. Garner was almost twenty-five years younger than Lawrence. "I can remember the old man," Lilly remarked. "He was . . . and that part was kind of disgusting . . . This old guy, butt naked, and you know, flab hanging all off and then . . ." His voice trailed off into laughter at the memory.[35]

Whatever the reasons were for taking the men to jail, that is where they headed next. Garner and Lawrence were cited for homosexual conduct. Eubanks was charged with filing a false report, a Class B misdemeanor punishable by a short prison term. Only Man #4 was released.

As the deputies prepared to leave the scene, Quinn advised them to wash their hands. "You have to wonder," said Quinn in an interview, " 'What have we touched? Have we come into contact with any fluids?' " In his patrol car, "I made sure I doused myself with sanitizer."[36]

By now the large police presence on the scene had drawn several of Lawrence's neighbors out of their homes, including Jeri Brock, the apartment manager. Brock, whose apartment was close to Lawrence's, came outside in her robe. "There was a lot of commotion, people outside, a lot of cop cars. I really didn't know a lot of what was going on at the time." She added, "Some of the cops were being kind of loud."[37]

According to the deputies, Lawrence defiantly refused to put on more than his underwear for his trip to jail, claiming that the deputies had no right to charge him for something he did in his own home. The deputies claimed that he refused to stand up and had to be physically lifted from the couch and carried to a patrol car by Tipps and Landry.[38]

Contradicting the officers' claims, Lawrence and Garner said the deputies refused to allow Lawrence to get dressed and that he was thus forced out of his home in his underwear and T-shirt with no shoes, socks, money, or identification. Lawrence acknowledged that he refused to walk and was indeed dragged down the cement stairs.[39]

Whichever version is true, a gathering crowd watched the spectacle as Lawrence, clad only in his skivvies, was brought downstairs in handcuffs, his legs scraping the cement, causing minor wounds and bleeding. It was humiliating. "How the hell did you tolerate that?" one of his neighbors later asked him.[40]

Afterward, the deputies insisted that Lawrence had not been abused. In fact, Quinn said that Lawrence could have been cited for resisting transport while under arrest, but that he did not add this to the sodomy charge because Lawrence "was doing all this to entice me to do something that could show I hated homosexuals."[41]

All in all, the police were in the apartment about forty minutes before they corralled the three defendants and placed them into the squad cars.[42] Garner remembered that he and Lawrence were placed in one car and Eubanks in another. Lawrence thought they were all in one car, which seems less likely given the cramped space, the availability of several police cars on the scene, and the animosity that had developed among the three. Quinn believed they were each put in separate patrol cars, with Eubanks riding in his own. In any event, the ride was a short one: the Wallisville substation was just two miles away. Along the route of surface streets, they passed the convenience stores, apartment buildings, and ranch-style homes common to the terrain in east Harris County.

According to both Lawrence and Garner, they still had no idea why they were being arrested. Inside the patrol car, they heard the police talking on their radios to officials in the department. They kept hearing references to "21.06," but were unsure what that meant.[43] The police did not explain it.

At the station, the three men were handcuffed to a bench. Lawrence continued to be angry and uncooperative throughout the standard intake procedures in which defendants are asked routine questions about their background, employment, and residence. As he had been in the apartment, Garner was quiet and cooperative. After answering questions from the booking deputy, the men were placed in windowless, spartan cells at the station. The whole episode consumed about two hours.

In his arrest report filed later that night, Quinn recounted the events:

Officers dispatched to 794 Normandy #833 reference to a weapons disturbance. The reportee advised dispatch a black male was going crazy in the apartment and he was armed with a gun.

Officers met the reportee who directed officers to the upstairs apartment. Upon entering the apartment and conducting a search for the armed suspect, officers observed the defendant engaged in deviate sexual conduct namely, anal sex, with another man.[44]

Quinn filed two identical affidavits, each concerning one sodomy defendant.[45] Both documents listed Lilly, and only Lilly, as a witness to the crime. Both were notarized by Sergeant Adams. The formal complaint against the men, a pair of additional documents signed by Quinn and notarized the same night by Adams, indicated that Quinn "has reason to believe and does believe that" each man "engage[d] in deviate sexual intercourse, namely anal sex, with member of the same sex (man)."[46] These are the only official sheriff's department documents the courts— including the U.S. Supreme Court—ever saw as the case worked its way through the judicial system.

In addition to his affidavit and formal complaint, Quinn also wrote up an Offense Report, a more detailed narrative of the night's events for internal department use only. It was filed at 3:22 a.m. on September 18, 1998, less than five hours after the arrests. Part of the multipage Offense Report simply listed the officers who were involved, the witnesses, and addresses for each person. Interestingly, the Offense Report listed Eubanks as living at Lawrence's address, indicating that they may have been roommates at the time. However, this was an error.

An "Investigative Narrative" in the Offense Report described the events. It is quoted in full.

OFFICERS DISPATCHED TO 794 NORMANDY #833 REFERNCE [sic] TO A WEAPONS DISTURBANCE. UPON ARRIVAL OFFICERS WERE SUMMONED AND DIRECTED TO THE UPSTAIRS APARTMENT BY THE REPORTEE WHO WAS LATER IDENTIFIED AS ROBERT ROYCE EUBANKS W/M 7-22-58.

OFFICERS VERIFIED THE REPORT VERBALLY AND MR EUBANKS REPLIED, "YES HE IS IN THAT APARTMENT UP THERE AND HE HAS A GUN."

OFFICERS KNOCKED ON THE DOOR AND ENTERED UPON FINDING IT UNLOCKED. OFFICERS BEGAN AN ARMED BUILDING SEARCH FOR THE SUSPECT WITH A WEAPON. OFFICERS FIRST OBSERVED A HISPANIC MALE LATER IDENTIFIED AS RAMON PELAYO-VELEZ 7-2-62 IN THE KITCHEN AREA TALKING ON THE TELEPHONE. OFFICERS SECURED THE FRONT BEDROOM AND PROCEEDED TO THE BACK BEDROOM OF THE FIVE ROOM APARTMENT.

OFFICERS UPON ENTERING THE BACK BEDROOM FOUND THE BLACK MALE AND A WHITE MALE ENGAGED IN DEVIATE SEXUAL INTERCOURSE NAMELY ANAL SEX. THE MALES WERE SEPARATED. THE BLACK MALE WAS IDENTIFIED BY TEXAS ID CARD [I.D. card number here] AS TYRON GARNER DOB 7-10-67. THE WHITE MALE WAS IDENTIFIED AS JOHN GEDDES LAWRENCE DOB 8-2-43. ALL PARTIES INVOLVED HAD BEEN DRINKING, AND WITH THE EXCEPTION OF MR. PELAYO-VELEZ, WERE EXTREMELY INTOXICATED.

OFFICER SEARCHED THE APARTMENT FOR THE ALLEGED GUN AND FOUND NO FIREARMS INSIDE. OFFICERS IN THE INVESTIGATION LEARNED THAT IT WAS AN APPARENT LOVE TRIANGLE AND MR EUBANKS CALLED BECAUSE HE WAS UPSET THAT MR GARNER AND MR LAWRENCE WERE HAVING SEX. MR EUBANKS IN HIS INTOXICATED STATE DENIED HAVING BEEN OUTSIDE THE APARTMENT AS OFFICERS ARRIVED.

OFFICER CONTACTED THE DISTRICT ATTORNEYS [sic] OFFICE AND SPOKE TO ADA WILLIFORD. MS WILLIFORD WAS ADVISED OF THE CIRCUMSTANCES AND ACCEPTED A CHARGE OF FALSE REPORT TO A POLICE OFFICER ON MR EUBANKS. OFFICER CONFIRMED WITH MS WILLIFORD THAT ELEMENTS OF HOMOSEXUAL CONDUCT DID NOT REQUIRE THE ACT TO OCCUR IN A PUBLIC PLACE. MS WILLIFORD AGREED THE ELEMENTS OF THE OFFENSE WERE MET.

OFFICER FILED CLASS C CHARGE OF HOMOSEXUAL CONDUCT ON MR GARNER AND MR LAWRENCE IN JUSTICE OF THE PEACE PRECINCT THREE POSITION ONE JUDGE MIKE PARROTT'S OFFICE.

ALL SUSPECTS WERE TAKEN INTO CUSTODY AND TRANSPORTED TO THE WALLISVILLE ANNEX FOR FILING OF CHARGES. MR. LAWRENCE RESISTED BEING HANDCUFFED AND HAD TO BE FORCIBLY RESTRAINED. MR LAWRENCE REFUSED TO COOPERATE AND WALK UNDER HIS OWN POWER. MR LAWRENCE WAS CARRIED TO THE PATROL CAR. MR LAWRENCE DRAGGED HIS LEGS AND FEET AS OFFICERS CARRIED HIM DOWN THE STAIRS AND ALONG THE SIDEWALK.

MR EUBAMKS [sic] WAS EXTREMELY BELLIGERENT AND VERBALLY ABUSIVE. MR EUBANKS HAD TO BE FORCIBLY REMOVED FROM THE PATROL CAR AT THE STATION. MR EUBANKS FELL TO THE GROUND CLAIMING OFFICERS ASSAULTED HIM AND HAD TO BE PICKED UP AND CARRIED A PORTION OF THE WAY INTO THE STATION. HE THEN BEGAN WALKING UNDER HIS OWN POWER. MR EUBANKS CLAIMED TO HAVE HIV, HEART PROBLEMS, EPILEPSY, AND ASTHMA. DUE TO HIS COMPLAINTS AND MR LAWRENCE RECEIVING ABRASIONS TO HIS LEGS WHILE BEING CARRIED, OFFICER CALLED NORTH CHANNEL EMS. NORTH CHANNEL EMS ARRIVED AT THE STATION TO CHECK BOTH MR LAWRENCE AND MR EUBANKS. BOTH INDIVIDUALS REFUSED TREATMENT. ALL SUSPECTS WERE LATER TRANSPORTED TO IPC.

NO ADDITIONAL SUSPECT OR WITNESS INFORMATION AVAILABLE.[47]

Because there was never an actual trial in the case, neither the Texas courts nor the Supreme Court ever saw this report. It contains many more details about the circumstances surrounding the arrest than were contained in the arrest reports for Lawrence and Garner, which the courts did see. (It did not, however, contain the details Quinn would later recount about the alleged crime.) Because Lawrence and Garner ultimately did not contest Quinn's claim that they were having anal sex, the bare-bones arrest report included all the information the courts needed to see as a matter of law.

Years after the sodomy arrests, the officers had no regrets about their actions. Quinn defended his decision to issue the citations to Lawrence and Garner and to take them to jail, stating, "When we review the entire record, the circumstances warranted what I did." As for his place in history, Tipps observed, "I was hired to do a job and I'm going to do my job, regardless. I was either at the right place at the right time or at the wrong place at the wrong time."[48]

7.

A Probable Explanation for
an Improbable Case

*B*EFORE CONTINUING THE STORY OF HOW *LAWRENCE* GOT TO THE
U.S. Supreme Court, we should pause to consider the implications
of the differing versions of events offered by the deputies and the defendants. This analysis takes us in two directions. One deals with speculation among some gay-rights opponents that Lawrence, Garner, and
their attorneys staged their arrest in order to challenge the constitutionality of the Texas law. The other concludes that Lawrence and Garner
most likely were not violating the Texas Homosexual Conduct law when
the police arrived.

Over the years since the events in John Lawrence's apartment, there
has been considerable speculation that *Lawrence* was a "cooked" case,
meaning that the officers' intrusion into Lawrence's home was deliberately provoked and elaborately planned by gay activists in order to test the
validity of the Texas sodomy law. Deputy Quinn himself suspected soon
after the arrest that *Lawrence* was a deliberate test case because of the
high-powered legal team brought in to defend the men.[1] William "Bill"
Delmore, the straitlaced Harris County prosecutor who handled the *Lawrence* case all the way to the Supreme Court, initially believed the cooked-
case theory, too. "I suspected that from the beginning," he said in an initial
interview about the case.[2] When news of the arrests hit the media in
November 1998, the chairman of the Harris County Republican Party,

whose party platform opposed repeal of the law, also speculated that the case was a setup. "The facts themselves sound suspicious," he charged.[3]

The speculation about a setup is calculated to minimize Lawrence and Garner's claims that the Texas sodomy law truly invaded their liberty or privacy as a practical matter.[4] In this view, they had to "invite" the invasion to be able to complain of it. It also supports the otherwise improbable Quinn and Lilly accounts that they actually observed Lawrence and Garner having sex. It provides a motive for the men to continue having sex while the deputies entered and searched the apartment. The speculation also draws sustenance from the common antigay stereotype that homosexuals are untrustworthy. They are, according to this perspective, conspiratorial, a group of people prone to intrigues, disguises, and lies.

From an outsider's perspective, there were several reasons to believe the case might have been a setup. Delmore, who later disavowed the setup theory,[5] cited the sheer implausibility that someone might be caught in the act of sex unless they wanted to be. "It is difficult to imagine circumstances in which people would continue engaging in the act with police in the apartment," he observed. "Most people would discontinue any sexual activity."[6]

There is support for the cooked-case speculation in the rarity of enforcement of sodomy laws against consensual, noncommercial adult sex occurring in the privacy of the home. The state claimed (incorrectly) that the Texas sodomy law, at least prior to 1994, had never been enforced in those circumstances.[7]

There is also support for this cooked-case speculation in the frustration of gay-rights advocates in Texas, whose earlier legal challenges to the law had been dismissed by the state courts for lack of "standing" precisely because there had been no enforcement.[8] The legal concept of standing requires that, in order to sue, a person must suffer an actual injury (for example, get arrested) rather than simply oppose the law on grounds of principle or on the grounds that he might one day be harmed by the law. Thus, to challenge the constitutionality of the state sodomy law, gay-rights activists needed someone to get arrested. Yet such arrests were exceedingly infrequent, and even more rarely brought to the attention of gay-rights lawyers before the cases were dismissed or fines were paid. One solution, then, would be to arrange an arrest in which police would be unwitting accomplices.

Despite all this speculation, *Lawrence* was not a test case. It was simply one of those rare, chance examples of sodomy-law enforcement—a bolt, so to speak, from the blue.[9] The cooked-case hypothesis suffers all the stock weaknesses of conspiracy theories: it relies on too many moving parts, counts on superhuman planning and coordination, founders unless flawlessly executed, and trusts that people are able to keep secrets.[10]

In other examples where prearranged test cases actually materialized, the parties involved had been active in the reform movements with which their test case was associated. In *Griswold v. Connecticut*, for example, the persons arrested for setting up a birth-control clinic in violation of a state anticontraceptives law, including Estelle Griswold, had long been active in the birth-control movement generally and in Planned Parenthood specifically.[11] Finding two people not previously involved in gay-rights activism who were willing to be initiated into their activism by being intruded upon *in flagrante delicto* by the police, to be arrested and hauled off to jail, to be convicted of a sex offense, and then to pursue litigation for years, with all the media exposure and loss of privacy that entails, beggars belief. It is possible, of course, but seems highly unlikely.

Consider that the person who reported an armed person in Lawrence's apartment, Robert Eubanks, would have had to be part of any conspiracy to test the law. It was his telephone call, after all, that started the chain of events. Eubanks admitted to the deputies *at the scene* that he was lying about an armed intruder,[12] was later convicted of filing a false report, and spent at least two weeks in jail. Eubanks, like Lawrence and Garner, had no prior involvement in gay-rights causes or organizations. It is unlikely that a nonactivist would have agreed to participate in such a way and suffer the penalty.[13] It's also unlikely that Eubanks would have admitted his false report at the scene, since this might have reduced the likelihood that the police would arrest Lawrence and Garner. Moreover, even the deputies' accounts of the events suggested an "innocent" (i.e., non-test-case) motivation for Eubanks's making a false report: he was jealous because he believed his boyfriend was flirting with another man.[14]

As the events of September 17, 1998, demonstrate, *Lawrence* would have been, at best, the clumsiest and most careless judicial test case ever planned in the history of the republic. Lawrence and Eubanks were intoxicated. "Why would you want them drunk?" noted Deputy Lilly, who rejected the test-case theory.[15] The sexual performers and their confederates would have needed to be stone-cold sober so that the directors could be sure all actors played their parts. Deputy Tipps, who also rejected the test-case theory, said they should be credited with "Academy Award winning" performances if they were simply acting out predetermined roles.[16] Man #4—the "Umbrella Man" of the great *Lawrence* conspiracy[17]—would also have been part of the plot.

Even if Lawrence and Garner managed to orchestrate a scenario in which Eubanks would call the sheriff's department with a false report and Lawrence and Garner would be seen having sex when the police arrived, they could never have been certain that the deputies would actually cite them and arrest them. Very few, if any, officers would actually cite people for having sex under such circumstances.[18] A test-case scenario would have been a very dubious enterprise at best, further reducing the likelihood that it is true.

The great conspiracy to set up the case would have needed to be kept secret among a significant number of participants—including not just Lawrence, Garner, and Eubanks, but also several gay-rights activists in Houston and an assortment of attorneys in Houston, Washington, D.C., and New York. Yet more than a decade after the arrest, not one person in this conspiracy has divulged anything about it. The conspiracy defies what we know about people: they are incapable of keeping a consequential secret for very long. And the chances that a secret can be kept secret diminishes with every additional person who knows about it.

Had gay activists wanted to set up a test case, it is unlikely they would have chosen Lawrence and Garner as the defendants. They were not a committed couple living a stereotypically "happy" life in a pleasant suburb. They were not involved in gay-rights causes and had no interest in them. They were not well educated or particularly articulate. They both had arrest records. Garner had no job and no permanent residence.

They were interracial and separated by twenty-five years in age. All of these factors would needlessly complicate the case for public-relations purposes.

Experienced gay-rights attorneys, like those at Lambda Legal, would instead have chosen two people in a committed relationship who could articulately plead their case to the media and embody the most powerful constitutional arguments the attorneys later made to the U.S. Supreme Court about gay relationships. Lawrence and Garner did not meet these criteria. Experienced attorneys would certainly not have picked a "lover's triangle" imbroglio to precipitate the arrest. And Eubanks would have been about the last person they would have picked to carry it all off. As Annise Parker put it, "If we wanted to set up the case, you would have gotten well-educated, articulate, pretty boys who would make it easy to raise money in the gay community."[19] Beyond the public-relations concerns and image concerns, Parker and others were worried at the time that, as nonactivists, Lawrence and Garner might be easily "spooked" by all the publicity and might back out of a lengthy and high-profile legal challenge.[20]

A dedicated conspiracy theorist could hypothesize that Lawrence and Garner were the perfect couple for a test case because they appeared *not* to be a perfect couple for a test case, even though this quickly becomes even more far-fetched. The idea would be something like the concept sometimes called the "expression game" in espionage. You try to fool the enemy. The enemy realizes you're trying to fool him. So you try to fool the enemy into thinking that you don't realize that the enemy realizes that you are trying to fool him. On and on it goes like that, an infinite regression. It works as a mind game between very sophisticated military intelligence analysts. But it doesn't work very well when you are trying to stage-manage anal intercourse, booze, jealousy, false police reports, and official overreaction.

Finally, as will be seen, even if everything else worked out, the power to prosecute a case would still be in the hands of Texas authorities. The government, at the beginning of the case, would have the power simply to dismiss the prosecution for any number of reasons entirely at its discretion and within its control.[21] All of the elaborate work to set up the case would come to naught.

To claim that gay-rights activists set up the bizarre and messy Lawrence and Garner arrest in order to challenge the state sodomy law is to say they possessed both superhuman brilliance and astounding incompetence. It is not a believable way to understand the case.

IT IS ALL too clear that Lawrence and Garner did not stage any sexual act for the purpose of testing the Texas sodomy law. In fact, it's unlikely they were even violating that law when the police entered Lawrence's apartment. If the case had gone to trial, the men's lawyers easily could have raised a reasonable doubt about whether the men were guilty. In an actual trial for their alleged crime, they would very likely have been acquitted. But given their desire to challenge the law and not the extravagant factual claims of the police, gay-rights attorneys had no interest in raising these questions. Simultaneously, given the prosecutors' desire to pursue the case, they had no desire to question the facts asserted by the officers, either. *Lawrence* advanced as a case because nobody wanted to know what the underlying facts were.

Only two deputies claim, as we've seen, to have actually witnessed Lawrence and Garner having sex: Quinn and Lilly. Neither of the deputies' accounts appears credible. Their accounts also conflict on the basic question of what they actually saw. This does not necessarily mean either man is consciously lying—people are capable of convincing themselves of just about anything and memory is unreliable—but it does seriously undermine their claims to have seen Lawrence and Garner having sex.

To accept Quinn's account, we have to believe that Lawrence and Garner

1. were having sex;
2. continued to have sex after the deputies entered Lawrence's apartment and announced their presence twice so loudly that anyone in the apartment could easily hear them . . .
3. with the door to the bedroom open about twenty-five feet away and lights on in the house . . .
4. with no interfering sounds such as a TV or stereo to mask the deputies' announcement;

5. then continued to have sex while Quinn and Lilly discovered a person standing in the kitchen near the bedroom, told him to put his hands up, and handcuffed him, all within a few feet of the open bedroom door;

6. then continued to have sex as deputies approached the bedroom door;

7. then continued to have sex after deputies turned on the bedroom light;

8. then continued to have sex while the deputies' guns were pointed at them and the deputies repeatedly shouted at them to stop having sex and shouted at Lawrence to "step back!";

9. then continued to have sex as Lawrence looked "eye to eye" directly at Quinn, and Garner exclaimed, "Oh!" at seeing the police;

10. then continued to have sex for "well in excess of a minute" overall, until . . .

11. deputies literally had to pull them apart.[22]

This version of events defies common experience and common sense. Perhaps parts of it could be passed over as the consequence of a failing memory of an event that occurred years before. (Quinn recounted this version of events to me in interviews first in 2003 and then again in 2005.) Perhaps what seemed to a shocked Quinn like "well in excess of a minute" during which he viewed live homosexual anal sex was really no more than a few seconds.

But parts of Quinn's account are very difficult to explain by fading memory or shock. It is not credible to claim that deputies had to pry Lawrence away from Garner, for example. Both Lilly and Tipps disputed this fanciful assertion.[23] They would surely remember if they had been obliged to pry apart two men having anal sex. This part of Quinn's story seemed like a conscious embellishment, one designed to put Lawrence and Garner in the worst possible light.

Yet Lilly's truncated account is not much more believable, consisting as it does of elements 1 through 6 above. The only significant differences between Quinn's account and Lilly's—aside from the rather big one of whether the men were having anal or oral sex—are that Lilly claimed the men immediately stopped having sex when the deputies entered the bedroom and claimed that deputies did not have to pull them apart. Both of these differences make Lilly's account more credible than Quinn's. But that still leaves Lawrence and Garner having sex *after* the deputies loudly announced their presence from a distance of about twenty-five feet and continuing to do so while Quinn and Lilly secured Man #4, just a few feet away from Lawrence's open bedroom door, all with the lights on in the adjacent rooms and no other sound in the apartment.

Others associated with the case have noted the improbability of this story. One source familiar with the case inside the Harris County judicial system relayed her reaction when she first heard the deputies' accounts: "My first thought was, 'That's a lie.' I don't care whether you're homosexual or heterosexual or like doing it with little puppies, when those deputies enter the apartment it's over."[24] Bill Delmore, the lead prosecutor, also expressed incredulity that Lawrence and Garner would continue to have sex when sheriff's deputies entered the apartment.[25] And even one of the first judges to hear the case in the Texas courts thought in retrospect that the deputies probably did not catch Lawrence and Garner in the act.[26]

There are four possible ways to understand the deputies' accounts. The first three—attempting to support the truthfulness of their accounts—are possible but not probable explanations. The fourth—which concludes Lilly and Quinn did not actually see Lawrence and Garner having sex—is more believable.

The first explanation is that perhaps Lawrence and Garner did continue to have sex after the deputies entered the apartment and announced their presence because Lawrence and Garner were oblivious of the announcement and of the deputies' other activities.[27] This is unlikely since all the officers said that they announced their presence loudly enough for anyone in the apartment to hear, there was no other sound in the apartment to cover the deputies' announcement, the door to the bedroom was open, and neither Lawrence nor Garner was hearing impaired.

On the other hand, Quinn wrote in his Offense Report, filed the night of the arrest, that the men were "extremely intoxicated."[28] (Tipps, Lilly, and Garner himself deny that Garner was drunk.) Both Lawrence and Garner admit they had been drinking and Lawrence, for his part, conceded that he was drunk. This makes the obliviousness explanation more plausible, since alcohol may have so impaired the men's judgment that they did not care who else was present in the apartment.

But even if the men were intoxicated, the Quinn account is still dubious. Not one but both men would have had to be so drunk that they were unable to respond as a rational person would under the circumstances. By all accounts, there was more than enough time to stop any sexual activity, even for two very drunk people.

The second explanation for Quinn's and Lilly's strange account is that perhaps Lawrence and Garner did continue to have sex after the deputies entered the apartment and announced their presence because they were caught up in a moment of sexual passion and could not stop themselves.[29] This, too, is possible, and a moment of heedless passion could have been lubricated by the men's alcohol consumption.

But this still assumes a degree of animalistic frenzy that seems improbable. Whatever passion Lawrence and Garner were enjoying at the moment was surely dissipated by the sound of a loud male voice announcing the presence of the "sheriff's department" and by the activities and words accompanying the deputies' encounter with Man #4. Moreover, the time that must have elapsed between the announcement and the moment the deputies actually entered the bedroom (just under a minute, according to Quinn) would have allowed passions to cool considerably.

Tipps estimated that only about thirty seconds passed between the time the deputies announced their presence (presumably, the moment when Lawrence and Garner would have realized the police were present) and the time Lawrence and Garner would have been observed (by Quinn and Lilly) having sex.[30] If Quinn and Lilly maintained that they went straight to Lawrence's bedroom upon announcing their presence, they would be more believable. But that is not the account they, the only two eyewitnesses, have offered.

And even thirty seconds, while brief in absolute terms, can be an eternity in real life. (Stop reading, count out thirty seconds, and then ask yourself whether this would be enough time to cease a sexual act.)

It's more than enough time for two people engaged in sexual activity, and suddenly conscious of loud, authoritative, and strange voices twenty-five feet away, to stop what they are doing.

The third explanation is that perhaps Lawrence and Garner did continue to have sex after the deputies entered the apartment and announced their presence because Lawrence and Garner were part of an elaborate scheme to set up a test case to challenge the constitutionality of the Texas sodomy law. Under this scenario, Lawrence and Garner *wanted* to be seen having sex so that they would be arrested for violating the law, an already discredited theory.

THE FOURTH AND FINAL explanation is that Quinn and Lilly simply are not telling the truth. Whatever Lawrence and Garner were doing when the deputies entered the apartment and announced their presence, they were not having prohibited anal sex (the Quinn view) or oral sex (the Lilly view) by the time the deputies made their way to the bedroom. Quinn made up the story because he was angry at Lawrence (and possibly for a number of reasons explored later in this chapter) and Lilly went along with it, allowing his name to appear as a "witness" to the alleged crime on Quinn's arrest report.

For many, the problem with this explanation is that it involves accepting that a law enforcement official fabricated evidence to issue a citation and make an arrest. But this may be less of a "problem" than one might suppose.

Police throughout the United States have been caught fabricating, planting, and manipulating evidence to obtain convictions where cases would otherwise be very weak. Some authorities regard police perjury as so rampant that it can be considered a "subcultural norm rather than an individual aberration" of police officers. Large-scale investigations of police units in almost every major American city have documented massive evidence of tampering, abuse of the arresting power, and discriminatory enforcement of laws.[31] There also appears to be widespread police perjury in the preparation of reports because police know these reports will be used in plea bargaining. Officers often justify false and embellished reports on the grounds that it metes out a rough justice to defendants who are guilty of wrongdoing but may be exonerated on technicalities.[32] Police fabrication of evidence is common enough to make it a plausible answer when no other theory appears to explain improbable officer testimony.[33]

Police misconduct against gay people specifically, including fabrication of "evidence" and entrapment of gay men for sex crimes, is common in American legal history.[34] For example, in the 1960s, New York police arrested hundreds of men each year on sodomy charges (usually for alleged conduct in public or semipublic places). Yet in all but one year, fewer than 10 percent of those arrested were charged, and fewer than 5 percent were ultimately convicted. Gays were arrested and detained as a harassment tactic when there was insufficient evidence for a conviction.[35] In Texas, a San Antonio park ranger testified that he had arrested more than 500 presumed gay men in a public park simply because "he wanted to rid the park of gays."[36] Many gay men charged with sodomy and other offenses have simply accepted plea bargains, reducing the possibility that the sufficiency and reliability of police testimony against them would ever be tested.[37] Police misconduct against gay men and lesbians has continued into the twenty-first century.[38] The Lawrence and Garner arrests may be just another episode in that sorry history.

Delmore doubted that the officers would have fabricated the story. "I can't imagine the officer making up the fact that he'd seen them having sex," said Delmore. "I don't have any reason to think it happened in this case." However, Delmore acknowledged that he never spoke to the officers involved in the arrest and knew very little about the circumstances of the arrest. "I wanted to know only what was in the record"—basically, the charge and simple factual allegations filed by Quinn—in order to preserve the state's argument that the record did not disclose whether the activity was truly in private, was consensual, was noncommercial, and so forth.[39]

Quinn himself firmly rejected speculation that Lawrence and Garner were not actually having sex when the deputies entered the apartment. "Why would I risk my career and reputation for that?" he argued. It's a very good question.

One answer is that, from the perspective of that night, it would have seemed unlikely that Quinn or Lilly were taking much of a chance on their reputations or careers by arresting these two men for homosexual conduct. Lilly was taking almost no chance, since he was not the lead deputy, never signed an affidavit swearing to any facts, and knew he likely would not be called to testify. He would never have to make a false statement.

Even for Quinn the risks would have seemed small. The offense was the equivalent of a traffic ticket. Even if the men demanded a trial, which would have seemed exceedingly unlikely at the time, it would be a deputy's word against the defendants'. And who were these defendants? They were obviously not rich or famous men. Moreover, they were homosexuals, a despised class of persons in the officers' milieu, who would probably meekly plead out the way so many before them had.[40] It was exceedingly unlikely that such men would even get a lawyer, or challenge their citations, much less take their case to the U.S. Supreme Court—akin to their being sent in a NASA rocket to the moon. They were easy marks, as gay men throughout history had always been.

There are several reasons that Quinn might have made up a story about seeing Lawrence and Garner having sex, and why Lilly might have acquiesced in that story. These motives can be found in the deputies' own accounts of what happened that night and in their expressed feelings about the events. Here are five, beginning with the most probable.

IT IS CLEAR that the deputies, especially Quinn, were angry and frustrated the night they took Lawrence and Garner to jail. They had to deal with a false report of a weapons disturbance, a potentially deadly situation for the officers and for anyone they encountered. Although Lawrence and Garner could not be blamed for the false report, they were part of the frivolous (to the deputies) "lovers' triangle" that led to it. Quinn acknowledged that the false report played a role in his decision to cite Lawrence and Garner and to take them to jail instead of simply issuing them a citation.

Furthermore, by all accounts (and total concurrence is rare in this story), Lawrence did not react placidly. He refused to cooperate in putting his clothes on, accused them of antigay harassment, and cussed at them. These acts amounted to uncivil disobedience on his part. Of course, if he was falsely charged with a crime in his own home, Lawrence's righteous anger was understandable. In an interview, Quinn conceded that Lawrence's uncooperative and belligerent actions and words factored into his decision to cite Lawrence and Garner and to take them to jail instead of simply issuing them a citation.[41]

From the deputies' point of view, they had been lied to, had put their lives and the lives of others at risk, and had been verbally abused for silly reasons. Their anger and frustration may have been taken out on Lawrence and Garner, who, as homosexuals, could plausibly be charged with the crime of acting on their homosexuality. They had probably been engaged in some sexual activity anyway, Quinn could have reasoned, making them no less guilty than if he had actually seen the act. A citation and arrest, from the deputies' perspective, may have been just punishment for those shenanigans. It was rough justice.

THE SIMPLE FACT is that, as the deputies themselves agreed, Lawrence and Garner were arrested because they were "a man and a man" having sex.[42] A man and a woman having sex in a discreet but public place, or two women having sex in their own home, would have drawn only an admonition. By itself, that is an acknowledgment that antigay animus led to the arrest. The thought of sexual acts between two men elicited a special revulsion from the deputies that helps explain why there ever was a *Lawrence v. Texas*.

As discussed in chapter 4, the Harris County Sheriff's Office had no policy prohibiting discrimination on the basis of sexual orientation, refused to give officers training to deal with the gay community, and had no openly gay deputies or other personnel. Antigay slurs and jokes were commonly heard among deputies. The deputies were ensconced in an antigay, hypermasculine world of good old boys.

Moreover, as chapter 4 also details, interviews with the deputies revealed their personal and deep discomfort with homosexuality. Quinn, Lilly, and Tipps made it clear that they regarded homosexual acts as morally wrong and each cited the Bible or their religious faith as reasons for that belief.[43] But beyond religious doctrine, their objections to homosexuality were visceral. None of them had known openly gay people when they were growing up in socially conservative areas. All three expressed unease at the thought of any physical proximity to gay men. They worried about being the object of sexual advances by homosexual males.

Events during the arrest itself confirmed that this revulsion toward gay men was at work. If Garner and Lawrence are to be believed, the deputies repeatedly used homophobic slurs like "fag" and "queer." Quinn's statements about the pornographic contents of Lawrence's home, including his derisive laughter at a sketch on Lawrence's wall, revealed great disdain for Lawrence's sexual orientation, not simply dislike for Lawrence's decorating taste. Quinn's own freely expressed fears about coming into contact with "fluids" from the men revealed irrational fear of their activity and perhaps of them as persons. Quinn's defensiveness about not wanting to give Lawrence room to claim antigay bias also conveyed his distrust of gays as manipulative and perhaps conspiratorial. Lilly said he could detect homosexuality by the disgusting smell in the apartment.

While it is difficult to accept that the deputies actually saw Lawrence and Garner engaged in sex, it is true that the men were scantily clad (perhaps hurriedly looking for their clothes inside a dark bedroom) when Quinn and Lilly saw them. Whatever Lilly saw, it shocked him so much that he "lurched back," according to Quinn. The very shock of seeing two adult men in a bedroom together, with the light off, may have awakened homophobic feelings.[44] That is one way to understand Lilly's "lurch back" upon seeing Lawrence and Garner. Discovering any couple engaged in sexual play would be startling, of course, but Lilly acknowledged that he probably wouldn't have had such an intense reaction if he had seen a man and a woman, or two women, having sex.

In fact, Quinn's account of the men as continuing to have sex for over a minute with deputies watching, shouting, guns drawn, and lights turned on, plays into stereotypes of gay men as so sex obsessed they are literally unable to control themselves. They are animals in their lust. Quinn's complaint that Lawrence and Garner lacked what he called "self-dignity" is significant. In this view, gay men lack the kind of self-respect and respect for others that ordinary people possess. They have no dignity.

Quinn could have expected that his version of events would be believed, since these stereotypes of gay men as sex obsessed are widely

shared.[45] The perception of gays as hypersexual is a defining characteristic of homophobia. As James O. Woods argued in his study of gay men
in American corporations, "Prevailing stereotypes about gay men (that
they are hypersexual, promiscuous, indiscriminate) further emphasize
the sexual aspects of their lives. The result is a tendency to hypersexual-
ize gay men, to allow their sexuality to eclipse all else about them, *even to
see sexual motives or intentions where there are none.*"[46]

From the deputies' perspective, then, it may have seemed obvious
that Lawrence and Garner had been having sex, or were preparing to do
so. Moreover, what they had been doing or were preparing to do was
morally objectionable and repulsive to the deputies. The fact that the
men had not actually been caught in the act was unimportant. They
were as good as guilty.

To be fair, the deputies claimed that they were not uniformly opposed to
all gay-rights measures. On a spectrum, Lilly seemed the most understanding and open to the idea of equality for gay people; Tipps, the most hard-
edged in opposition; Quinn, somewhere in between. All opposed gay
marriage but, perhaps surprisingly, Tipps and Quinn said they supported
allowing gay people to serve in the military (Lilly worried that gays might
be attacked by straight soldiers). Lilly thought people should be able to have
sex in their homes without government interference. He also thought people did not choose to be gay because he'd seen signs of it in "little bitty kids."

CLOSELY RELATED to the homophobic motive, there might also have
been an element of what is known as "gender anxiety" at work in the
case. As discussed in chapter 4, both Quinn and Lilly harbored very traditional attitudes about the proper roles, attitudes, dress, and manner of
men and women.

Both men perceived themselves as masculine and, indeed, both men
presented themselves in traditionally masculine ways. Quinn was particularly upset when his masculinity was challenged, as it was when one
citizen taunted him for not being "man enough" to arrest her.

Lilly articulated even more disgust for gender nonconformity. What
bothered him most about many gay men, he said, was that they are
effeminate. As a kid, he remembered another young boy who exhibited
what he called "feminine twists" that unsettled him.

Garner was one of those guys with "feminine twists." Quinn described him as a "naggy bitch." In Garner, the deputies would have seen one of the things they most abhor about homosexual men: their tendency to adopt the manner, voice, and passivity associated with women. Garner was a feminized male. While Lawrence's back talk upset the deputies, at least he was man enough to defend himself and his home. From the vantage of the police, Garner just stood by and took the abuse and orders they inflicted. Lawrence could be respected at some level, even as his sexuality was reviled; Garner did not even deserve this grudging respect.

WHEREVER GAY PEOPLE have been discriminated against, those at the lowest end of the economic scale have been among the hardest hit. According to historian Martin Duberman, the patrons at the Stonewall Inn, who rioted against police harassment and sparked the modern phase of the gay-rights movement, were from the economic and social margins of life.[47] It is they who most often proved vulnerable to, and were undefended against, police harassment.

In the same regard, there is evidence that economic class may have played a role in the *Lawrence* arrests. Lawrence and Garner were neither wealthy nor well educated. It is no accident the arrests occurred in a lower-middle-class area rather than in a tony Houston neighborhood like River Oaks, with its large houses and broad lawns occupied by CEOs, successful lawyers, and millionaire doctors. Police charging crimes against wealthy home owners could expect the residents to fight back with ample resources. Lawrence and Garner, by contrast, could be expected to do nothing. Yet Lawrence and Garner, like the patrons at the Stonewall Inn and like so many generations of gay people before them, resented their shabby treatment.

Beyond that, the lead officer in the case, Quinn, approached his job differently on the east side of Harris County than he would in wealthier (and more white) areas on the west side. East Harris County residents, he claimed, were less likely to speak to police in a respectful manner, were more prone to resist orders, and were generally less deferential. Quinn adapted to the difference by getting tougher on residents in east Harris County. This he attributed to "something in my personality" that would not tolerate disobedience. To Quinn, Lawrence's foul language and defiance of his authority would have been typical of the area, and Quinn would have reacted in his customarily rough way.

FINALLY, IT IS POSSIBLE that complex racial feelings—unstated and perhaps subconscious—entered the decision to cite the men and take them to jail. Race consciousness was present at the start of the events, when the sheriff's department received a report that "a black male" was "going crazy with a gun." In fact, as noted in chapter 5, it is possible Eubanks used a racial slur when he made the report.[48]

Lawrence's apartment was in a working-class neighborhood, an area that is very traditional in its attitude toward gays. It is also racially polarized. The Harris County Sheriff's Office reflected those attitudes.[49] Lawrence was white and Garner was black. Few have commented on the fact that they were an interracial pair or on what role that might have played in the relatively harsh treatment they received. However, one gay-rights activist familiar with the sheriff's department suspected a simple reason that might have caused the deputies to fabricate a story about seeing sexual activity: "Black guy, white guy, apartment, naked. That's all you need."[50] This suggests that a mix of homophobia and racism may have been at work.[51]

If racism was present, however, it was not as simple as white deputies inflicting their racist views on an interracial couple. Although Quinn was white, Lilly was black. This, too, added a potential racial element to the case. It is possible that Lilly, coming from a socially conservative and religious black community,[52] was especially offended by the sight of a black man engaged in what he considered a morally objectionable sexual act with a white man. This offense may have been aggravated because the black man was playing the receptive (passive, subordinate, female) role to the white man during sex.[53] At the scene of the arrest, Lawrence was aggressive and belligerent (masculine); Garner was passive and cooperative (feminine). Lilly was clearly bothered that Garner was very effeminate, which suggests that gender anxiety and racial pride may have produced a toxic mix.

In Houston, there had long been friction between mostly white gay-rights advocates and blacks. The 1985 referendum on the city's gay-rights ordinances reflected this antagonism. As we saw in chapter 2, black leaders, especially black ministers like Floyd Williams and C. Anderson Davis, strongly opposed antidiscrimination laws protecting gays. To the vast majority of black religious leaders, homosexuality was immoral and should not be tolerated.

Implicit in the criticisms of gay-rights laws was the idea that homosexuality was a phenomenon peculiar to whites. Gays were "them," not "us." The problem was that Garner, as a gay black man, disproved this fiction. For Lilly, Garner's homosexuality may have been experienced as racial betrayal.

This is speculation. The deputies have not admitted that race influenced the arrests, nor would they be expected to admit it if it had. Neither Lawrence nor Garner recalled any racial slurs during the arrest or during their time in prison. "I was not worried about racism at that moment," said Lawrence about his encounter with the deputies. We cannot know with any certainty what role race may have played. The possibilities are intriguing but are ultimately unknowable. If race played any role, it was very complicated and is unlikely ever to be acknowledged explicitly by law-enforcement authorities or anyone else involved.

As we have seen, the arrest of John Lawrence and Tyron Garner for sodomy was not the work of gay-rights masterminds scheming for ways to challenge the Texas Homosexual Conduct law. It was, in all probability, based on an invention of sheriff's deputies who were angry about, among other things, the drunken machinations and insolence of three homosexuals. The Lawrence of *Lawrence v. Texas* claims that the alleged sex never took place. There is an abundance of evidence to support his denial, some of it circumstantial and inferential, some of it obvious at the time, and some of it emerging only later. But there is no reason, other than blind faith in the word of two sheriff's officers with several reasons to misrepresent what they saw, to believe that there was any actual sex in the U.S. Supreme Court's heralded sexual freedom decision.

8.

The Homosexual Status Law

*S*UPPOSE SHERIFF'S DEPUTIES DID INDEED CONCOCT A STORY ABOUT
seeing sex they never saw. Suppose they used their discretion
against Lawrence and Garner at every step. Suppose they did this simply
out of spite, or for homophobic, sexist, classist, or racist reasons. One
might say that none of this much matters, except perhaps to history buffs
trying to understand the story. The point, one might continue, is that the
police claimed to have seen something, the defendants were charged,
they challenged the law as unconstitutional, and won. If the police were
telling the truth, they correctly charged the men, and the *Lawrence* decision stands as a repudiation of the law under which they were convicted.
If the police were lying, they falsely charged the men, but the *Lawrence*
decision still stands as a repudiation of the law. Either way, antigay sodomy laws are now unconstitutional. There is no going back. Perhaps the
background facts, including the improper acts and motives of a handful
of police officers, make no difference for the legacy of *Lawrence v. Texas*
and contain no larger lesson for the law.

And if sheriff's deputies did not actually see Lawrence and Garner
having sex, that does not necessarily mean the men were innocent. If
they were having anal or oral sex with each other when the police
entered Lawrence's apartment—or indeed at any other time or any
other place in Texas—they broke the state's sodomy law whether the
deputies saw them or not.

In other words, the hypothesis that Lawrence and Garner were not caught in the act by the police may be correct but inconsequential. However, that would be a facile conclusion. It matters a great deal—sociologically, politically, culturally, and even legally—if events produced a false and abusive arrest of two gay men in a private home for sodomy.

Start with the observation that American law is not designed to catch and punish every instance of illegal conduct. Nothing short of a totalitarian state could do that. It is designed to prosecute persons when there is a reasonable basis for believing they have committed a crime, and then to convict them when there is no reasonable doubt that they are guilty. An arrest cannot even be made unless there is probable cause to believe a crime was committed.[1] If the deputies saw Lawrence and Garner having sex, the standard was obviously met. But if deputies only saw Lawrence and Garner naked in a bedroom with the lights off, that standard was not met—at least not without more information indicating they had engaged in impermissible anal or oral sex.[2] Too many other possible explanations intrude, including that they were engaged in sexual play, such as mutual masturbation or kissing, that did not violate the Texas law, even for same-sex participants. If the deputies did not see the act of anal or oral sex, as claimed, they did not have probable cause to make an arrest and there could be no subsequent prosecution. *Lawrence* would never have happened.

Even if Quinn and Lilly actually saw Lawrence and Garner having sex, that does not explain the decision to issue citations to the men and it certainly does not explain the decision to take them to jail for the night. The fact that someone is caught breaking the law does not mean he will be cited for it, as anyone who has gotten a warning for speeding can attest. Moreover, under similar circumstances, many deputies would not have even cited Lawrence and Garner, much less arrested them.[3]

Something made *Lawrence* different from other cases involving mildly discouraged sex—like an opposite-sex couple parked on a dark country lane. On its surface, the Texas sodomy law dealt only with conduct. It was, after all, called the Homosexual *Conduct* law. As the name suggests, it was formally about prohibiting certain types of same-sex sexual conduct. If persons engaged in that prohibited conduct, they violated the law—no matter whether they were actually gay or were straight and experimenting or were settling for second-best sex. If they did not engage in that conduct, what explains the deputies' decision to cite the men and to take them to jail?

The deputies were partly motivated by contempt for gays, especially gay men, as I suggested in the previous chapter. Thus, the discretion built into law enforcement may have been abused by authorities harboring prejudice against the class of persons targeted by the law. One of the sources of that prejudice is surely the very law to be enforced, a law that singled out gay people both on its face and in its practical effects. A law of the type under examination in *Lawrence*—one that is rarely enforced but packs a strong cultural message about the group it affects[4]—may or may not be adopted because of simple antigay hatred.[5] But it will be peculiarly susceptible to animus in its enforcement, as appears to have happened here. In other words, the law itself may be a violation of the Constitution, but it invites and creates more violations by the authorities who enforce it.

This background reveals how gays were both better and worse off in states with sodomy laws than the Court imagined. They were better off because if sheriff's deputies did concoct a story about seeing sex, *Lawrence* shows once again how rare it must be for law enforcement authorities to be legally present in a home when two people are having sex, much less to *witness* the act so that they have the clear constitutional authority to arrest the pair. The chance of being caught by police in the act of sodomy in a private home was like the chance of a lightning strike. Gay persons could rely on this improbability in making decisions about what Justice Kennedy in his *Lawrence* opinion called "the most private human conduct, sexual behavior, and in the most private of places, the home."[6]

But for gay men and lesbians, their legal status was even worse than the Supreme Court knew. What gay people could not factor into decision making about private life was the opportunity the law afforded, and the incentive it gave, for abusive enforcement. Any law may be abused; evidence can be fabricated against anyone. But the danger is especially acute where the law has taught prejudice against a class, where enforcement is rare, where the activity itself is considered not just illegal but deeply shameful and literally indefensible, and where the effect of this shame is to inhibit all challenge. It is for these very reasons, among others, that the American Law Institute recommended the decriminalization of sodomy in the Model Penal Code five decades ago, writing:

> To the extent . . . that laws against deviate sexual behavior are enforced against private conduct between consenting adults, the result is episodic and capricious selection of an infinitesimal fraction of offenders for severe punishment. This invitation to arbitrary enforcement not only offends notions of fairness and horizontal equity, but it also creates unwarranted opportunity for private blackmail and official extortion.[7]

At a minimum, *Lawrence* involved these very problems of "episodic and capricious selection," accompanied by "arbitrary enforcement."

But the enforcement of the Texas law in this case also involved much more, a deeper malignity within the state's criminal code, and one that had inoculated it from meaningful challenge. Because of the deep shame it instilled in its targets, the law insulated itself against the checking function that our criminal procedural guarantees are supposed to serve.[8] The *Lawrence* Court glimpsed this truth when it observed that the state sodomy law was "an invitation to subject homosexual persons to discrimination both in the public and private spheres."[9] But what the Court could not have known was that this perversion of the public and private spheres likely touched the very enforcement of the law under review.

If citizens cannot trust that laws will be enforced in an evenhanded and honest fashion, they cannot be said to live under the rule of law. Instead, they live under the rule of men corrupted by the law. Gay citizens, as demonstrated by the underlying facts of *Lawrence*, lived in a parallel world where principles of honesty and impartiality in law enforcement thought to apply to everyone did not in fact apply to them. That is, prior to this final act of perversion by law enforcement authorities and its repudiation by a Court not even aware of the extent of the law's depravity, gay people cannot be thought to have been full citizens at all.

What was nominally a law criminalizing homosexual conduct in fact was a law criminalizing the status of being homosexual. In Texas, *being* gay became a crime. As John Lawrence responded when his partner, Jose Garcia, asked why they had been charged, "We were arrested for being gay."[10] In a technical sense that was untrue, but in the real world, simply being gay was a crime in Texas. The Homosexual Conduct law was, in practice, a Homosexual *Status* law.

Lawrence, in this light, was not simply a case of enforcing a bad law. It was a case of corruptly and capriciously enforcing a bad law. It was not just an invasion of "liberty," as the Court thought. It was the deformation of the basis for all liberty: order under law. It was not simply a law prohibiting certain specified sexual activities between specified persons, it was aimed at the very persons themselves. *Lawrence*, therefore, involved a double perversion of law. It was worse than we knew.

Part Three

...

AFTER THE
ARRESTS

9.

From the Jail to the Bar

W HATEVER HAPPENED THAT NIGHT IN JOHN LAWRENCE'S APART-
ment, the case was now in the Texas judicial system. If *Lawrence v. Texas* was going to be anything more than another forgotten
Class C misdemeanor, the clock was now ticking toward a deadline just
weeks away.[1]

At the Wallisville substation two miles from Lawrence's apartment,
Lawrence and Garner were shackled to a bench along with the evening's
other alleged criminals. Sheriff's department personnel asked the men
standard questions about date of birth, current address, phone numbers, height and weight, and so on. Their possessions, including Garner's wallet and watch, were taken and placed in bags. After being
processed at the substation, they were taken to the Harris County jail in
downtown Houston, where they were offered a shower in one of the
jail's communal facilities.[2] Thus, having just been arrested for having
sex, Lawrence and Garner were now encouraged to shower together.

After cleaning up, the men were given standard orange jail jumpsuits. They were provided mattresses and a blanket for the night. Lawrence was so bruised and sore from his encounter with the police that he
could not carry his mattress. At his request, Lawrence was taken to the
"gay tank," a separate holding cell for gay inmates who might otherwise
be harrassed and abused. Garner was taken to a large cell with a general
inmate population, full of men arrested for public intoxication and other
minor offenses.

The next day, September 18, Lawrence and Garner were taken to an initial arraignment. This initial hearing took place in a small courtroom at the jail where, one by one, numerous people charged with petty offenses were called by the hearing officer to stand up, walk to the front, have the state's charges against them read aloud, and declare whether they plead guilty, not guilty, or pleaded "no contest." Most defendants, including Lawrence and Garner, had no legal representation at the hearing. Many simply pleaded guilty or no contest and paid their fines.[3] Such behavior is standard in any urban courtroom.

The hearing officer called Lawrence to the bench and the D.A. announced the charge of "homosexual conduct" against him. "There was an audible gasp in that courtroom," Lawrence recalled. The D.A. then read Quinn's short affidavit stating that the officers had observed Lawrence and Garner having anal sex. That's the moment Lawrence understood the charge for the first time. "I thought, 'My god, we didn't have sex.' "[4] The hearing officer, Carol Carrier, acting as a judge, asked Lawrence how he would plead. "Not guilty," Lawrence responded. Garner also pleaded not guilty.

There are many reasons that Lawrence and Garner might have pleaded not guilty the day after their arrests and before they had legal counsel. Perhaps they believed this was the best way to preserve their case until they could contact a lawyer. Perhaps they believed that in having anal sex in Lawrence's home they had done nothing wrong, or at least nothing that should be a crime. These would have been fairly sophisticated and calculated motives for two "guilty" men who had no representation and no knowledge of the law, standing in orange jumpsuits before a judge and next to a county prosecutor. The most obvious inference from a "not guilty" plea, of course, is that they were saying they were not guilty. Lawrence and Garner were asserting their factual innocence. The arraignment was the first time they heard Quinn's claim that they had actually engaged in anal sex, rather than the more nebulous "homosexual conduct," which could refer to any number of same-sex activities, or the even more mysterious reference to "21.06." Later, represented by attorneys eager to challenge not the factual basis for the arrests but the constitutionality of the law, their pleas changed to no contest.[5] But the earlier not-guilty pleas are the closest thing we have to a statement from Lawrence and Garner, immediately after the arrests, about what actually happened.

The fact that they pleaded not guilty and later denied they were having sex does not establish their innocence, of course. Perhaps they had actually been caught in the act and were avoiding the truth. Perhaps they were ashamed to admit what they had done in an open court full of strangers. But their not-guilty pleas are one more bit of information that tends to undercut the received version of what happened in Lawrence's apartment.

Carrier scheduled another arraignment in the court of Justice of the Peace Mike Parrott for October 5, just over two weeks away.[6] Parrott's court was in the same building as the Wallisville substation, where Lawrence and Garner had been taken immediately after their arrest. If their case was to go anywhere, the arrest of these two men with no previous connections to any gay-rights organization would somehow have to be brought to the attention of gay-rights advocates and then given to lawyers equipped to handle it. If the case had made it to the justice of the peace without the guidance of gay-rights lawyers, there was a very real chance it would have been dismissed and lost its place in history.[7]

After the arraignment, the men were taken back to their cells to stay until their release late that night, after midnight. Lawrence was given an old pair of blue jeans, but still had no shoes. By then, his feet were hurting. He and Garner hailed a cab and went back to Lawrence's apartment. Lawrence retrieved his wallet, which had been left behind with his clothes when he was arrested twenty-four hours before, and paid the driver. Garner slept on the living room sofa. The next day he took a bus back to his brother's house, where he had been staying. Except for their meetings with attorneys, the men rarely saw each other after that night. Except for one meeting with attorneys on October 12, Lawrence never again saw Eubanks.

Over the next few days, Lawrence began receiving telephone calls and mail from attorneys wanting to represent him. He ignored the calls, knowing that the attorneys had gotten his name and phone number from the public arrest records and were simply looking to collect fees. He had time to wait and decide what he wanted to do, although challenging the constitutionality of the state sodomy law was not on his mind. He distrusted attorneys.

Lawrence did, however, call his stepfather to tell him that he had been arrested. "For what?" his dad asked. "Because I'm gay," Lawrence replied. His father told him that he would pray about it and knew his son would make the right decision about what to do. He told Lawrence to expect a telephone call from someone offering to help. "My dad was very religious and I think he was praying for a miracle to happen," recalled Lawrence.[8]

Lawrence waited until Jose Garcia returned from visiting his family in Durango to tell him about the incident. It was not the sort of thing he wanted to explain over the phone. "Tyron and I were arrested for being gay," Lawrence told him. "What do you mean?" asked Jose. Lawrence recounted the events, including how the police had falsely charged them with having sex. Jose took it well, Lawrence recalled, fully accepting that he would not have had sex with Garner.[9]

MEANWHILE, THE CASE was registered on the docket for Judge Mike Parrott, where it would be processed by Parrott's staff. Among these was thirty-eight-year-old Nathan Broussard, who had been a file clerk in the office for five years.[10] Broussard, a Catholic Cajun from southern Louisiana, had met his partner, Mark Walker, on the Tuesday before Thanksgiving in 1986 while bartending at JR's, a popular Houston gay bar. They moved in together two weeks later, yet he remained closeted on the job.

Two years older than his partner, Walker was a sergeant in the Harris County Sheriff's Office, where he had worked since the early 1980s. He was a demanding "drill sergeant," as Broussard termed it, known to enjoy hunting, and was widely respected and trusted by all on the job. Walker and Broussard, both physically imposing men, were extremely discreet with sheriff's deputies and court personnel about their homosexuality and their relationship. Few in either workplace knew they were a couple. The men were aware such a revelation could have cost them their jobs. (Walker frequently heard deputies under his supervision use words like "fag," especially when telling jokes or talking about prisoners.) Neither man was active in gay-rights causes.[11]

Broussard and Walker knew Joe Quinn quite well, both personally and by reputation in the department. Ironically, Walker had been assigned as Quinn's supervisor on the night shift in an effort to rein him in. "Mark was about the only one that could keep him sort of under control because Mark really wasn't scared of anybody," Broussard remembered. "He'd tell it like it is. He was very blunt." In fact, Walker constantly complained about Quinn. Of course, at the time, Quinn had no idea that either Walker or Broussard was gay, much less that they were lovers.

On Friday morning, September 18, Broussard came into the offices of Judge Parrott in the Wallisville substation, prepared for an ordinary workday. There, waiting on the fax machine, he saw the charges Quinn had filed for "homosexual conduct," sent to the office from a clerk at the county jail at 2:27 a.m. Broussard's job, in part, was to ensure that charges assigned to Judge Parrott's court were properly coded in the county's computer system. But there was no updated code in the system for homosexual conduct, apparently because such charges were so rare. "I thought it was rather embarrassing because I didn't know the charge had existed myself." He called the county jail and said, "Surely this isn't a good charge." But the clerk confirmed that it was.

Broussard had no idea of the legal significance of what he had just seen. Still, it was intriguing enough that he showed the complaint to Sheryl Roppolo, the office manager, as soon as she walked in the door. When Judge Parrott came into the office that morning, she told him about the case. Like Broussard, Parrott was oblivious of its import.[12]

Broussard called Walker at home to tell him about Quinn's actions. "You're not going to believe what Quinn did now," he told Walker. He then explained the arrest for anal sex. "It fits," replied Walker. "I've got to see this." Broussard then faxed the charges to Walker at their home. Walker made some calls to people he knew in the sheriff's department to find out more about what happened, but he did not want to arouse suspicion—he was still closeted.

Early that evening, Walker and Broussard made their weekly trip to Pacific Street, a local gay bar. The two-story bar was large and dimly lit. The first floor combined a bar area with a dance area.

Lane Lewis, a bartender at Pacific Street, was active in the gay civil rights movement, including the Houston Gay and Lesbian Political Caucus. By then, Broussard and Walker had known Lewis for years and gossiped and bantered with him when they came in. "You could talk to him about more than just what you were drinking," recalled Broussard. Lewis was very much abreast of what was happening politically and in the gay community. When they arrived that night, they mentioned the arrest for sodomy and the charges under Section 21.06. Lewis looked astonished. As far as anyone knew, there had not been an arrest for private sodomy in Texas for many years. "He was kind of excited," Broussard remembered, "like someone told him what he was getting for Christmas."

It had never occurred to Broussard or to Walker that gay-rights activists needed an actual case to challenge the law. Lewis, of course, knew that gay activists in Texas had been waiting for years to get a sodomy case based on an arrest of two adults in the privacy of the bedroom. At that moment, in the midst of what Broussard called a "gossipy" conversation, *Lawrence v. Texas* was set on a legal trajectory no one there could have anticipated.

Lewis asked Walker to fax him a copy of Quinn's complaint, which recited the basic allegations that officers had entered Lawrence's home and witnessed him and Garner engaged in the criminal offense of homosexual conduct. The release of this information to Lewis at this early point in the case was probably "not proper," Broussard admitted, but the information would soon enough be public as an arrest and complaint record.[13]

When Lewis went home that night, the arrest report was waiting on his fax machine. Lewis saw the names of John Lawrence and Tyron Garner, whom he had never heard of before the incident. He called Broussard and Walker, declaring with obvious excitement, "I think this may be a Supreme Court case."[14]

To any student of gay life and history, the fact that a critical moment in the case took place in a gay bar should not be surprising. Such venues had long been the site of much-needed socializing and information sharing in an era of repression. "[B]ars were the first institution in the United States that contradicted . . . stigmas and gave gay Americans a sense of pride in themselves and their sexuality," wrote historian Allan

Bérubé. "In a nation which has for generations mobilized its institutions toward making gay people invisible, illegal, isolated, ignorant and silent," the establishment of gay bars was a political act, "the first stages in creating the roots of America's national movement for civil rights for gay people."[15]

In an age where gay political organizations were few and small, bars were also an important gathering place for political organizing. Gay historian John D'Emilio, for example, has provided a memorable portrait of San Francisco's Black Cat bar in the early 1960s. José Sarria, a singer at the bar, would end his performances by leading the patrons in a round of "God Save Us Nelly Queens." With vice squad officers present taking names, the song was a way of saying, "We have our rights too."[16] When Sarria ran for city supervisor in 1961, he collected signatures for his petition to run for office by approaching the patrons of the city's gay bars. D'Emilio concludes: "[Sarria's] candidacy, although it garnered only 6,000 votes, was the hot topic in the bars that fall, forcing patrons to think about their identity, their sexual orientation, in political terms."[17]

It's thus unsurprising that the modern phase of the gay civil rights movement began in a bar, New York's Stonewall Inn in 1969. Gay bars helped form gay communities in major cities across the nation.[18] While many patrons may have perceived the bars simply as a place to unwind or to pick up others of the same sex, the gay bar had a catalyzing effect on its patrons. The most nonpolitical gay people have never really been able to escape the politicization of their lives by those who detest them. So it was in *Lawrence*.

Shortly after learning of the sodomy arrests at the bar, and possibly as early as Saturday, September 19, Lewis called Garner at the number supplied on the arrest report. There was no answer. He next called Lawrence.[19] "I am not a lawyer," Lewis explained in the message. "I am a gay activist and I would like to talk to you." Lawrence's first thought was "What the fuck is a 'gay activist'?" But something about Lewis's message made his call stand out from the others. "I think it was the sincerity in Lane's voice," he said. "The way he explained things, the way he put things. And he wasn't an attorney. And so I knew he was not out to make a buck."[20] Over time, Lawrence and Garner, both unfamiliar with the world of lawyers and gay-rights causes, would come to trust Lane

Lewis more than anyone else involved with the case. It was an important human connection in the first weeks and months after the arrest. Early on, Lewis was the glue that kept the case together.

Within the next few days, Lawrence returned Lewis's call. As they spoke, Lewis scribbled notes of the conversation on the faxed arrest report. He explained to Lawrence that he had obtained the report.[21] A surprised Lawrence asked, "How did you get it?" Lewis replied, "I can't tell you." He reiterated that he wanted to help Lawrence, that he was not an attorney, and that Lawrence could hang up if he wanted to. He offered to get Lawrence an attorney who would represent him free of charge and suggested that his case could lead to a Supreme Court decision that would get rid of sodomy laws across the country. If Lawrence didn't like the first attorney, Lewis said, he could get another one.

Having recently been released from the county jail, still tired and bruised, Lawrence remained angry about the arrest.[22] He was also concerned, as countless gay men facing criminal charges for sexual conduct had been before him, that he might lose his job because of it. Lewis warned Lawrence about the possibility of enormous media coverage. They then talked about what had happened the night of the arrests.

There were indications the case might run into complications. Lewis recorded in his notes that Lawrence told him they were "not guilty" and that he "was not having sex."[23] According to the notes, Lawrence claimed that "Tyrone [sic] was in the living room when police came in— John was in bed." Lewis, who had no formal legal training, could not have known whether this might endanger the whole case, but he knew it was a potential problem.[24] The case had to get in the hands of experienced lawyers as soon as possible.

Lawrence agreed to meet Lewis at eleven that night, in the parking lot of the hospital where he worked, after his shift ended, in order to talk more about the case. The encounter cemented Lawrence's trust in Lewis's good faith and knowledge.[25] As Lawrence went, so went Garner— thus, at this moment, *Lawrence v. Texas* was effectively in Lewis's hands.

IO.

From the Gay Bar to the Bar

$\sim\!\!\sim$

IMMEDIATELY AFTER HIS MEETING WITH LAWRENCE, LANE LEWIS knew he needed to get advice from some old hands in the Houston gay civil rights movement. He leaned toward calling Mitchell Katine, a well-known and well-regarded local gay attorney, but first there were people he trusted even more.[1]

Among the inner circle he relied on that very same night was Ray Hill, the gray-bearded grizzly bear of a man and veteran of the local gay-rights movement. Born in 1940, the Houston native had been involved in practically every gay organization ever created in the city. He was the one who kicked off the 1977 march against Anita Bryant with a defiant speech. He was also an adviser to local adult businesses where police frequently conducted sting operations looking for men having sex in video stalls.[2] Never publicity shy, he also had a deep political consciousness and innate ability to understand others' motives and feelings. Although some people called him a self-promoter, he was also utterly fearless in defense of the weak and unpopular. He was, as Annise Parker put it, "the biggest pain in the butt," but he was fighting for gay rights when few others were willing to do so.[3]

Hill's personal story reflected the diversity of America's gay world, a culture that defies simple stereotyping. An evangelical preacher in his teens, he still spoke in the cadences and with the fervor of the devout. He made a lot of money, as he put it, "saving souls, five dollars a piece. Shrinking hemorrhoids without surgery." He came out to his family when he was eighteen. His mother took a long drag from her cigarette and a sip of her coffee and said, "Well, that's a relief." "What?" he asked. Late 1950s Houston was not a tolerant time and place for homosexuals, especially in the blue-collar, religiously devout area in which he lived. "We noticed that you kind of dress up more than the other boys in the neighborhood and we thought you were pretending to be wealthy and we aren't," she explained. "We were afraid you might grow up to be a Republican."[4]

In the late 1960s Hill became a gay-rights activist. He'd been to the Supreme Court, and won, in *Houston v. Hill.*[5] In that case, Hill was arrested for berating a police officer while the officer was trying to arrest a friend of his. "Why don't you pick on somebody your own size?" said Hill, who was six feet tall and weighed more than 200 pounds, taunting the officer. Arrested for disorderly conduct, Hill countered that his First Amendment rights had been violated. The Court agreed, holding that the law under which he had been prosecuted was so broad it might be used to punish protected speech.

Lewis wanted Hill's advice when he called that night to tell him about two guys who had been arrested in an apartment for sodomy. "That's bullshit," Hill replied. "Nobody gets arrested for that. Did you wake me up in the middle of the night for a weenie-wiggling case in the goddamn bookstore?" Eventually, Lewis persuaded him that this was an arrest for private acts. Hill suggested that Lewis call Katine, especially since Katine practiced at a law firm headed by Gerald Birnberg, who had represented Hill in his Supreme Court case.[6]

A man on a mission, Lewis next called Annise Parker, the former president of the Houston Gay and Lesbian Political Caucus who had been elected to the city council the year before. Parker had been involved in citizen review boards for complaints against officers in the Houston Police Department and led training for recruits on how to deal sensitively with racial minorities and gay people. She had suggested Lewis as her replacement on the citizen review board when she ran for office.[7]

Lewis reached Parker at her office in Houston's limestone city hall. He described the arrests and the rough treatment to which Lawrence and Garner were subjected. As one of the frustrated gay advocates looking for a chance to undo the sodomy law, Parker could not believe what she was hearing. "Tell me it's not a Houston police officer who did this." Reassured that it was a county sheriff's deputy, she then asked Lewis to describe the defendants. "These are basically blue-collar guys. I think one of them has been to jail before," he commented. "One of them is black." The interracial element, they agreed, could complicate things with the public and even with the gay community, which they believed could be just as racist as the general public.

"What do I do?" he asked her.

Parker told Lewis that they needed to get an attorney immediately. "We just have to make sure we don't mess anything up," she told him. She suggested Mitchell Katine because, although he was not a criminal defense attorney, he was "ambitious" and his law firm would support him. She closed the conversation with a warning to Lewis. "Make sure you babysit these guys. Whatever you do, don't let them just plead out and disappear."[8]

These conversations confirmed Lewis's initial inclination to call Katine. Mitchell Katine, who had been born in Miami in 1960, first came to Houston in 1982 to attend South Texas College of Law. Fresh out of law school, Katine worked on HIV and AIDS issues, both as a lawyer and as a volunteer visiting the AIDS floors of local hospitals. The law firm he worked for told him that they were afraid he would get AIDS and spread it around the office. Katine then moved to Gerald Birnberg's firm, handling real-estate litigation and employment discrimination cases.[9]

Like Hill and Parker, Katine could hardly believe what he was hearing. He figured the case must involve public lewdness or some other complicating factor. Lewis faxed Katine the arrest report and his own handwritten notes of his conversation with Lawrence.[10]

But Katine was still wary of taking on the case because he wasn't a criminal defense lawyer. He called Hill to discuss his reluctance, which provoked the irascible gay-rights veteran. "No, you're not a criminal lawyer," Hill retorted. "I wouldn't hire you to represent me in a traffic case. But, son, if you let this case slip through your fingers, when you die they won't remember your name thirty minutes after you're dead. But if you take this case and see that it's done the right way, they'll carve your name in marble."[11]

Buoyed by this pep talk, Katine marched down to the office of another attorney in the Birnberg firm, David Jones, who *was* experienced in criminal law. In more than two decades of practice, Jones had handled everything from public lewdness cases to capital murder trials throughout the county. Although he had never seen a prosecution for sodomy between consenting adults in a home, he knew the local judges, the dockets, the personalities, and the procedures of the local courts.[12]

When Katine told him about the case, Jones thought it had potential to go to the Supreme Court, but it might be thrown out by one of the "eccentric" JP judges in the county. He advised that, if the defendants wanted a jury trial, they would be entitled to one in the JP court and again at the next level, the county criminal court. But he cautioned that a trial should be avoided. Jones was especially concerned that the case not be subjected to the intense factual examination of an actual trial "because you might win by causing the jury to doubt that Lawrence and Garner had sex"—that is, they might win the case *but lose the cause*.[13]

As word seeped out, several local gay attorneys urged Katine to drop the case. They argued that it was not the right time to challenge the Texas sodomy law in court. The state and federal courts, they opined, were still too conservative. And the Supreme Court was far from a sure bet. They worried that the case might end up making more "bad law," setting new antigay precedents that would reverberate throughout the legal system and be used as a basis for yet more discrimination against gay men and lesbians. That is exactly what had happened just twelve years before in *Bowers v. Hardwick*, when the Supreme Court upheld Georgia's sodomy law in an especially dismissive way. Although Katine agreed that this was indeed a danger, he concluded that the risk was worth it. Even if they lost, there was value in simply educating the public about the existence of the sodomy law in Texas.[14]

Undaunted, Katine contacted Suzanne Goldberg, a senior staff attorney for Lambda Legal, the national gay legal advocacy group. While there were well-regarded heterosexual attorneys in his own office, including the lead partner, Gerald Birnberg, Katine wanted gay lawyers to lead the effort:

> The case isn't just about the law. This case is about sociology, feelings of people in our country, religious issues, political issues,

family issues. And it needed to be handled by a person or an organization that can appreciate all the ramifications that a case like
this involves, as opposed to a lawyer thinking, "This is just a case
about the law and let's just argue the legal issues, and we'll do the
best we can."[15]

From the beginning, *Lawrence* was about more than constitutional
theories and doctrines. It was about lives. Nobody could better understand how important it was to be rid of sodomy laws than a gay person
who had lived through the consequences of being criminalized. Lambda
combined the rich legal talent and personal commitment Katine thought
would be needed.

Suzanne Goldberg started at Lambda in 1991, the year after graduating from Harvard Law School. Goldberg had a quick intelligence and an
encyclopedic knowledge of the law, not to mention an instinct for tactical advantage.

Lambda's national headquarters were on Wall Street in New York.
At the time of the Lawrence arrests, the group also had regional offices
in Los Angeles, Chicago, and Atlanta. Its budget was in the low seven
figures and it employed only about a dozen lawyers, but its attorneys
handled a myriad of gay-rights claims that arose at the state and federal
level, and in every area of the law, civil and criminal. Lambda's lawyers
across the country held a weekly conference call to review the status of
ongoing cases and to decide which new cases should be taken. Since
every case involved expense and precious lawyer time, hard choices had
to be made. Often meritorious claims had to be rejected.

Working out of Lambda's head office, Goldberg handled a mix of
cases, including HIV discrimination, domestic partnerships, immigration
matters for binational couples, asylum claims, the military's exclusion of
openly gay personnel, and state antigay initiatives. She had learned from
Tom Stoddard, the executive director of Lambda when she began working there, how to be what she called a "political lawyer." By this, she
meant a lawyer not simply attuned to the legal merits of a case and the
value of that case to the specific clients involved, but devoted to the larger
cause and political impact of the litigation. Suing might help clients, or it
might not, but either way it could help highlight the underlying issue to

the public, to legislatures, and to the judicial system—including other lawyers, clerks, and judges. Back in the early 1990s, for example, she worked on a case challenging the insurance company practice of limiting AIDS coverage to $5,000 per year while coverage for other catastrophic illnesses was capped at $1 million per year. She lost in the lower courts but appealed to the Supreme Court, knowing that the Court would almost certainly refuse to hear the case, as it did. Nevertheless, Lambda's effort highlighted the discriminatory practice and had the effect, she believed, of influencing the subsequent interpretation of federal law.[16]

Goldberg had also worked on the legal challenge to Colorado's Amendment 2, passed in a referendum by voters in 1992, which stripped from gay men and lesbians all civil-rights and antidiscrimination legal protection. In a historic victory for the cause of gay rights, in 1996 Justice Anthony Kennedy wrote for the Court in *Romer v. Evans* that Colorado had violated the Equal Protection Clause.[17] The decision prompted Lambda to redouble its efforts to find a vehicle for overturning sodomy laws in America.

By September 1998, Goldberg had honed her skills on a handful of legal challenges to state sodomy laws, including cases in Montana, Tennessee, and Arkansas.[18] The goal was to get a case back to the Supreme Court and persuade the Justices to overrule the Court's 1986 *Bowers v. Hardwick* decision.[19] All these cases, however, had one weakness in common: nobody had actually been arrested for violating a state sodomy law. Instead, in the cases Lambda pressed, the plaintiffs were arguing that the very existence of sodomy laws inflicted collateral injury on them by making it harder to get jobs, complicating efforts to obtain custody of their children, and marking them as presumptive criminals in the eyes of the state and their fellow citizens. These were certainly real harms, but they were not the kind of direct injuries inflicted by the law that federal courts are generally willing to consider when being asked to hold a law unconstitutional. Someone had to be arrested for actually violating a sodomy law.

By the autumn of 1998, the painstaking progress against sodomy laws had almost ground to a halt. The states retaining such laws were resisting change to their statutes. Neither their courts nor their legislatures were very responsive to critiques of the laws. Then, Goldberg got the call from Mitchell Katine one warm afternoon in late September.[20] After hearing Katine present Lawrence and Garner's story—the circumstances of the arrest, the fact that the men had been treated roughly, that they were angry about this treatment, that neither was a gay-rights activist but felt that the events had violated what Goldberg called their "internal sense of justice and fairness"—she felt instinctively that this case held promise. The men had been arrested. They had been charged with a crime. The law was directed solely at gay sex. The Harris County district attorney's office, whose head was an elected Republican, seemed likely to pursue the prosecution. The Texas courts, which had been taken over in partisan judicial elections by conservative Republicans, were likely to uphold the state law. All of that could clear a path to the Supreme Court.[21]

In Goldberg's view, it helped that the legal stakes were low for Lawrence and Garner personally. At most they were looking at a $200 fine, not several years in jail, as other state sodomy laws called for. This alleviated whatever conscientious doubts the lawyers might have had about not challenging the factual basis for their arrests and instead going straight to the constitutional arguments. Nevertheless, Goldberg acknowledges that the nonlegal stakes for Lawrence and Garner were real. Whatever the underlying truth, they were making a public declaration that they engaged in same-sex sodomy. It meant coming out as gay to the entire nation. Lawrence, for one, was still somewhat closeted on the job and to some members of his family.

Katine reassured Goldberg that his colleague David Jones was an experienced criminal defense lawyer who could get them through the thicket of the lower Texas court system. In those lower courts, the vaunted constitutional arguments would be subordinate to technical procedural questions and knowledge of how local courts actually work. At the end of the call, Goldberg told Katine that she was almost certain Lambda would take the case, with him and Jones serving as local counsel, but that she had to consult others in the office.[22]

Goldberg walked three doors down to the office of Lambda's supervising attorney, Ruth Harlow. Harlow was born in Michigan in 1961. Measured in her rhetoric, which was nevertheless laced with a dry wit, she gave the impression that she was at least two steps ahead of you. And that wasn't just an impression—as a legal thinker and strategist, she had been several steps ahead of just about every opponent she had faced.

Five years after graduating from Yale Law School, inspired by the openly gay law professor William Rubenstein, Harlow went to work for the lesbian and gay rights subdivision of the American Civil Liberties Union. Among other things, she led successful litigation against efforts to ban gay student groups from public schools and colleges. For example, Alabama had passed a law barring such groups on the grounds that its members violated the state sodomy law. She assisted an HIV-positive inmate in Texas who was convicted of attempted murder because he spit at a guard. In another Texas case, she worked on an appeal for a man named Calvin Burdine, who was sentenced to death for the murder of his same-sex lover. His trial was plagued by multiple problems. During testimony, his lawyer, who referred to Burdine as "fairy" and "faggot," had fallen asleep. Echoing arguments considered at the time the state enacted the Homosexual Conduct law, the prosecutor argued to the jury that a life sentence would be inappropriate because putting a gay man in prison was like putting a kid in a candy store. The judge also allowed evidence of Burdine's prior sodomy conviction to be introduced. Courts eventually ordered a retrial, where Burdine was once again convicted, but this time sentenced to life in prison.[23]

During her time at the ACLU, Harlow met semiannually with representatives of other gay legal groups, such as Gay and Lesbian Advocates and Defenders in Boston, the National Center for Lesbian Rights in San Francisco, and Lambda. These "round-table meetings," as Harlow called them, were designed to share information about cases, discuss strategies, and coordinate efforts as much as possible. They sometimes involved gay-rights litigators and law professors like Rubenstein, William Eskridge, Nan Hunter, Arthur Leonard, Nancy Polikoff, Andrew Koppelman, and Evan Wolfson. Mostly, however, the round-table discussion included only the actual litigating attorneys in the main legal organizations. The meetings fostered a degree of collegiality and cooperation rarely seen in gay political circles. It led, for example, to effective coordination among lawyers from Colorado, Lambda, and the ACLU in *Romer v. Evans.* In short, the round-table meetings were "a big factor in the effectiveness of gay-rights litigation overall."[24]

In 1996, Harlow moved to Lambda as a managing director, in charge of supervising the half-dozen or so lawyers in the New York office. Like Goldberg, Harlow had previously worked on sodomy cases from states like Oklahoma, Montana, and Kentucky. After the *Romer* decision that May, the ACLU and Lambda decided that the next step would be to go after same-sex-only sodomy laws. As they saw it, since the Supreme Court had struck down antigay discrimination in *Romer*, the logical extension would be to strike down an antigay classification in a criminal sodomy statute. Thus, the lawyers envisioned a challenge primarily under the U.S. Constitution's Equal Protection Clause.[25]

Lambda began trying to find plaintiffs in states with same-sex-only sodomy laws who would sue without having to be arrested and without other complicating factors, like public lewdness, force, prostitution, or public solicitation. To overcome the legal barriers to a civil suit, they needed plaintiffs who would be willing not only to endure the public glare but to declare openly that they regularly violated their state's sodomy law. However, many people—for instance, parents who might lose their children in custody fights because the court deemed them presumptive criminals—might be very reluctant to make such a public statement. In short, gay-rights groups needed plaintiffs with little to lose.[26]

Harlow immediately realized the Houston arrests might end up in the Supreme Court, but she was also cautious. Many things could go wrong. As Harlow and Goldberg assessed the case that day, they worried that there was still no guarantee that Lawrence and Garner would go through with a protracted legal battle. There was always the possibility that "someone in Texas would come to their senses and stop the prosecution." The lawyers might make a technical mistake that would ruin their opportunity to launch a head-on constitutional challenge.[27]

And there was, as Harlow acknowledged in an interview, some doubt about what had really happened in Lawrence's apartment. There were the issues of whether the police had caught the men in the act, had perhaps exaggerated what they had seen, or had simply presumed that the men must have been having sex.

But for Harlow, these were not important questions. She was several degrees removed from the quotidian facts and the actual defendants. Goldberg, Katine, and Lewis would be more directly involved in all of that. For Harlow, and for Lambda more generally, the case was going to be about the state's power to discriminate against gay people by interfering in their private lives. If the police claimed to have caught them in the act, that was all Lambda needed. Whether those facts were correct was the state's problem; Lambda would let the case proceed on the premise that the police had seen Lawrence and Garner and had properly charged them under the Homosexual Conduct law, but that the police had no power under the Constitution to arrest them for private sexual activity. And if the police were lying, that made it "a further misuse of their power and a further reason to get rid of the law so that they could never fabricate such things."[28]

There was never any question Lambda would take the case. This was the spark the gay-rights movement had been awaiting for more than a decade. Lambda's involvement was formally approved by its legal director, Beatrice Dohrn, and its executive director, Kevin Cathcart.[29] Suzanne Goldberg would be the front-line attorney, charged with overseeing the work of Katine and Jones as they navigated the lower-court minefield of Texan justice. Meanwhile, the initial arraignment hearing scheduled in Mike Parrott's JP court, at which Lawrence and Garner would once again have to declare whether they were guilty, had been delayed two weeks, to October 19. *Lawrence v. Texas* had some breathing space.

Back in Houston, Lawrence called Garner to explain what was happening. Garner was content to let Lawrence make decisions for them about the case. Lawrence decided they should at least meet with the lawyers to hear them out.[30]

On October 12, 1998, the first meeting of the defendants and their lawyers finally occurred. Lewis, Lawrence, Garner, and—to everybody's surprise—Eubanks arrived at Katine's office. Still smarting over Eubanks's role in causing all of their problems, Lawrence was unhappy to see him there.[31] Katine was also distressed that Eubanks had come. "Who is this? What is he doing here?" Katine asked. Garner explained that Eubanks was his boyfriend. But Eubanks was not Katine's client in the sodomy case, and the lawyers knew that anything said in Eubanks's presence might not be protected by the attorney-client privilege. Besides that, Eubanks was in their view erratic, untrustworthy, and had a heap of legal trouble on his own. On September 21, after spending three days in jail, Eubanks had pleaded no contest in county criminal court to the Class B misdemeanor of filing a false report to a peace officer. He was sentenced to thirty days in jail but was released early and was assessed court costs of $189.25. Now Eubanks was at best a distraction, at worst a threat to their success. He was sent to the lobby to wait.[32]

Lawrence repeated what Lewis had already told the lawyers: he and Garner were not having sex.[33] Katine and Jones explained three legal options. They could plead guilty and pay fines. At that point the case would be over and the men would have a Class C misdemeanor on their records. But no trial would be necessary, and thus there would be no danger of testimony about their private lives.[34]

They could plead not guilty and request a trial to contest the allegations made by police. If Quinn had ever been brought to a witness stand, an experienced lawyer like Jones could have made mincemeat of his salacious tale of animalistic lust. On the other hand, a trial would mean exposing the unseemly facts of the case—the drinking, the fighting, the jealousy, the gay porn, the specific sexual allegations, and the cussing. All of this would be embarrassing and very public. If the pair were acquitted, they would not have to pay a fine and would not have a conviction added to their existing records. But their victory against the factual allegations by the police would mean that the sodomy law remained on the books to be used against others in the future.[35]

Finally, they could plead no contest, meaning that they would not deny the allegations made by the police and there would be no trial. This would have the same legal effect as a guilty plea, but could not be used against them in the unlikely event of a civil case that might later be filed against them. Under a no contest plea, the case would be handled by lawyers who would argue in legal briefs that the law itself was unconstitutional. It was a clean option: none of the messiness of their lives and their conduct need ever be brought to light; they would simply stipulate to the facts in Quinn's short, public complaint and admit to nothing else. Their privacy would be respected, Jones reassured them.[36] It was clear that the lawyers had a high-powered legal team now stretching all the way to New York ready to help them with this third option.

Katine and Jones studied the reactions of Lawrence and Garner. Both men were stone-faced. The lawyers said that they would shield them as much as possible from the media and that all questions from reporters should be referred to them. But obviously the case would be widely reported. Neither Lawrence nor Garner ever wanted to become famous. They did not want to speak in front of cameras. While they were upset about the arrests, they did not have the "fire in the belly" reaction of activists ready to take on the legal system. They were not looking to make history with their case.

Lawrence, in particular, was worried that the case might affect his job.[37] He recalled his thinking at the time:

> The Supreme Court was the furthest thing from my mind at that point. *I wanted to get out of the court. I wanted it to be over with.* I wanted to get it out of the way because people at work . . . I had told one person at work, the manager, what was going on and so the bombshell went and hit her. And I didn't even tell my best friend at work.[38]

Lawrence also seemed "embarrassed" to be involved in the case, according to Jones. After all, it was a case in which (as Jones saw it) Lawrence was alleged to have been having sex with a much younger man, one from what most people would regard as a lower station in life. Jones speculated that Lawrence may also have been uneasy about the fact that his alleged sexual partner was black. Lawrence had been marinated in the racial attitudes and stereotypes of his upbringing in small-town east Texas. However, nothing Lawrence actually said indicated that he was uncomfortable with the interracial aspect of the case.[39]

Garner was mostly quiet, as he would be for the next five years. He was polite, Jones remembered, but also "had a street savviness to him that made him seem much older than his years." He seemed less fearful of the fight and less concerned about publicity, perhaps because he had less to lose. He was unafraid of describing his past, including his run-ins with the law. He didn't speak much, "but when he did speak he was much freer; he had a more vivid way of expressing himself."[40]

After the lawyers finished making their pitch to pursue the constitutional route, they left the room. With their appearance in the JP court scheduled for just a week away, on October 19, it was time for a decision. Lawrence, Garner, and Lewis were left alone in the conference room, where Eubanks rejoined them. Lewis looked warily toward Eubanks, the man whose bizarre telephone call had started everything. "I could smell bourbon on him across the room," he recalled. "Man, he made us nervous."[41] He was kept out of future proceedings.

Lawrence and Garner did not really know the lawyers, and Lawrence was suspicious of them, yet they had already come to trust Lewis. He spoke to the men for about fifteen minutes. He told them that what he was about to say might sound corny. He then quoted the famous line from John F. Kennedy's inaugural address, "Ask not what your country can do for you but what you can do for your country." Invoking the history of the gay civil rights movement and its early pioneers, he told Lawrence and Garner to "think about all the gay and lesbian people who stuck their necks out so you could enjoy whatever freedom you have." He told them about the Mattachine Society, one of the earliest gay-rights organizations, and about Harry Hay, one of the movement's earliest leaders. He told them how these pioneers had hidden in basements to have meetings, about the Stonewall Riots in New York in 1969, in which bar patrons had publicly resisted abuse by the police and sparked the modern phase of the gay civil rights movement. He told them the story of Harvey Milk, the first openly gay elected official in San Francisco, who was gunned down by a homophobic colleague in 1978. Lawrence and Garner knew none of this history. "They went above and beyond the call of their duty," Lewis pleaded. "I'm asking you to go above and beyond the call of your duty. Think how far we've come from all that, but think how far that really is. You were drug out of your home." Then he added, "You tell me to stop and I'll pull the plug."[42]

Lewis hit a nerve with the men. Lawrence explained what finally persuaded him:

> If it could happen to me, a poor little guy who worked forty hours
> a week and lives in his own house, and for someone to barge in
> and make this kind of accusation and to literally, you know . . .

anyone else—this probably could have destroyed somebody's life. They would have shuttered themselves in and committed suicide. And I said no. No.[43]

But for the intervention of Lewis, Garner might have simply paid the fine. "But I didn't have money at the time of the arrest," he added. He was not concerned about the media—he had no reputation to protect. He was not worried that his family would find out—his mom and dad were sick most of the time and he had to take care of them. They never read about the case or talked much about it. He was not concerned about losing a job—he didn't have one. "I didn't worry about nothing."[44]

He was driven by what Goldberg called an internal sense of justice. As Garner himself explained it:

> I realized how important it was. For an outdated law like that to make it all right for the police or government to walk into your house . . . you know, uninvited. I think that was just a wrong thing on the police part. I think they was just wrong. I felt like I had been taken advantage of. To get an outdated law like that off the book, I believe this is worth it to a lot of people.[45]

Having said everything he could, Lewis asked the men, "Is this something you would be willing to move forward on?" Just casual acquaintances three weeks before, Garner and Lawrence were being asked to commit to a long-term, high-profile court case in which their names would be forever linked. They looked at each other and nodded *yes*.[46]

When Jones and Katine returned, Lewis announced that Lawrence and Garner had decided to take their advice and challenge the sodomy law. The attorneys were elated, and the case was able to proceed.

Throughout these early stages, Lewis acted as Lawrence and Garner's friend, confidant, public-relations manager, and chauffeur. He made sure they got to court appearances and meetings with attorneys. They followed his instructions. The three men agreed to speak to media exclusively through Lewis. He gave them instructions that if any media called, they were to be directed to him or the attorneys. "Once you start talking," Lewis warned them, "they will be at your house, at your job, and everywhere else." Neither Lawrence nor Garner ever threatened to withdraw from the case.[47]

With the lawyers involved and media exposure imminent, Lawrence, Jose Garcia, and the defense team decided that Jose's existence would not be divulged. For one thing, Jose's homosexuality was not known to his traditionalist Mexican family. Lawrence warned Jose that he might be among those "mediatized" by reporters. "I don't want them in the apartment," Jose insisted. Throughout the litigation, however, Jose wanted to be informed about what has happening and asked Lawrence to "bring stuff home and tell him about it."[48]

Undoubtedly, knowledge of Lawrence's relationship with Jose would also have further complicated public relations by (falsely) raising the specter that Lawrence had cheated on his long-term partner. There was no need in the litigation—either as a matter of law or as a matter of image—for this additional distraction.

In New York, Lambda was also concerned that Eubanks was a "wild card" who might say anything to the media. Even Lawrence and Garner were shielded from media scrutiny. "After one press conference, a decision was made with the clients that the focus would not be on them personally," remembered Harlow. Instead, the focus would be on the actions of the state of Texas. The media was largely compliant with the request that the men's privacy be respected, which surprised the attorneys at Lambda. Reporters did not dig into the background of the story, which was a "huge factor" in letting Lambda control the narrative of the case.[49]

Not far into the case Lawrence received a phone call from his younger brother. "I'll come over and pay that damn fine," he offered. "Well, it's too late," Lawrence replied, "I'm sorry. This is going to go where it has to go because I'm not going to tolerate it."[50]

Into the Texas Courts

WITH LAWRENCE AND GARNER ON BOARD FOR A CONSTITU-
tional challenge to the state sodomy law, the defendants now
had to face the Texas judicial system. Only if they lost in Texas could
they hope to get to the Supreme Court. As it would turn out in the initial
stages, however, Texas judges were much more sympathetic than they
imagined. Defying preconceived stereotypes, they were not the bigoted
country bumpkins that Lambda's lawyers were warned to expect.

The day after the Houston attorneys met with Lawrence and Garner,
David Jones requested and obtained a delay in their first formal court
appearance, at which they would once again enter a plea.[1] It was
rescheduled to November 6 and eventually to November 20.

This first judicial stop was at the lowest court in the state system, the
Justice of the Peace (JP) court.[2] These courts handle certain small civil
claims and minor criminal cases. Their dockets include evictions, traffic
tickets, bad checks, truancy, public intoxication, threats, and simple
assault (where no weapon is involved). Many of the petty criminal cases
involve charges against minors from troubled homes who have misbe-
haved at school. Defendants can request trials, including a trial by jury
or a trial in which the JP judge himself decides whom he believes. JP
courts are not "courts of record," meaning that there is no official transcript of the proceedings. Of the sixteen JP judges in Harris County, most
did not even have law degrees.

Justice of the Peace Mike Parrott was one of the JPs who was not a lawyer. He'd become a JP judge in 1991 because he wanted to help local juveniles, many of whom ended up in his courtroom for minor offenses. Parrott was raised in east Harris County during the era when black people were known as "niggers" and "fag" and "queer" were acceptable terms. "We were so poor we put an extra 'o' in it," he recalled. A high school football star, he was still a jock in the eyes of his office manager, Sheryl Roppolo. However, defying the caricature of a good old boy, Parrott had a live-and-let-live decency about him. A conservative Democrat, he was impressively tolerant toward gay men and lesbians. "That's the life they choose," Parrott said. "As long as they do it in their homes, and not in front of me or my family or on TV." He joked that he felt "the same way about Republicans." On the morality of homosexual acts, Parrott said, "They'll deal with that at another time, when they die."[3] He supported allowing gays to serve in the military and thought the government should not tell adults what they can do in their bedrooms. He resisted supporting same-sex marriage, yet said he would have had a hard time denying marriage to his clerk Nathan Broussard and Broussard's partner, Mark Walker. It made no difference to him that two of his clerks were gay. For him, the personal was not political.

Parrott's courtroom wasn't a marble-and-mahogany palace of justice. Rather, it was a big unremarkable room in the Harris County Jim Fonteno Courthouse Annex, a large complex of unremarkable rooms containing administrative offices, the Wallisville substation of the HCSO, and the holding cells where the defendants had been taken the night of their arrests. From the outside, the building had the charm of a strip mall. On the inside, it lacked even that.

Not until forty-eight days after the arrests, on November 5, did the *Houston Chronicle* report on the sodomy case, but it showcased the matter on its front page. The story quoted Mitchell Katine: "This is just unbelievable that in 1998, this sort of arrest could happen. All those people who have said over the years that this statute is never enforced need to realize that that's not true."[4]

Soon after the arrest, the county's top prosecutor, Harris County District Attorney John B. Holmes Jr., had learned about the charges. He called Bill Delmore, the head of the appellate section of the D.A.'s office, to ask whether the statute was constitutional. In Delmore's two decades of service at the D.A.'s office, he had never encountered such a case. Delmore responded that he did not know whether the law was constitutional but remembered there had been some litigation about it. He then did about an hour's worth of research. "The Fifth Circuit says it's constitutional," he reported back to Holmes, referring to the federal appeals court's 1985 decision in *Baker v. Wade*.[5] "That was the end of the conversation," Delmore remembered.[6]

Holmes freely conceded that the law might be unfair, but told the newspaper that his office had no choice. "We're supposed to presume that these laws are constitutional," Holmes explained to the *Chronicle*. "If we just say, 'Let this thing go away,' then we're not really complying with the law and I'm not comfortable with that." He continued, "But I've always said that the best way to get rid of a bad law is to enforce it. . . . We plan to go forward."[7] Later that week, Holmes told the *Dallas Morning News*, "I'm not sure I agree with government regulating private sex acts between consenting adults, but it's not my call."[8] In fact, the prosecutor's office did have the discretion to drop the case entirely, but Holmes's early law-and-order declaration was beginning to back the office into a corner. After all the publicity, remembered Delmore, "it would have seemed almost a little cowardly for us to fail to defend the constitutionality of the statute."[9]

Nevertheless, the case stirred controversy within the D.A.'s office itself. There were many prosecutors who told Delmore the statute was "ridiculous" and "that we had no business trying to defend it."[10] Meanwhile, Ray Hill was already strategizing as he talked to reporters about the case. He hoped that the men would be convicted so that they could test the constitutionality of the law, saying, "I'm concerned the judge is going to throw it out."[11] Newspapers around the state and country and news agencies like Reuters picked up the story,[12] so that by mid-November, Roppolo was fielding daily inquiries from reporters about the coming court date for the arrests.[13]

Suzanne Goldberg flew in for the arraignment on Friday, November 20. The JP court appearance would last only a matter of minutes, just enough time for the pleas to be entered, and would involve no briefing or legal arguments. Lambda maintained tight control over the cases it managed, and the *Lawrence* case had the highest priority. Even though the initial arraignment promised to be uneventful and unimportant, nothing could be allowed to go wrong or be left to chance.

While they had previously talked on the phone, Goldberg had not met the defendants, Lawrence and Garner. That happened for the first time at a breakfast with Katine and Jones the morning of the arraignment. She came from a very different world than the one inhabited by her clients. She was educated, intellectual, politically engaged, and extremely articulate. Yet Goldberg and her clients bridged these differences and developed a mutual admiration. She was impressed by her clients' quiet, reserved, and polite manner. She appreciated their willingness to challenge the law.[14] At the same time, Goldberg impressed the men as smart and capable. "When I first met her, I fell in love," remembered Lawrence.[15]

Surrounded by attorneys, Lawrence and Garner were nervous and on their best behavior. When they arrived at the Wallisville courthouse, they were besieged by media, including a half-dozen television cameras. There were also a handful of religious fundamentalists holding up antigay signs, like "God Hates Fags." The defense team walked through the media and protesters into the courtroom without answering questions.[16]

Parrott's court was not usually of much interest to local media. Reporters requested that they be allowed to film the proceedings, but the JP refused to let cameras in his courtroom. However, he did tell them they could film outside through the small crack in the space between the two front doors to the courtroom, he recalled with a mischievous grin.[17]

In the courtroom itself, there was already a smattering of people contesting their speeding tickets.[18] The allegations against Lawrence and Garner involved much more intimate matters. They were charged with a crime for their private sexual conduct. The contrast "highlighted the outrage of the law and the arrest, and of the treatment of gay people in Texas," observed Goldberg.[19]

Announcing the case of *State of Texas v. Tyron Garner*, Judge Parrott called the defendant to the bench. Accompanied by his three attorneys, an unusual event in this court, Garner walked up. The D.A.'s office was represented by Brett Ligon, who headed the prosecutors handling cases in the JP courts.[20] Judge Parrott read aloud the charge of homosexual conduct against Garner, and asked how he would plead. Jones informed the court that Garner would plead no contest. (Recall that both men had pleaded not guilty at their jailhouse arraignment the night after the arrests.) This surprised Parrott, who expected the men to plead not guilty and ask for a trial.[21] The attorneys advised the judge that they would waive any right to a trial at which testimony would be taken. Everyone—including, by now, Parrott—was aware that Parrott's court was just a stepping-stone to the real battle over the larger constitutional questions.

Judge Parrott then announced that he would fine Garner $100 plus court costs of $41.25. This was lower than the maximum monetary penalty for the offense. Now it was simply a matter of approaching the court clerk to pay the fine. Garner stepped away. This brief process was repeated for the case of *State of Texas v. John Lawrence.*[22]

However, David Jones quickly realized there was a problem. Judge Parrott, he advised Goldberg and Katine, had set the fines too low, at amounts that would not allow the defense to take the case to the court of appeals. If they couldn't do that, their precious opportunity to change constitutional law would be over. The fine needed to be greater than $100.[23] They were a mere penny short of a potential constitutional transformation.

Parrott had stepped off the bench for a few minutes and was about to reconvene the court to dispense with more cases. In the back of the room he could see the defense team and Assistant District Attorney Ligon excitedly conferring. The defense attorneys then approached Parrott and asked whether they could set aside the $100 fine so that a larger fine could be imposed. It was the first and only time Parrott could remember a defendant's own attorneys asking for a *higher* fine. Incredulous, Parrott confirmed that the state's D.A. would agree to the imposition of a higher penalty. He then set the fine at $125, plus court costs, for each defendant.[24] Katine wrote a check from his firm's account in the amount of $332.50 to cover the fine and the appeal bond for both men.

Some time after the arraignment, Parrott discussed the case with Quinn, who had been in the courtroom in case his testimony was needed. Quinn denied rumors and some press reports that the deputies had "busted down" Lawrence's door to enter the apartment.[25] As Parrott playfully put it: "Lawrence was the only one with forcible entry, if you know what I mean."[26]

After the arraignment, Goldberg made a short statement to the press about the importance of the case. "We believe the law is an outrageous intrusion into the private liberties of lesbian and gay Texans, and it's unconstitutional for this law to single out gays and criminalize their behavior," she declared. "This 'homosexual conduct' law treats lesbians and gay men as second-class citizens. It stigmatizes them as law-breakers and is used to discriminate against gays and lesbians in employment and housing."[27] Goldberg was effectively previewing the arguments Lambda's attorneys would be making to courts for the next four years.

Realizing how significant the case could become, reporters wanted to know whether they were headed to the Supreme Court. "Certainly, this case could raise an issue that goes past the Texas Court of Criminal Appeals and to the U.S. Supreme Court," Goldberg responded. "But that's a long way down the road and it's impossible to predict if that will happen at this point."[28]

While Goldberg was speaking, Lawrence and Garner stood by silently. In response to questions, Lawrence described the police raid as "sort of Gestapo." Garner told a reporter for the Associated Press that "I feel like my civil rights were violated and I wasn't doing anything wrong."[29] After this unscripted moment, which came close to a public denial of the charges, the defense lawyers decided the men would say nothing further in public about the case.[30]

Back at his office, Harris County D.A. Johnny Holmes argued that critics of the law should try to get it repealed in the legislature, not in the courts. He added that the legislature had resisted such changes for decades. These, too, were among the arguments the prosecution would be making to courts for the next four years.

ON THE DAY of the hearing, it was already clear that there was an inescapable political dimension to the case. After all, Texas is a state where all judges are elected in partisan races, running either as Republicans or Democrats. A cornerstone commitment of the Texas Republican Party was its opposition to homosexuality. It specifically opposed repeal of the state sodomy law because, the party platform declared, homosexual sodomy "tears at the fabric of society, contributes to the breakdown of the family unit, and leads to the spread of dangerous communicable diseases." It declared homosexual behavior "contrary to the fundamental, unchanging truths that have been ordained by God, recognized by our country's founders, and shared by the majority of Texans."

Reflecting the views of his party, Harris County GOP chairman Gary Polland, a Jewish criminal defense attorney in a party dominated by fundamentalist Christian conservatives, told the press that the state sodomy law was not unconstitutional and should not be repealed. (Of course, an elected party chair like Polland could not say otherwise.) "We think it would definitely send a wrong message and signal a continuing deterioration of morals in our society," he stated, asserting that privacy was not an issue in the case because the sexual conduct of the men became public when police entered the bedroom.[31]

Religious-conservative groups influential in the state GOP were also quick to defend the Texas ban on gay sex. The president of the Texas Eagle Forum called homosexual practices "unnatural and unhealthy" and said the law reinforced the distinction between traditional married couples and homosexual ones. The head of the American Family Association of Texas declared that homosexuality "speaks for a person's character" and argued that gays should be denied child custody and some kinds of jobs.[32]

The Texas GOP and the religious conservatives backing it fueled the case by opposing all efforts to repeal the law in the state legislature (including such efforts while the case was pending) and, as we shall see, by pressuring elected Republican judges on the appeals court to uphold its constitutionality. In this way, they too, albeit unintentionally, gave us *Lawrence v. Texas.*

Just three days after the JP court hearing, on November 23, two events simultaneously demonstrated the promise and potential perils of the Texas sodomy challenge. That day, the Georgia Supreme Court held that state's sodomy law unconstitutional.[33] The Georgia law had been at issue in the Supreme Court decision in *Bowers v. Hardwick* declaring that states could ban gay sex even in the home. Now the Georgia law was gone, but for the time being at least, the harmful 1986 precedent set in *Bowers* remained. Still, the demise of the Georgia law was cause for celebration among the defense lawyers because it further eroded legal support for sodomy laws. The legal momentum was on their side.

That same morning, however, Tyron Garner was arrested and charged with assaulting Robert Eubanks. According to a police report, the men, apparently having resolved their differences, had gone out drinking together on Sunday night, November 22, and had returned to the Montagu Hotel, a transient residence where they were now living. They got into an argument and started fighting. According to Eubanks, Garner swatted him with a belt. Eubanks waited for Garner to go to sleep and then, as he had done before, called the police. Garner was arrested at about two o'clock Monday morning.[34]

The team now challenging the sodomy law had to come up with some way to discount the story. It was not a strictly legal problem for their sodomy case, of course, but it might diminish popular, and even judicial, sympathy for their clients. "No one should be surprised there is some tension between the two," David Jones explained to the media, since Eubanks "wrongfully" put Lawrence and Garner in jail. In fact, it is not known whether the men were fighting over the bogus call that led to Garner's arrest for homosexual conduct. Jones continued, "I am very suspicious of anything that comes out of the mouth of that guy."[35] On Tuesday, the charges were dropped and Garner was released from jail. "I'm very relieved this assault charge is over with," Katine said. "Now we can focus on the homosexual conduct case and move forward with that."[36] However, the incident was reported in both the *Houston Chronicle* and the *Dallas Morning News*.

The coinciding legal victory in Georgia and public-relations contretemps in Houston encapsulated the sodomy case. Even as legal progress was being made, keeping a lid on the tumultuous private lives of John Lawrence and Tyron Garner was going to be a persistent headache. The response of the lawyers was to clamp down even harder on any public inquiry into the men or their arrests. The focus must be on the perfect case, not the imperfect clients.

The Constitutional Case Takes Shape

THE FIRST SUBSTANTIVE CONSTITUTIONAL ARGUMENTS IN *LAWRENCE v. Texas* sprouted in the Harris County Criminal Court, housed along with several courtrooms and administrative offices in downtown Houston. In Texas, the petty offenses heard in JP courts must be heard *de novo* (anew) in these county criminal courts before further appeals, if any, are pursued. Defendants effectively get a second bite at the apple, with another opportunity to plead and another opportunity to request a full trial by judge or jury. The county criminal court pretrial arraignment, the third appearance at which the men would enter a plea, was scheduled for December 22, 1998. It would be held before a judge with an actual law degree in a courtroom that actually looked like one, a considerably more formal and traditional setting than the JP court. This time, moreover, there would be a court reporter present to transcribe the proceedings. The court clerk's "record" of the case, along with a transcript, is what any appeals court might actually see. As a legal matter, therefore, the proceedings in the county criminal court were potentially far more consequential than those in the Justice of the Peace court. For lawyers seeking a win for their cause in higher courts, the county criminal court was another potential roadblock.

The Lawrence and Garner cases, which were still officially separate matters in the Texas judicial system, were initially assigned to the court of Judge Hanna Chow, a Democrat who had held her position in County

Criminal Court #5 since 1986. As it happened, however, Chow had been defeated on November 3 in her reelection bid—a victim of the 1998 Republican sweep of all Harris County offices, including judicial positions. Her replacement, a conservative Republican named Janice Law, would take office in January. With Law's impending takeover, Chow asked Sherman Ross, a longtime colleague, to handle the sodomy cases in his court, County Criminal Court #10. "She [Chow] knew I would call it [the *Lawrence* case] properly and Judge Law at the time was an untested, unproven jurist," Ross, a moderate Republican, said in an interview.[1]

In the county criminal courts, the state is represented by prosecutors assigned to handle cases that come before a particular judge. In Judge Chow's court, Angela Jewel Beavers was the D.A.'s chief prosecutor.[2] A no-nonsense, smart, and respected assistant district attorney with a strong presence and reserved prosecutorial demeanor in the courtroom, Beavers was also a lesbian whose sexual orientation was then unknown in the D.A.'s office.[3]

In other words, a lesbian would be prosecuting two gay men charged with having sex under an antigay sodomy law in a landmark case that had the potential to eliminate such laws. David Jones recalled that Beavers understood what the stakes were and understood that the defendants' attorneys wanted the case to continue to higher courts. As such, she did not go out of her way to create difficulties for the defense team, and assisted it in understanding the procedures of the county criminal court.[4] Jones did not suggest that Beavers did anything improper, and indeed carrying out her duty to prosecute the case was fully consistent with the defense team's independent interests in having it prosecuted.

When Beavers learned of the assignment, she thought, "What are the odds?" She claimed she was not eager to handle the sodomy case and certainly did not go looking for it. "I didn't feel like it was going to be helpful to my career in the D.A.'s office," she remembered. "I didn't even want it to be there." Nevertheless, when the case was transferred to Judge Ross's court, she decided to continue prosecuting it because, she asserted, she was already familiar with it, had spoken with Katine, knew it would be a high-publicity case, and "felt strongly about the issue of sodomy laws."[5]

As a chief prosecutor in the county criminal court, Beavers was, however, responsible for looking at the facts of a case, the defendant's criminal history, and other factors to negotiate a plea agreement with the defendant's lawyer. This agreement could include anything from a dismissal of the charges to a small fine to jail time. Such plea agreements, rather than full trials, are the way most criminal cases are handled. If the prosecutor and defense lawyer can't agree, the case moves to trial. If they do agree, the judge must then approve the agreement before it is enforceable.[6]

Beavers talked about the case with Katine, whom she had not previously known. He told her what the defense planned to do: challenge the law's constitutionality in Judge Ross's court, plead no contest to the charge and the factual allegations by the police, and move on to the court of appeals. If Beavers had wanted to frustrate the goals of the gay-rights attorneys, Jones stressed, she could have insisted on a fine so low it would have been below the amount needed to qualify for an appeal.[7] However, it would have been exceedingly unusual for a prosecutor to demand a fine *lower* than the one insisted upon by defense counsel, and the defense attorneys wanted a fine large enough to remove any doubt about their ability to appeal. A $200 fine for each defendant was acceptable to both sides, so there was not much else to negotiate.[8]

There was one other potential complication. As chief prosecutor, Beavers had the discretion to dismiss the criminal charges against Lawrence and Garner before any trial or plea could be entered. This is called a *nolle prosequi*, a Latin term meaning "unwilling to pursue." If Beavers filed a *nolle prosequi*, and Judge Ross accepted it (as he surely would have),[9] the case would come to an end and there would be little chance to challenge the state sodomy law. Defense counsel could have done nothing to reinstate the prosecution. Lawrence and Garner would have "won" and would not have been able to appeal their victory.[10]

A prosecutor might refuse to pursue a case for any number of reasons. She might conclude that further expense of time and money by the D.A.'s office would be wasted, as in circumstances where a conviction seems very unlikely. A critical witness might be unavailable or unwilling to testify. The crime victim might not want to proceed. Or the prosecutor might think that a key witness's testimony—even a police officer's—would not be credible. Thus, if the sodomy case had moved toward trial and Beavers had concluded that, say, Quinn's account was not believable, she could have dismissed the case at that point. However, it never went that far because Lambda was unwilling to challenge Quinn's story; thus, Beavers had no need to interview Quinn and hear his version of events.

A chief prosecutor at Beavers's level would not have the option to refuse to pursue a case because she believed the law itself was unconstitutional. Beavers opposed the state sodomy law, but this had nothing to do with her obligations as a D.A., as she saw it. "Our job is to uphold the laws of the state of Texas, not to pass judgment on what the legislature decides," she maintained in an interview.[11] She was doing her job, defending the state. If defending the state aligned with the cause of gay rights, that's just the way it was, she insisted.

Beavers also said that she would not dismiss a prosecution because the cost of pursuing the case seemed out of proportion to the triviality of the offense.[12] In this case, it was obvious that the D.A.'s office would be spending a large amount of attorney time defending a Class C misdemeanor, but Beavers said that the ultimate cost of defending the law was "definitely not" a consideration in *Lawrence*.

One possible reason Beavers never considered cost was that she wanted the case to proceed in order to permit a sodomy law challenge. But there's another, more likely, reason that the cost of defending the case was not a consideration: it would have been politically unpopular in Texas to back off on a sodomy prosecution, especially after the case hit the media.[13] Johnny Holmes himself had committed the D.A.'s office to defending the constitutionality of the law as soon as the press asked him about the case early in November 1998. Holmes, a Republican in an elective office, could hardly do otherwise.

In the weeks after the JP court arraignment, Lambda's lawyers put together what amounted to their first legal brief in the case, a motion to have the prosecutions of Lawrence and Garner "quashed"—dismissed— because the Texas sodomy law violated their state and federal constitutional rights.[14] The seven-page briefs, one for each of the two cases, were filed on December 16.[15] In an early preview of the arguments they would make before the Supreme Court in *Lawrence v. Texas* four years later, they offered two main reasons why the law was unconstitutional.

First, Lambda argued that the state Homosexual Conduct law violated the "equal protection of the law" guaranteed by both the federal and Texas constitutions.[16] The U.S. Constitution forbids a state to "deny to any person within its jurisdiction the equal protection of the laws." The Texas Constitution, originally written in the nineteenth century, guarantees that "all free men, when they form a social compact, have equal rights."[17] It declares that "no man, or set of men, is entitled to exclusive separate public emoluments, or privileges, but in consideration of public services." Texas was among the states in the 1970s to add an "equal rights amendment" to its own constitution. This amendment specifically banned certain forms of discrimination: "Equality under the law shall not be denied or abridged because of sex, race, color, creed, or national origin."[18]

Lambda argued that the Texas law violated these equality provisions because it "classifies and criminalizes consensual sexual acts, including those in private, according to the sex and sexual orientation of those who engage in them."[19] Texas could not discriminate based on sex unless it had an "exceedingly persuasive justification"[20] for such discrimination. And, on the basis of the Supreme Court's then-recent decision in *Romer v. Evans* striking down an antigay state constitutional amendment,[21] Texas could not "single out" and "disadvantage" gays and lesbians without at least some "legitimate purpose" for doing so.[22] The state of Texas, Lambda asserted, had no legitimate purpose for banning only consensual gay sex.

Lambda next argued that the Texas Homosexual Conduct law violated the right to privacy guaranteed by both the U.S. and state constitutions. This right, Lambda asserted, protected individuals "from state interference in personal, important decisions about their most intimate relationships and the ways in which they choose to express themselves through consensual sexuality." This due process right to privacy "is particularly strong in one's own home and in similarly private settings."[23]

The problem with Lambda's sexual privacy argument, as it recognized,[24] was that the Supreme Court itself had held that gay people had no such right in 1986 in *Bowers v. Hardwick*.²⁵ Lambda flatly told the county criminal court that *Bowers* was "wrongly decided." Of course, as the lawyers knew, a county criminal court in Texas had no power to "underrule" the Supreme Court. The attack on *Bowers* would have to wait until 2003.

In sum, Lambda's briefs to quash outlined the main arguments it would be making for the next few years. The twin pillars—equal protection and the due process right to privacy—were there. The assault on the *Bowers* decision, which had been decided by a Supreme Court whose composition and knowledge of gay people had dramatically changed over twelve years, was there. The particulars of the argument would change, as would the priority given to the main arguments, and many details had yet to be filled in. But the constitutional basics were in place in December 1998.

The D.A.'s office made no response to Lambda's arguments. There was nothing unusual in this. "In criminal law, we hate to write [briefs]," noted Beavers, who was responsible for handling literally dozens of minor criminal cases every day in the court.²⁶ Besides, everyone knew that a criminal court judge was highly unlikely to hold the law unconstitutional, no matter how strong Lambda's arguments were.

With the constitutional complaints on file, the time came for the defendants' appearance in Sherman Ross's court. Ross had a keen mind combined with a droll manner, all coated in a fairly heavy Texas drawl. He had an excellent reputation for fairness and legal skill among the lawyers who practiced in his court. By 1998, he was no stranger to gay people. He had known gays professionally. He and his wife occasionally went out to eat with their next-door neighbors, a gay couple. Ross had a "laissez-faire" attitude about the subject. "I can't think of any time that I was directly affected by someone's sexual preference," he maintained.²⁷

In his seventeen years as a judge and in his fifteen years as an attorney before that, he had never heard, until now, of a prosecution for violation of the Homosexual Conduct law. But Ross had seen cases where police officers were lying. He could not dismiss a case on his own, but he could grant a motion to exclude an officer's testimony from a trial. If he thought an officer was lying, he could also "put pressure on the D.A. that this [was] a bullshit case. The ones I feel are outright lying I just made it real clear to the D.A. that they better dismiss the dadgum case." The D.A. herself may dismiss a case if she believed an officer was lying. "I remember one case where the D.A. after direct examination of the police officer is looking at the offense report, looking back at the officer, looks back at his offense report, and starts writing out a *nolle prosequi*," Ross said.[28]

Ross speculated that the arresting police officers in the sodomy case "probably" never saw Lawrence and Garner having sex or were at the very least "embellishing," but he never got to hear Quinn's or Lilly's testimony.[29] The *Lawrence* case never got that far in his or any other judge's court. The gay-rights attorneys made certain of that.

On December 22, Ross's courtroom was crowded with defendants waiting to be arraigned on various minor criminal charges, their attorneys, and—on this day—the media. Lawrence and Garner, "the center of the whole controversy,"[30] nervously waited to be called.

Beavers and the defense attorneys consulted briefly before the hearing to confirm their agreement. Goldberg, meeting Beavers for the first time, realized that she might be a lesbian.[31] When they were called, Lawrence, Garner, Goldberg, Katine, Jones, and Beavers approached the judge's bench. Goldberg immediately introduced into evidence Quinn's Offense Reports for both Lawrence and Garner. Ordinarily, the D.A. would be the one to introduce the police officer's formal complaint and affidavit to support the charge, but Goldberg was taking nothing for granted. She knew this would be the defendants' one and only chance to make sure the perfect facts were adequately supported in the record for the appeal.[32] Since the defense team was introducing the state's own supporting affidavits, Beavers had no reason to object to them.[33]

Goldberg next noted that Lambda had filed constitutional objections to the prosecution. Even though the Lambda brief had been filed only six days before the hearing, Beavers didn't protest the lack of time to prepare a response. An objection would only cause delay and there was no need for that. Beavers and Goldberg also told Judge Ross that they had previously agreed not to make any oral arguments about the briefs to quash.

"The Court has reviewed the Motions," Ross announced, "and respectfully denies them."[34] This is exactly what everyone—defense attorneys and prosecutor alike—expected. In an interview, Ross maintained that a county criminal court judge has no authority to hold a state law unconstitutional. Such a ruling would have to come from the court of appeals, he believed.

It was then time for Lawrence and Garner, each uncharacteristically and somewhat uncomfortably dressed in a jacket and tie, to enter their pleas. The pleas had previously been arranged among Ross, the D.A., and Goldberg. The ensemble was acting out a script.

Ross turned to Garner. "Let me ask them individually what their pleas are. Mr. Garner?"

"Yes, sir."

"How do you plead, sir?"

"No contest."

Ross next looked at Lawrence. "Mr. Lawrence?"

"No contest." These were the last words Garner and Lawrence ever said in court about their case.

Even though Lawrence and Garner had just conceded the state's case against them, it was still formally necessary to have the facts read aloud for the court reporter to transcribe. Beavers began recounting the substance of Quinn's allegations: "Your honor, 'officers were dispatched to 794 Normandy, Number 833, in reference to a weapons disturbance.'" She continued reading as she got to the allegation of sexual conduct. "'On entering the apartment and conducting a search for the armed suspect, officers observed the defendants engaged in deviate sexual conduct, namely, *oral* sex.'"[35]

Goldberg, listening closely to every word, immediately caught the error. "Excuse me," she interrupted, "your honor, it was, the police report says '*anal sex*.'" For Goldberg, who had written a lot of sodomy law briefs, it was an odd moment. "Reinforcing the oral/anal sex distinction was not something I had envisioned in my life as a lawyer," she remembered.[36]

"I'm sorry, anal sex," Beavers continued, embarrassed by her slip of the tongue.[37] She did not know it at the time, but Beavers had confused the very two acts at issue later in the conflicting memories of Quinn and Lilly. She repeated the underlying point for emphasis, so that there was no doubt they had violated the terms of the Homosexual Conduct law. "Both defendants were engaged in 'deviate sexual conduct.'"

"All right," said Ross, looking at the defendants. "I find you guilty." He next confirmed with Katine, Goldberg, and Jones that they had agreed to a $200 fine for each defendant. Ross could have rejected the "no contest" plea if he thought it was not in the interests of justice, as in a case where he believed the defendant did not understand what he had agreed to or in a case in which he did not believe there was enough evidence to support the conviction. He could also have set the fine lower than the defendants and state had agreed they should pay. A conservative Republican judge, or the D.A.'s office, for that matter, who feared the political problems that might be created by the prosecution or who believed higher courts might hold the law unconstitutional could have acted strategically to end the case. But there would be none of that on this day. Ross winked at Jones as if to say that he understood his court was just a stopping point on a longer mission.[38]

"I'm ready to sentence both the defendants," said Ross, turning first to Tyron Garner. "Mr. Garner, having been found guilty of the offense of Homosexual Conduct, the court assesses your punishment at $200." Ross looked at Lawrence. "Mr. Lawrence, having been found guilty of the offense of Homosexual Conduct, the court assesses your punishment at $200. All right. The hearing is concluded."

Lawrence, Garner, each of their attorneys, and Beavers now signed a standard plea form.[39] As part of the standard form, the defendant waives his right to trial by jury, forgoes any right to challenge the testimony of the witnesses against him, and surrenders his right to remain silent. He also agrees that his attorney has properly represented him and that he has discussed the charges and plea with his attorney.

Finally, in the standard form signed by Lawrence and Garner, the defendant agrees to the following statement: "I confess that I committed the offense as alleged in the State's information and that each element of the State's pleading is true." Although it's unlikely the men had carefully considered this statement before they signed, surrounded as it was by preprinted legalese, Lawrence and Garner had officially agreed that they had indeed violated the Homosexual Conduct law. Since there was no other way to allow their case to proceed to an appeal on the constitutional claims, this was a necessary concession, even if it was factually incorrect.

As Lawrence, Garner, and their attorneys started to walk out, the court's bailiff stopped them. "You have to be fingerprinted before you go," he instructed them. This was the moment the two men realized that they were now convicted criminals in the eyes of Texas.[40]

Fingerprinting completed, the men and their attorneys went outside, where a group of reporters wanted to hear from them. Once again, Goldberg did almost all of the talking, explaining what had happened and promising a continued challenge to the law. Lawrence uttered an unremarkable sentence or two, causing the reporters' microphones to whip over to him. Garner said nothing.

13.

The Politics of Law

T HERE ARE FOURTEEN COURTS OF APPEAL IN TEXAS, ARRANGED TO cover the vast expanse that constitutes the state. Two courts, the First and Fourteenth Courts of Appeals, concurrently cover ten counties in southeast Texas, including Harris County. Appellate cases, whether involving civil or criminal matters, are randomly assigned to these two courts. After the brief stop in Judge Ross's county criminal court, *Lawrence* wound up in the Fourteenth Court of Appeals.

For the first half of 1999, the New York defense lawyers and the Harris County D.A.'s office exchanged volleys in legal briefs. The already limited participation of John Lawrence and Tyron Garner in their own case was ending. David Jones was also no longer needed. Even Mitchell Katine was now relegated to the sidelines as Lambda's intellectual team—the Harvard-educated Suzanne Goldberg and the Yale-educated Ruth Harlow—took full control.

On March 18, 1999, the Lambda lawyers asked the court to consolidate the Lawrence and Garner cases into one appeal.[1] A week later, the appeals court granted the unopposed request, and the case officially became *Lawrence v. Texas*.

Lambda's twenty-six page appellate brief, filed on April 16, 1999, was drafted principally by Goldberg with characteristically active editing and revision by her supervisor, Harlow. Additional input came from such other experienced Lambda attorneys as Patricia Logue, head of the group's Chicago office. The defense of two gay men convicted of having anal sex was for now entrusted entirely to lesbians.

Lambda's brief described Lawrence and Garner as "gay men" and "long-time friends,"[2] not as boyfriends, partners, or lovers. It declared that the police had entered Lawrence's home "unannounced," which was not verifiable in the public record, and "uninvited," which was true but legally irrelevant since the police had been directed into the apartment on a legitimate though mistaken search for an armed black man. The brief repeated Deputy Quinn's claim that he found the men engaged in anal sex, but did not state whether the claim was correct.[3]

The brief expanded on the basic themes of equal protection and privacy asserted in the county criminal court. The strategic issue was how to frame these arguments in a way that courts would accept. This called for careful thought and drafting, a skill Lambda's lawyers had honed in numerous sodomy cases before *Lawrence*.

Lambda argued that the Texas Homosexual Conduct law, by its very title and by its prohibition on gay sex alone, was aimed squarely at "those who have a same-sex sexual attraction, i.e., lesbians and gay men."[4] It emphasized that the identical conduct, oral and anal sex, was perfectly legal in Texas for heterosexuals.

The law was thus a form of sexual-orientation discrimination. Much of gay legal scholarship for two decades had been an effort to show that antigay discrimination was like race- or sex-based discrimination, in that it disadvantaged a group long targeted in the law, that the group was politically weak, and that the defining characteristic of the group (whether race, sex, or sexual orientation) was unrelated to merit or the ability of individuals in the group to contribute to society.

There were a couple of practical problems with this argument. First, few courts in the United States in 1999 regarded antigay discrimination as presumptively forbidden by the U.S. Constitution. Certainly no Texas court had ever held that the state constitution forbade it. Courts are reluctant to stake out entirely new legal territory.

Second, the legal consequences of such a new position were unpredictable and potentially far-reaching. If a court held that antigay discrimination was impermissible, what would become of the recently enacted "Don't Ask, Don't Tell" policy barring service by gay military personnel? What would happen to laws defining marriage as a heterosexual institution? The gay-marriage issue had hit the national consciousness a few years before, prompting Congress to pass the 1996 Defense of Marriage Act, which defined marriage as the union of one man and one woman under federal law and allowed states to disregard gay marriages validly performed in other states. Lambda knew courts would fear the implications of ruling that antigay discrimination was generally impermissible. So Goldberg and Harlow relegated the argument for "heightened scrutiny" of antigay discrimination to a footnote.[5] They did not want to give up entirely on the argument but they also did not want to highlight it.

Continuing on its theme that the Texas statute denied equality under the law, Lambda argued that it deserved especially rigorous judicial skepticism because it contained a sex-based classification: whether the law forbade certain sexual conduct depended entirely on the biological sex of one's intimate partner. In a similar way, Lambda noted, the Supreme Court had struck down laws banning interracial marriage as racial discrimination even though such laws equally prohibited both whites and nonwhites from interracial marriages.[6]

The idea that laws singling out gay men and lesbians constitute "sex" discrimination had also long been a favorite of legal academics looking for some judicial way to undermine antigay public policy.[7] Goldberg and Harlow, along with practically the entire gay legal establishment, certainly accepted the intellectual foundations of that argument. However, they were attorneys arguing a case, not professors writing a law review article. They recognized that the argument suffered from the same practical flaws as the argument that sexual-orientation discrimination itself was presumptively unconstitutional: few courts had yet accepted the idea of antigay discrimination as sex discrimination.[8] Judges feared its larger implications for other areas of public policy, especially marriage.[9] Avoiding the marriage issue was a continuous effort throughout *Lawrence*.

Nevertheless, Goldberg and Harlow decided to make the sex-discrimination argument in their brief. Texas, they reasoned, was one of those states where it made most sense to make the argument: its constitution specifically guaranteed that "[e]quality under the law" could not be denied "because of sex."[10] The argument was thus on firmer textual ground than the argument about sexual orientation, a protection unmentioned in the state constitution. Of course, they also knew that if the Texas courts accepted the state constitutional argument they would be denied their larger goal of reversing *Bowers v. Hardwick* in the U.S. Supreme Court. But then at least the Texas Homosexual Conduct law would be history—no small triumph in itself. The benefit of winning thus outweighed the "harm" of winning only in the Texas courts.

Lambda asserted that the state had no legitimate reason for singling out gay sex as criminally prohibited. The only reason for the ban Texas had offered in previous cases challenging the state sodomy law was protecting "public morality." Goldberg and Harlow anticipated, correctly, that this would once again be the reason offered for the law. They were ready for it:

> First, "public morality," when offered to justify a law's different treatment of people who engage in the same acts, reflects an improper effort to give legal effect to societal biases or dislikes. Second, "public morality" does not even rationally explain this law. It cannot properly be invoked here to support criminalization of the very *private* conduct affected by Section 21.06.[11]

In other words, using "morality" to treat the same acts differently depending on who engages in them amounted to nothing more than a cover for hatred against the criminalized group. And hatred cannot constitutionally justify a law. Since there was nothing "public" about the conduct the police claimed to witness, defending the law on public-morality grounds made no sense, either. There was, in short, nothing "public" or "moral" about the "public morality" claim.

This argument elided the possibility that even private behavior might ultimately affect the content of morals embraced by the public. Private racism may seep into the public realm. Similarly, private antigay attitudes undergird public discrimination against gay men and lesbians. The core objection to the state sodomy law was that antigay morality was bad morality, a point not directly confronted by Lambda in its briefing. That would have been too aggressive a claim to make in 1999.

Lambda's second argument, also elaborating a point made in Judge Ross's court, was that the Homosexual Conduct law violated the fundamental right to privacy protected by the U.S. and state constitutions. "Engaging in sexual relations with another consenting adult inside one's home is one of the most private, intimate types of conduct imaginable," Lambda claimed.[12] Texas courts were free to construe the state's own constitution to protect *more* liberty than was protected by the federal constitution.[13]

But as a federal matter, Lambda's privacy argument was on even thinner ice than its equality argument. In *Bowers v. Hardwick*, the Supreme Court had already rejected the claim that the right to privacy protected "homosexual sodomy." Goldberg and Harlow nevertheless criticized *Bowers* on several grounds—grounds that anticipated Justice Anthony Kennedy's own rejection of *Bowers* four years later. First, they argued that *Bowers* was badly reasoned and inconsistent with the Court's precedents protecting a right to privacy. Second, commentators and scholars had almost unanimously criticized the decision. And third, the Court itself had undermined *Bowers* in 1996 by rejecting a state constitutional amendment targeting gays in *Romer v. Evans*.[14] All of these considerations, and more, were eventually used by the Court to overrule *Bowers* in *Lawrence*.

Lambda questioned *Bowers* in large part to make sure that it did not waive the argument "should this case reach the U.S. Supreme Court."[15] But it also flatly urged the Texas Court of Appeals to "reject *Bowers* as an inaccurate interpretation of the federal protection [of privacy] and construe the state right [to privacy] consistent with the dissent in that case."[16] This was a bold suggestion. Among all courts, the Supreme Court has the final say on the meaning of the U.S. Constitution. Lambda wasn't quite advocating that the Texas court rebel against the Supreme Court, but it was skirting the edge.

Against this, the Harris County D.A. had to defend the law's constitutionality for the first time.[17] Bill Delmore, the head of the appellate division in the office, volunteered to handle the appeal. After moving to the area in grade school, Delmore attended private Catholic schools and graduated from the University of Houston Law School in 1981.

By November 1998, when it had begun receiving media inquiries, the D.A.'s office had realized that *Lawrence* was no run-of-the-mill misdemeanor case. Delmore wanted to take charge of the appeal personally because he knew there would be substantial media coverage and he did not want the office to be embarrassed in the case. In his view, it needed to be handled by a supervisor to make sure things were done well. In an interview he asserted that one principle guided him up to the Supreme Court:

> One goal I had in this was that we were going to take the high road. We were not going to descend to the level of name-calling. We were not going to write anything that [would offend] people in the gay community, including in the legal community that happened to be gay. . . . I didn't want to make any statements that made us appear to be anything other than professional and kind of dispassionate about it. Professional prosecutors rather than zealots.

Delmore thought that much of Lambda's brief was very good, including the expected arguments about privacy and equality. But in Delmore's view, the sex-discrimination argument, based on the Texas equal rights amendment, was "complete bullshit." The Homosexual Conduct law was not sex-based discrimination, he thought, because it was not aimed at women or men as a class. It treated men and women equally. The fact that the state constitution disapproved of sex discrimination did not mean it must ignore biological differences. For Delmore, as for many other lawyers and judges around the country, the sex-discrimination argument had what William Eskridge has called a "transvestic quality": it was a gay-rights argument dressed up in the garb of sex discrimination.[18] Delmore devoted only a paragraph to rebutting the argument in his reply brief.[19]

Delmore still had a critical decision to make. How could the government justify an antigay sex law? What government interest was there in forbidding anal and oral sex in private, and only between two people of the same sex?

Delmore researched the issue and decided the only legitimate basis for defending the law was public morality, a justification that had been used in every state's defense of its sodomy laws. The argument was basically that a majority of the people of a state, acting through their elected representatives, could decide that an activity should be criminalized based solely on their view that the activity was immoral. If they did not like something, if they believed it to be wrong—for whatever reason— they could make it illegal. Even if the activity did not hurt anyone else, it could be prohibited. Similarly, Delmore relied on "the promotion of family values" as a reason for the state law,[20] although he later acknowledged that the reference was "a really vague phrase."[21] It had rhetorical and political appeal, perhaps, but no substantive content Delmore could articulate. He made no effort to explain the reference in the D.A.'s brief.

Delmore defended morality-based criminal law with a list of historic Texas statutes that was, to say the least, odd. Examples of morals-based legislation in the past included, he noted, prohibitions of sodomy; working, horse racing, or bowling on Sunday; miscegenation; fornication; keeping a disorderly house (an antiquated reference to using a home in ways that create a public nuisance like prostitution); abortion; seduction; leading "an idle, immoral, or profligate life"; gambling, telling fortunes, or begging; exhibiting a film of a prizefight; participating in a roping contest; operating a pool hall; injuriously affecting the morals of female employees; and for women, "travel[ing] from place to place" in order to participate in a "dancing performance."[22] Many of these examples actually highlighted the ridiculousness of past efforts to enforce morality apart from any tangible harm to others. Some of the laws would now be regarded as clearly unconstitutional, either because they violate a fundamental right (the abortion prohibition), discriminate on the basis of sex (the dancing troupe law), or violate both the Equal Protection Clause and the Due Process Clause (antimiscegenation laws). So obviously anachronistic and troubling were many of these examples that Delmore's brief, also signed by Angela Beavers, could be regarded as slyly critical of morals-based legislation.

Some of Delmore's colleagues and many conservative academics and interest groups regarded reliance on morality alone as a mistake. They were afraid that courts would want to hear some kind of harm-based justification for the law and might strike it down if there were none. They urged Delmore to argue, among other things, that the law was a reasonable way to protect the public from sexually transmitted diseases, especially AIDS.[23] This "public health" rationale had been successfully used by states defending their sodomy laws in the past.

But Delmore thought the public health arguments "were really too silly to be made and I didn't want to make them." The reason was simple: even if it was true that gay men ran higher risks of STDs, the laws were so rarely enforced they could hardly make a difference. Additionally, Delmore had "read somewhere [that] AIDS is almost nonexistent in the lesbian population. So why subject lesbians to this great restriction on their personal privacy to avoid the spread of a disease that's nonexistent in their community? It doesn't make any sense." The public-health argument also seemed like gay-baiting to Delmore. He was not willing to do any of that in his brief.[24]

As for the right to privacy, Delmore relied on *Bowers v. Hardwick* and other cases to point out that sodomy laws had been around for a very long time and were perfectly within a state's authority. He characterized the case narrowly as involving "a right to engage in homosexual anal intercourse,"[25] similar to the way the Supreme Court itself had characterized the issue in *Bowers*, and in contrast to Lambda's comparatively desexualized claim that the case involved a right to "intimacy." As for the notion that the Texas law violated the equal rights of gay men and lesbians, Delmore noted that courts had never treated antigay laws as skeptically as they had treated racist or sexist laws.[26]

The thrust of the brief urged judicial restraint. It was up to legislatures, not courts, to decide how to make public policy and how to draw lines between permissible and impermissible activities. If the Texas Homosexual Conduct law was archaic or bad policy, the remedy was to repeal it through the state legislature, not to overturn it by judicial decree.[27]

Delmore outlined his proposed defense of the Texas law to D.A. Johnny Holmes. "I'm not going to get into a bunch of name-calling," Delmore told his boss. "I'm not going to invoke a bunch of religious stuff. We're going to limit this to the position that public morality is something that you basically leave to the legislature for the line-drawing process and that's gonna be it." Holmes emphasized that he expected Delmore to write as a "scholar." Other than that, the arguments sounded fine to him.

Delmore personally wrote the court of appeals brief in two weeks. He solicited and received almost no input from anyone else. Staffing on cases in the D.A.'s office is typically light, caseloads are heavy, and during the time he was working on the *Lawrence* Class C misdemeanor, Delmore also had briefs due in a robbery case, an aggravated sexual assault case, two murder cases, and a capital murder case.

Reading Delmore's handiwork, Goldberg was not surprised that the D.A.'s office had omitted any reference to public health. There was no evidence that sodomy laws protected public health in any way, much less that they helped prevent the spread of HIV. The D.A.'s decision to leave out such an argument, as Goldberg saw it, probably reflected one of two things. Either the D.A.'s office wanted to focus on its best argument without the distraction of a "ridiculous" claim about public health, or it was doing the minimum necessary to defend the law in order to maintain political credibility.[28] It was throwing the case without appearing to do so.

On July 16, Goldberg and Harlow filed a response to the Texas reply brief, focusing on Delmore's morality justification. A morality justification was not enough to save the constitutionality of laws that forbade only some people to do the same act others could do, Lambda retorted. Unlike laws cited by Delmore prohibiting incest or drug use, which apply to everyone, the Texas law applied only to gay people.[29] A law barring only same-sex incest or forbidding drug use only by homosexuals would not truly defend any morality.

In response to Delmore's argument that antigay sex laws were not "so strange or foreign as to be irrational," Lambda noted that for the first 114 years of the state sodomy law's existence it applied regardless of who committed the acts. "The same-sex-only prohibition is itself relatively strange and foreign," Lambda archly responded.[30]

Summer turned to early fall as the two sides waited for some word on what the appeals court would do. In early October, the court of appeals informed Lambda and the D.A.'s office that the appeal was set for oral argument on November 3, 1999, in front of a three-judge panel. The three judges, all Republicans, were Chief Justice Paul C. Murphy and Justices John S. Anderson and J. Harvey Hudson.[31]

The backgrounds of the judges are worth noting. Anderson, a graduate of the University of Texas School of Law, was fifty-four and had been on the court of appeals since 1995.[32] Hudson was three years younger than Anderson, and had also been on the court since 1995. He had graduated from the South Texas College of Law and had worked for the Harris County D.A.'s office for five years.[33]

At sixty-four, Murphy was the oldest of the trio and had been on the court the longest. He was the only one of the three who agreed to be interviewed about *Lawrence*. A self-described "country lawyer," he was actually born in Houston, graduated from the University of Houston Law School in 1962, and had begun practicing in the Huntsville area in east Texas in 1972, handling a wide variety of cases, as attorneys in small towns tend to do. By 1999, he knew gay people professionally, both among court personnel and lawyers; one of the court's employees was a lesbian raising a child with her partner. Murphy also had gay acquaintances— friends would be too strong a word—and did not believe homosexuality was immoral. He also believed gays, like all "red-blooded and patriotic Americans," should be allowed to serve in the military.[34]

Murphy was instrumental in getting the Republican Party off the ground in southeast Texas in the mid-1970s, just as conservative Democrats were starting to bolt for the GOP. At the same time, religious and moral traditionalists began organizing to resist the sexual revolution of the 1960s and '70s. The Texas Homosexual Conduct law was one consequence of this revived traditionalism. In the South, social conservatives found a sympathetic forum in a Republican Party still starved for votes. The final break between conservatives and the Democratic Party at the federal level came after 1976. That year, Jimmy Carter, a born-again Christian from Georgia, was the last Democrat elected with the support of most of the South. Yet his presidency bitterly disappointed Southerners and moral traditionalists, who had imagined he might be one of them. By 1980, these trends converged to produce a landslide victory for Ronald Reagan, who swept the South. Republicans began winning state offices, as conservative Democrats switched parties.

Supported by the grassroots activists he had marshaled, Murphy won election to the court of appeals for the first time that year. But Murphy himself was not a religious conservative. He cared little about the social issues that motivated them.

At the state GOP convention in 1984, Murphy was chairman of the platform committee and supported a plank advocating a ban on abortion except in cases of rape, incest, and danger to the life of the mother. To many people, this would seem a solidly conservative view of abortion. But it was not good enough for the new religious conservatives in the party, who demanded that abortion be banned *in all circumstances*. Murphy was conservative but not conservative enough for them. They attempted to defeat him in his judicial reelection bid by running more conservative opponents against him in the Republican primary, but they failed.

WHILE THE COURT of appeals was awaiting the argument, Suzanne Goldberg went on personal leave from Lambda, and Ruth Harlow stepped forward to handle the oral argument.[35] Harlow soon had a discouraging conference call with gay-rights attorneys and activists in Houston, most of whom were Democrats with little understanding of the internal tensions and fissures within the GOP. Painting all Republican judges with a broad brush, and seemingly unaware, for example, of the nuances of Chief Justice Murphy's standing in the party, they warned Harlow in a conference call to expect a "disaster" at the oral argument. Harlow had no reason to doubt them. She steeled herself "in case it got very uncomfortable."[36]

On the day for argument, November 3, Harlow and Delmore encountered a horde of media at the downtown Houston courthouse. The small courtroom on the ninth floor was packed with law students and gay-rights supporters.[37] Although the lawyers could not have known it at the time, this was the only oral argument they would get until they reached Washington.

From the start of her argument, Harlow was impressed with the respect, knowledge, and interest shown by the judges. They had read the briefs closely, were familiar with the issues, and began asking sophisticated questions. They focused a surprising amount of their questioning on the sex-discrimination argument under the Texas equal rights amendment. The judges were receptive to the arguments Harlow was making and the responses she gave to their questions, which surprised her in light of what she had been led to expect.[38] Satisfied that she had done her best, Harlow sat down.

Delmore delivered his rebuttal, which, by his own account, was not his best effort.[39] Harlow, describing his argument as "workmanlike," suspected that Delmore lacked any real enthusiasm for defending the law. "He was doing his job, but it was not an impassioned defense of the law," she remembered. "He knew what we were doing and there seemed to be a glimmer of sympathy there."[40] The D.A.'s office was letting its own in-house lawyer defend the law with little or no input from the outside and seemingly without adapting strategies and arguments from other states' cases.[41]

As we have seen, Delmore had vetoed any public-health argument for the law in his brief, and he did not try to resuscitate it in the oral argument. Under questioning from the judges, he made another important and surprising concession. The Texas law, he said, could not survive "heightened judicial scrutiny." That is, if the judges decided that the law discriminated on the basis of sex, decided that antigay discrimination was itself constitutionally suspect, or decided that the defendants had a fundamental right to their own private sex lives, the state of Texas could not come up with an overriding, "compelling" reason to prohibit the defendants' private sexual conduct. Delmore told the court that he could not "even see how I could begin to frame an argument that there is a compelling state interest" for banning gay sex. "There is no evidence on the record to support a compelling need for this legislation," he told the judges.[42] Delmore had planned to make the concession about heightened scrutiny in advance if he was asked about it (he was later harshly criticized by social-conservative groups for making it) and had cleared it with Holmes.[43] But the concession surprised just about everyone else in the courtroom. Texas, like other states, had defended its law forcefully in every other legal challenge. Now it seemed to some observers that the state was giving up.

The best he could do, Delmore conceded, was argue that the law was not completely irrational and that protecting morality was a legitimate, but not especially strong, reason to ban same-sex sexual conduct.[44] His entire case rested on the idea that there was no sex discrimination in the law, that antigay discrimination was itself constitutional, and as the U.S.

Supreme Court itself declared in *Bowers*, that there was no "fundamental right to homosexual anal sex."

Delmore also claimed that the state Homosexual Conduct law did not single out gays because it equally prohibited bisexuals and heterosexuals from having homosexual sex. Harlow scoffed at this notion in her rebuttal, comparing it to the idea that a law against going to Roman Catholic mass applied equally to non-Catholics.[45]

With the ninety-minute oral argument over, the defendants and the state now had to wait what must have been agonizing months for the court's decision. Meanwhile, legal victories for gay rights mounted elsewhere. In late December 1999, the Vermont Supreme Court declared that gay couples must be given the same rights as married straight couples under state law.[46] The state legislature responded by creating "civil unions," a status that allowed same-sex couples to obtain equal benefits and privileges for the first time in any state.

At the same time, *Lawrence* itself remained a volatile case as the tumultuous life of Tyron Garner continued to unravel. In the new year, Robert Eubanks sought a court order to keep Garner away from him. In his affidavit, Eubanks accused Garner of several beatings and a sexual assault: Garner "punched me on my left eye two times" in January 2000; beat him with a hose in 1999 while "using crack and drinking"; beat him with a belt in 1998 (as mentioned earlier); and, in May 1998, four months before the sodomy arrests, "stabbed me on my right ring finger with a box cutter, . . . grabbed a hot iron and burned me," and "then sexually assaulted me." The judge granted Eubanks's request for a temporary restraining order, but the matter was dropped after Eubanks's lawyer withdrew, saying she could not locate him for a scheduled hearing.[47] Nevertheless—and bizarrely—Garner and Eubanks continued to live together. The allegations in Eubanks's affidavit surfaced in the media, causing more public-relations problems for the gay-rights lawyers. Their clients were unpredictable, their lives a bit unstable. Up to now, all of the surprises in the case had been bad ones.

However, the Republican judges were about to change that. They had not yet made up their minds about the case. Even after the oral argument at the panel's so-called postsubmission conference, the outcome was still uncertain. Justice Anderson was assigned to write and circulate an opinion, which the other two judges could then either accept or reject.[48]

Anderson's draft opinion declared the Homosexual Conduct law unconstitutional as sex discrimination under the Texas equal rights amendment. After reading it, Justice Hudson quickly announced he would vote to deny the appeal, because he didn't think the state's voters had intended to make homosexual sodomy legal when they voted for the that amendment. With Anderson voting to strike down the state sodomy law and Hudson voting to uphold it, Justice Murphy became the deciding vote.

Murphy voted to strike it down. What ultimately convinced him about the law's unconstitutionality was the way it selectively aimed at one group while decriminalizing many other sexual offenses. It was manifestly unfair, he concluded.

> When that penal code was revised in 1974, they decriminalized bestiality, adultery. They decriminalized alienation of affection and heterosexual sodomy. They decriminalized all that. And I kept thinking that if they decriminalized all those things that one would normally say are immoral, then why did they leave this one in? There had to be a reason. And the religious right, so to speak, never seemed to understand that the legislature decriminalized all these other offenses and left this one standing. And nobody could explain to me why.[49]

Without realizing it, Murphy had stumbled upon the core truth about Texas's Homosexual Conduct law. It was inexplicable on any rational ground of public policy. Its logic was beyond reason. It was beyond religious doctrine or traditional sexual morality, neither of which, on their own terms, justified a law targeted solely at gay people. Murphy could not describe the real reason that the law stood. But he knew that what the state was telling him about the law—that it was just a standard moral judgment—could not be true. He had the insight to see that some shadow was moving in the darkness. That shadow was a simple disgust for a group of people—gay people, and especially gay men—a disgust that had outlasted every moral principle, every religious doctrine, and every public-policy mandate that had been summoned to justify it. Stripped down to its essentials, the Texas Homosexual Conduct law was revealed to this "country lawyer" in its unseemly nakedness, one of the last living remnants of a vanishing world.

On June 8, 2000, in a 2–1 vote, the Fourteenth Court of Appeals ruled in favor of the defendants. However, Justice Anderson's opinion for the majority avoided federal constitutional issues. He first noted what had caught Murphy's attention: Texas had decriminalized anal and oral sex between men and women in 1974 for the first time in 114 years, ever since the state sodomy law was initially enacted. Since then, these same acts remained illegal only if performed between two men or two women. "Thus, the distinction between legal and illegal conduct was not the act, but rather the sex of one of the participants," wrote Anderson. Lawrence and Garner were treated differently from others "solely on the basis of their sex."[50] It did not matter that two men and two women were equally prohibited from oral and anal sex, just as it did not matter in *Loving v. Virginia* that antimiscegenation laws had applied equally to whites and nonwhites.[51] The court of appeals had thus accepted the basic structure of the sex-discrimination theory that gay-rights advocates had been advancing, to little effect, for two decades. The court was among the few in the country ever to validate this argument. It meant that heightened judicial scrutiny would apply to the court's analysis of the law.

Texas had no compelling reason for discriminating on the basis of sex, Anderson concluded, citing Delmore's "surprising" concession. In a line that would be echoed three years later in Justice Kennedy's U.S. Supreme Court opinion, Anderson distanced the court from any argument about the (im)morality of homosexual acts. "[I]t is not the judiciary's prerogative to condone or condemn a particular lifestyle and the behaviors associated therewith upon the basis of our moral belief."[52]

The court deployed arguments associated with both constitutional conservatism and liberalism. For example, Anderson said the court was simply following the literal language of the state equal rights amendment.[53] Strict reliance on the text of a constitution or statute—even if it produces unusual, unexpected, or less than optimal results—is a hallmark of strict constructionism, which is most often associated with conservative judicial theory. Deploying such an argument in the service of a "liberal" result disoriented some conservative critics. At the same time, in another passage presaging the Kennedy opinion, the court observed that the state constitution was an "organic document" meant "to govern society and institutions as they evolve through time."[54] This living constitutionalism, the idea that courts should interpret a constitution in light of changed circumstances, is most often associated with more liberal judges.

Justice Hudson dissented, arguing that Anderson and Murphy had "blindly" followed the "bare words of the [state equal rights] amendment, giving them absolute effect."[55] Going beyond the text, Hudson asserted that the voters of Texas had intended to benefit women, not gay people, when they overwhelmingly passed this amendment in 1972. Women's equality, not gay rights, had been the underlying purpose.[56] Hudson was undoubtedly correct about the expected application of the amendment. He wanted the court to interpret the text in a way that made the most sense of its basic purpose, regardless of what the words literally required. It was a rare example of a judge rejecting a gay-rights claim on essentially liberal legal grounds.

Hudson went on to recount the history of the legal condemnation of homosexual conduct, going back to the foundations of Judaism and Christianity. He cited Montesquieu's condemnation of unnatural sex acts, the Justinian code of Roman law, the ancient Goths, English common law, American colonial law, and state sodomy laws. Echoing Chief Justice Warren Burger's concurrence in *Bowers v. Hardwick*, Hudson noted Sir William Blackstone's reference to sodomy as "the infamous crime against nature, committed with either man or beast."[57]

Hudson went even further, suggesting that morality should not be a "relative, highly mutable concept." It "must rest upon divinely instituted principles." Hudson thought that decriminalizing homosexual conduct would reflect a destructive moral relativism, contrary to the laws of God. He proposed that rather than expanding personal autonomy and privacy, the state legislature might want to recriminalize "other forms of consensual sexual conduct that are currently permissible under the law." Of course, it was highly unlikely that the Texas legislature would actually impose criminal sanctions on their own preferred sexual conduct, but Hudson was content to leave such matters to their wisdom.

It was up to the Texas legislature to decide what's immoral and act accordingly, "protecting virtue and restraining evil,"[58] even if it chose to restrain only the vices of a small minority. "[W]e must assume for the purposes of our analysis that homosexual conduct is morally reprehensible."[59]

Hudson's opinion was essentially a sermon, placing homosexual sinners in the hands of an angry legislature. The history it cited failed to convey the complexity and comprehensiveness of sodomy laws. Its jurisprudence was activist in its willingness to downplay the actual words in the law, nostalgic in its clinging to a legal idyll, and myopic in its ignorance of equality under law. Its morality was blind to the American liberal tradition of entrusting virtue to individuals, families, and churches rather than to the state. It recalled a past that was already fast fading in a country where popular TV shows like *Will & Grace* featured openly gay characters. (The series had debuted September 21, 1998, four days after Lawrence and Garner were arrested.) Hudson, like Justice Antonin Scalia three years later, was already worried about a future taking shape beyond the demise of sodomy laws, one that included gay marriage.[60]

The Fourteenth Court of Appeals's ruling, for now, would apply only to the fourteen counties in southeast Texas that it covered. *Lawrence* was not yet a statewide victory for gay advocates.

Hudson's dissent was the kind of analysis Ruth Harlow had expected she would get from a Texas appellate court full of elected Republicans. But Hudson had been outvoted by his two fellow Republicans, Anderson and Murphy. The result reinforced Harlow's "general faith in the judiciary and in humanity."[61] Even in a state like Texas, with strong ideological pressure at work, it was possible for judges to step outside their political commitments and reason to a result based on law rather than on what their own preferences might dictate. That June, the gay-rights movement enjoyed an unexpected, premature, yet incomplete victory over sodomy laws. But the Texas Republican Party was about to throw a lifeline to the sodomy law—and thus unintentionally to the cause of gay rights at a national level.

As it turned out, the Texas GOP met for its biennial state convention in Houston just days after the court of appeals decision was released. By

2000, religious conservatives had engineered a nearly complete take-over of the state party apparatus, even if not quite all Republican office-holders had fallen in step. They controlled the party's agenda and its platform, which included everything from repeated invocations of biblical authority and rejection of the separation of church and state to urging the United States to quit the United Nations. They had successfully fought to include in the party platform a strong condemnation of homosexuality and any effort to ameliorate the status of gay people. Since 1996, the state party had even refused to give the gay Log Cabin Republicans a small amount of rented booth space in the vendor area outside the convention floor.[62]

As the 2000 state convention opened, defending the state sodomy law from "activist judges" was at the top of the agenda for those who controlled the party apparatus. Eight days after Justice Anderson's surprising decision striking down that law, Texas Republicans adopted a platform denouncing homosexuality even more harshly than in the past:

> The Party believes that the practice of sodomy tears at the fabric of society, contributes to the breakdown of the family unit, and leads to the spread of dangerous, communicable diseases. Homosexual behavior is contrary to the fundamental, unchanging truths that have been ordained by God, recognized by our country's founders, and shared by the majority of Texans. . . .
>
> Texas Sodomy Statutes—The party opposes the decriminalization of sodomy.

The platform could be considered nothing less than an antihomosexual manifesto, an antigay agenda. As *Lawrence* proceeded through the courts, the Texas GOP's response to cultural change was to resist at every stage. No quarter would be given; no compromise considered.

Many state party activists had a very hard time understanding why elected Republican judges would vote contrary to the party platform. They believed legal decisions should reflect the party's political preferences. That was the point of working so hard to screen and elect judges. So the state GOP had a special message directly for Justices Anderson and Murphy. "We publicly rebuke judges [sic] Chief Justice Murphy and

John Anderson, who ruled that the 100 year-old Texas sodomy law is unconstitutional, and ask that all members of the Republican Party of Texas oppose their re-election."[63] Unfortunately for party leaders, the deadline had passed for a candidate to run against Anderson, who had already won his primary and was unopposed for reelection in November 2000. Murphy was up for reelection in 2002 (he would announce his retirement in January 2001). But the party's actions put *all* elected Republican judges on notice that they had better not rule against the state sodomy law or they would face opposition and probable defeat in their next primary.

The political machinery of the GOP was beginning to grind against the appeals court. On June 23, the Harris County D.A.'s office asked the entire Fourteenth Court of Appeals, composed of nine judges, to overrule the panel decision. While that request was under consideration, Harris County GOP chairman Gary Polland and Paul Simpson, an attorney who was county party treasurer, drafted an angry letter intended to be sent to Justice Anderson. It demanded that Anderson either resign or reverse his ruling on the sodomy law. His decision, the letter said, was "the worst kind of judicial activism" and contradicted the "will of the people"[64]—as if judges should take polls before deciding cases.

But there was some discomfort within the party itself over Polland and Simpson's letter. Polland tried to get the GOP chairmen in the other thirteen counties covered by the Fourteenth Court of Appeals to cosign the letter. But some of them balked, responding that they did not think it appropriate to get involved in judicial matters and they believed they should defer to the judges' legal expertise. The letter was never officially sent. However, someone faxed a draft to Anderson's office.

When Murphy, who had been away on vacation after the decision came down, returned to work, he was dumbfounded by the backlash. Some of his associates and friends told him that they wished he had voted to uphold the law. He rejected the criticism from what he called "ultraconservatives" in the party that he was a judicial activist. "We were doing our duty as judges, not 'activism,' but what we were sworn to do," he remembered. "And one of those duties was to declare an unconstitutional statute unconstitutional." He resented the scolding from a party that he had served so long and so faithfully.[65]

A little over a week after news of Polland and Simpson's letter broke in the media and less than a month after the state GOP's warning to judges, the Fourteenth Court of Appeals announced that all nine of its judges would reconsider Anderson's opinion. The Harris County D.A.'s office, which was also feeling the political heat from the party, turned up the burner in defense of the state sodomy law. On August 23, Bill Delmore filed with the court his brief focusing on the sex-discrimination argument that had been accepted by Justice Anderson.[66]

On the heels of the GOP's harsh rhetoric on the subject, Delmore's arguments now acquired a harder, almost mocking, edge: "The appellants are effectively arguing that under the Equal Rights Amendment, human sexual activity must be regarded as a calculus of disembodied organs and orifices in which the sex of the participating individuals cannot be legally acknowledged."[67] As we have seen, nothing like the disembodied-organs-and-orifices taunts had appeared in Delmore's earlier briefs.

Delmore also suggested a new reason that the state might want to ban homosexual sex: it was not reproductive. "Because sexual activity between persons of the same sex cannot lead to reproduction, there is a long-standing consensus that such activity is unnatural and immoral," Delmore wrote. The argument was similar to one often made in Catholic theology and in natural-law philosophy. The state sodomy law, according to Delmore, was "thus based solely upon a recognition of the 'reproductive differences between the sexes.'"[68]

This new argument was remarkably flawed. Neither homosexual nor heterosexual anal sex is reproductive. Neither homosexual nor heterosexual oral sex is reproductive. But under the state Homosexual Conduct law, only the former varieties of sex were forbidden. The state still could not explain the reason for the different treatment. The Harris County D.A. appeared to be grasping for arguments to give the full court of appeals a legal basis to reverse course.

On September 13, the nine-judge Fourteenth Court of Appeals announced that it would issue an opinion without even hearing oral argument in the case. This was an unusual treatment of a high-profile case involving a serious constitutional matter. It was a sign that the rest of the appellate court might not be willing to consider seriously the arguments made against the sodomy law's validity. There was nothing for either side to do but wait for the full court's opinion.

While *Lawrence* was under consideration *en banc*, a horrific assault reminded the defense team that the clean legal arguments masked complicated and ultimately tragic human lives. Sometime late in the evening of October 10–11, 2000, Robert Eubanks, the man whose drunken telephone call had set off the whole case, was savagely assaulted by an unknown assailant or group of assailants. Tyron Garner later speculated that Eubanks had probably been catching a bus when he "mouthed off" to somebody, something he frequently did.[69] Garner also thought it might have been a gay-bashing. Bloodied and only semiconscious, Eubanks apparently crawled to the apartment he shared with Garner. Scrapes found on his hands and knees were consistent with that theory. Garner called 911 and Eubanks was transported to the hospital at 4:15 a.m. on October 11.

While Eubanks was laying unconscious for days in a Houston hospital, Eubanks's family forbade Garner to see him. In fact, Eubanks would never regain consciousness and died on October 14. Garner was excluded from the funeral, although the family never explained why. If the family were uncomfortable with Eubanks's homosexuality, Garner's presence would be the living embodiment of the deceased's deviance.[70] It would not be surprising if Garner's race was also a factor. Additionally, Garner was initially a suspect in Eubanks's murder, although a grand jury refused to indict him. If the family suspected Garner was the murderer, their reluctance to let him visit Eubanks in the hospital or attend the funeral was understandable. Whatever the case, Eubanks's autopsy described massive head injuries likely inflicted by a blunt instrument—possibly a baseball bat or similar bludgeoning device.[71] The murder remains unsolved.

On November 7, 2000, Justice Anderson was reelected. It had helped, of course, that he was unopposed and that it had been too late for anyone else to qualify for the ballot when he issued his controversial decision in the *Lawrence* case. Anderson told Murphy that the political reaction to their decision worried him, because it meant he would not have the party's support in the future.[72] This was exactly the kind of reaction that state GOP leaders wanted to induce in their elected judges.

Tyron Garner, in front of his brother's house, 2005.

John Lawrence in the Navy, age seventeen, 1961.

Ray Hill, in front of an adult arcade, 2005.

Annise Parker, 2005.

Deputy Joseph Quinn, Harris County Sheriff's Office, 2005 (in front of the stairs leading to John Lawrence's apartment).

Deputy Donald Tipps, Harris County Sheriff's Office, 2005.

The door to John Lawrence's apartment.

TWO BEDROOM • TWO BATH
995 SQUARE FEET

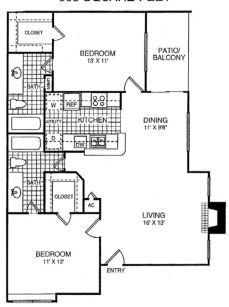

Floor plan of John Lawrence's apartment. (*Colorado Club Apartments*)

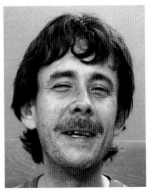

Mug shots of John Lawrence, Tyron Garner, and Robert Eubanks (left to right), September 18, 1998.

The building that houses the Wallisville substation of the Harris County Sheriff's Office and the courtroom of Judge Mike Parrott.

Nathan Broussard in his office, 2005.

Mitchell Katine (left) and John Lawrence.

Mitchell Katine and Suzanne Goldberg. (*Provide Mitchell Katine*)

Judge Sherman Ross of Harris County Criminal Court #10.

William Hohengarten of Jenner & Block, 2007.

Ruth Harlow of Lambda Legal, 2005.

Judge Paul C. Murphy (retired), of Texas's Fourte Court of Appeals, 2007.

The Supreme Court building at night. (© *Rudy Sulgan / Corbis*)

Inside the Supreme Court.
(© *Richard A. Bloom / Corbis*)

Official portrait of the Justices of the Supreme Court, 2002–03 term.
(© *Jason Reed / Reuters / Corbis*)

Supreme Court Associate Justices Anthony M. Kennedy and Sandra Day O'Connor attend the groundbreaking ceremony for an expansion of the Supreme Court building in Washington, D.C., June 17, 2003. (© *Brooks Kraft / Corbis*)

Chief Justice Rehnquist in his chambers. (© *Lynn Johnson / National Geographic Society / Corbis*)

Associate Justices Ruth Bader Ginsburg and Stephen Breyer. (© *Jim Bourg / Reuters / Corbis*)

Justice David H. Souter. (© *Matthew Cavanaugh / epa / Corbis*)

Justice John Paul Stevens relaxing in his chambers. (© *Lynn Johnson / National Geographic Society / Corbis*)

Justice Scalia at a National Italian American Foundation event in Washington, D.C. (© *Jonathan Ernst / Reuters / Corbis*)

Charles Rosenthal, Harris County D.A., faces the media after Supreme Court oral argument, March 26, 2003. (*Provided by Mitchell Katine*)

Paul Smith and Ruth Harlow face the media after Supreme Court oral argument, March 26, 2003. (*Provided by Mitchell Katine*)

John Lawrence (left) and Tyron Garner at the rally in Houston after the *Lawrence* decision, June 26, 2003. (© *Erich Schlegel / Dallas Morning News / Corbis*)

Rally after the *Lawrence* decision. (© *Rick Friedman / Corbis*) / (© *Reuters/Corbis*)

From left: John Lawrence, Mitchell Katine, and Tyron Garner riding in Houston's gay pride parade on June 28, 2003. (© *Reuters / Corbis*)

That same election day, the voters of Harris County chose a new district attorney to replace the retiring Johnny Holmes. Born in Alice, Texas, in 1946, Charles A. "Chuck" Rosenthal had graduated, like Justice Hudson, from the South Texas College of Law and had been a prosecutor in the county D.A.'s office since 1977. An excellent jury-trial lawyer with a folksy manner and heavy Texas drawl, he was something of a playboy and prankster. In 1995, he actually set off firecrackers in the stairwell of the D.A.'s office. Even though it occurred soon after the Oklahoma City bombing had destroyed a federal courthouse, Rosenthal excused the incident as a harmless joke. Shortly after he was elected to head the prosecutor's office that sends more convicts to death row than any other in the nation, Rosenthal defended the death penalty as a "Biblical proposition."[73]

Another four months passed after Rosenthal's election while the D.A.'s office and Lambda lawyers waited for a decision from the court of appeals. On March 15, 2001, by a 7–2 vote, the *en banc* court reversed its three-judge panel, upholding the state Homosexual Conduct law. When the appeals court had taken an early vote, some of the judges were on the fence[74]—but in the end only Anderson and Murphy dissented.

Hudson, who had previously been in the minority, now wrote the majority opinion, reiterating many of the points he had made in his dissent the summer before.[75] There was no right to private homosexual conduct. And there was no impermissible discrimination in the state sodomy law. Not only was the state legislature free to criminalize conduct based on its immorality rather than on its harmfulness to others, it was also free to say that the same conduct could be made criminal for some people but not for others. The "state could rationally conclude that 'homosexual sodomy' is a different, and more reprehensible, offense than 'heterosexual sodomy.'"[76] The legislature may declare that some acts are simply more egregious than others without giving any reason for that declaration. Homicides, for example, may be first-degree felonies, second-degree felonies, or entirely lawful (as in the case of self-defense).[77]

Anderson scoffed at this rationalization for the state's focus on homosexual sex "as nothing more than politically-charged, thinly-veiled, animus-driven cliches."[78] He wrote that he was bound by the judicial code to decide cases regardless of his own views of morality and "without bias or prejudice."[79] His dissent hinted that the judges in the majority were running in fear for their political lives.

Murphy also suspected that this fear of political retribution, inspired by the county GOP letter and the state GOP convention, had driven the outcome. In states with partisan judicial elections, it's reasonable to think that partisan considerations will enter the judge's decision-making process.[80] Frank Harmon, a lawyer and well-connected Republican political consultant in Houston, agreed that political pressures might have influenced the outcome of the *en banc* vote: "Some of these guys [on the Fourteenth Court of Appeals] do think about their political futures and would have gotten themselves into a heap of trouble" if they had voted to strike down the Texas law.[81]

Five of the seven judges in the majority felt that kind of charge against the court was so objectionable that they needed to respond specifically to it. In a concurring opinion by Justice Leslie Brock Yates, they rejected the notion that the appeals court had succumbed to political pressures. They noted that the state rules governing judicial conduct required them to resist "'partisan interests, public clamor, or fear of criticism.'"[82] They acknowledged that "attacks on the judiciary, like the one following the panel opinion, may have the effect of increasing the potential that the public's confidence in our courts will diminish because of a perception, however erroneous, that we have made a political decision, not a legal one."[83]

The answer to this corrosive perception of the judiciary, suggested by an *amicus* brief that had been filed on behalf of Lawrence and Garner, might have been to affirm the panel's decision as a way to show judicial solidarity and resistance to political pressure. But, referring to the Polland and Simpson letter, the concurring judges disagreed that the proper answer was a public show of solidarity with their beleaguered colleagues:

> [T]he response to such a reckless and irresponsible act cannot be that we ignore our duty to decide the law we have been entrusted to interpret. Attempts to politicize this opinion—regardless of their origin—have no place in our decisionmaking process, nor are attacks from opposing interests immune from creating the

very same perception in the mind of the public that may now exist as a result of earlier inappropriate attempts to influence this decision.[84]

No matter what they did, suggested the judges, the court would be vulnerable to the charge of having acted politically. If they overruled the panel opinion, they would be seen by some as caving in to political pressures. If they upheld the panel opinion, they would be seen by others as digging in their heels against public pressure. The best answer was to decide the case based on their best judgment of what the law required, "not because of political pressures, as amicus curiae has suggested, but despite them."[85] Nevertheless, in this politicized sodomy law case, they could not escape the suspicion that they had applied the law in the manner most consistent with their reelection prospects.

In Texas, the highest court dealing with criminal law issues is the Court of Criminal Appeals, which sits in Austin. The court has long had a bad reputation among lawyers, on both the defense and prosecution side, for inconsistent and political decisions. Again, all nine judges on this court are elected, and when *Lawrence* reached them, all were Republicans.

On April 13, 2001, in what's known as a petition for discretionary review, Lambda asked the criminal appeals court to reverse the appeals court's decision. The petition, largely restating Lambda's previous arguments, was drafted by Lambda Supervising Attorney Susan Sommer and Harlow. The Harris County D.A.'s office tried to downplay the significance of the appeal to the state's highest criminal court, treating it like just another appeal out of the many it handled. Bill Delmore told the media that the D.A.'s office typically didn't respond to discretionary review petitions. "We receive so many that we can't respond to all of them and if you do respond to one, you're typically calling attention to the case." However, he conceded, "this is such an unusual case, we may respond to it. I'll just have to take a look at what the other side has filed and make my decision based on that."[86] Eventually the D.A.'s office decided not to respond. It was entirely up to the court whether to take up the case and, if so, whether to entertain oral arguments from the contending sides.

Just two weeks earlier, the Netherlands had become the first country in the world to recognize same-sex marriages. Five days after Lambda's appeal, on April 18, the Texas House Committee on Criminal Justice, in fact, voted to repeal the state sodomy law. Two Republicans joined five Democrats on the committee in a 7–2 vote to repeal the law.[87] But in the face of opposition from both conservative Democrats and the state GOP; the bill later died in the full state House of Representatives.

The matter of *Lawrence* stayed with the Court of Criminal Appeals, which said nothing for more than a year. In that time, however, the world seemed literally to change. A tropical storm caused five billion dollars of damage to the city of Houston. Then, the September 11 terrorist attacks occurred. The United States launched a retaliatory war against Al Qaeda and the Taliban in Afghanistan. All of this passed with no word from the Court of Criminal Appeals.

Then on April 17, 2002, a full year after Lambda's attorneys asked the court to hear the case, it finally responded, denying Lawrence and Garner's petition without hearing any oral argument or even asking the parties to submit briefs on the issue. The state's highest criminal court gave no explanation for its decision not to hear the case. It was a remarkably cavalier act by the court. This was the first and only time it had the opportunity to consider the constitutional validity of the law. A few years before, the Texas Supreme Court (the state's highest court in civil matters) had refused to rule on the state sodomy law in a civil case precisely because, it declared, the constitutionality of a criminal law was the province of the Court of Criminal Appeals.[88] Now that very court refused even to ponder the issue.

The parties were left to guess at the court's thought process. Even as gay-rights claims were being seriously considered by courts and legislatures around the country, the Texas court seemed to be saying that the *Lawrence* case was unworthy of its time and attention. It's unclear why the court needed a year to make the decision not to make a decision or even think about making a decision. It was a judicial back-of-the-hand, a silent version of Justice Byron White's declaration in *Bowers v. Hardwick* that the constitutional arguments against homosexual sodomy laws were "at best, facetious."[89]

Not surprisingly, Ruth Harlow regarded the criminal appeals court's refusal to hear the case "a major abdication of judicial responsibility, given that the other Texas high court had said that the only court that can review this [law] is the Court of Criminal Appeals."[90] Bill Delmore, too, thought the judges were "big chickens" for avoiding the merits in *Lawrence*. "It's so typical," he observed with disdain. "They have a history of avoiding the hot potato cases if they can."[91]

With the final court in Texas now out of the way and the state sodomy law still standing, the next stop, and last hope, was the U.S. Supreme Court.

14.

The Constitutional Mainstream

T HE YEAR 2002, THE PENULTIMATE ONE FOR SODOMY LAWS IN America, saw a dismissive rejection of gay-rights litigants from the highest criminal court in Texas and uncertain prospects in the U.S. Supreme Court. It was hardly clear that the Court would be willing even to consider the case and doubtful that, upon rethinking the matter, it would be willing to overrule its own decision from sixteen years earlier in *Bowers v. Hardwick.* By the end of the year, however, the tides had changed and the constitutional arguments for Lawrence and Garner had been shaped and sharpened into a presentable form for the Supreme Court.

As their lawyers carefully controlled the legal narrative of their case, John Lawrence and Tyron Garner continued to lead lives whose narratives could not be so easily controlled. In 2002, Garner's parents grew gravely ill: his father's leg was amputated and his mother lost her voice. Neither of them followed developments in their son's case. In fact, they never talked about it, and it's not clear that they even knew Garner was involved in a historic challenge to the Texas sodomy law. By the time the *Lawrence* decision came down in June 2003, both of his parents would be dead.[1]

In 2002, John Lawrence, too, was preoccupied with matters other than his challenge to the state sodomy law. He was running up credit card debt and had declared bankruptcy by the time his namesake case was decided.[2] He was saved from eviction from the Colorado Club Apartments only by the rules protecting debtors in a bankruptcy proceeding.[3]

Lawrence's stepfather had predicted that he was going to lose in the Texas courts. "Then where does it go?" his dad asked. "Supreme Court," Lawrence replied with his characteristic verbal economy. "Well, there's your chance," his dad said. But Lawrence's stepfather never got to see his son's legal victory, dying in a car crash in 2002.[4]

Under the best circumstances, victory in the United States Supreme Court is hugely improbable. There is no right to have an appeal actually considered by the Supreme Court. Litigants who lose in the lower courts must petition the Court for what is known as a writ of certiorari, a request for the Court to review the case (a "cert petition"). The decision whether to entertain arguments on the merits is left entirely to the Court's discretion. At least four of the nine Justices must agree to hear the case. Only about 1 percent of the more than 8,000 petitions filed annually with the Supreme Court are granted. If the court grants the petition, it then orders the contending sides to file briefs and sets a date for oral argument. But the easiest way out of a complicated and controversial matter is simply for the Court to refuse to hear the case and thus say nothing either way.

There was no real question that Lambda would file a cert petition. Some gay-rights lawyers and law professors worried, however, that it might be too soon to ask the Court to reverse *Bowers v. Hardwick*.[5] "I don't think it is clear-headed behavior to take this to the Supreme Court now," said Emory University School of Law professor David J. Garrow, the author of *Liberty and Sexuality*, a highly regarded book on the Court's major privacy cases. He doubted that Justice Sandra Day O'Connor, who voted with the majority in *Bowers* to uphold sodomy laws, would now reverse herself. Justice Kennedy, the other possible swing vote on the issue, was not on the Court when *Bowers* was decided. In Garrow's view, he was also unlikely to vote to reverse *Bowers*. In fact, Garrow noted that of the dissenting Justices in *Bowers*, only Justice John Paul Stevens still served on the Court in 2002.[6] Garrow's doubts were reasonable, and he was hardly alone.

The greatest danger for gay-rights advocates was that four Justices would agree to hear the case, but that there would not be the necessary five votes to hold the Texas law unconstitutional. Instead, the Court might end up reaffirming a decision, *Bowers*, that had done extensive damage in almost every area of the law. But having brought the case this far, and looking at developments in society and the law since 1986, Lambda concluded that the risk was worth it.

Lambda lead attorney Ruth Harlow believed that, in addition to securing the support of longtime gay-rights advocates and organizations, it was important to enlist experienced Supreme Court litigators from Washington's legal establishment. There were several elite law firms and lawyers who would fit that description. These were generally attorneys who attended the highest-ranked schools, made excellent grades, clerked for well-known judges, landed lucrative jobs at influential and well-connected firms, and excelled in practice. Among those she first consulted was William M. Hohengarten, an appellate attorney at Jenner & Block. Harlow had known Hohengarten since 1992, when they worked briefly together for the ACLU gay-rights project under Bill Rubenstein.

Bill Hohengarten was born in St. Paul, Minnesota, in 1960. After graduating from Yale Law School, he worked for a law firm in New York before clerking with Justice David Souter in 1996–97. That was the term in which the Supreme Court decided *Washington v. Glucksberg*,[7] which concluded that a state was free to ban physician-assisted suicide and that constitutionally protected "fundamental rights" were only those deeply embedded in the nation's traditions and history. After his clerkship ended, Hohengarten joined Jenner, a law firm that represented many business clients in the Supreme Court.[8] So far removed was he from the day-to-day grind of gay-rights litigation that, before getting the call from Harlow, Hohengarten hadn't even heard of the Texas case.

Initially, Jenner was to be one of several firms serving in a *pro bono* advisory capacity for the final phase of the case. But after a few weeks, Harlow hired the firm to serve as Lambda's co-counsel. Harlow trusted Hohengarten's judgment and experience and had a good working relationship with him. She wanted a firm that would understand the case as the product of an entire movement, not just a particular criminal proceeding. And she wanted someone who understood that this was "a Lambda case," meaning that Lambda would retain ultimate control and remain the face of the litigation.[9]

Hohengarten brought a wealth of Jenner experience with him,

including Paul Smith, a firm partner and veteran Supreme Court advocate, and associates Dan Mach and Sharon McGowan. In 2002, Jenner also had a pool of exceptional summer associates (law students working there between school years) from the best law schools in the country. Four of these summer associates—Lindsay Harrison from Harvard, Luke Platzer from Stanford, Lee Taylor from Columbia, and Scott Wilkens from Harvard—each worked on distinct legal questions to help prepare the cert petition in *Lawrence*. Harrison wrote a memorandum on the legitimacy of the state's interest in preserving "morality." Paltzer wrote about the various "collateral" harms caused to gay men and lesbians by the very existence of sodomy laws, even when they weren't enforced against private sexual conduct.[10] Wilkens tackled the significance of post-*Bowers* due process cases for challenging the Texas statute (for example, *Planned Parenthood v. Casey* and *Washington v. Glucksberg*). Taylor worked on the question of *stare decisis*—the legal doctrine under which the Court usually stands by its own precedents—and specifically whether the Court would overrule *Bowers v. Hardwick*. He concluded that it probably would not, a widely accepted conclusion.[11]

So as it prepared to take *Lawrence* to the Supreme Court, Lambda was mobilizing an army of experienced litigators and top-notch law firms, all with strong educational backgrounds and a deep commitment to the cause.

Through the summer of 2002, the *Lawrence* team worked on researching and drafting their cert petition. Meanwhile, on July 5, Lambda's lawyers, led by Susan Sommer, scored another victory against sodomy laws when the Arkansas Supreme Court struck down that state's version of the Texas Homosexual Conduct law.[12] The plaintiffs in that case had not been arrested, as in Texas, but the Arkansas court was willing to decide the issue anyway. While the ruling, decided under the Arkansas state constitution, obviously did not bind the Supreme Court on a matter of federal constitutional law, it did reinforce the basic idea that sodomy laws were a relic of the past. There were now only four states that criminalized gay sex as a distinct category: Kansas, Missouri, Oklahoma, and Texas.

The cert petition, which is really a brief explaining the significance of the case and the reasons the court should rule in favor of the petitioner, was the product of considerable thought and refinement. It reflected decisions on everything from what theme to create to what should be included and excluded, and from what should be put in a footnote rather than in the main body of the brief to what priority should be given to the arguments.

The overarching theme of the case, which the Lambda and Jenner lawyers developed in each of their briefs to the Supreme Court, was that the United States had progressed well beyond the crude and cruel antigay posturing represented by the Texas sodomy law. Harlow saw it this way:

> If you frame the case in terms of "Does the government belong in your bedroom?" 75 to 80 percent of America will say no. And "Should there be different rules for gay people than there should be for straight people?" most people will say, "No, that sounds fishy." So we thought the questions were easy questions. And we wanted the case to be positioned as if the Court were catching up to society, as opposed to pushing the Court to do something that would be leading society.[13]

The Court was now behind the times. The country had left its decision in *Bowers v. Hardwick* and the few remaining state sodomy laws on the trash heap of a discredited and bigoted past. Whatever Americans thought of homosexuality and the morality of specific homosexual acts, this was not a controversial case for 80 percent of U.S. citizens. The government should keep out of adults' bedrooms and should treat everybody the same. In striking down the Texas law, the Court would simply be catching up.

In order of priority and likelihood of success with the Court itself, Lambda and Jenner suggested that the Court should address three issues:

> 1.   Whether Petitioners' criminal convictions under the Texas "Homosexual Conduct" law—which criminalizes sexual intimacy by same-sex couples, but not identical behavior by different-sex couples—violate the Fourteenth Amendment guarantee of equal protection of the laws?
> 2.   Whether Petitioners' criminal convictions for adult consensual sexual intimacy in the home violate their vital interests in

liberty and privacy protected by the Due Process Clause of the
Fourteenth Amendment?

3.   Whether *Bowers v. Hardwick*, 478 U.S. 186 (1986), should be
overruled?[14]

Ruth Harlow wrote the first draft of the equal protection section of the
brief; Bill Hohengarten, the first draft of the due process and *Bowers* sections. The drafts were then circulated to the rest of the "inner group,"
which included Pat Logue in Lambda's Chicago office, Susan Sommer,
and Paul Smith.[15] Drafts were also circulated to prominent law professors who had worked on gay-rights cases, including Laurence Tribe (the
Supreme Court advocate for Michael Hardwick in *Bowers*), Nan Hunter,
and Bill Rubenstein. However, nothing major in the briefs changed
because of outside advice. No major arguments or subarguments were
added. No major case citations were inserted. Based on the outside
reviews, the inner team of Jenner and Lambda lawyers was reassured
that they had written a very good petition.[16]

On the first issue, equal protection, the *Lawrence* team was careful to
pick the battles it thought it could win. Its basic argument was the same
one made in the lower courts: the state of Texas had no rational basis for
treating homosexual sodomy differently from heterosexual sodomy. The
state's interests, promoting public morality and the traditional family,
amounted to nothing more than "a statement that the legislature wants
the criminal code to include this condemnation."[17] If that circular justification were enough to avoid invalidation, "any discriminatory law
could be justified with the statement that the legislature considered it
'moral' to disadvantage the targeted group."[18]

Consistent with the "following—not leading" theme, it is noteworthy
that the equal protection argument minimized two other theories popular in academic writings and supported, in principle, by the Lambda and
Jenner attorneys themselves.[19] These were the arguments that the Texas
law represented impermissible sex discrimination and that it was sexual-
orientation discrimination that should be treated as constitutionally
offensive as sex or race discrimination themselves. Let's look briefly at
each of these downplayed legal theories.

The *Lawrence* team had quickly rejected reliance on a sex-discrimi-

nation argument, which essentially asserted that the Texas law impermissibly classified people based on their biological sex because it specified
the sex of the sexual partners they could choose.[20] Suzanne Goldberg
had been a proponent of this argument, but (as was mentioned earlier)
she was only peripherally involved in the case at this point, and even she
acknowledged that its prospects for success were limited.[21] While it had
won the day briefly with two judges in the Texas Court of Appeals, that
result was a rare success for the argument in courts, and the *Lawrence*
team concluded it was unlikely to be followed by the Supreme Court.
Whatever the caricature of it offered by some critics, the Supreme Court
is ordinarily a cautious, minimalist, and incremental institution. A sex-
discrimination argument would immediately call into question many
more laws in an obvious way. For judges and laypeople, the argument
seemed "too cute or too fine" as a way to fend off what were basically
antigay laws.[22] So, however popular it might be among academic theorists, it "wasn't the argument of the sloggers in the courthouses because
it was ahead of the [popular] consciousness," Ruth Harlow said.[23] For
the Court to rule on sex-discrimination grounds would be leading the
country down a new path, not catching up. So that form of equal protection argument was relegated to a footnote on page 22 of the brief.[24]

The cert petition also downplayed the argument that discrimination
based on sexual orientation should be presumptively unconstitutional—
subjected to "heightened" or "strict" scrutiny. Again, the lawyers on the
Lawrence team fully agreed with the argument in principle. The main
problem with it, like the sex-discrimination claim, was its aggressive-
ness. It would potentially call into question other forms of discrimination against gay men and lesbians, such as the ban on military service
by openly gay personnel and possibly the restriction of marriage to heterosexual unions. The argument for heightened judicial scrutiny of
sexual-orientation discrimination, too, would make the Court a leader,
not a follower. So this argument was limited to one paragraph at the
very end of the discussion of equal protection.[25]

If the Court wanted to go down one of these more adventurous
paths—sex discrimination or heightened judicial scrutiny of antigay
discrimination—it was free to do so. The attorneys for Lawrence and
Garner offered the Court the opportunity, but they believed that was not

the most likely way the Court would go.[26] Moreover, they worried that emphasizing heightened scrutiny might generate anxiety in the Justices, especially the swing voters on the Court, Kennedy and O'Connor. "You had more to lose than to win by pushing those thoughts," recalled Hohengarten. In particular, the team "absolutely wanted to reassure the Court that it was not deciding the marriage issue in this case."[27] The arguments were crafted to allow the Court to strike down the Texas law without necessarily leading the way to gay marriage.

On the second big issue in the case, whether the Texas law violated the constitutional rights to privacy and liberty, the cert petition described the law as invading "private, adult sexual intimacy," an "intimate realm of personal autonomy, family, and relationships," and "personal dignity."[28] The attorneys carefully minimized references to the specific sex acts criminalized. The brief mentioned anal or oral sex just four times, twice to describe the content or history of the Texas law,[29] once to discuss the prevalence of these acts among heterosexuals,[30] and once in a quotation from Deputy Quinn's arrest report.[31] The acts were not mentioned at all in the constitutional analysis. The team wanted the Court to see *Lawrence* as a case about families and relationships, not about sex—except insofar as sex instrumentally served the goals of individual autonomy and relationship formation.

On the third big question, whether the Court should overrule *Bowers v. Hardwick*, the *Lawrence* team emphasized how much had changed in the country's perception and treatment of gay people since 1986. "*Bowers* is out of step with the vast majority of the States," the cert petition asserted, noting that only thirteen states still had sodomy laws, in contrast to the twenty-four that did when *Bowers* was decided.[32] The brief criticized *Bowers* for minimizing the claim for adult intimacy as merely a right to "homosexual sodomy." It also emphasized subsequent developments in the Court's own case law, including its abortion decision in *Casey* in 1992 and its decision in the antigay Amendment 2 case, *Romer*, in 1996.[33]

The underlying point, however, was not about legal or constitutional doctrine, or even about the Court's own precedents. "Since 1986," the cert petition argued, "the country has developed a more accurate understanding of gay and lesbian couples and families—neighbors, friends, relatives, and coworkers who live their lives more openly."[34] The *Lawrence* team knew that the Justices themselves were far more familiar with gay people than they had been in 1986. Many former law clerks for the Supreme Court were gay. Some of these law clerks were enlisted to review the petitioners' briefs in *Lawrence v. Texas* to help craft arguments that would appeal to the Court—especially to O'Connor and Kennedy.[35]

The cert petition also highlighted changes in state laws since *Bowers* had been decided. Many local and state governments now had domestic partnership ordinances. Even a federal law, named after a beloved gay chaplain who died in the terrorist attack on the World Trade Center on September 11, 2001, allowed federal death benefits to surviving same-sex partners.[36] All but one state allowed gay adoptions and many now allowed second-parent adoptions; gay people served as long-term foster parents; and the 2000 census showed that there were gay couples in more than 99 percent of the nation's counties.[37] "For adults in gay and lesbian families, as in all families, sexual intimacy is a basic component of stable, healthy relationships," the brief concluded, rebutting the charge in *Bowers* that there was no connection between the right of gay adults to have sex on the one hand and the formation of families and the raising of children on the other. "Much has changed since *Bowers*," but anachronistic and harmful laws like the one in Texas persisted.[38]

Where the Court in *Bowers* saw only gays having sex, the Court now should see gays having relationships. Hohengarten, in particular, pressed for a "mainstream presentation" of the issues, to "drive home the message that gay people are essentially just like everybody else," including in their sexuality and relationships.[39] The only difference was in the choice of partner. In an interview about the case, Hohengarten contrasted this approach to one that might emphasize, for example, "special sexual communities for gay men or something like that." That would not be helpful with the Court, since it would "conjure up lots of images of whatever scene in San Francisco. That was not what we wanted to conjure up here."[40]

A caricature of "San Francisco values"—a throwback to the Republican election themes from 1984, and understood as a particular form of sexual obsession and license and an abandonment of social and familial responsibilities—had often been used to stigmatize gays. This very stereotype was used in Houston and throughout Texas in opposition to gay-rights measures, and indeed had informed the attitudes of the arresting officers when they encountered gay men in John Lawrence's apartment. Now, when the Justices considered the case, the *Lawrence* team wanted them to be thinking of relationships "just like" straight relationships, not homosexual leather or bondage fetishists.

To the extent that the members of the Court believed that what they were being asked to protect in *Bowers* was *difference*, they were less likely to grant it constitutional protection. To the extent that the Justices now believed what they were being asked to protect in *Lawrence* was *sameness*, they could perhaps be persuaded to extend it constitutional protection. Whether the doctrine was equal protection or due process, whether the goal was eradicating antigay stigma or protecting fundamental privacy, the essential task was to have the Court see the case as a protection of similarity. Homosexuals were virtually heterosexuals, and for that reason deserved the same treatment. The nation had come to understand that fact. This was the framework for the constitutional argument in *Lawrence*.

Having done their best to get the Court to pay attention to the case, the *Lawrence* team filed its cert petition on July 16. They thought they were most likely to get the Court to hear and rule on the equal protection issue, in part because of the obvious inequality of the Texas law and in part because they did not expect the Court would overrule *Bowers*.[41] But for now they waited.

ON THE OTHER SIDE of the case stood Bill Delmore, nearly alone, in defense of the Texas sodomy law. The first instinct of Harris County D.A. Chuck Rosenthal was to hand the case off to the state attorney general, a position then held by Republican John Cornyn, a former Texas Supreme Court justice. This was, after all, a challenge in federal court to a state statute. The case had statewide implications, Rosenthal reasoned, and would thus better be handled by the state rather than by one county.[42]

But Cornyn's office refused to take responsibility for defending the law. The reason it declined the case is unknown, but politics provides a possible explanation. Cornyn was then running for U.S. Senate and, Delmore later speculated, he might have regarded the case as too "controversial." Delmore noted in an interview, "A lot of people in the community felt strongly that the statute didn't belong on the books. The *Houston Chronicle* and other publications were coming down on the side of those challenging the law."[43] Cornyn's campaign later said that he supported the state sodomy law.[44] That would have been a popular stand—indeed a necessary one—to take within the state GOP, whose biennial convention took place in June 2002. But perhaps Cornyn didn't need the additional headache of the lawsuit and the general perception that he was an anti-sex crusader.

Harris County D.A. prosecutors didn't want to be seen as crusaders, either. The office would do what was necessary to defend the law, as it believed it was obliged to do, but no more. In contrast to the careful and thorough preparation by Harlow, the D.A.'s office did not mobilize prominent law firms or lawyers to support the law. It did not get advice from religious-conservative groups about what arguments should be made in the Supreme Court. Delmore did most of the Supreme Court work by himself, with help from one other assistant district attorney, Scott Durfee.

Delmore had the option to file a brief opposing Supreme Court review of the case. It was better, he reasoned, as it had been with the Texas Court of Criminal Appeals, not to magnify the importance of the issue to the Justices by filing such a brief. If Texas treated the issue as unimportant, it was even more likely that the case would be one of the roughly 7,900 that the Court refused even to consider every year.

However, on September 19, 2002, the Court requested that Texas respond to the cert petition. This did not mean the Court would agree to take the case, but it did indicate the Justices were sufficiently interested that they wanted to hear Texas explain why they should not consider the matter. For a busy prosecutor, the case had become a persistent time drain. Delmore did not need the added work. "I've got plenty of real, serious crimes to worry about every day," he said.[45]

In the end, however, Delmore wrote the state's response to the due process arguments. Scott Durfee mostly handled the equal protection claims. Chuck Rosenthal, the Harris County district attorney, relied on Delmore to describe the arguments to him but was otherwise uninvolved. He did not actually read the briefs before they were filed in the Supreme Court.[46] This was a remarkable degree of inattention to a major case, filed under his name, and which he ultimately decided to argue himself. As he had before, Delmore resisted entreaties from religious-conservative groups to defend the statute by arguing that it protected public health from communicable diseases spread through homosexual sex.[47]

In response to the due process argument made by gay-rights attorneys, the D.A.'s office relied primarily on history. "In light of the fact that homosexual anal sodomy was viewed as criminal behavior under state law and the common law for a period of centuries," the state's brief stated, "that conduct could not conceivably have achieved the status of a 'fundamental right' in the brief period of sixteen years since *Bowers* was decided."[48] Statements like this relied on the *Bowers*-era understanding of the history of sodomy laws.

In response to the equal protection argument, the state repeated its responses in the Texas courts that the same-sex-only sodomy law did not discriminate on the basis of sexual orientation. It would equally punish homosexual conduct by heterosexuals or bisexuals. Indeed, citing work by the famous sex researcher Alfred Kinsey, the state argued that as much as 50 percent of the population was not exclusively heterosexual.[49] Even if the law did discriminate against gay people, the D.A. claimed, that was not constitutionally problematic. As it had argued in the Texas courts, the state asserted that its interest in morality was enough to validate the law.[50] Under the circumstances, argued the state, the Court should let the issue be resolved democratically in the state legislature.[51]

On October 21, 2002, Delmore filed his brief opposing certiorari. After doing so, he told the *Houston Chronicle* that the D.A.'s office had defended the law "reluctantly," saying that "we're stuck with it." He continued, "The Legislature had decided it. We may not necessarily agree with it. We may not be enthusiastic about enforcing it or prosecuting it, but the district attorney doesn't get to pick and choose which laws to defend."[52] It was not a rousing endorsement of the statute.

Two weeks later, the *Lawrence* team filed a response to the state, emphasizing a variety of mistakes and omissions in the D.A.'s brief.[53] Now the lawyers on both sides had to wait to see whether the Court would give the case full consideration.

As stated earlier, it takes four Justices to grant certiorari in a case—

but five to win. Since the Justices do not discuss in advance how they will ultimately vote in a case prior to taking it, they must make an educated guess about whether at least four others will agree. While Justices do get to know one another's views as they serve together over time, they cannot be certain of the result in many close cases. Sometimes they misjudge the likely votes of their colleagues. In *Bowers*, for example, the Court initially voted not to hear the case. But Justice Byron White, who wanted to uphold sodomy laws, persuaded Chief Justice Warren Burger and Justices William Rehnquist and Thurgood Marshall to vote for cert.[54] Of these four, only Justice Marshall eventually voted to strike down the laws. It seems clear that Justice Marshall miscalculated the likelihood that four of his colleagues would go along with him.[55] In retrospect, his vote to grant cert, a vote cast with the best of intentions, did lasting and comprehensive harm to gay and lesbian rights.

On December 2, 2002, the Supreme Court granted Lawrence and Garner's request for certiorari, including the reconsideration of *Bowers v. Hardwick*.[56] "Now we had this historic thing on our hands," remembered Jenner partner Paul Smith.[57] Gay-rights supporters around the country were ecstatic. The American Civil Liberties Union and the Human Rights Campaign, the country's wealthiest gay-rights group, praised the move. It meant that *Bowers* itself was now on the table. "We had a strong feeling that we would succeed on some issue," recalled Hohengarten.[58] But the fact that the Court agreed to consider the issue anew, as in *Bowers* itself, hardly assured success on the merits. Even the Court's inclusion of the *Bowers* issue did not necessarily mean much because the Court rarely narrows the issues presented by the parties when granting cert.[59]

THE JENNER AND LAMBDA lawyers now had forty-five days to write their brief on the merits of the three questions and to line up *amicus* briefs to be filed by organizations that supported the challenge. To a large extent, the petitioners' fifty-page brief, filed on January 16, 2003, restated the arguments from the cert petition, only in denser, more citation-laden prose. It repeated the overall theme that the Court would be following, not leading, the country if it struck down the Texas sodomy law. It paid considerable attention to the history of discrimination against gay men and lesbians. It spelled out the ways in which the law had changed in response to empirical learning about gay life in America. And it discussed the many reasons why *Bowers* was wrongly decided and should now be overruled.

The brief also continued to highlight the importance of sex to long-term relationships and therefore to the stability of families. Here, the team departed from what it regarded as the apologetic tone of the argument for Michael Hardwick, the defendant in *Bowers*, who had been arrested and charged under a Georgia sodomy law for allegedly having oral sex in his own home. In that case, as the *Lawrence* lawyers viewed it, Hardwick's defenders presented sex as something embarrassing or even shameful that had to be tolerated as the price of living in a libertarian society. Striking down the Texas law was not simply a matter of liberal tolerance. Gay sex was normatively good, both for individualistic and communitarian reasons. But the brief carefully focused on sex as normatively desirable in connection with stability, commitment, and family—not in connection with a broader sexual liberation.

As it had been in the cert petition, the sex in the *Lawrence* brief was "clothed." The brief fully articulated the mainstream presentation the inner team had begun to sketch in the cert petition. "We did not want to give the impression that we were backing away from the subject of sex," affirmed Ruth Harlow, "but we also wanted to clothe it in a phrase that wouldn't just be saying 'anal sex' or 'oral sex.'"[60] Here, the advocates distanced themselves from the actual circumstances in which the police and the defendants played out their drama in September 1998. Words like "intimate" and "intimacy" (used 60 times in the brief) and "relationship" (35 times) replaced references to specific sexual acts. This intimacy was "private" or a matter of "privacy" (70 times) and was connected to "families" or "family" (15 times). Protecting a right to sex was important not because it represented sexual freedom as a form of recreation, or a rebellion against Victorian strictures, or because it was pleasurable, but because it was the kind of thing that mature, responsible adults do when leading mature, responsible lives. As before, there would be no defense of "San Francisco values" here. Paul Smith reconstructed the thought process:

We sat down and we had these lines of cases [dealing with family, procreation, the home, and bodily integrity] and we tried to make our best story out of it. We came down focusing less on sexual acts and more on relationships and families on the theory that that was a more appealing way to talk about these things. . . . So we focused on the family concept a great deal, which obviously resonated with Justice Kennedy.[61]

The *Lawrence* team was making the most conservative argument possible for a constitutional right to sex. Overturning the Texas law would be a vindication of traditional American values—like respect for individual autonomy, privacy, relationships, the home, and families—in a changed world. The petitioners' brief was not the rejection of morality in favor of immorality or even amorality. It was an embrace of neotraditional morality.

There were many critics of the mainstream presentation and the Kennedy opinion it would generate. Some of these critics worried that it gave homosexuals only a freedom to be safe and sanitized. It made them acceptable only to the extent that they adopted traditional (and heterosexual) norms. Sex was a private matter and for persons in relationships. The resulting opinion recognized only a "domesticated liberty," as one post-*Lawrence* academic critic put it, not sexual freedom as intrinsically good.[62]

Whatever the merits of that critique, it never seriously entered the petitioners' brief-writing process in *Lawrence*. The Jenner and Lambda lawyers were trying to get rid of a bad law in a deeply conservative Court, one that was unlikely to base its decision on the need for a new horizon of sexual liberty. Besides, as Smith put it, the mainstream presentation was right as matter of principle. It was not just smart tactics. "We were trying to communicate something about what the real importance of sexuality is in people's lives and that it was the basis of family. We thought that at this point the Justices would understand that relationships are just as important to gay people as they are to straight people."[63]

There were some refinements and other noteworthy omissions in the argument. First, the brief now placed the due process argument ahead of the equal protection claim. This was not so much to emphasize the fundamental-rights argument—the Lambda and Jenner lawyers still believed they were most likely to persuade the Justices on equal protection grounds—but because it was a better way to frame the important personal interests in the case. It was a better way to tell the story. The Court needed to understand *why* the equal protection violation mattered: it involved conduct of an intensely personal and private nature.[64] "We wanted the Court to understand the harms that sodomy laws caused to same-sex relationships," said Harlow.[65]

The fundamental right to "adults' private, consensual sexual choices" was now grounded in three types of liberty interests: intimate relationships, bodily integrity, and the sanctity of the home.[66] The *Lawrence* team knew that the Court's cases involving "bodily integrity"—the right to resist state control of one's body—were "not a perfect fit."[67] There was considerable debate over whether to include them at all. But in the end, the inner team decided that including the argument would emphasize for the Court how profoundly personal the expression of one's sexuality is, as well as how much the Texas law was an affront to personal dignity. The state of Texas was literally exerting control over a person's body through its sodomy law. It needed to have a strong justification for doing so.

The *Lawrence* team decided to avoid reliance on the Court's decision in *Roe v. Wade*, which held that women have a fundamental right to abortion under the Fourteenth Amendment's Due Process Clause. The *Roe* decision was mentioned only five times in the entire brief, and not once in a substantive way. The word "abortion" was never used. The team opted instead to emphasize past decisions involving contraception, like the case establishing the right to marital privacy, *Griswold v. Connecticut*,[68] and the case extending the right to unmarried people, *Eisenstadt v. Baird*.[69] The brief also relied heavily on *Planned Parenthood v. Casey*,[70] a 1992 decision jointly authored by Justices Kennedy, O'Connor, and Souter, in which the Court upheld a right to abortion even as the Justices admitted moral and jurisprudential doubts about abortion rights. The brief described *Casey* only as protecting individual autonomy against state interference, without mentioning a woman's right to choose whether to terminate her pregnancy. Indeed, the one arguable reference to *Casey* as a reproductive-rights decision noted the comparative strength of the state's interest in protecting "the potentiality of human life," in contrast to Texas's weak interest in protecting public morality.[71]

The reason for this reticence about *Roe* was clear. "It has obviously continued to be a very controversial strain of constitutional law," Harlow said, "and if we could avoid getting mired in that, we were happy to do so."[72] The "closeting" of *Roe* was a significant event for a gay-rights brief. For decades, many academics and activists linked abortion to gay rights, both because the linkage illustrated a common theme of individual choice and because the linkage showed solidarity between gay-rights supporters and the women's rights movement. Now, in the most important gay-rights case yet to reach the Supreme Court, the lead attorneys were rhetorically downplaying ties with both sex discrimination as theory and with reproductive choice as practice.

In contrast to some briefs in which lawyers make every conceivable argument, hoping that something will work, the *Lawrence* team omitted also-ran arguments. For example, no serious consideration was given to arguing that the Texas sodomy law inflicted "cruel and unusual punishment" on Lawrence and Garner in violation of the Eighth Amendment. The case involved a mere $200 fine, after all, not the potential twenty years' prison sentence of the Georgia law in *Bowers*.[73] Additionally, the Jenner and Lambda lawyers never seriously considered an argument based on desuetude, a legal doctrine under which a criminal law is held unenforceable because it is rarely enforced. While the Texas law was rarely enforced, and while this fact raised the risks of arbitrary police action, that by itself would have been a "very difficult argument to make," recalled Paul Smith.[74]

The arguments based on sexual-orientation discrimination and sex discrimination, twin pillars of gay-rights legal theory for decades, were reduced to one sentence each and placed in a single footnote.[75] (An argument that the Texas law discriminated on the basis of sex was made in an *amicus* brief filed on behalf of the National Organization for Women.) Since the cert stage, Bill Hohengarten had advocated arguing for heightened judicial scrutiny of discrimination based on sexual orientation. An antigay sodomy law was ready-made for such an argument and the petitioners certainly laid the groundwork by outlining the history of discrimination against gay people, along with the persistence of antigay animus. But after discussions with allies at the Boston-based Gay and Lesbian Advocates and Defenders and the ACLU, even he was finally persuaded that the petitioners were not going to pick up additional votes that way.[76]

Paul Smith remained unapologetic about not making more ambitious constitutional claims. "We thought this was our great chance to get rid of sodomy laws. We weren't worried about establishing a precedent for the eleven other things that came after that," he explained. "You have to take these things one day at a time. The idea that we would actually get rid of *Bowers* seems sort of commonplace now," Smith noted, "but at the time it seemed absolutely enormous."[77] In the end, pursuing the case as a matter of sex discrimination or sexual-orientation discrimination deserving extraordinary judicial action would be asking the Court to lead the country, not to follow it. The country was ready to end sodomy laws, but it was not yet there for the rest of the so-called gay agenda.

The brief ended with a powerful denunciation of the Texas law, melding the due process and equal protection arguments into a unified constitutional theme.

> [The Constitution] is a critical guardian of liberty as well as equality. It defends against unreasonable exactions by the State because it "requires the democratic majority to accept for themselves and their loved ones what they impose on you and me." The Texas Homosexual Conduct Law makes a mockery of that principle. Just as the majority may not decide that the availability of divorce or education is critical for the majority itself but then deny those benefits to a few, so Texas may not determine that freedom from state intrusion into the private sexual intimacy of two consenting adults is an important aspect of liberty for most of its citizens, but then deny that liberty to a minority—particularly a minority historically subject to discrimination. Consensual sexual decisions are too clearly matters for individual decisionmaking, not for imposition by the State. The discriminatory criminal law at issue here seriously diminishes the personal relationships and legal

standing of a distinct class, and under the Fourteenth Amendment cannot stand.[78]

Beyond writing the main petitioners' brief, the challengers needed to coordinate *amicus* briefs—legal arguments from individuals and groups who are not formally parties to the litigation but who have some interest in the outcome. A phalanx of prominent organizations, professors, and law firms volunteered their support as soon as the Court announced it would hear the case. They were virtually begging to be part of the attack on the Texas law. Susan Sommer was put in charge of the *amicus* effort, assisted by attorney Brian Chase.[79] Chase, a moderately conservative young litigator, had just been hired to help open Lambda's new regional office in Dallas.[80] Like the main brief, *amicus* briefs were due on January 16, 2003.

Sommer, the only heterosexual with a significant role among the lawyers attacking the sodomy law, was born in New York City in 1961. She had known Ruth Harlow since they were roommates at Yale, both graduating from law school in 1986. She had come to Lambda in 2000, replacing Suzanne Goldberg. A married woman with three children, Sommer had no gay or lesbian relatives. For her, achieving equality for gay people was a matter of improving the world her children would grow up in. Most of her work before *Lawrence* involved challenges to state sodomy laws, including as the main attorney in the recent successful challenge to the Arkansas statute. Around the Lambda office, she had acquired the nickname "Sodomy Girl." She was now to be "the *Amicus* Queen."[81]

Sommer's job was to fill the holes in the petitioners' arguments. She made sure that potential *amici* understood the main themes and theories of the case. Beyond that, the petitioners needed the *amicus* briefs to accomplish several things. First, they wanted a relatively small group of elite briefs so that each would get read and make some independent contribution. This meant discouraging some enthusiastic supporters who wanted to file briefs. One of these was the New York City Bar Association. "That was definitely a group where we said, 'Don't do your own *amicus* brief,' because saying that lawyers in New York City support getting rid of the Texas sodomy law is not really going to add anything," remembered Harlow.[82] In the end, they held the number to sixteen outside briefs.

Second, each of the *amicus* briefs also needed to make a distinct substantive contribution. The *Lawrence* team wanted briefs fleshing out historians' perspectives on sodomy laws (to correct the misrepresentation of that history in *Bowers*), presenting psychological and medical research on homosexuality and relationships, outlining the views of gay-friendly religious groups, explaining developments in international law, and so on. Even in the fifty pages they were given for their main brief, the petitioners could not fully address all of these matters. To this end, important briefs were filed by the American Psychological Association, the American Public Health Association, several professors of history, and Amnesty International.

Several prominent religious denominations joined one of the *amicus* briefs against the Texas sodomy law, including the Episcopal Church, the United Church of Christ, and a several liberal Baptist organizations. However, two religious groups that had been expected to sign on did not do so. These were the Methodist Church, which had filed an *amicus* brief supporting the claim of a gay scoutmaster in *Boy Scouts v. Dale*,[83] and the Presbyterian Church, which had filed an *amicus* brief opposing the Georgia sodomy law in *Bowers v. Hardwick*. The reason these groups did not sign on to the Texas sodomy challenge cannot be known for sure, but it may be that their earlier gay-rights advocacy had drawn considerable internal dissent.

Third, the *amicus* briefs needed to impress on the Court the real-world impact of sodomy laws. Even many gay-rights supporters regarded sodomy laws as a largely symbolic intrusion since they were rarely used to prosecute anyone for having sex. It was important to show the Court that the very existence of sodomy laws created numerous problems for gay men and lesbians. Several *amicus* briefs helped do that.

Finally, the *Lawrence* team wanted the *amicus* briefs to demonstrate the broad and mainstream political opposition to sodomy laws. The American Bar Association filed an *amicus* brief for the petitioners, a signal to the Court, if it needed one, that support for gay rights was now the default position of the American legal establishment.

Supporting gay rights was also not a radical or leftist political cause anymore. "There was some effort made to have more unusual voices," as Ruth Harlow put it, like right-leaning groups. These included libertarian think tanks (the Institute for Justice and the Cato Institute) and Republicans (the Republican Unity Coalition [RUC] and the Log Cabin Republicans).[84] On the morning of the *Lawrence* oral argument, the *Wall Street Journal* published an op-ed by former senator Alan Simpson, who had cosigned the RUC brief, in which he stated that "[h]omosexuality should be a non-issue inside the GOP. That is, no special preferences, but also no special penalties. No mandatory quotas, no enforced diversity or diversity police; just live-and-let-live. That, in my judgement, is the proper Republican vision of equality."[85]

The op-ed used language inspired by RUC co-chair Charles Francis, a partner in a Washington-based Republican lobbying firm and a longtime friend of the Bush family. In a private letter to Francis, former president Gerald Ford agreed with what he called "gay equality before the law." He supported the challenge to the Texas law and was almost persuaded by Francis to sign the RUC's *amicus* brief. However, Ford decided to lend his name to another case on the Court's docket, one involving the constitutionality of affirmative-action admissions policies at the University of Michigan, and he did not want to dilute the significance of his contribution there.[86]

"Those briefs were important to show just how widespread the feeling was that these kinds of laws crossed the line," said Harlow, referring to the right-leaning *amicus* briefs.[87]

The law firms, lawyers, and law professors preparing the sixteen *amicus* briefs were among the most respected in the country.[88] They were immediately recognizable to the Justices. Some of the authors were former Supreme Court clerks. Notable individual authors included former solicitor general Walter Dellinger and law professors William Eskridge, Pam Karlan, Bill Rubenstein, and Laurence Tribe. This was the legal equivalent of a combined land, sea, and air assault by sophisticated twenty-first-century weaponry on a ramshackle nineteenth-century edifice.

ON JANUARY 16, 2003, with the filing of hundreds of pages of carefully edited and researched briefs, reflecting the learning of scholars and writers at the top of their fields, the legal establishment of the United States landed thunderously on the desk of Bill Delmore. His brief, and any *amicus* briefs supporting Texas, were due February 18. However, despite the immensity and the sophistication of the legal challenge to the Texas sodomy law, Delmore once again made no effort to get outside help for his constitutional arguments. He made no effort to encourage or to coordinate *amicus* briefs supporting the law. He stuck with the original plan to defend the Texas law on grounds of public morality and "protecting families," which he still recognized was a vague phrase.[89]

Delmore continued to handle the due process argument for a fundamental right, while Scott Durfee reworked the state's response on equal protection. Delmore characterized Lawrence and Garner's behavior as "a form of extramarital sexual conduct" that had long been prohibited in the law, along with other forms of such conduct. There could not possibly be a long-standing, "fundamental" right to engage in it.[90]

Rather than describing the issue as whether there is a right to engage in "private consensual sexual intimacy with another adult," as the petitioners described it, Delmore incorporated the caveats in the petitioners' brief. The right would not extend to prostitution, incest, or adultery, for example, because these implicate additional state concerns (beyond mere morality). "In short, the petitioners are asking the Court to recognize a fundamental right of an adult to engage in private, non-commercial, consensual sex with an unrelated, unmarried adult."[91] In a sense, this recharacterization of the right was helpful to the petitioners, who wanted to avoid having the Court view the case as involving a fundamental right to homosexual sodomy or a fundamental right to homosexual oral and anal sex. Elsewhere in the brief, however, Delmore drew on *Bowers* to describe the petitioners' claim as seeking a "right to sodomy" and "a right to engage in homosexual anal intercourse."[92] Delmore quibbled over whether the official record in the case showed that the sex really did involve noncommercial, consensual sex in private between two unmarried, unrelated homosexuals.[93] But this quibbling never gained traction in the Supreme Court.

In response to the notion that changes in American attitudes toward gay people and in American laws governing sexuality over the past few decades had changed the due process analysis, Delmore had a clever response similar to the one Justice Scalia would use in dissent: "The petitioners mistake new growth for deep roots."[94]

Delmore furthermore argued that gay sex had no constitutional value: "The conduct at issue in this case has nothing to do with marriage or conception or parenthood and it is not on a par with these sacred choices. Homosexual sodomy cannot occur within or lead to a marital relationship. It has nothing to do with marriage or children."[95] These claims could have been made in 1986, when they would have gone undisputed except by gay-rights advocates. But Delmore did nothing to rebut the extensive briefing by the petitioners and their *amici*, which showed that there actually were many gay families, that these families were raising large numbers of children, and that sex played a role in gay relationships similar to the one it plays in straight relationships. Delmore's brief was on *Bowers* autopilot.

In the equal protection section of the brief, drafted by Durfee, the state's earlier arguments were mostly repeated. But there were a couple of puzzling additions. The brief stated that *Bowers* "stands alone as the only modern case in which this Court has approved moral tradition as a submitted rational basis for legislation." This was true, and perhaps an example of admirable candor, but it was an odd way to defend the Texas law when *Bowers* itself had been brought into question. In fact, it's a sentence one might have expected to see in the *petitioners'* brief.

Another strange section of the brief argued that Section 21.06 was actually an attempt to *liberalize* the state's sex laws regarding homosexuality. Not only had Texas reduced the punishment for anal and oral sex, but it had allowed "kissing" and "sexual stimulation of another person of the same sex with hands or fingers."[96] The great moral traditions of Texas were offended by homosexual anal and oral sex, in other words, but were unperturbed by homosexual mutual masturbation. Unintentionally or not, the brief served only to highlight the selective nature of the moral defense of the law.

Near the end of the state's brief, Durfee made a novel claim:

[A]lthough the statute is unlikely to deter many individuals with an exclusively homosexual orientation, the Legislature rationally could have concluded that section 21.06 would be effective to some degree in deterring the remaining population (i.e., persons with heterosexual or bisexual orientation) from detrimentally experimenting in homosexual conduct.[97]

This was a concession that the law was unlikely to prevent much of the conduct Texas regarded as immoral. The possibility that the state might prohibit homosexual conduct only as an indirect way to save heterosexuals from unspecified "detriment" showed just how irrelevant gay people were to any concern of the state. They were such a hopeless group that the state did not even bother to save them from the consequences of their own conduct. The state did not simply malign gay men and lesbians in its law. It did not simply neglect their interests, needs, relationships, and families. Even on its own terms, as spelled out in the D.A.'s brief, it *malignly neglected* them.

WHATEVER MALIGNITY COLORED the D.A.'s defense of the sodomy law, however, paled next to the revulsion against homosexuality expressed in the *amicus* briefs supporting Texas. No major private law firm filed an *amicus* brief for Texas. With two obvious exceptions—Jay Alan Sekulow, head of the religious-conservative American Center for Law and Justice, and Robert P. George, a prominent Catholic natural-law academic—few of the authors were well-known to the Court. While the main religious-conservative groups were represented, along with several obscure ones, no organization outside this religious-conservative spectrum supported Texas. "It was remarkable how all the big-name law firms in town [Washington, D.C.] were on our side and nobody was on their side in the end," noted Paul Smith.[98] Antigay argument was no longer acceptable in polite, elite society in Washington, D.C., or among the top law firms in the country. Too many gay attorneys had come out of the closet in major law firms, most of which now had antidiscrimination policies and domestic-partnership benefits. Too many young heterosexual lawyers for whom homosexuality was a nonissue had moved up into positions of authority in these firms. Clients were demanding diversity among the teams of lawyers who worked for them. Every law school, under a mandate of the American Bar Association, banned sexual-orientation discrimination in recruiting and hiring. All of these developments had seeped into law firm culture so thoroughly that defending an antigay sodomy law was virtually unthinkable.[99]

The *amici* supporting Texas, however, inhabited a very different world, characterized by religious devotion and social conservatism. The *amicus* briefs described homosexuality as a dangerous and unnatural maladjustment, a contagious and filthy thing to be discouraged by the state. Several of the briefs claimed that gay men were carriers of HIV who were deliberately infecting the heterosexual population and seeking infection for themselves ("bug chasing," a sensationalistic phenomenon in which uninfected men deliberately had sex with positive partners was mentioned by several of the *amici* supporting Texas),[100] and that they disproportionately suffered anal cancers and "gay bowel syndrome,"[101] a long discredited diagnosis. The states of Alabama, South Carolina, and Utah suggested that homosexual sodomy, unlike heterosexual sodomy, entailed "severe physical, emotional, psychological, and spiritual consequences."[102] Liberty Counsel, an organization founded in 1989 to "restore the culture one case at a time," said gay men were hyperpromiscuous and diseased.[103] Even lesbians faced higher risks of cancer, Hepatitis C, and bacteria vaginosis, it averred.[104]

Liberty Counsel unearthed a satirical piece titled "The Homosexual Manifesto."[105] The Manifesto had originally appeared in the Boston-based *Gay Community News* in 1987 under the pseudonymous byline "Michael Swift.[106] The Manifesto was a send-up of the conspiratorial and hysterical views of homosexuality promoted by groups like Liberty Counsel itself.[107] Liberty Counsel quoted liberally from the piece:

> We shall sodomize your sons, emblems of your feeble masculinity, of your shallow dreams and vulgar lies. We shall seduce them in your schools . . . in your seminaries, in your youth groups, in your movie theater bathrooms . . . in your houses of Congress, wherever men are with men together.

This sexual exploitation and recruitment would be the result of eliminating sodomy laws, as Lawrence and Garner were asking the Court to do. Again, Liberty Counsel quoted the Manifesto:

> All laws banning homosexual activity will be revoked. Instead, legislation shall be passed which engenders love between men. . . .
> There will be no compromises. We are not middle-class weaklings.
> . . . Those who oppose us will be exiled.

Next the homosexuals would come after families and religious traditionalists. "The family unit, which only dampens imagination and curbs free will, must be eliminated," continued the Manifesto, as quoted faithfully by Liberty Counsel. "All churches who condemn us will be closed."

While the brief acknowledged that the manifesto was "satirical," Liberty Counsel claimed that it "is at the same time shocking in its assertions while revealing for its similarities to the political agenda advanced today by homosexual groups." For professional antigay groups, the manifesto was the long-secret "gay agenda"—the Protocols of the Elders of San Francisco.

Another brief claimed that closeted homosexuals, like an unseen army of Manchurian deviants, infiltrated organizations so that they could seize control. "The organization would thus appear to reflect the percentage of homosexuals in the general public," said the brief cosigned by the Traditional Values Coalition (TVC) and others, "yet be entirely in the political control of 'gay' activists."[108]

The *amicus* briefs also contained dire warnings of "slippery slopes." Striking down the Texas sodomy law would mean legalizing, they warned, gay marriage, prostitution, adultery, necrophilia, bestiality, possession of child pornography, incest, and pedophilia.[109] Even fictional towns on TV sitcoms and Saturday morning cartoons would not be safe from the homosexual menace. The Center for Law and Justice International was concerned about the effect a pro-sodomy ruling might have on Mayberry because it would mean that "Aunt Bea has a constitutional right to sexual intimacy with Andy."[110] The Flintstones, too, would be imperiled. Adulterous foursomes would now be constitutionally protected, at least in animation. "[Adultery] laws would arguably 'burden' Fred's and Wilma's constitutional right to intimacy with Barney and Betty, individually or all together.[111]

In the world of the *amici*, then, homosexuals were freakishly promiscuous, conspiratorial, diseased, mentally ill, and a threat to society (and especially children), as well as absorbed by what one brief termed "Dionysian self-interest."[112] The petitioners were insisting on a right "to place their male reproductive organs in the anus of another human being."[113] Sodomy, said the American Center for Law and Justice (founded in 1990 by Reverend Pat Robertson), is "an abusive act, i.e., a misuse of the organs involved."[114] More abstractly, Robert George asserted on behalf of the Family Research Council that it was "impossible for them [two persons of the same sex] to enter into bodily communion."[115] Even if gays could be protected from discrimination at work, "needing a job is different from 'needing' to be sodomized," opined the TVC brief.[116]

These *amicus* briefs replayed, in almost every respect, the campaign to reverse the city of Houston's limited antidiscrimination laws in the fall of 1984. They echoed the hoary arguments long used to justify sodomy laws and other forms of discrimination against gay men and lesbians: they were diseased, sick, contagious, mentally ill, proselytizing, immoral, self-absorbed, sexually compulsive and obsessive, conspiratorial, dangerous to children, and generally a menace to society.

Realizing how far removed the *amicus* briefs were from the actual lives of gay men and lesbians, from the perceptions that an increasing majority of Americans had toward gay people, and from the world the Court had come to know, Lambda greeted each new *amicus* brief almost with delight. These briefs were helping reinforce the charge that the Texas law was based on animus and uninformed bigotry against gay men and lesbians. "Oh goody, another one," Susan Sommer remembered thinking. "Make our day. File another brief."[117] Bill Hohengarten believed that comparing the *amicus* briefs on both sides showed "where the educated America stands."[118]

Bill Delmore, for his part, was embarrassed by many of the *amicus* briefs supporting the state sodomy law. There were a couple of helpful briefs offering scholarly arguments "on why we shouldn't go wild in recognizing substantive due process rights." However, the others were at best a distraction, at worst a detriment to the more careful and limited arguments he was making. He especially disliked "the ones that went off on the medical and psychiatric studies." He also refused to engage in "name-calling arguments" like those found in the *amicus* briefs.[119] They were antigay crusaders. Delmore wanted nothing to do with that crusade.

The *Lawrence* team was ready for the "slippery slope" alarms sounded by Texas and its *amici*. In a Reply Brief filed on March 10, the petitioners dismissed as "chimeras" the coming tide of bestiality, prostitution, incest, adultery, and bigamy. "Comparison of the intimate relations of two human beings—married or unmarried, same-sex or different-sex— with bestiality is simply offensive," they wrote. "Nor do the other kinds of laws in the [litany of dire predictions] involve such a wholesale and devastating burden on individual liberty as here—where *all* same-sex partners are prohibited, for a vast range of intimate acts." In the case of some of the horribles conjured by supporters of the Texas law, a state's constitutional defense might well be stronger.[120] Nor was gay marriage an issue, the petitioners contended. "Petitioners here assert a shield to be free from government interference, not any right to affirmative state recognition or benefits."[121]

The Jenner and Lambda lawyers clarified that the case was not a constitutional referendum on all morality-based justifications for law. States were free to enact laws based on morality. However, they asserted that a discriminatory moral code—i.e., moral condemnation of one group but not another for the very same conduct—merely expresses disapproval or negative attitudes toward the *group* condemned.[122]

This was a bit of an evasion. Morality by its very nature is "discriminatory," and may even be said to discriminate against the "group" that violates it. The Jenner and Lambda lawyers were drawing a very fine line between moral disapproval expressed in law (constitutionally permissible) and impermissible animus covered as moral disapproval (constitutionally impermissible). Justice Kennedy's eventual opinion in *Lawrence* also glossed over this difficulty.

The petitioners' Reply Brief dispensed with the public-health arguments in the *amicus* briefs by attacking the medical and scientific credentials of the religious and advocacy groups making them. It also noted the illogic, as Delmore himself recognized, of prohibiting all same-sex conduct despite the fact that lesbians had lower rates of HIV infection than gay men or heterosexuals. Moreover, the public-health arguments were based on outright falsehoods (like a single lurid article in *Rolling Stone* about "bug chasers") and inaccurate stereotypes and generalizations about gay people. Relying on the public-health professionals among its own *amici*,[123] the petitioners charged that banning same-sex sodomy actually inhibited efforts to protect public health because it forced people into the closet.[124]

The Reply Brief by Jenner and Lambda was the last one before the Court. Now that the briefs were filed, it was time to get ready for oral arguments before the Justices.

15.

Mismatch at the Supreme Court

———

A CHASM OF WORLDVIEW AND APPELLATE EXPERIENCE SEPA-
rated the lawyers who squared off over the constitutionality of
the Texas sodomy law on March 26, 2003. That was no accident. For
each side, the process of choosing the oral advocate mirrored the brief-
writing process. For Lambda, the decision was calculated, methodical,
extensively discussed, a product of consultation, and designed to maxi-
mize the chances of success. For the Harris County D.A.'s office, the process was haphazard, idiosyncratic, insular, and unreflective.

There was no shortage of excellent candidates to argue against the
constitutionality of the Texas sodomy law. One obvious choice would
have been Professor Laurence Tribe of Harvard Law School. Extremely
intelligent and knowledgeable, with a gift for words and remarkable
intellectual agility even by the high standards of appellate advocacy,
Tribe had written the best-known modern treatise on constitutional
law.[1] He was considered a leading authority in the area and had argued
many cases before the Supreme Court.

Tribe's work on *Bowers v. Hardwick* had given him an immediate facil-
ity with the underlying doctrinal controversies. But reviews of his performance in that case were mixed. While gay-rights advocates had been
ebullient immediately after the oral argument,[2] they were ultimately disappointed. Justice Lewis F. Powell Jr., the swing vote in the case, panned
Tribe's "usual overblown rhetoric" but did concede that he had focused
narrowly on the precise issue of state power before the Court.[3] A former

clerk for Justice White, who wrote the opinion upholding the Georgia sodomy law, was even more critical. "Tribe blew his oral argument," opined Andrew Schultz. "He was flailing from the very beginning."[4]

Unlike his successors in the *Lawrence* litigation, Tribe failed to draw attention in his oral argument to the tremendous changes in the country that had already occurred since the early 1960s, like the removal of homosexuality from the list of mental disorders by the American Psychiatric Association in 1973. He also failed to articulate clearly what Powell needed in order to side with Hardwick: "a limiting principle" that would allow states to continue to criminalize incest, bigamy, and bestiality—the very "slippery slope" fears the *Lawrence* team would be so well prepared to swat away.[5]

To be fair, it's not clear that the most silver-tongued orator or dazzling constitutional lawyer could have persuaded the Court to overturn the Georgia law in 1986. It was a little too soon. The Court and its members needed more time and experience with actual, known gay people before they could associate homosexuality with families and appreciate the importance of intimacy for gay couples and individuals.

Tribe approached the *Lawrence* team, asking to handle the oral argument.[6] He believed deeply in the cause. He was obviously experienced. A second chance would allow him some personal redemption. However, gay-rights advocates in the *Lawrence* litigation were not enthusiastic about having Tribe take the baton again. He had not been involved in the case up to that point. A few doubted his ability to take it on and do it well. Much had changed since 1986, both on the Court and in the field of gay-rights advocacy. A new face was needed, they believed, to reflect these profound changes.

Several members of the team, including Ruth Harlow and Bill Hohengarten, thought it was important to have a gay person present the oral argument. This alone was a significant change from 1986. A gay person would embody the very argument being made. He or she would give it a personal dimension and passionate intensity that a sympathetic straight person might not.[7]

There were a couple of obvious candidates who fit this criterion. Bill Hohengarten was one possibility, but he himself quashed that idea immediately. While he was an experienced appellate advocate and had clerked for Justice Souter, he had never argued a case before the Supreme Court. This was *Brown v. Board of Education* for gay rights, which made it both a great opportunity and a terrifying burden. Hohengarten did not want that responsibility at this stage in his career.[8]

Ruth Harlow was also an obvious choice. She knew the case better than anyone else. She had successfully argued it in the Texas Court of Appeals. She had drafted and edited all of the briefs. She was a lesbian. She also worked for Lambda, which had taken ownership of the litigation. But Harlow, too, had never argued before the Supreme Court, and she feared that her profile as a gay-rights activist was too high. "Whether I saw myself as the legal director of Lambda or not, that is how I would have been viewed the moment I opened my mouth," she reflected. She worried that her own passion and single-minded focus, which had brought the case to the Court, would undermine her credibility once there.[9]

It was important for the person to be known to the Court, and preferably for reasons unrelated to gay causes. The person had to walk the fine line between being gay and being *too* gay—that is, being too closely identified with the cause of gay rights. The advocate needed a veneer of objectivity and detachment. The movement had come a long way since 1986, and there were now openly gay advocates who had achieved a certain stature in the legal profession apart from their sexual orientation or gay-rights advocacy.

The person who met all of those requirements was Paul Smith, a tall, red-haired man who exuded confidence, communicated experience, and inspired trust. Born in Salt Lake City in 1955, he was a Presbyterian who had graduated from Amherst in 1976 and had attended Yale Law School, where he was editor-in-chief of the law journal. After graduating in 1979, he clerked for Justice Lewis Powell, a year when Smith was barely conscious of his own homosexuality. He married in the 1980s, got divorced, and finally came out as a gay man in the early 1990s.

After his clerkship, Smith became a litigator in Washington, D.C. He was hired as a partner at Jenner & Block in 1994, where he handled both business litigation and appellate work and became a co-leader of Jenner's Supreme Court practice. From 1986 to 2003, Smith argued eight cases in the Supreme Court, all on behalf of commercial clients, and filed more than one hundred cert petitions or briefs opposing certiorari.

Other than a select group of lawyers at the Justice Department, few attorneys could boast as much experience in the Supreme Court.[10]

Prior to *Lawrence*, Smith did only limited gay-rights work, mostly writing briefs for the American Psychological Association in *Romer v. Evans*, the case challenging Colorado's Amendment 2, and in several lawsuits challenging state sodomy laws. Smith was mostly unknown among gay-rights advocates, a fact that raised eyebrows among some of the external advisers to the *Lawrence* team.[11]

However, Harlow had no doubts about him. "She had to sell it to [Lambda Executive Director] Kevin Cathcart, who was never one of my great friends," Smith remembered, "and for institutional reasons it was difficult for Lambda not to be the face of the case completely."[12] When Harlow offered Smith the argument in January 2003, he immediately accepted.

Under the best circumstances, in an "ordinary" business case, argument before the Supreme Court is daunting. The first time Smith argued a case before the Court he got what he called "psychological laryngitis" for the preceding twenty-four hours. *Lawrence*, however, was no ordinary business case. Even though he would not be a first-timer before the Court in March 2003, the persisting legacy of *Bowers v. Hardwick* would weigh heavily on him. Every word he uttered would be scrutinized.

There would also be an extra personal burden for Smith to stand before the Court and argue against *Bowers*. Ironically, he was just one of a long series of closeted gay men and lesbians who had clerked for Justice Powell in the decade before the *Bowers v. Hardwick* decision. Smith had not come out to Powell during his 1979–80 clerkship. In retrospect, Smith thought it possible that he himself didn't realize he was gay at the time, which might be so given his subsequent marriage. When Powell was considering what to do with the Georgia sodomy law in 1986, he discussed the case with Cabell Chinnis, a gay man who was one of his three clerks that term. A genteel Southerner, Powell told Chinnis that he didn't understand homosexuality and that he had never met a homosexual. Although Chinnis toyed with the idea of coming out to his boss, thinking it might have an effect on Powell's views, he—like Smith and his other gay predecessors—did not reveal his sexual orientation.

As the personal drama of his clerk played out unbeknownst to him,

Powell teetered in the *Bowers* case, now veering toward upholding the law, now ready to strike it down. He had originally voted to strike down the Georgia law, but changed his mind. Years later, he confessed publicly that he had made a mistake.[13] For that reason alone, the decision not to come out to Powell haunted Chinnis and the leaders of the gay-rights movement.[14] As an intellectual and constitutional matter, perhaps, it should not have mattered that Chinnis or any of Powell's former clerks like Paul Smith were gay. But the experience of the gay-rights movement was that coming out mattered a great deal for others people's perceptions of homosexuality. Time after time, polls showed that Americans who said they had relatives, friends, or neighbors who were gay had more favorable opinions about homosexuality and gay-rights issues than those who said they didn't know anyone gay. It became a truism in the gay-rights movement that for straight people familiarity led to greater acceptance.

The sequence of events involving Powell and his vote in *Bowers* was well-known to gay-rights litigants. That Paul Smith was yet another of those former Powell clerks who never revealed his sexual orientation to the Justice added to the pressure he felt as he prepared for the oral argument. It was *his* Justice who had cast the deciding vote in *Bowers*, and now he would be the one to stand before the Court and the country to tell the Justices that *Bowers* had been a historic mistake with terrible consequences. For Smith, Powell was "looming in the background, psychologically."[15] For professional but also for these deeply personal reasons, Smith had to take on the argument.

In early March, there were three formal practice sessions for the *Lawrence* team. In each of these "moots" (as they are known among appellate lawyers), Smith presented the case for Lawrence and Garner before a panel of three or more "judges," lawyers and academics who would try to expose weaknesses and pose difficult questions. One moot, held at Georgetown Law School in front of about forty law students, included Professor David Cole in the role of a skeptical judge. Another, held at Jenner & Block, included Don Verrilli, the firm's co-chair (with Smith) of the Supreme Court practice, and Roy Englert, a conservative gay attorney with a Supreme Court practice.[16] Authors of the *amicus* briefs supporting the petitioners also participated. Before and after the moots, there was extensive discussion of questions that should be expected and the best ways of phrasing responses.

Smith spent the three full weeks before the *Lawrence* argument preparing for it, an extraordinary investment of *pro bono* time by a lawyer at an elite law firm. The day before the argument Smith stayed home and kept entirely to himself, looking through the briefs and relevant cases. "By that time you're sick to death of all the materials, but you can't think of anything else," he recounted. He went to bed early but was wide awake by 3 a.m., his mind racing. "You just pace, you sort of think about the same things over and over again," Smith remembered.[17]

A HALF CONTINENT AWAY, both geographically and experientially, the Harris County D.A.'s office was also preparing for the Supreme Court oral argument.[18] After the D.A.'s briefs were filed, Bill Delmore went to Chuck Rosenthal's office to talk about the case. Rosenthal had approved the outlines of the argument in the D.A.'s briefs but had not read them before the filing. "We've got another decision to make," Delmore told Rosenthal.

"What's that?"

"We need to think about the oral argument." Delmore outlined three possibilities for handling the argument. "One is that Scott [Durfee] or I could do it."

"Yeah, you do it," Rosenthal snapped, without waiting to hear what the other options were.

Delmore persisted. "Okay, but let's talk about the other options because one is that we could get outside help." There were indeed many experienced and able appellate and Supreme Court lawyers and law professors who would argue the case for Texas, if called upon. "There's a group of people who are the go-to guys in the Supreme Court," he informed Rosenthal. "There'd be nothing disgraceful in taking advantage of that and enlisting somebody to do it. And we'd have to talk about who we would want to represent our interests, somebody we trust to not embarrass us or say anything we disagreed with." The latter point seemingly ruled out many of the authors of the *amicus* briefs.

Rosenthal had little patience for extended conversations about any case, but Delmore pressed on. "The third option of course is for you to do it." He paused, trying to gauge Rosenthal's reaction, and then continued. "You're the elected district attorney. It would be your prerogative if you want to do this. It's a pretty big deal, you know. It's basically a historical event." Delmore waited again for some response.

"Okay, well I'll run those past some people and I'll get back to you," Rosenthal replied, abruptly terminating the meeting.

The next day Rosenthal and Delmore were discussing another case over the telephone. Toward the end of the conversation, as Delmore recalled it, Rosenthal casually said, "Oh, by the way, what you were talking about yesterday. I think I'll do that."

Delmore didn't know what he was referring to. "I'm sorry, Chuck. You'll do what?"

"Well, the argument. I'll do the argument."

Rosenthal was indeed an excellent trial court lawyer. With his folksy phrases, deep voice, and rich Texas drawl, combined with his passion for putting offenders behind bars, he connected effectively with jurors in criminal cases. But he had never argued a case in the Supreme Court. Indeed, he had little if any experience in any appellate court, state or federal. His debut as an appellate advocate would be in the Supreme Court of the United States.

"Isn't that amazing?" recalled Delmore, with an expression revealing more disdain than amazement. Rosenthal's lack of appellate experience concerned a great many people on Texas's side in the case, not the least of them Delmore himself, a seasoned appellate lawyer.

After a couple of days, Delmore went back to Rosenthal's office to discuss the oral argument. "Chuck, I'm a little bit worried about your decision to do this," he said, broaching the topic as delicately as he could. He wanted to give Rosenthal a face-saving way to bow out of the argument. "If you're doing this because you feel I'm not sufficiently gung-ho about this case," Delmore continued, referring to teasing he had received around the office and the county's courts that he had conceded too much in the case, "I can do it differently. You tell me to do it differently and I will." Rosenthal replied that he had no problem with Delmore's handling of the case but wouldn't budge on his determination to argue it himself.

So, with no experience of his own in the Supreme Court, Delmore now had the task of preparing another novice in a landmark case. "It's almost like they're speaking their own language" in the Supreme Court, said Delmore. "It'd be like going to France and doing an oral argument in a language you had a couple of months to learn."

Rosenthal's tutorial consisted of two moots at the D.A.'s office and three external moots. A pair of the external moots were held at South Texas College of Law in downtown Houston, with a mix of law professors, authors of the *amicus* briefs, and local judges. The last external moot took place at the Heritage Foundation, a prominent conservative think tank in Washington, D.C, just days before the oral argument. Based on Rosenthal's poor performance at the moots, there was considerable concern about his readiness for the actual argument.

The other part of Rosenthal's preparation was to review two large binders containing highlighted copies of past decisions related to the case. One, prepared by Delmore, addressed due process; the other, put together by Durfee, equal protection.

Delmore correctly surmised that the attorneys for Lawrence and Garner were, as he put it, more "sophisticated" in their preparation. "The courthouse is practically burning down around us on all the other stuff we do. I think we did as much as we could," he observed, laughing. "I mean, five moots on a Class C misdemeanor?" In the end, Delmore spent more time on *Lawrence* than on any case he had ever handled, including capital murder cases. In a role reversal that gay men and lesbians of an earlier era could hardly have imagined, Delmore disclosed that the D.A.'s office had "the feeling we were underdogs" going up against the cream of the nation's legal crop.

THE DAY FOR oral argument in *Lawrence v. Texas*, March 26, was a bright spring morning, with temperatures nearing 70 degrees. The Iraq war had begun one week earlier, consuming most of the attention of the media and the public at large. At the Supreme Court, however, all eyes were on a battle of a different sort, a cultural and legal one with historic implications.

The building housing the Supreme Court is an imposing structure resembling an ancient Greek or Roman temple. Directly across the street is the Capitol. Marble steps lead up to the Court's front entrance, flanked by two seated figures representing Justice and Law. A passerby must look up to see the building, which makes its appearance even more imposing. The words EQUAL JUSTICE UNDER LAW are emblazoned on the pediment.

On the morning of the argument, Ruth Harlow, Pat Logue, Mitchell Katine, and John Lawrence ate breakfast together before heading to the Jenner offices, where Paul Smith had already been for several hours pacing out his argument.[19] The group then traveled the short distance to the Court by taxicab, arriving at about 8:45 a.m. There, they took photographs and greeted some of the hundreds of supporters lined up to witness the event. It was Lawrence's first visit to the Supreme Court.[20]

Everybody connected to the issue on Lawrence and Garner's side wanted to be present, from attorneys representing the parties and the *amici* to law students, law professors, and others who had given a substantial portion of their professional lives to gay-rights issues. The Court has seating for 250 public visitors, but as in every high-profile case many of the seats were reserved ahead of time for guests of the Justices, members of the Supreme Court bar, and the press. Probably no more than 100 seats were available on a first-come, first-served basis to the general public, and people had been in the queue for those all night.

At the front of the line was Lindsay Harrison, the summer associate from Harvard who had written one of the research memos for the cert petition at Jenner.[21] After having driven from Boston with some classmates, Harrison arrived at 9 a.m. the day before the argument, and they inaugurated the line. She and her friends were put in charge of maintaining a list of those who arrived after them. By evening there were more than 100 people waiting, almost all of them supporters of the challenge to the Texas sodomy law. They spent the night in sleeping bags or sitting on blankets or folding chairs; even after registering on Harrison's list, no one was allowed to leave for more than one hour at a time. The mood was festive, upbeat, anxious, and excited. Someone in line with a guitar serenaded the group with folk songs and civil-rights anthems, as if the 1960s had briefly flowered once again in the twenty-first century.

Even before the petitioners arrived, Harrison and her friends had spotted another major figure in the upcoming events. Chief Justice William Rehnquist, a large and commanding man now stooped slightly with age, appeared for his daily walk around the Court building.

Appointed a Justice by Richard Nixon in 1971, and promoted to Chief Justice by President Reagan fifteen years later, he had served longer than anyone else then on the Court. A judicial conservative who favored states' rights against federal power and opposed what he saw as the creation of new constitutional rights, he had dissented in landmark cases like *Roe v. Wade*, but had increasingly been in the majority as he was joined by five Reagan and Bush appointees between 1981 and 1991. Rehnquist voted to uphold Georgia's sodomy law in *Bowers* and was now seen as a likely vote to uphold the Texas sodomy law. He vanished back inside, but he could not have missed the hundreds of people waiting to get in.

Sometime that morning about a dozen antigay protesters led by the seventy-three-year-old Rev. Fred Phelps, the leader of the Westboro Baptist Church in Topeka, Kansas, arrived, accompanied by some young children. The group held up signs referring to the Bible and its condemnation of Sodom, and bearing slogans like "God Hates Fags" and "AIDS Is God's Revenge." Other signs attacked America itself for its excessive tolerance of homosexuality. A young girl held aloft the message "Thank God for Sept. 11."[22] Another sign said, "God Destroyed the Shuttle," referring to the recent crash of the *Columbia* space shuttle. The antigay protesters distributed leaflets warning that the United States would lose the war in Iraq, among other calamities, if the Supreme Court ruled in favor of the so-called sodomites. They stomped on an American flag.[23] Marge Phelps, one of the reverend's daughters, mocked the Supreme Court's opening greeting to courtroom observers. "Oyez! Oyez!" she yelled, "All you having business before this Court draw nigh and bend over."[24]

For the hundreds of gay-rights advocates in line, there was nothing new about any of this. They had long ago habituated themselves to such protesters at gay pride parades and other events. Mostly amused by the Phelps clan, some had their pictures taken beside them, as if posing with circus acts.[25] Their optimism was not going to be spoiled by this preacher and his followers.

But the tourists and others walking by that morning, who had no idea what was happening, were nonplussed. They found the signs and chants of the Westboro contingent offensive. Many passersby let the antigay protesters know exactly what they thought. Just as the Phelps clan began an off-key rendition of "God Hates America" (sung to the tune of "God Bless America"), a group of about fifteen black high school girls in matching uniforms, on a field trip, happened to be walking by. They began reciting "The Pledge of Allegiance" to drown out the anti-American song.[26] It was a spontaneous encounter of pitched intensity few would forget.

By the time the marshal of the Court began letting members of the public through the front door of the Supreme Court building, around 9:30, the list of people waiting to get in had grown to about 400. The line stretched down the entire block in front of the Court. Those too far back in line to get a seat were allowed, following standard Supreme Court practice, to stand at the rear of the courtroom for three minutes to watch the argument. Then they were shuttled out so that the next group could watch.

PAUL SMITH, the unflappable Washington appellate lawyer, and Chuck Rosenthal, the drawling Texas trial attorney, met for the first time in the lawyers' lounge, a small antechamber for oral advocates off of the main courtroom, around nine o'clock that morning. They chitchatted politely with the other lawyers in the room, including Delmore, Harlow, Hohengarten, Logue, and the attorneys representing the parties involved in the other case that was being heard that morning. Lawrence took a seat in the courtroom, waiting. As is customary, the Court's clerk, William Suter, delivered a primer on procedure. He reminded them about who would speak in what order, explained the system of small lights at the lectern that inform the lawyer when his time is almost up, cautioned them not to spill their water, and so on. Following a Court tradition, the clerk asked if anyone needed a button sewn, and then gave the lawyers ceremonial quill pens to mark the occasion. Suter, who knew Smith from previous arguments, joked about how there was nothing big on the Court's agenda that day, nothing of major importance. "He had a sense of history being made, too," recalled Smith. After fifteen minutes in the lawyers' lounge, all the attorneys filed out to take seats in the courtroom.[27]

The courtroom itself is 82 feet by 91 feet, a grand but surprisingly small setting. Sitting in the audience, one is close enough to the Justices to take note of their facial expressions. The windows to the side are dressed in red velvet drapes. The top of the courtroom's walls is lined by friezes representing famous lawgivers and other historical figures, including Hammurabi, Moses, Solomon, Lycurgus, Solon, Confucius, Augustus, Justinian, Muhammad, Charlemagne, William Blackstone, John Marshall, and Napoleon. To some, the decor befits the solemnity and importance of the proceedings. To others, the room is overly fussy or even pompous, looking as if the Justices should enter riding elephants.

At the front of the room the Justices sit behind an elevated, curved bench, each in a high-backed wood chair upholstered in black leather. They peer down upon the lawyers and the spectators. The Chief Justice sits in the middle, presiding over the argument. The Associate Justices flank him on either side, from most senior to least. Attorneys argue behind a lectern positioned directly in front of the chief Justice. The pair of Associate Justices at either end of the bench are at almost ninety degrees from the speaker, just within his or her peripheral vision. The effect is to almost encircle the attorney—undoubtedly, an intimidating experience for the uninitiated. Counsel, up to four lawyers each for the petitioners and respondents, sit at tables positioned on either side of the lectern. Each side gets thirty minutes to make its presentation to the Court.

In the courtroom, the lawyers and audience members nervously waited for the Justices to enter for the first argument. At ten o'clock, the Court's marshal asked everyone to rise. As the Justices entered, he declared, "God save the United States and this honorable Court."

The first case heard that March morning involved a claim that prison inmates had a constitutional right, under the Due Process Clause and under the First Amendment's protection of intimate association, to receive in-person visits.[28] The tone of their questions suggested that the Justices were skeptical of these novel claims, which wasn't an encouraging sign for Lawrence and Garner, to the extent it mattered at all for their case. However, prisoners' rights to associate with others weren't really comparable to the claims of Lawrence and Garner, who lived as adults in free society, not in a jail. Additionally, the state had significant penological interests (not a bare "morality" interest) in maintaining prison security.

When the first argument concluded, the lawyers in the *Lawrence* case took their seats. Rosenthal and Delmore sat at the respondents' table. Smith, Harlow, Hohengarten, and Logue sat at the table for the petitioners' counsel. Smith was keyed up but no longer nervous. Like a kicker about to boot a last-second field goal that could win a game, he was left alone to his own thoughts. He turned back to Mitchell Katine, seated just behind him in the audience, and handed him one of the quill pens he had been given by the Court's clerk.[29] It was a recognition of Katine's role in the early stages of the case and an appreciation of his selflessness in stepping aside to let others take charge.[30]

Susan Sommer, the "Sodomy Girl," sat next to John Lawrence, the convicted sodomite, holding his hand through much of the argument. She had brought a picture of her husband and children as a good luck charm.[31] Lawrence, unrecognizable to most of the audience, was awestruck:

> Have you ever had that magical moment that just said "We're here"? We're going to hear what they have to say. This is the court of the land. And they're listening to a case of some little two guys from Texas that supposedly broke a law that was stupid to be on the books in the first place. You get to hear the justices. You get to see the true court system of the United States at work.[32]

The Court had unalterably changed since it decided *Bowers* in the mid-1980s, not simply in its membership (only Rehnquist, John Paul Stevens, and Sandra Day O'Connor remained from the 1985–86 term) but in its knowledge of gay people. A deep transformation in American culture and politics had brought about a profound shift in the Court's perception of gay men and lesbians. As Smith waited to deliver his argument, someone in the audience whispered in his ear that Justice O'Connor had recently sent a baby present to one of her former clerks and that woman's same-sex partner.[33] It was an encouraging sign, and a mark of how far things had come since 1986, when O'Connor had been among the five Justices to uphold the Georgia sodomy law. The

Justices could pick out many familiar faces: friends, law professors, eminent lawyers, and former clerks, many of them openly gay. Lawrence himself was certain that Justice Ginsburg smiled at him.[34] It was no longer possible to say that the intimate lives of gay men and lesbians had nothing to do with families and relationships, as the Court had facilely asserted in *Bowers v. Hardwick*. However, that fact alone did not guarantee a win.

THE *LAWRENCE* ARGUMENT commenced at 11:09 a.m.[35] Chief Justice Rehnquist, in his authoritative baritone, announced, "We'll hear argument next in No. 02-102, *John Geddes Lawrence and Tyron Garner v. Texas*."[36]

Paul Smith stepped up to the podium, arranged his notes for a moment, and looked down at his prepared remarks. "Mr. Smith?" Rehnquist said, signaling him that he could begin. His first few sentences were carefully scripted. The veteran Supreme Court advocate looked directly at the Justices and began to speak slowly and deliberately, picking up speed as the argument proceeded:

> Mr. Chief Justice, and may it please the Court. The State of Texas in this case claims the right to criminally punish any unmarried adult couple for engaging in any form of consensual sexual intimacy that the State happens to disapprove of. It further claims that there's no constitutional problem raised by a criminal statute that is directed not just at conduct, but at a particular group of people, a law that criminalizes forms of sexual intimacy only for same-sex couples and not for anyone else in the State who has the right to make a free choice to engage in the identical conduct.

Smith quickly previewed the two basic constitutional arguments against the Homosexual Conduct law. Adults, he argued, had the "fundamental right" to "be free from unwarranted State intrusion into their personal decisions about their preferred forms of sexual expression." But even if they did not have such a right, Texas had "no legitimate and rational justification" for treating same-sex couples differently from others. These were the two basic arguments Lambda had been making for more than four years, from the time Lawrence and Garner appeared in the county criminal court.

Ninety seconds into Smith's presentation, the first interruption came. Rehnquist challenged the idea that there was any historical basis for a fundamental right to "the kind of conduct we're talking about here," which "has been banned for a long time." Smith was ready for that objection and corrected Rehnquist's understanding of the history, repeating the argument from the briefs that *Bowers* was wrong: "Sodomy was regulated going back to the Founding for everyone and indeed the laws in the nineteenth century didn't focus on same-sex couples."

Justice Scalia, who had joined the Court just after it decided *Bowers* and was now the intellectual leader of the Court's conservative wing, jumped into the argument. A former law professor, he was also the most active questioner on the Court, capable of finding and exploiting weaknesses in almost any argument. He was a devout Catholic with a judicial philosophy emphasizing judicial restraint, the text of the law, and the original meaning of the Constitution. His opinions, especially dissents, featured lucid, pungent prose. He was, in short, the most intimidating figure on the Court.

Scalia pointed out that whatever else the law had prohibited, it did not permit gay sex. That proved there could be no historical right to such conduct. "What more do you need than that?"

But Smith pointed out that if the long history of sodomy laws was enough to justify the Texas law, it would also be enough to justify banning such conduct by *married couples*, who were also covered by the old sodomy laws. Yet, Smith noted, Texas had conceded that the state could not outlaw marital sodomy.

"They [Texas] conceded it. I haven't conceded it," retorted Scalia, generating an audible disquiet in the courtroom. Scalia was implicitly suggesting that even *Griswold v. Connecticut*, which protected a married couple's right to privacy, a case that was a canonical precedent in modern constitutional jurisprudence, might have been wrongly decided. Such a position would put him at the extreme margins of even conservative judicial thought, which had grudgingly accepted *Griwsold*.

"Your Honor," Smith replied, catching the radical implication in Scalia's question, "that may well be true" but "I was working with the assumption that there may be Justices of the view that married couples do have such a right." Of course, Smith was speaking of seven out of the nine Justices, all except Scalia and Justice Clarence Thomas, who surely would not reject a right to privacy protecting married couples, notwithstanding antediluvian sodomy laws. It was a very polite way of letting Justice Scalia know that the petitioners were not counting on his vote. The next question, suggested Smith, was whether the right to adult sexual intimacy extended *beyond* married couples to include unmarried people. And that issue, he noted, had been decided in *Eisenstadt v. Baird.*

Even when sodomy laws were on the books in all fifty states, Smith remarked, the laws were unenforced except in cases involving minors and rape. However, this was an essentially negative argument by itself. For the Court to recognize a right as fundamental, it needed to understand the right not merely as a negative (the absence of state repression in the form of mass arrests), but as an affirmative (the presence of actual societal respect for the right). Smith smoothly translated the lack of enforcement of sodomy laws from a negative into an affirmative tradition of protection. "So you really have a tradition of respect for the privacy of couples in their home, going back to the Founding. And I think then what began to happen in 1960 was a recognition that we should take that tradition and turn it into positive law on the books" by actually repealing sodomy laws. This trend was "a recognition that it's not consistent with our basic American values about the relationship between the individual and the State."

Smith's invocation of the nation's values provoked Justice Scalia, whose understanding of the the term was grounded in traditional morals and long-standing practices. To undermine Smith's reliance on sodomy-law decriminalization, Scalia now raised what may be the most notorious analogy ever used in a Supreme Court oral argument.

"Well, it depends on what you mean by 'our basic American values,'" he began, in a tone almost mocking Smith's interpretation of such values. "I mean, suppose all the States had laws against flagpole-sitting. At one time, you know, there was a time when it was a popular thing and probably annoyed a lot of communities, and then almost all of them repealed those laws. Does that make flagpole-sitting a fundamental right?"

Audience members stirred again, exchanging astonished looks and a few nervous giggles. Was Justice Scalia really talking about sitting on flagpoles in a case about anal sex? Some observers would later say that Scalia's analogy was an unintentional, subconscious, Freudian moment. "It was just beyond analysis," Harlow maintained, not a deliberately chosen allusion to anal sex. It showed "just how far from reality he may be at times." He "thinks so rigidly about logic, right answers, and so it was bizarre."[37] Others thought the double meaning was intentional, an instance of Scalia's intellectual playfulness, a clever joke and perhaps an attempt to throw Smith off his game. It was not the first time Scalia had used phallic imagery in a sexually charged context. For instance, in a case challenging a ban on public nudity on free-speech grounds, Scalia had asserted the law was constitutional under the First Amendment because it would apply equally to "unclothed purveyors of hot dogs and machine tools."[38]

Whether a self-consciously sexual joke or not, Scalia's reference to flagpole-sitting was certainly calculated to belittle the importance of sexual expression in gay people's lives by comparing it to a passing fad, like playing with hula hoops, donning bell-bottom jeans, or decorating with lava lamps.

Justice Scalia's analogy also subtly denigrated the constitutional challenge by conjuring an image of a graphic sexual act. Justice Scalia himself never referred to the matter at hand as "anal sex," preferring to call it "that conduct" in a way that seemed to indicate his own discomfort. His analogy was "a way of reminding everyone we're talking about fucking, about one guy sitting on another guy's flagpole, not 'liberty' and not 'intimacy,'" observed Lindsay Harrison.[39] It implicitly took the *Lawrence* case back to the Lawrence bedroom.

Smith caught the double meaning in Scalia's question but did not smile or otherwise visually react to it, even as the audience behind him did. "I just played it straight, so to speak," he recalled.[40] Not missing a beat, he responded to Scalia with noticeable exasperation. "No, Your Honor. But the Court's decisions don't look just at history, they look at the function that a particular claimed freedom plays in the lives of real people. That's why contraception became an issue. That's why abortion became an issue." It was a rare reference to abortion in the oral argument.

Smith explained that sexual intimacy was connected to personal autonomy, relationships, and even the moral upbringing of one's children. "It's about basic questions of what kind of a family you're going to live with and other intimate associations," Smith averred, drawing a connection between sodomy and family that the Court had explicitly rejected seventeen years before. Unlike their predecessors a generation ago, however, not even the Court's conservatives challenged the idea that gay people were a part of something that could properly be called families.

Instead, Justice Scalia returned to the idea that a fundamental right had somehow been created by a lack of sodomy-law enforcement. "It seems to me what you would need is evidence that when the police discovered this matter, they said, 'oh, well, these are not laws that we enforce.' I don't see any evidence of that sort." In fact, if the Harris County D.A.'s office can be believed, very few police in Harris County would have enforced the law in most instances where they saw someone engaged in homosexual conduct.[41] The examples Scalia said Smith needed were no doubt legion, but were not something law enforcement authorities could be expected to divulge in court filings. There was no "evidence" for Smith to cite that would satisfy Scalia's burden of proof.

Instead, Smith had prepared for Scalia's objection with a different answer. If police were serious about stopping private sodomy, they could treat it like drug use in the home, a matter that had certainly been the subject of active investigation and prosecution. The fact that police did not treat sex in the home that way suggested that they had absorbed an uncodified tradition of letting adults make their own decisions about whom to have sex with.

Smith was now eleven minutes into his presentation. He had not once been shaken or presented with an unexpected argument from the Court. In fact, only the Court's confirmed skeptics, Scalia and Rehnquist, had asked him anything. Justice Clarence Thomas, another likely vote against Lawrence and Garner, rarely asked any questions at oral argument. Smith had not needed the help of the Court's liberal Justices. He was handling the master inquisitor, Justice Scalia, all on his own.

Speaking more quickly and urgently than before, he was not nervous but still had much to say in the rest of his half hour. Shifting deftly to the equal protection argument, he reiterated the view that the Texas law impermissibly discriminated against same-sex couples.

Justice O'Connor, who was widely regarded as one of the two swing votes on the Court, asked in her flat Arizona accent, "What about a statute that covered both [homosexual and heterosexual intercourse]?" O'Connor, the first woman appointed to the Supreme Court, was now seen as a moderate conservative; she often focused on the specific facts of cases rather than on sweeping theories of constitutional law. The only former legislator on a Court full of judges, professors, and lawyers, she was pragmatic rather than dogmatic.

During her fifth term on the Court, O'Connor had voted with four conservatives to uphold the Georgia sodomy law, which had equally applied to opposite-sex and same-sex sodomy. But since then, she had also voted to reaffirm the right to abortion in *Planned Parenthood v. Casey*. Even more important, in 1996 she voted in *Romer v. Evans* to strike down Colorado's Amendment 2, which had stripped gays of all civil rights protections. These votes and others upset judicial conservatives, who found her unreliable and erratic.

Smith answered that a law banning both heterosexual and homosexual sodomy would be unconstitutional under his first argument because it would intrude on all adults' right to sexual intimacy. "Right," replied O'Connor. That was the argument she had voted to reject in *Bowers*.

Justice Anthony Kennedy now spoke up for the first time. Like O'Connor, Kennedy had been appointed by President Reagan, in 1988. But Kennedy was nominated only after the far more consistently conservative Robert Bork had been rejected by the Senate. If Bork had taken the seat instead of Kennedy, he would almost certainly have voted to uphold the Texas sodomy law. More conservative than O'Connor, Kennedy had nonetheless voted with her to reaffirm *Roe v. Wade* in *Planned Parenthood v. Casey*. He was also the author of the majority opinion in *Romer*, a fact that gave great hope to the *Lawrence* team because it meant they had a chance at getting six Justices to strike down antigay discrimination.

The full concentration of court observers fixed on Kennedy, whose vote everyone knew might determine the outcome. Kennedy sought a clarification about the relationship between the equal protection and due process arguments, referring back to O'Connor's question. "If the statute covered both [heterosexual and homosexual sodomy], would there be an equal protection argument?" It was to be his only question during Smith's presentation and left maddening uncertainty about his ultimate vote.

Smith responded that there would be an equal protection problem with a general sodomy law if *in practice* the state enforced the law only against same-sex couples. The problem, as Smith defined it, was that the Texas law was a classification of *people*—and a minority to boot—not simply a classification of *conduct*. This got at the root problem of the Texas sodomy law because its effect was to stigmatize an entire group associated with a criminal behavior, no matter how responsible they were as citizens.

Justice Scalia asked whether Smith's argument might lead to the invalidation of rape laws, which he said classically "requires the penetration of the female sex organ," but did not include homosexual rape. This was the one question of the day Smith had not anticipated and, he later acknowledged, he fumbled the answer.[42] The state would have to justify such an omission, he answered. It might think that homosexual rape was "not a problem that needs to be addressed" or that homosexual-rape victims are "more able to protect themselves" than women being raped by men. Smith might have instead challenged the very premise of Scalia's question by noting that all forcible sex, homosexual or heterosexual, would violate general state laws against sexual assault.

But, continued Scalia, couldn't the state declare that it regarded the same conduct when performed by some people as "more . . . more . . . more . . ."—he sputtered, searching for a word—"more odious"?

This was another argument for which Smith had prepared. It was made in the D.A.'s briefs as a way to distinguish heterosexual sodomy from homosexual sodomy. Heterosexual sodomy might be bad (state law called it "deviate sexual intercourse," after all), the D.A. argued, but homosexual sodomy was worse (state law called it "deviate sexual intercourse" *and* slapped on a criminal fine). A majority should not be able to give itself full freedom to engage in certain conduct but prohibit it to a minority for no better reason than, as Smith characterized it, "we want it that way."

That characterization of the state interest in defending morality clearly irked Justice Scalia. "I mean you can put it that way, but society always . . . in a lot of its laws makes these moral judgments. You can make it sound very puritanical, the . . . you know, the laws . . . the laws against bigamy, I mean, who are you to tell me that I can't have more than one wife, you blue-nose bigot?"

Smith was now responding in rapid-fire style. He distinguished laws against bigamy as involving marriage, which is created by the state itself. Smith was reassuring the Court that a ruling for Lawrence and Garner would not necessarily undermine the existing understanding of marriage.

Justice O'Connor jumped back in. With audience members straining to squeeze meaning from her every word, she asked, "Well, in order to win under an equal protection argument, do you have to apply some sort of heightened scrutiny?" Smith reassured her that no heightened scrutiny would be needed. The Court would not have to declare gay people were a special, protected class. The Texas law as written was irrational because it was based on no more than "distaste" or "disapproval."

That was the last colloquy with Justice O'Connor in the oral argument. It gave little hint about how she would vote, although it did suggest she was looking for the narrowest possible way to reject the Texas law and was leaning toward an equal protection holding. Ruth Harlow, among others, was disappointed in O'Connor's focus on equal protection because it signaled there had been little "evolution" in her thinking about fundamental rights since her vote to uphold sodomy laws in 1986. Smith concluded only that she had been noncommittal in her questions.[43]

The problem was that if "morality" was a good enough reason to deny homosexuals a fundamental right to have sex, as Justice O'Connor agreed in *Bowers*, then the same morality might be good enough to make gay sex alone a crime. Justice Scalia saw the potential significance of O'Connor's question. For Lawrence and Garner to prevail even on their equal protection argument, the Court would have to overrule *Bowers* on the morality issue, Scalia said. The clear but unstated implication was that Justice O'Connor would have to publicly admit her error in *Bowers* if she were to vote against the Texas sodomy law. She could not get around such an embarrassment simply by pretending she was deciding a different constitutional question. Whether equal protection or due process was the basis for the attack, the morality defense was the same.

Smith wanted to salvage O'Connor's vote, to allow her to save face while voting for his clients. The Court knew "the reality of what the world is like," he said, appealing to O'Connor's pragmatism in contrast to Scalia's theorizing. Reminding the Court of *Romer v. Evans*, he noted that "some line-drawing can be very harmful." While the Texas law dealt only with sex, it had "collateral effects," including loss of gay parents' right to visit their children, denial of custody, and loss of public and private employment.

The mention of children prompted a potentially momentous question from Rehnquist. "If you prevail, Mr. Smith, and this law is struck down, do you think that would also mean that a State could not prefer heterosexuals to homosexuals to teach kindergarten?"

This was dangerous territory for gay-rights advocates. In all of their preparations, the attorneys for Lawrence and Garner anticipated questions about the effects of sodomy legalization on children, but not this precise question about gay teachers.[44] It was the second and last point in the argument at which Smith seemed to stumble.

Smith had a difficult split-second decision to make. He knew that the subject of homosexuals teaching kids was a volatile one, since it raised all of the recruitment and molestation concerns that had always lurked in the background in discussions of antigay public policy. Recall, for example, the pamphlet distributed during the Houston antidiscrimination referendum in 1985 that had featured a young girl cowering in a corner as a shadowy figure wielding a hatchet closed in on her. Smith did not want to scare the Court, or get into complicated questions of whether sexual orientation is genetic or developed, chosen or unchosen, fixed or immutable. At the same time, he did not want to concede that a state could ban gay teachers or lend legitimacy to the underlying homophobia implicit in such a ban. The careers of gay teachers had been ended and their lives ruined by irrational fears. "So the question is, do I take this on?" he pondered as he prepared to answer. "Or do I just let it go and stick on the topic? And what will people say later on about what choice I had made?"[45] There was not much time to think; an answer would be expected immediately and any hesitation might signal weakness in his case.

Smith cleared his throat. "I think the issue of . . . of preference in the educational context would involve very different, uh, uh, criteria, Your Honor, very different considerations," he began. "The State would have to come in with some sort of a justification."

Scalia saw an opening. "A justification [for a state law preferring heterosexuals in teaching] is the same that's alluded to here, disapproval of homosexuality."

Under Lambda's approach to *Lawrence*, mere "disapproval of homosexuality" translated into unreasoned prejudice against a minority, an impermissible governmental objective. Smith invoked that idea, calling such a justification "highly, highly problematic." The government would need to show a "more concrete harm to the children in the school."

Scalia answered that the concrete harm of allowing gay people to teach schoolchildren was that "the children might . . . might be induced to"—again, he seemed hesitant to say what was really on his mind—"to follow the path of homosexuality."

Some spectators in the courtroom groaned and shifted in their seats. What would their advocate say about this long-standing recruitment canard, with its implicit homophobia? "Here I am representing the [gay] community," Smith remembered. "There are probably 100,000 gay kindergarten teachers out there and the idea that having a gay teacher is going to turn a lot of people gay in kindergarten is remarkably ignorant." Smith no doubt shared the courtroom's disdain, frustration, and even anger at Justice Scalia's line of questioning. But as a professional advocate who owed the Court and the occasion a high degree of decorum and respect, he had to restrain himself regardless of his personal feelings. He could not call a sitting Supreme Court Justice ignorant. He could have explicitly said that banning gay schoolteachers was simply irrational and that there was no justification for it. But he did not want to risk getting mired in a fight about sexual-orientation discrimination in teacher hiring. "I could have got myself in trouble" in the oral argument.[46]

Smith confronted Scalia's gay-conversion fears, but quickly shifted back to his underlying criticism of the group hostility reflected in state law. "I think the State has to have a greater justification for its discrimination than, 'we prefer pushing people towards heterosexuality.'" That was just another way of saying "we don't like you." It was a frank assertion that heterosexuality enjoyed no special status in constitutional law and that state attempts to establish it as preferred were also unconstitutional unless the state had some reason other than a bare desire for the preference itself.

Justice Ruth Bader Ginsburg, her careful locution delivered in a New York accent familiar to court observers, asked Smith to make the straightforward case for overruling *Bowers*. The diminutive Ginsburg was the first Jewish woman appointed to the Court, by President Bill Clinton in 1993. Decades earlier, she had been turned down as a law clerk to Justice Felix Frankfurter, despite her Harvard credentials, because she was a woman. Notwithstanding this setback, she built a distinguished legal career advocating for women's equality, teaching law school, and judging. She and Justice Scalia were good friends, even though the two were far apart in their politics and judicial philosophies.

Smith summarized the arguments for overruling *Bowers* as they had been laid out in the briefs. His argument was now moving with freight-train intensity. He passionately declared that the *Bowers* court had misunderstood "the realities of gay lives and gay relationships." As the Justices looked upon a courtroom full of gay people they personally knew, including Smith himself, he implicitly invoked their very presence, drawing inspiration and strength from them:

> I submit it has to be apparent to the Court now that there are gay families; that family relationships are established; that there are hundreds of thousands of people registered in the Census who have formed gay families, gay partnerships; many of them raising children; and that for those people, the opportunity to engage in sexual expression as they will in the privacy of their own homes performs much the same function that it does in the marital context; that you can't protect one without the other; that it doesn't

make sense to draw a line there and that you should protect it for everyone; that this is a fundamental matter of American values.

Smith's words were the culmination of decades of legal and political struggle. They were all the more resonant because they connected homosexuals' search for love and companionship to national ideals found in the constitutional commitment to "liberty" and "equal protection," underscoring the words of the Declaration of Independence that "all men are created equal." Furthermore, they connected gay sex to relationships, families, and children. These were all "American values."

Smith was determined not to let the oral argument degenerate, as he believed it had in *Bowers*, into a discussion of whether and where the state must permit what some people thought was a "disgusting" activity to take place. In a hotel room? in a mobile home? in a public restroom? Locational privacy—the privacy of the home itself—was important; but it was not the main issue.[47] Smith articulated the substantive idea that sexual intimacy among gay Americans was a *good* thing, not merely a *tolerable* thing.[48] Focusing on liberal toleration and locational privacy, as Laurence Tribe did in 1986, may have been the best strategy at the time. However, for the *Lawrence* team, Smith asserted, "it was not the way we wanted to talk about it in 2003."[49]

There was a limit on how far the attorneys for Lawrence and Garner would go in affirming the normative value of gay relationships. Smith had suggested that gay relationships and families were "much the same" as marriages but, he later insisted, they were not trying to set up a constitutional argument for gay marriage.[50] Harlow agreed, maintaining that the references to marriage were "definitely not intended to plant the seed for future marriage litigation."[51] That would disquiet the Court, or at least Justices O'Connor and Kennedy, who had to be persuaded to take the incremental step of invalidating the Texas law. Arguing for same-sex marriage would be asking the Court to lead the nation, not follow it. Getting rid of an anachronistic sex law would be following the nation, not leading it. That was the essential theme of the case, and the arguments needed to support that theme.

In the oral argument, Smith returned to this "following, not leading" narrative. While it had decided to protect rights to contraception and even abortion, he remarked, the Court had left an odd silence in its jurisprudence by not flatly declaring that adults had a right to private sexual intimacy. "And I submit to you, while the Court has left that unanswered, the American people have moved on to the point where that right is taken for granted for everyone," Smith averred, improvising the phrase about Americans having "moved on."[52] "Most Americans would be shocked to find out that their decision to engage in sexual intimacy with another person in their own home might lead to a knock on the door, as occurred here, and a criminal prosecution."

Scalia tilted one last time at Smith's argument. Were adultery laws also unconstitutional? Could a state prefer heterosexual and marital sex over homosexual sex?

Smith used this question as an opportunity to respond to the expected "slippery slope" arguments. As for things like adultery, incest, prostitution, and bestiality, the balance of state interests in regulation on the one hand and personal interests in liberty on the other would be different than for the Texas law. "Either there's very little individual interest [in engaging in the other acts], or there's very heightened state interest [in regulating them], or both, in all of those cases."

Having used twenty-six of his allotted thirty minutes, Smith saved his remaining time for rebuttal. A monsoon of words and arguments, drawing from a lifetime of personal and professional experience, had just washed over the Court. Delmore thought Smith did an excellent job but that he had talked too fast, which "detracts a little bit from the force of the individual thought."[53] As Smith resumed his seat, he appeared satisfied with his performance. Harlow, impressed by his effort and relieved that no great concession had been wrangled from him, passed Smith a note: "Good job!"[54]

CHUCK ROSENTHAL WAS looking up at a mountain of obstacles. He had the precedent of *Bowers* on his side, but it had been battered in briefs and in a barrage of sophisticated arguments about language, society, and history. He had three certain votes on his side (Scalia, Rehnquist, and Thomas), but four certain votes against him (Stevens, Ginsburg, David Souter, and Stephen Breyer); the other two might be winnable but were drifting to the other side (O'Connor and Kennedy). He had a moral argument on his side, but it was a peculiarly selective morality.

What he did not have on his side was experience or appellate polish. He also did not have a command of constitutional law, or as it turned out, even a deep understanding of his own state's laws. He was arguing that Texas should be able to criminalize something that most people, not just inside the courtroom but in the country, believed was none of the state's business.

The Chief Justice looked at Rosenthal and, in his authoritative baritone, announced flatly, "Mr. Rosenthal, we'll hear from you." Rosenthal, who had injured his foot and was in a brace, limped up to the podium. As he approached, he noticed a watch on the floor beside the lectern. He looked at Rehnquist, who was waiting for him to begin, and said, "Excuse me just a moment." Seconds ticked away. Bending over to pick up the watch, he said, "Mr. Marshal?" and offered it to the Court's security personnel. They had no idea what he was talking about.

Rosenthal then turned around toward Smith and, extending the watch, asked, "Is this yours?" Smith shook his head. Rosenthal wheeled around to face the audience, still holding up the watch. "Somebody want this watch?" he asked. Tall and handsome in a weathered way, Rosenthal had the look of a courtly gentleman who seemed totally lost and confused. Nobody claimed the errant watch. Thirty seconds had passed since Rehnquist had asked him to begin, an eternity in a Supreme Court oral argument when the Justices have fixed their gaze upon an attorney.

It was an inauspicious but richly symbolic beginning to the defense of the state sodomy law in the Supreme Court. Texas appeared to be fumbling around. The time allotted for its defense was ticking away on an abandoned watch. There were no takers. Just a bemused silence greeted the state.

Rosenthal turned to face the Justices again. He laid the watch beside the podium, and oriented himself toward Rehnquist. In his rich and deep lilt, a bit garbled but soothing and authoritative, perfect for addressing a Texas jury, he began at last. "Mr. Chief Justice, and may it please the Court," he said, pausing briefly. He resumed, a hint of anxiety in his voice:

> The State humbly submits that enforcement of Texas Penal Code Statute 21.06 does not violate the Fourteenth Amendment of the Constitution because this Court has never recognized a fundamental right to engage in extramarital sexual conduct and because there is a rational basis for the statute sufficient to withstand equal protection scrutiny.

Rosenthal was reading from a prepared text, a practice the Justices dislike. He had not even bothered to memorize his opening remarks, which experienced members of the Supreme Court bar recommend for a first-time advocate. These were the kinds of mistakes that a veteran Supreme Court advocate, or at least a well-prepared one, would never make. Rosenthal continued with the idea that the Constitution nowhere mentioned "privacy" or "sexual conduct." Any constitutional protection that went beyond the words of the Constitution needed some basis in the Court's own decisions or "the history of our people."

Trying to sound like a constitutional scholar, he continued. "The Court has maintained that designation of a liberty interest is done"—he corrected himself—"*not* done with impunity." The word "impunity" was out of place. Perhaps he meant "imprecision," which would have been a forgivable error if he were speaking extemporaneously rather than from a script the state had months to prepare. "But only those interests that appear to be carefully identified asserted rights should be drawn and should be considered as liberty interests," he said, apparently relying on the Court's decision in *Washington v. Glucksberg*, which Justice Kennedy had joined.

Then the confusion began, as Rosenthal tried to quibble over the facts of the case. "The record in this case does not particularly show which rights the petitioners are asking to uphold," he asserted.

Justice Scalia interrupted, a quizzical look on his face. "I don't understand what you mean by that. Aren't we clear what right they're seeking to uphold?" Scalia certainly did not agree with the petitioners, but he was clear about what he thought they were asking for: a right to engage in homosexual sodomy. It was not good news for Texas that its single most important ally on the Court was dissatisfied.

"But there's nothing in the record to indicate that these people are homosexuals," Rosenthal replied, pressing Texas's vain argument that there was nothing in the record establishing that the conduct was private, consensual, and noncommercial. The Justices looked at him "like he was crazy," Smith remembered.[55]

One homosexual act does not necessarily mean a person is homosexual, the D.A. explained. "It's our position that a heterosexual person can also violate this code if they commit an act of 'deviate sexual intercourse' with another of the same sex." Sitting in the press section, National Public Radio's Nina Totenberg, a longtime Supreme Court reporter, dropped her head into her notes, as if she thought Rosenthal was hopeless.[56]

Scalia scowled at Rosenthal. The petitioners, he noted, were arguing that either heterosexuals or homosexuals should have a right to commit homosexual acts.

The Court was expecting to hear Rosenthal argue the fundamental-right issue, not the equal protection issue, but the Texas D.A. was jumbling the two. He should have clarified that and explained that gay people as a group were not isolated, despite what Smith had argued. Instead, Rosenthal offered that the lack of evidence about the petitioners' sexual orientation meant the Court could not give them "a specific form of relief."

This made no sense because the requested "relief"—what the petitioners wanted the Court to do—was clear. They wanted their convictions reversed and wanted the Court to declare the Texas law unconstitutional. Whether they were gay or bisexual or heterosexuals experimenting with gay sex made no difference in the remedy they sought. Justices Ginsburg and Souter pointed that out. At last Rosenthal made the distinction between status and conduct, arguing that the law did not criminalize people based on their sexual orientation, but his argument was already sinking.

Justice Kennedy entered the fray. He had a halting, stuttering manner of speaking, like a person trying not to give away his views or commit himself prematurely to a position. He hedged and qualified almost every statement. He also spoke with a nervous speed, clipping off the end of words in a rush to get to the next thought. The effect could be confusing, even for practiced oral advocates. "Well, I . . . I can see that your point may have some relevance on the equal protection side of the equa-

tion," Kennedy began, referring to Rosenthal's status/conduct distinction. "Some relevance. I don't think it may be control—It . . . it doesn't
seem to meet the argument that's made under the, um, the substantive
liberty part, of, of the argument with reference to *Bowers*."

Rosenthal asked "I beg your pardon?"

Kennedy clarified that Rosenthal wasn't addressing the argument
that *Bowers* should be overruled. Rosenthal replied that the state believed
Bowers was "good law" and should indeed not be overruled. "But that
question is certainly clearly before us," Kennedy observed. "I mean this
is your statute. You convicted the people for these acts and you have to
be . . . you have to defend it." This was the last thing Kennedy said during
the oral argument. It gave the *Lawrence* team and gay-rights advocates
in the courtroom some hope that he was seriously considering the reversal of *Bowers*.

Rosenthal tried to explain why *Bowers* should be upheld. Nothing in
the history or traditions of the United States had changed, he said.
"Physical homosexual intimacy" was not part "of the fabric of American values." The fact that various states had decriminalized sodomy did
not mean that "extramarital sexual relations" were constitutionally
protected.

Scalia was again perplexed. "I'm sorry," he interrupted. "The argument [for the petitioners] is [that] tradition doesn't matter." Was Rosenthal saying that public attitudes toward homosexuals had changed or
not? "Do you think there's public approval of it?"

"Of homosexuals, but not of homosexual activity," Rosenthal replied.
He did not seem to understand that Scalia was trying to help him, something Justices frequently do at oral argument when they believe their
own views are not being adequately defended.

"What do you base that on?"

Rosenthal was getting confused again. "I beg your pardon?"

"What do you base that on?" repeated Scalia, growing more frustrated by the moment. "There ought to be some evidence which you can
bring forward" to show that homosexuality was still disfavored by the
American people. If Rosenthal wasn't knowledgeable enough to make
the argument, Scalia would start making it for him. He observed that
Congress had refused to protect "sexual preference" as a protected class

alongside race, sex, and other personal characteristics. By describing homosexuality as a "preference" rather than an "orientation," Scalia was hinting that he did not believe it was a matter beyond individual control. Just because the states had not rigorously prosecuted sodomy did not mean they approved of it, he added. It was a different way of making the point about flagpole-sitting.

"Well, certainly," Rosenthal agreed meekly, adding that "just because someone has decriminalized sodomy doesn't mean that they embraced that practice as something that ought to be taught in the schools, as was mentioned before." Once again, children were props in a decidedly adult sodomy-law drama.

Justice Breyer, who was presumed to be sympathetic to Lawrence and Garner, had lost all patience with Rosenthal. His face long and sunken, Breyer generally spoke even more quickly than Kennedy, employing a more steady stream of words, arguments, and verbalized parentheticals. More than any other Justice, he had the habit of introducing strange, otherworldly hypotheticals. He could be very hard to follow in an oral argument.

Breyer wanted Rosenthal to respond directly to Smith's arguments about why *Bowers* should be overruled. He summarized the petitioners' arguments, highlighting the danger that even if people were not actually prosecuted, "they fear they might be, which makes it a possible instrument of repression in the hands of the prosecutors." This last point touched on the background facts of the arrests on September 17, 1998, in a way that Breyer intuited but could not have fully appreciated. "Now, that's the kind of argument that they're making [to overrule *Bowers*]. Harmful in consequence, wrong in theory, understating the constitutional value. All right—now how do you respond to that?" Breyer finally asked.

When Rosenthal began his response with a detour into the level of misdemeanor for sodomy in Texas, Breyer cut him off. "I would like to hear your . . . your straight answer to those points."

The savvy audience immediately caught the inadvertent double entendre in "straight answer" and erupted in laughter. Nothing was getting by them. Every nuance and allusion in every question was drawing their rapt attention. It was as close as one could get in the august confines of the Supreme Court to the combination of sophistication and humor one might encounter at a screening of *All About Eve* to a gay audience at the Castro Theater in San Francisco.

Breyer was taken aback by the mirth. He quite clearly did not intend the double meaning and did not get the joke. He might have thought the audience was laughing, however, perversely, *at him*. He reclined in his chair, a puzzled and slightly wounded look on his face. As Rosenthal began his response, Justice Thomas, sitting next to Breyer, leaned over and whispered the explanation in Breyer's ear. Thomas, a conservative, was more culturally attuned than Breyer, who nodded and mouthed the word "oh" as Rosenthal spoke.

Breyer never got his "straight" answer, but he did get a heterosexual one. "It's our position that the line should be drawn at the marital bedroom, through which we can . . . through the law enforcement or anyone else cannot pass unless something illegal happens inside that bedroom," responded Rosenthal, lapsing into sentence fragments and awkward locutions.

Rosenthal added that the state of Texas had an interest in "the preservation of marriage, families and the procreation of children."

Justice Ginsburg did not believe Texas had a law banning gay sex so that people would get married and have children. In her patient, low-key voice, she zeroed in on the point about children. "Does Texas permit same-sex adoptions? Two women or two men, to adopt a child or to be foster parents?"

Rosenthal candidly admitted, "I don't know the answer to that, Justice." Mitchell Katine, sitting in the audience, wanted to jump out of his chair and shout, "Yes! Texas allows gay couples to adopt." He and his partner had, in fact, just obtained such an adoption through a state judge.[57] They were an example of exactly the kind of change that had transformed gay life and the judiciary's perception of it since 1986, when the Court casually asserted that their lives had nothing to do with families.

Ginsburg undoubtedly knew the answer, too, or she wouldn't have asked the question. She pressed the issue to its logical conclusion. "Well, in portraying what Texas sees as a 'family' and distinguishing both married and unmarried heterosexual people from homosexual people," she explained to Rosenthal, "those things wouldn't go together if the State at the same time said, 'same-sex couples are qualified to raise a family.'"

Scalia tried to salvage some state interest in distinguishing gay sex from heterosexual intercourse. "You're fairly certain that they can't procreate children, aren't you?" he asked, drawing audience laughter at Rosenthal's expense.

"We are sure that they . . . that they can't do that," Rosenthal answered sheepishly.

For the first time, Justice John Paul Stevens spoke up. Stevens had been appointed by President Ford in 1975. Considered a moderate conservative when he ascended to the Court, he had over time become a liberal stalwart.

"Does Texas prohibit sexual intercourse between unmarried heterosexuals?" he asked in his distinctive Midwestern accent. He was slyly making the point that the Texas law was aimed at homosexual status, not a particular conduct.

"It used to," Rosenthal responded. He did not mention that Texas decriminalized fornication in 1973, the same year it criminalized gay sex.

"What about adultery?" asked Scalia, who probably assumed that Texas still did so and thus that Texas was still enforcing some aspects of traditional sexual morality besides the ban on gay sex. Scalia was apparently unaware that Texas had also repealed its adultery law the same year it made homosexual conduct a crime.

"Adultery is not penalized in Texas," said Rosenthal, quickly adding, "but it is certainly not condoned in Texas." There was more laughter from the audience. The argument for Texas was unraveling with every question as Rosenthal was forced to acknowledge that the state had decriminalized many of the archaic sex offenses that once marked the boundary of traditional sexual morality. Yet for some reason that Rosenthal still had not explained, the state clung to its prohibition on gay sex alone.

The "adultery" moments in the *Lawrence* oral argument, like so much else in the case, paralleled *Bowers v. Hardwick*. Michael Bowers, Georgia's attorney general, defended the state law in 1986 on moral grounds even as he was secretly conducting an adulterous affair, then criminalized in the state.[58] Similarly, years before he defended the Texas

Homosexual Conduct law on moral grounds, and unknown to everyone else in the courtroom that day, Chuck Rosenthal had carried on an adulterous affair with his secretary.[59] There was deep historical irony in having an adulterer defend traditional morality by prosecuting sodomites. Adulterers, by having sex outside of their marriages, were their own brand of sodomites.

Justice Breyer pounced on Rosenthal's defense of marriage. Protecting marriage could not be the justification for an anti-gay-sex law because the state didn't criminalize all sex outside of marriage. It couldn't be about children because gay people were allowed to adopt children. And it couldn't be about procreation since the law didn't ban all non-procreative sex, including oral and anal sex among heterosexuals.

"So what is the justification for this statute?" he wanted to know. "Is this simply, 'I do not like thee, Doctor Fell, the reason why I cannot tell'?" The rhyme from Mother Goose amused the audience. Could Texas, for example, say "it is against the law at the dinner table to tell really serious lies to your family?"

The D.A. fumbled, responding that such a law would not be rational. "Oh, really?" said Breyer, with mock surprise. "It's certainly immoral to tell very serious, harmful lies to your own family under certain circumstances and around the dinner table. Some of the worst things can happen." He cited a possible moral law, a ban on "cheating," a hypothetical whose irony in Rosenthal's case would be revealed four years later.

Seeing Rosenthal's flailing, Justice Scalia came to the rescue. State power to enforce morality could be justified if the state had long been thought to possess the power to pass the law in question. "I don't know of a 200-year tradition of laws against lying at the dinner table."

NOW BEGAN A COLLOQUY in which the Justices effectively argued among themselves, using Rosenthal as a foil.

Justice Stevens noted that bans on interracial marriage were justified by moral concerns. "I don't suppose you're going to argue that Loving against Virginia was incorrectly decided, are you?" Certainly not, Rosenthal replied. Scalia interjected again, noting that *Loving v. Virginia*, which invalidated a ban on miscegenation, involved racial discrimination.

In his calm New England tone, Justice Souter intervened, asking,

"When did Texas select homosexual sodomy as a subject of specific criminal prohibition?" He knew that the answer was, of course, 1973. "When was the first statute passed? I think 200 years was mentioned." The question now became a rebuttal to Scalia. "Was there a law in the books in 1803?"

Missing the import of the question—that the state Homosexual Conduct law was a recent enactment, not a long-standing one—Rosenthal replied matter-of-factly that Texas did not exist in 1803.

Justice Scalia chuckled. "It's a trick question, Mr. Rosenthal," he said to chortles in the audience. "Don't fall into that trap."

With Rosenthal silent, Souter continued. "When did they single out homosexual sodomy?" Rosenthal responded finally that Section 21.06 was adopted in 1973. "So the issue here," Souter concluded, "doesn't have much of a long-standing tradition specific to this statute, does it?" Rosenthal conceded that the specific law did not have a long pedigree but that Texas had long regarded homosexual conduct as "immoral and unwholesome."

Justice Breyer pointed out that during World War I some states banned the teaching of German because they regarded it as immoral, but the Court struck down those laws as unconstitutional. Could the state do anything it wanted simply by claiming morality as support for its action? "You've not given a rational basis except to repeat the word 'morality,'" Breyer charged.

Justice Scalia did not wait for Rosenthal to reply, asserting that the "rational basis" was that the state thinks it is immoral, "just as the State thinks adultery immoral or bigamy immoral."

"Or teaching German," Breyer interjected, smiling. The audience was enjoying the jousting among the Justices, who were no longer even feigning interest in Rosenthal's responses. The oral argument had become practically a law school classroom.

Scalia began to respond to Breyer. "Well, that—"

Rehnquist interrupted Scalia, looking at the forlorn Rosenthal and admonishing his colleagues, "Maybe we should go through counsel."

Returning to the morality theme, Souter clarified the issue. "When the State criminalizes behavior as immoral, customarily what it points to is not simply an isolated moral judgment or the moral judgment alone, but it points to a moral judgment which is backed up by some demonstration of harm to other people." This is the harm principle (although Souter did not use that term): the state permissibly acts to prevent *harm* to people, not simply to enforce *the majority's own preferences* about how others should behave. "What kind of harm to others can you point to in this case to take it out of the category of simple moral disapproval, per se?" asked Souter.

The Harris County D.A. was at a loss. Morality had been the state's only justification for the law from the beginning of the case. It was the only reason given for the law in the state's briefs. If that wasn't good enough, Texas would lose. So Rosenthal stretched, bringing in matters that nobody previously had brought into the case. The law might be useful, Rosenthal speculated, as a way "to discourage people who may be in jail together" or others who "want to experiment from doing the same kind of thing."

The specter of gay jailhouse romps was greeted with silence from everyone in the courtroom.

The state could also prevent people from harming themselves, Rosenthal offered, by taking drugs. Now at least Rosenthal had grasped a possible harm-based analogy. But what was there in homosexual conduct, Souter wanted to know, comparable to the harm caused to the body and mind by taking drugs? Souter paused, waiting for a reply, but Rosenthal was silent. "I mean, I don't see the parallel between the two situations," he added.

Rosenthal skated out tentatively onto the thinnest ice, where Delmore had deliberately refused to go because he considered it silly. "Well, not . . . not only do we say that morality is a basis for this, but of course the amicies[60] have raised that there may also be health considerations. I don't know whether there are or not." He quickly retreated. "That's not the State's claim, but I can't say that it's not true." This was an equivocal defense, at best. It was going nowhere. Souter referred to the *amicus* brief filed by professional medical authorities arguing that state sodomy laws were "directly antithetical to the health claim." Additionally, if the spread of communicable diseases was really the concern, Souter noted, "the law would not be restricted to homosexuals."

Rosenthal tried one last time to distinguish homosexual conduct from other types of sexual activity. Heterosexual sodomy, he suggested, "can lead to marriage and to procreation." Apparently, Rosenthal meant that if an unmarried man and woman performed oral sex on each other, it might eventually lead them to get married. Or, perhaps, if a man anally penetrated his wife, he might be tempted to try vaginal inter-course, too.

Ginsburg saw an inconsistency in the procreation justification, since those unable to procreate were allowed by Texas to have sex. Texas had abandoned the procreative ideal of sex. "Whatever that line might have meant in times gone, it certainly isn't true that sexual relations are for the purpose of procreation, and anything that is not for that purpose is beyond the pale," she concluded.

Once again, Texas had no reason to single out gay sex. Not even the conservative Justices were helping Rosenthal now. He was all alone.

Having been batted around for almost his full thirty minutes, Rosen-thal sought to return to his prepared remarks. He argued that the case was not like *Romer v. Evans* which, he said, invalidated a state law that classified people on the basis of their sexual orientation—not their sex-ual conduct—and "excluded a certain class of people from the political debate." Texas, by contrast, had recently passed a hate-crimes law giving special protection to people attacked because of their sexual orientation. "So I don't think we can say across the board that there's some sort of Texas policy that we're trying to overall discriminate against homosexu-als as a group," he said.

Not even this was allowed to pass unnoticed. Ginsburg noted that, if a gay person wanted to run for political office in Texas, his opponent could dismiss him as a "lawbreaker." Rosenthal replied that openly gay people had been elected to public office in Texas. (By March 2003, for one, Annise Parker held an at-large seat on the Houston city council.)

His time running out, the accomplished jury-trial attorney delivered his summation:

I'm sure it's obvious to this Court that the issues of homosexual rights are highly emotional for the petitioner and their support-ers. But equally anxious in this Court's . . . for this Court's deci-sion are those who are, number one, concerned with the rights of

States to determine their own destiny, and, two, and possibly more important, those persons who are concerned that the invalidation of this little Texas statute would make marriage law subject to constitutional challenge.

Justice Scalia would end his dissenting opinion in *Lawrence* with the same warning about gay marriage. Much more than the defense of an unenforced and symbolic sodomy law was implicated by the case. If gay sex was a constitutional right, and there was no basis for distinguishing it from heterosexual married intercourse, then marriage itself was on trial.

But Rosenthal went even further, concluding his argument with a warning that children were in danger of sexual exploitation. "Then again, how far behind that can there be other acts of sexual gratification brought for constitutional challenge also? There's already movements to lower the age limit of consent for children engaged in sexual practices," he cautioned, without specifying which "movements" he was referring to. In times gone, as Ginsburg might have put it, there was no need to be specific or cite any evidence to justify fear of homosexuals. Such fears needed no defense. The hoary stereotype of gays as a threat to children, rising from their squalor to "sodomize your sons," as the satirical "Homosexual Manifesto" said, had long been a potent weapon against even modest efforts to lift antigay stigma and end discrimination. A ruling for Lawrence and Garner, Rosenthal persisted, would "disenfranchise 23 million Texans who ought to have the right to participate in questions having to do with moral issues."

There was an anachronistic quality to Rosenthal's appearance before the Court. His cavalier efforts and thin arguments, unburdened by learning and experience with actual homosexuals, would have been more than sufficient decades earlier. Indeed, they were just good enough to command a bare majority of the Court seventeen years before. But the time had passed for breezy assertions that anything the state called "morality" could justify any discrimination whatsoever against gays. There was arrogance and insult in the state's presumption that it could say whatever it wanted, march in with an ill-prepared but folksy defender, and walk out with an unearned win.

Even before Rosenthal sat down, partisans were appraising his performance. Hohengarten thought "it was a classic case of a political hack being in way over his head and having no clue about how to litigate a case in the Supreme Court."[61] Delmore, sitting just a few feet away, was impressed by the "dignity" Rosenthal brought to the argument and the "physical courage" he showed because "he was still recovering from some health problems." Other than that, Delmore would not comment on the quality of the argument itself—a damning politeness on Delmore's part.[62]

The Chief Justice put the Harris County D.A. out of his misery with a quick "Thank you, Mr. Rosenthal."

Smith had four minutes remaining for a rebuttal, if he wanted to use it. Rosenthal hadn't landed any punches and there was nothing much in O'Connor's or Kennedy's questions to address. There was a rationale for declining to rebut Rosenthal and simply letting his callow performance speak for itself. However, Smith decided that in a case of this monumental importance, he could not simply surrender a precious four minutes.[63] He was especially keen to rebut fallacies about public-health threats. In particular, Smith noted the low incidence of sexually transmitted disease among lesbians, the trump card played anytime gay male profligacy was introduced in debates about homosexuality. The Justices, in turn, had no further questions for him.

Since Rosenthal was not entitled to a further response, Rehnquist concluded the session. "Thank you, Mr. Smith. The case is submitted." The marshal asked the audience to rise, and the Justices filed out of the room.

In the entire hour of argument, the words "anal sex" and "oral sex" were never mentioned. That, by itself, was a sign of how much the discussion about gay people in legal circles had shifted from sexual acts to intimacy and respect, personal dignity and family. The names of John Lawrence and Tyron Garner were also never mentioned. The case had been abstracted away from what had or had not happened that September night in Lawrence's apartment. The case had become far more consequential than their fates. The strategy devised in the early stages of the case to shine a harsh light on the Texas law rather than focus on the defendants appeared to have worked.

The oral argument in *Lawrence v. Texas,* as one veteran watcher of the Supreme Court put it the next day, was "a mismatch of advocates to a degree rarely seen at the court."[64]

Although hardly alone among the audience, John Lawrence was ecstatic. "I was totally impressed," he said of Smith. "He knew how to come back at them. It was like he was reading their minds." He was confident of victory, as was everyone else on the gay-rights side.[65] As Smith returned to the lawyers' lounge to get his coat and other belongings, members of the team and spectators began hugging and congratulating him. There was a sense on the petitioners' side that if something were going to derail the case, it would have come up in the questions from Kennedy or O'Connor.[66]

Smith was confident about his own performance. He had gotten skeptical but courteous questions from Rehnquist and even from Scalia, who had asked twenty-three of the thirty-five questions put to him. "I didn't have the sense that they were really trying to make me look bad," he remembered. He sensed that they respected him and the historical weight of the moment.[67] Scalia and Rehnquist seemed simply to be performing their expected roles as skeptics of what they regarded as new constitutional rights. There was a perfunctory—and resigned—quality to their resistance.

The *Lawrence* team walked out of the Supreme Court building into a warm Washington spring day. Supporters and even some reporters cheered as they emerged. There, on the steps of the courthouse, crowded by onlookers, they held an informal press conference. In front of the cameras Smith consciously adopted a "very severe expression" befitting the seriousness of the occasion. But inside, as he later commented, he was as relieved and as hopeful as everyone else.[68]

At a celebratory lunch for Lambda and its supporters near the Supreme Court, gay-rights supporters were doing high fives in expectation of a victory. The only questions for most seemed to be: On what basis would the Court strike down the Texas sodomy law? Would the Court actually overrule *Bowers v. Hardwick?*

However, activists with long memories recalled an earlier day, almost exactly seventeen years before, when they burst from the same courtroom expecting a win in a sodomy case. "I felt very good during the oral argument in *Bowers,*" Laurence Tribe had said.[69] The gay men and lesbians watching in the courtroom also thought they had won. They thought Tribe had parried every legal thrust. They, too, had a postargument "triumphant lunch" at a café blocks from the Supreme Court.[70] A generation earlier, it seemed that sodomy laws were about to be eradicated.

Not everyone welcomed the possibility that *Lawrence* might bring the end of sodomy laws, of course. Among many others, Senator Rick Santorum later brought up *Lawrence v. Texas* in an interview with a reporter for the Associated Press. He denied there was a constitutional right to privacy and worried about the implications of a pro-sodomy decision for traditional marriage. A ruling against the Texas sodomy law, he warned, might mean constitutional rights to bigamy, polygamy, incest, adultery, and "man on child, man on dog, or whatever the case may be."[71]

Knowledgeable court watchers knew that a quick decision in a case of such magnitude was unlikely. But as April stretched into May, and May into early June, there was still no ruling. The Court's term was slated to end in late June, and as that date approached, the Justices began issuing new opinions every week, with no word about *Lawrence v. Texas*. Ruth Harlow started to worry. If the case had been an easy win, she wondered, why was it taking the Court so long?[72] Even Smith was nervous. Some of the initial confidence in the outcome dissipated. An agony of anticipation planted itself in the minds of gay-rights supporters.[73]

A poll released after the oral argument revealed that 74 percent of Americans opposed laws making homosexual sex a crime.[74] Americans had moved on from their past, at least in this respect. The *Lawrence* team was counting on the Supreme Court to follow them.

16.

Respect for Their Private Lives

*E*ARLY IN THE SUMMER OF 2003, THE UNITED STATES WAS AT A
crossroads. In Iraq, a growing insurgency was goaded by the president to "Bring 'em on." The University of Michigan waited to hear, as
did schools across the country, whether the Supreme Court would allow
it to consider race in its admissions decisions. And two men in Houston,
backed by millions of gay men and lesbians across the country, awaited
word on whether the state could criminalize their sex lives.

Lawrence v. Texas was now entirely in the hands of a court that, seventeen years before, dismissed the notion that gays had a right to sexual
privacy and liberty that the state was bound to respect. As they waited
for a new decision from the Justices, both gay-rights advocates and their
opponents were aware of the stakes. If the Justices upheld *Bowers v.
Hardwick*, they would be reasserting the principle that a small minority's
freedom to engage in the most intimate activities was a matter of majori-
tarian grace. And this grace could be extended or withheld based not on
whether these intimacies were benign, beneficial, or harmful, but simply
on the fact that the majority wanted it that way. For another generation,
at least, the lives of gay citizens in those states that retained sodomy
laws would be left to the discretion of law enforcement authorities who
could exercise that power with mercy or malignity. Even in those states
without sodomy laws, the fact that the Supreme Court had reaffirmed
the power of the state to act in this way would mean that the claims of
gay citizens to legal and constitutional equality in every other area of

life could be discounted. On the other hand, if a majority on the Court could be persuaded to reverse *Bowers* and strike down state sodomy laws, the result would unleash the potential for further political and legal changes in the years to come.

Because the Justices' deliberations are secret, we do not know with certainty how discussions developed in the Court regarding *Lawrence v. Texas.* There is no audio or video recording of the Justices' decision-making process. Some Justices preserve their private papers, including internal memoranda and drafts of opinions, and release these after their deaths; others do not. In any event, nothing about the Court's internal deliberations of *Lawrence* has been made public so far.

Based on standard Supreme Court practice, however, a few reasonable assumptions can be made about how events unfolded after the oral argument on March 26.[1] The Justices likely did not confer about the case with one another before the oral argument, although they would have discussed it with their own law clerks. No Justice would have known how the others, including Kennedy and O'Connor, would vote.

Each Justice would have been able to make assumptions about how others would ultimately rule based on whether a Justice had voted to grant cert, but these assumptions are hardly infallible. For example, according to the Lambda and Jenner attorneys, it's unlikely that Kennedy and O'Connor would have voted to hear the case if they were simply going to reaffirm *Bowers* and uphold the Texas Homosexual Conduct law. There was no disagreement on the issue among the federal appellate courts, for example, a common reason that the Supreme Court intervenes. So if one or both of them voted for cert, that was a good indication they were leaning against the Texas law. However, we do not know which Justices voted to grant cert. It may simply have been the Court's four liberals, leaving open the possibility that Kennedy and O'Connor, forced to decide the case, would side with Texas. Or the Court's three conservatives and one of the others might have voted to grant cert.

The Justices' intentions most likely were not revealed to one another until they met in what's called the Justices' conference. This conference is held on Wednesday and Friday afternoons when the Court is in session. At the Wednesday afternoon conference the Justices consider arguments heard on Mondays and Tuesdays. At the Friday conference they consider cases heard on Wednesday. Thus, in *Lawrence*, this critical postargument conference probably occurred on March 28.

The Justices' conference is held in a huge formal conference room in the chambers of the Chief Justice. Only the Justices themselves are present. There are no marshals, clerks, secretaries, or other Court personnel in attendance. The Chief Justice calls the meeting to order. The Justices shake hands in a ritual display of their mutual respect and collegiality. They first consider the week's cert petitions, deciding whether to accept or to reject new cases.

They then present their views on the cases undecided since their previous conference. Starting with the Chief Justice and continuing in descending order of seniority, each briefly gives his or her analysis of the case. The Justices do not interrupt one another. At the time *Lawrence v. Texas* was decided, the order of seniority was Rehnquist, Stevens, O'Connor, Scalia, Kennedy, Souter, Thomas, Ginsburg, and Breyer. The nine Justices had all served together for almost a decade, a period of stability in the Court's membership unknown since the early nineteenth century. Indeed, they knew one another well, and some had become friends across ideological lines, like Justices Ginsburg and Scalia.

Having presented their views on the case, the Justices would next take an actual vote, again starting with the Chief Justice and continuing in descending order of seniority. In *Lawrence*, Chief Justice Rehnquist voted to affirm the decision of the *en banc* Texas appellate court, Justice Stevens voted to reverse that decision, and so on, until all had spoken.

Once the vote is taken, the Chief Justice—or the most senior Justice in the majority if the Chief Justice is dissenting—assigns a Justice on his side of the outcome (including, at his option, himself) to write an opinion. In *Lawrence*, Justice Stevens assigned Justice Kennedy to write the majority opinion. Since he was dissenting, Rehnquist could have assigned Justice Scalia to write the dissent; or, given his passionate feelings about the case, Scalia might simply have volunteered.

After the conference, a clerk for the Justice assigned to write the opinion would have produced the first draft, subject to substantial revision. (Of the Justices on the *Lawrence* court, only Stevens typically wrote the first draft of his own opinions rather than relying on a clerk to do so.)[2]

The four clerks hired annually by each of the Justices can have an influence, even though in a big case like *Lawrence* it is unlikely that their views
changed anything in the outcome. In the year *Lawrence* was decided,
three of Justice Kennedy's four clerks were, in fact, conservatives.[3]

The Justices writing the majority and dissenting opinions then circulate their drafts to the other Justices for comments and revisions. Any
Justice can write a separate concurring or dissenting opinion expressing
his or her own views of the case. Occasionally, votes change after the
initial conference, as happened when Justice Powell initially voted to
strike down the Georgia sodomy law in *Bowers*, then changed his mind.
But that is the exception. It's likely that no Justice subsequently changed
his or her vote on *Lawrence* and thus that the fate of the Texas sodomy
law was sealed at the Justices' conference on March 28, 2003.

The outcome was, of course, unknown outside the Court. There is
no advance notice of when a decision in a case will appear. There is no
e-mail, telephone, or fax alert sent to the media or even to the lawyers
involved. To announce their opinions, the Justices take their seats in
the courtroom on certain mornings of the week beginning at ten
o'clock. The Chief Justice announces which case has been decided
without revealing the outcome, and then turns to the Justice who has
written the majority opinion. That Justice reads a summary and
selected portions of his or her decision. If they feel especially strongly
about a case, dissenting Justices sometimes reply by reading a summary and portions of their dissent. The full text of the opinions is then
released to the public.

The only way to hear the actual announcement of the decision in a
particular case is to show up on a day scheduled for the reading of opinions and hope the decision is among those released. Often, one must
leave the Supreme Court building having heard nothing and then return
again for the next announcement day. This happens over and over. Paul
Smith, Bill Hohengarten, and Dan Mach from Jenner showed up on
opinion-reading days toward the end of the term, just in case *Lawrence*
was announced.[4]

The final week of the Court's 2002–03 term began on Monday, June 23.
Opinions were scheduled to be announced that day and on the final day of
the term, Thursday. The two most anticipated major decisions by then

were *Lawrence v. Texas* and the pair of companion cases involving affirmative-action admissions policies at the University of Michigan, *Grutter v.
Bollinger*[5] and *Gratz v. Bollinger*.[6] Attorneys for both the Michigan cases
and the *Lawrence* case showed up on Monday hoping to hear their respec-
tive results. The Court announced its decisions that day in the Michigan
cases. It was a split doubleheader, with Justice O'Connor as the deciding
fifth vote for the majority in both cases, siding with the liberals to uphold
the law school's race-conscious admissions policy but siding with the conservatives to strike down the undergraduate school's race-conscious
admissions policy. Justice Kennedy joined the Court's conservatives in both
cases. By itself, this augured little for *Lawrence* because Kennedy had long
sided with conservatives in cases regarding racial issues.

But there was no announcement about *Lawrence* that day; it would
have to wait until the Thursday session. Gay-rights supporters realized the decision was going to be handed down right before the annual
gay-pride celebrations traditionally held the final weekend of June to
commemorate the Stonewall Riots in New York in late June 1969. Anticipating a jovial celebration that Sunday, a supporter from Parents, Families and Friends of Lesbians and Gays remarked, "I don't want the
Supreme Court to pee on our parade."[7]

Those familiar with the malarial heat of the nation's capital in late
June were not surprised by the hazy and humid air of Thursday, June 26.
The temperature was already in the low eighties that morning as gay-
rights attorneys, academics, and law students began filling the courtroom to hear what the Justices would say. The main Jenner lawyers were
there, including Smith and Hohengarten, along with most of the law
students working for Jenner that summer. Ruth Harlow flew in from
New York. She was greeted by a court clerk she didn't know who smiled
and said, "Good luck to you today."[8] Laurence Tribe, on the losing end
seventeen years earlier, also took a seat. Notably absent were Lawrence
and Garner, who did not have the time off from work or the resources to
fly to Washington to hear something they would soon enough learn by
television or telephone. Also absent were all but a handful of supporters
of the Texas sodomy law. In contrast to the day of the oral argument,
the courtroom was not quite full.

With the audience in place by ten o'clock, Pamela Talkin, the Court's marshal, told everyone to rise as the Justices entered. Audience members searched their faces for any sign, any subtle smile or frown, that might reveal what was going to happen, but the Justices were inscrutable. Chief Justice Rehnquist started with the announcement of opinions in other cases. As these were revealed, Hohengarten began a maddening internal guessing game. The Court usually begins the daily readings with opinions by the most junior Justices and moves up in seniority. Justices Breyer and Ginsburg had already announced opinions in cases heard the same week as *Lawrence* back in March. That meant two of the Court's liberals had to be crossed off the list of authors. Not a good sign, he thought.[9]

Then, as Chief Justice Rehnquist said "The opinion of the Court in No. 02-102, Lawrence against Texas . . . ,"[10] Hohengarten and the other team lawyers caught their breath, waiting to hear who the author would be. "I'm thinking," Hohengarten recalled, "'Oh my God, it's Justice Thomas!' because he was the next most senior Justice and he had not done an opinion from our sitting. My thought was, 'We've lost.'" The next instant he hoped perhaps Thomas had been persuaded by the arguments of his former clerk Erik Jaffe, the principal author of the RUC *amicus* brief supporting the petitioners. But it was improbable that they had actually gotten Thomas's vote, and even more improbable that he would write the opinion striking down the Texas law on constitutional grounds.[11]

Rehnquist continued, ". . . will be announced by Justice Kennedy."

The room tensed up. The anticipation felt by people who had worked on the case for almost five years, and on the larger cause for longer, was palpable. The lawyers for Lawrence and Garner still did not know which way the case would come out. The fact that Justice Kennedy, a pivotal Justice, had written the opinion did not necessarily mean they'd won. Along with O'Connor, Kennedy could have sided with the conservatives and been assigned by Chief Justice Rehnquist to write the opinion upholding the Texas sodomy law in an effort to keep him on the conservative side, a common tactic in the assignment of opinions to wavering Justices. But it was equally true that Kennedy could have been assigned to write the opinion by Justice Stevens, the most senior liberal, to keep him on the liberal side.

Meanwhile, at Lambda's headquarters in New York, Susan Sommer was watching CNN and refreshing her web browser every few seconds to find out the result.[12] In Houston, Mitchell Katine was in his office with local reporters, TV news cameras trained on him to capture the moment of victory or defeat.[13] John Lawrence was rousing himself from bed, having worked until late the night before, waiting for the call.[14] Living in the same modest two-bedroom apartment in which he'd been arrested for homosexual conduct, he was told by Harlow on a conference call the night before to expect a decision that morning around 9 a.m. (CDT). Tyron Garner was staying with his brother and had also heard from the lawyers that the decision would come soon.[15]

With the other Justices looking out at the audience, Justice Kennedy began reading from his prepared statement, including a summary and excerpts from the opinion. His voice had "an uncharacteristic quaver":[16]

> The question before the Court is the validity of a Texas statute making it a crime for two persons of the same sex to engage in certain intimate sexual conduct. In Houston, Texas, police officers were dispatched to a private residence in response to a reported weapons disturbance. The right of the police to enter does not seem to have been questioned at any stage in the case. Now, the police entered the apartment where one of the petitioners, Joseph Geddes Lawrence, resided. The officers observed Lawrence and another man, Tyron Garner, engaging in a sexual act. Garner is also one of the petitioners here. Lawrence and Garner were arrested, held in custody overnight, and charged under the Texas criminal statute.

This was all the Supreme Court knew about the facts of the case. So far, nothing Kennedy had said gave away the result. He was in the middle of what seemed to partisans on both sides like a tortuous and interminable windup. Kennedy continued his stroll through the case background, describing the constitutional claims and the proceedings in the Texas courts. Then he said:

We conclude this case should be resolved by determining whether the petitioners were free as adults to engage in this private conduct in the exercise of their liberty under the Due Process Clause of the Fourteenth Amendment, and for this inquiry, we deem it necessary to revisit this Court's holding in *Bowers*.

Two minutes into the presentation, this was the first hint that the Court might rule against Texas. Kennedy's usual nervous manner and speech patterns were even more noticeable, especially as the subject of *Bowers* came up. Hearing these words, Harlow and others in the gallery began to realize they might actually win.[17] Kennedy laid out the factual similarities between *Bowers* and *Lawrence*, both involving consensual sex between two adult men in the privacy of a home. Still, Kennedy had not actually said the Court was going to overrule *Bowers*. He continued:

> The *Bowers* court rejected the petitioner's claims under the Due Process Clause. The *Bowers* court began its discussion as follows: It said, "The issue presented is whether the federal Constitution confers a fundamental right upon homosexuals to engage in sodomy and hence invalidates the laws of the many states that still make such conduct illegal and have done so for a very long time."

This was the sentence in the *Bowers* decision that had stung for seventeen years. It had belittled the lives of gay men and lesbians, many believed, and cast them as outsiders to American law and heritage. It hurt to hear it again, even now.

Kennedy drew a deep breath. Then he exhaled. "That statement, in our view, discloses *Bowers'* failure to appreciate the extent of the liberty at stake."

It was at this moment that perceptive observers like Smith and Harlow realized what was happening. The result in fundamental-rights cases builds from the framing of the issue. If *Bowers* got that wrong, as gay advocates had been arguing since the day it was decided, the Court had been wrong. Tears were beginning to well up in the eyes of many in the courtroom. Expectations surged as Kennedy elaborated on *why* the *Bowers* majority had framed the issue incorrectly:

To say the issue in *Bowers* was simply the right to engage in certain sexual conduct demeans the claim put forward, just as it would demean a married couple were it to be said that marriage is simply about the right to have sexual intercourse. The laws involved in *Bowers* and here are, to be sure, statutes that do prohibit a particular sexual act. Their penalties and purposes, though, have more far-reaching consequences, touching upon the most private human conduct, sexual behavior, and in the most private of places, the home. The statutes seek to control a personal relationship that is within the liberty of persons to choose without being punished as criminals.

The Justices, just a few feet away from those in the front row, could easily see the effect the ruling was having on the gallery. Hohengarten tried to check any visible display of his own emotions. He didn't want Justice Souter, his old boss, to see him crying. In fact, Souter knew Hohengarten was gay, knew how passionately he felt about the case, and also knew, through the grapevine, that Hohengarten played a very significant role in it. But it was no use. The moment overwhelmed the best efforts of many gay-rights advocates to conceal their feelings.[18]

Kennedy reviewed the history of sodomy laws, declaring that *Bowers* had overstated its claim that laws against homosexual conduct "as a distinct matter" had ancient roots. He acknowledged that many people had moral objections to homosexual conduct and that such views were important to them. But, he averred, "the issue is whether the majority may use the power of the state to enforce those views on the whole society."

Changes in American law over the past fifty years, the Associate Justice said, "show an emerging awareness that liberty gives substantial protection to adult persons in deciding how to conduct their private lives in matters pertaining to sex." Kennedy singled out for criticism Chief Justice Burger's concurrence in *Bowers* invoking centuries of Western tradition purporting to treat even consensual homosexual acts as worse than rape. Kennedy explained that *Bowers* was inconsistent with the Court's own previous decisions in *Griswold, Eisenstadt, Roe,* and *Carey v. Population Ser-*

vices.[19] Since *Bowers*, the additional precedents of *Casey* and *Romer*, which Kennedy himself had endorsed, further undermined it.

Kennedy acknowledged that the Texas sodomy law might be unconstitutional under the Equal Protection Clause. As everyone later learned, that was the basis for Justice O'Connor's lone concurring opinion in *Lawrence*.[20] But, he said, "it is our view that the instant case requires us to address whether *Bowers* itself has continuing validity." Now, more than seven minutes into his delivery, Kennedy uttered the words gay Americans and their supporters had waited a generation to hear:

> We conclude the rationale of *Bowers* does not withstand careful analysis. *Bowers* was not correct when it was decided and it is not correct today. It ought not to remain binding precedent. *Bowers v. Hardwick* should be, and now is, overruled.

Overwhelmed by what was happening, many of the gay and lesbian advocates sitting in the gallery were now openly sobbing. This display of unbridled emotion was exceedingly unusual in the Court's history.[21] The Court is typically a place for a particularly joyless and solemn dignity, where reasoned analysis is supposed to prevail over emotion. Justice Kennedy saw, and obviously felt, the reaction of the gallery. He seemed almost to choke up himself, catching his words as he said that *Bowers* was wrong "when it was decided and it is not correct today."

It is rare enough for the Court to overrule itself. It is rarer still for the Court to confess that it was wrong from the beginning. Even in *Brown v. Board of Education*,[22] in which it overruled its infamous decision upholding segregation, *Plessy v. Ferguson*,[23] the Court did not quite confess that it had been wrong from day one.[24] This was as close as the Court would ever get to an apology to gay and lesbian Americans for the wrong, and for the harm, it had done them. Lawrence and Garner, Kennedy said, were "entitled to respect for their private lives." No longer, he declared, could the state "demean their existence or control their destiny by making their private sexual conduct a crime."

In his written opinion, released that morning, Kennedy stressed the importance of relationships, a word he mentioned eleven times. Thus,

Kennedy noted that sodomy laws "seek to control a personal relationship," that the government could not define "the meaning of the relationship or . . . set its boundaries," and that "adults may choose to enter upon this relationship."[25] While Kennedy's language did not always make it clear what he meant by "relationship," the overarching impression left by his opinion was that he meant more than fleeting sexual encounters of the sort Lawrence and Garner (might have) engaged in. "When sexuality finds overt expression in intimate conduct with another person," he wrote, "the conduct can be but one element in a personal bond that is more enduring."[26]

The Court's opinion in *Lawrence*, despite protestations to the contrary,[27] was at root a verdict about the content of morality in a world where gay men and lesbians were no longer at the fringes of life and culture. It was a judgment that gay sex, too, might lead to—and might be an integral part of—lasting relationships. The opinion implicitly recognized that gays might aspire to formal recognition—marriage—although Justice Kennedy remained carefully agnostic on that issue. Gay sex was not constitutionally protected merely because a free society must allow people to do objectionable things in the exercise of their own autonomy. It was constitutionally protected because it was normatively right, just as it was for heterosexual couples who might decide to marry. It was part of the good life. This was the moral code adopted in *Lawrence*. Traditional sexual morality would have to accommodate itself to this realization, but this did not mean that the concept of sexual morality was at an end. The very idea that gay sex could be the glue of an "enduring bond" between same-sex partners was exactly what the *Lawrence* team wanted the Court to grasp. The mainstreaming strategy had paid off.

The tremor in his voice returning, Kennedy closed with thoughts about the larger meaning of the Constitution's protection of liberty:

> It is the promise of the Constitution that there is a realm of personal liberty which the government may not enter. Had those who drew and ratified the Due Process Clauses of the Fifth Amendment or the Fourteenth Amendment known the components of liberty in its manifold possibilities, they might have been

more specific. They did not presume to have this insight. They knew times can blind us to certain truths and later generations can see that laws once thought necessary [or] proper in fact, serve only to oppress. As the Constitution endures, persons in every generation can invoke its principles in their own search for greater freedom.[28]

Just over nine minutes, and 400 years, had passed as Kennedy closed. Smith and Harlow, both reserved and serious in their courtroom demeanor, steeled themselves against any public display of their own emotions. This composure was remarkable especially for Harlow, who had borne the weight of the case from the beginning, and now was relieved of the "pressure and responsibility." Farther back in the room, Laurence Tribe, the man who had lost a battle that probably could not have been won in 1986, was obviously moved by the experience.[29]

The *Lawrence* team wanted to burst out of the courtroom, but etiquette demanded that they sit through the rest of the morning session. This included Justice Scalia's reading of his dissent, an unusual act that indicated how vehemently he rejected the outcome.

By turns dismissive, angry, and sarcastic, Scalia chastised the Court for effectively decreeing the "end of all morals legislation." Traditional morality, as he argued in his written dissent, was all that stood between society and a long list of horrors, like masturbation (already legal everywhere), fornication (already legal in most states, including Texas), adultery (already legal in most states, including Texas), bigamy, adult incest, obscenity, and even bestiality (decriminalized in Texas). He charged that the Court had "taken sides in the culture war" between traditional morality and the latest moral fads and fancies. Relying on standard tropes used to influence the broader public, he intoned that many Americans did not want known homosexuals to work in their businesses, serve as scoutmasters for their children, be teachers in their schools, live as boarders in their homes, or serve in their military. Homosexuals lead "a lifestyle they believe to be immoral and destructive."

In an obvious reference to the lopsided support for the petitioners from the American legal establishment, he charged that the Court was "imbued" with "the law profession's anti-anti-homosexual culture." He resented the fact that the elites of the legal profession had so completely abandoned his version of traditional sexual morality.

Justice Scalia closed with a prophecy about the coming battle over gay marriage:

> The Court today pretends that . . . we need not fear judicial imposition of homosexual marriage as has recently occurred in Canada. At the end of its opinion, the Court says that the present case "does not involve whether the government must give formal recognition to any relationship that homosexual persons may seek to enter." Do not believe it. Today's opinion dismantles the structure of constitutional law that has permitted a distinction to be made between heterosexual and homosexual unions. . . . One can believe that this case does not involve the issue of homosexual marriage only if one thinks that principle and logic have nothing to do with the decisions of this Court. Many will hope that, as the Court comfortingly assures us, that is so.

While Justice Kennedy made no direct mention of gay marriage, Justice Scalia was interpreting the decision as leading to just that. His intention, no doubt, was to point out how ridiculous the Court's opinion was. If it led to something as radical as gay marriage, it could not be right. But ironically, Scalia's words would be quoted by gay advocates in the future to prove that *Lawrence* was, in fact, the natural prelude to marriage.

Chief Justice Rehnquist and Justice Thomas also signed Scalia's dissent. Justice Thomas wrote separately to say that the Texas law was "uncommonly silly" and that, if he were a legislator, he would vote to repeal it. But he was not a legislator, just a judge. He saw no right to privacy in the Constitution and thus no basis for striking down the state sodomy law.[30]

Still, even with Scalia's peroration on sodomy and marriage complete, the audience could not leave the courtroom. A few more decisions were announced before Rehnquist brought the session, and the Supreme Court's 2002–03 term, to a close. He gave customary thanks to the Court's staff for their work that term. Then he announced that there would be a retirement. Gay-rights supporters in the room momentarily feared that he might reveal the retirement of one of the members of the five-vote majority to overturn *Bowers*, like the eighty-three-year-old Justice Stevens, whose replacement would have been nominated by President George W. Bush.[31] This would put *Lawrence* in some danger even before the ink had dried on the opinion. However, it was the Court's librarian who was stepping down. The announcements concluded, the marshal banged her gavel. The spectators rose to their feet as the Justices exited.[32]

The attorneys, media, and other observers could finally leave. As they bounded out, the *Lawrence* attorneys were entering a new land of constitutional protection they had helped shape. Even before they left the courtroom, the opinion was released to the media and CNN had reported the result. The news was running riot across the airwaves and the Internet, charging the electronic world.

JOHN LAWRENCE'S ALARM went off a few minutes before nine o'clock. He turned on CNN, but there was no decision yet. "And I rolled over and said, 'Okay fat ass, you can get five minutes of sleep. Then you got to get up.'" He had not yet snuggled into the pillow when the anchor announced that the Supreme Court had struck down the Texas sodomy law. "I came out of that bed," he recounted, chortling, "and I fell on the floor!"[33]

At Katine's office, everybody was waiting for a call from Lambda telling them what had happened. At 9:12 a.m. (CDT), the phone rang. It was Katine's mother, saying she had just heard on MSNBC that they won. She didn't know the vote or the basis for the decision, but she knew her son, now the father of an adopted child, had prevailed. Quickly, congratulatory phone calls and e-mails began pouring in. Katine called Lawrence and then Garner, who was just getting out of bed. "We won!" said Katine. "We won the case!"[34] Garner jumped out of bed and knocked on his brother's door, telling him to turn on the television.[35]

Leaving the classical Corinthian confines of the Supreme Court the normally impassive Ruth Harlow got a bear hug from an emotional Laurence Tribe. For Professor Tribe, a combatant for a living Constitution who bore the scars to mark his efforts, it must have been a bittersweet day. Harlow joined the legal team's celebration lunch at a local restaurant. After lunch, she was marooned all afternoon and evening in TV and radio studios, performing her duties to the end.

If *Lawrence v. Texas* were to become the gay-rights movement's *Brown v. Board of Education*, Ruth Harlow was a good candidate to be its Thurgood Marshall. Like Marshall, she had toiled for years to advance the cause in the courts. She endured second-guessing and doubts about her choices from many on her own side. She faced an opposition that believed she was trying to force upon them a moral vision they found repugnant. She was the lawyer who had done more than any other to make the day possible. She was satisfied that, if nothing else, the Court had wiped away the stain of *Bowers* and had "evened the playing field" for gay men and lesbians.[36]

Upon leaving the courtroom, Bill Hohengarten had immediately opened his cell phone to call his partner of twenty years and tell him the good news. This was the day, Hohengarten remembered, when they "stopped being second-class citizens." At Jenner's offices, practically the whole firm was celebrating the *Lawrence* decision, as well as another victory for the firm in a death-penalty case.

At Lambda's New York headquarters, staff members huddled around Susan Sommer's office waiting for the news. "We won!" she announced to cheers and clapping.

Suzanne Goldberg, who walked through a throng of antigay protesters with Lawrence and Garner at the Justice of the Peace court in 1998 and laid the foundation for the arguments that ultimately persuaded the Supreme Court, was in her office at Rutgers Law School when she heard the news. She told the *New York Times*, "It removes the reflexive assumption of gay people's inferiority. *Bowers* took away the humanity of gay people, and this decision gives it back."[37]

Chuck Rosenthal made no public appearance, but released a statement: "I am disappointed that the Supreme Court justices who voted in favor of the reversal did not allow the people of the state of Texas, through their elected legislators, to determine moral standards of governance for this state."[38] He wanted nothing more to do with the case. He was reelected to a four-year term as the Harris County D.A. in 2004, but by 2007 had renewed his amorous affections for his secretary. The next year, he resigned in disgrace after a series of scandals involving pornographic and racist e-mails sent from his office computer, substance-abuse problems, use of his office computer for political campaigning, and a threat of a contempt-of-court citation for deleting 2,500 e-mails during a federal investigation of his activities. A lawsuit by a former city council member seeking Rosenthal's ouster for "official misconduct" alleged that he had consumed alcohol while performing his duties from 2001 to 2007, which covered the time he was defending the morals of Texas in *Lawrence*. Rosenthal blamed prescription drugs for impairing his judgment. After his resignation, ironically, he pleaded for the media to respect his "privacy" as he tried to "restore my family as a unit."[39]

Bill Delmore was in his office at the Harris County D.A.'s headquarters answering e-mails and reading cases when the news came in. "Obviously I am a little bit disappointed in the outcome because of the amount of work we put into it," he told the *New York Times*.[40] But he had expected to lose. "Is it important in that we're not getting any more Class C misdemeanors for homosexual conduct? Well no, because we didn't get any before," he remarked later. "Is it important to people in the gay community with regard to where they're going from here? Yes." But for him, "the important thing was that we attempted to strike a blow for state legislatures and against judicial overreaching—and we failed."[41] He was not worried about declining moral values, but about increasing judicial activism. Delmore said very little to the media about the case after *Lawrence* but did express "relief" that he could finally "leave the social implications and philosophy and all that behind, and just focus on putting the bad guys in prison."[42]

Deputy Joe Quinn, whose uncommon arrest of Lawrence and Garner produced an extraordinary Supreme Court case, had figured the men would just pay their fine. That is, he expected them to bow out quietly until "the media and the ACLU and Lambda got a hold of it." (In fact, the ACLU did not handle the case.) As soon as he learned they were involved, he thought, "Oh my God. This is going to be blown out of proportion." The threesome of the media, the ACLU, and Lambda had come to the rescue of that other "triangle kind of thing"—Lawrence, Garner, and Eubanks. For years afterward, people in the sheriff's department teased him. "There goes the Supreme Court deputy."[43]

Quinn claimed to be of two minds about the verdict in the Supreme Court. On the one hand, "if you just look at the way it's written [the Equal Protection Clause], there is no equal protection here. They don't ban that activity for heterosexuals. It isolates the homosexual." On the other hand, "the states themselves should have the right to make their own laws." He added, with words that would horrify James Madison, "But then again, we are one nation governed by a Supreme Court, so I have to live by it." Looking back at the convoluted events and tension-filled moments involving Lawrence and Garner that led to their arrests, Quinn observed that "it's unfortunate it had to happen over something stupid that could've cost them their lives."[44]

Deputy William Lilly, the only other officer who claimed to have seen Lawrence and Garner having sex, agreed with the Supreme Court's decision. As a police officer, he didn't like to "invade people's privacy" and regretted that that's what they had done in this case. "We had to do our job as far as answer the weapons disturbance, but the homosexual conduct in private was their business," he said, obviously chagrined by what had happened. "I've always felt that way." He also thought morals-based laws were a bad idea. "We're trying to enforce morality in America and that's become a huge problem in this country. If you have kids and they're doing things that's immoral, it's not my job as a police officer to enforce this. That's the parents' job."[45]

Deputy Donnie Tipps, who was also there the night of the arrest but did not claim to witness the crime against nature, remained unequivocal and curt about *Lawrence*: "I don't agree with it." He made the status/conduct distinction more concisely than did the Harris County D.A.'s office in its briefs. "I don't agree with homosexual conduct, either. Nothing against homosexual *people*." Asked about the right to privacy, he opined, "There are some things that don't need to be done in your home and this is one of them."[46]

Word of the *Lawrence v. Texas* decision spread through each of the Texas courts touched by the case. Nathan Broussard, the court clerk whose actions helped keep the case going, received a call at the office from a good friend. "Congratulations!" the friend exulted.

"What are you talking about?" asked Broussard.

"Y'all won y'all's case!"

Broussard, who dealt with scores of cases every week, still didn't know what he was referring to. "It went through the Supreme Court and they overturned it," the friend explained.

Broussard realized that the Court must have held the state sodomy law unconstitutional, although he still didn't appreciate the full impact of such a decision. To him, it proved that while the judicial system may have some leaky pipes, it works. "And what's even cooler is most of the appointees were appointed by conservative presidents," he observed, noting that Reagan had nominated Kennedy and O'Connor, and that Ford had picked Stevens, "which leads you to believe that they still have an open mind and they actually still have a love of the law and of human rights."[47] He called his partner, Mark Walker, the brawny sheriff's sergeant who had divulged the sodomy arrest to bartender-activist Lane Lewis and set the case in motion. Closeted, they had both endured repeated fag jokes from the sheriff's deputies. At last, they were now legal in Texas. But their liberation was brief. Within a few months, Walker had died of complications from AIDS.

Mike Parrott, the burly justice of the peace, torn between his traditional upbringing and his friendships with gay people, the man who had to increase the fine to help ensure the case would go up on appeal, was listening to traffic citations the morning *Lawrence* came down. His top administrator, Sheryl Roppolo, who had assiduously followed the case, approached the bench and slipped him a note. "It was just a stepping-stone is all it was," Parrott said of his court.[48] In recognition of his role in the *Lawrence* case, he was asked to be a grand marshal in the Houston gay pride parade to be held later that year. But he politely declined.[49]

Angela Beavers, the lesbian who prosecuted the alleged sodomites but opposed the sodomy law, was happy with the outcome. "The judicial system worked," she concluded.[50]

Sherman Ross, the county criminal judge who presided as Beavers read the homosexual conduct charges, heard the news from an assistant D.A. during a court session. Years later, he smiled impishly remembering the moment. "Send Angela Beavers my regards," he said.[51]

Justices Murphy and Anderson, the two state appellate judges who ruled against the state law on sex-discrimination grounds and were then subjected to a torrent of state GOP criticism, were vindicated. But Murphy didn't see why the Supreme Court had to dwell on the historical background of sodomy laws, drawing a distinction between sodomy laws that broadly prohibited nonprocreative and nonmarital sex. All one really had to know to decide the case, he reasoned, was that Texas and its legions of moralizers let people have sex with animals. End of story. "We tried to keep it as short and simple as we could," said Murphy.[52]

Elsewhere in Houston, Annise Parker was sitting in her chambers at the Houston City Council when she got the news. The gay community had been dealing with Section 21.06 for so long that she didn't know whether to cry or celebrate. She slumped in her chair. "I just wanted to be quiet and be alone for a few minutes," she remembered. Then she called her partner of almost two decades and lamented, "Too bad we haven't violated 21.06 more often, because now it's gone."[53] Six years later, she would be elected mayor of Houston.

Religious conservatives around the country were predictably infuriated.[54] In the afternoon, according to one account, several religious-conservative clerks for the Supreme Court, including one of Kennedy's, prayed together at the Court, asking God to forgive the Justices for making sexual licentiousness a constitutional right.[55]

The United States Conference of Catholic Bishops called the decision "deplorable."[56] Pat Robertson denounced the Supreme Court as the "tyranny of a nonelected oligarchy" rending the "moral fabric of the nation."[57] Others said it was "anti-Biblical" and an "attack on Christianity."[58] Scott Lively, director of the Pro-Family Law Center, fumed that the decision "would have terrible consequences for our nation." Jerry Falwell, founder of the Moral Majority, said it would hurt families, lead to bestiality, and overall "was as bad a day as we've had since *Roe v. Wade*."[59] One antigay group warned that it was worse than *Roe*, calling it a "moral 9/11."[60] Fred Phelps, the Kansas pastor and antigay zealot whose church serenaded gay supporters and passersby with anti-American songs the morning of the *Lawrence* argument, foretold doom: "It's the death knell of American civilization," he said. "It's a covenant with death and an agreement with Hell."[61]

Not all conservative Christians, however, opposed the ruling. Arkansas governor Mike Huckabee, whose own state's sodomy law had been ruled unconstitutional the year before, told a radio audience, "What people do in the privacy of their own homes as adults is their business."[62] John Lawrence's Southern Baptist preacher called him the day of the decision and said, referring to antigay protesters and the religious support for the state sodomy law, "John, there's good Christians and there's bad Christians." Lawrence responded, "I've met most of the bad ones."[63]

At the White House, President Bush's spokesperson, Ari Fleischer, dodged questions about the decision. The president opposed every major item on gay-rights groups' wish list, from a repeal of "Don't Ask, Don't Tell" to enactment of antidiscrimination laws, but his press secretary pointedly declined to comment on *Lawrence v. Texas*. Fleischer would say only that the administration did not file a brief in the case. But even that silence was something of a change from Bush's stance as governor of Texas in the 1990s, when he had opposed repeal of the sodomy law because he said it was a "symbolic gesture of traditional values."[64] Charles Francis, the co-chairman of the Republican Unity Coalition, commented, "I hope the giant middle of our party can look at this decision not as a threat but as a breakthrough for human understanding."[65]

Across the country, in places where there had been no sodomy law for decades, and in others where gay sex was still a crime not fit to be named, gay men and lesbians celebrated. In Chicago, in the first state to repeal its sodomy law (forty-two years earlier), more than a thousand people packed into the corner of Halsted and Roscoe, the center of the city's gay community.[66]

In Seattle, the local gay men's chorus held an impromptu concert on the federal courthouse steps. They sang "You Can't Stop the Beat" from the musical *Hairspray* as a crowd of hundreds laughed, clapped, and danced.[67]

In North Carolina, gay-rights supporters hailed the decision. The state's sodomy law, which formally forbade both heterosexual and homosexual activity, had been used by landlords to deny housing to gay couples because they claimed that renting to homosexuals would aid and abet the commission of felonies. In another case, a North Carolina judge had stripped a father of custody of his two sons when he admitted having sex with his partner.[68]

In Alabama, another of the thirteen states whose sodomy law was now unconstitutional, the decision promised the end of the harshest forms of legalized discrimination. The year before, in a concurring opinion, Alabama Supreme Court Chief Justice Roy Moore used the law to decry the "inherent evil" of homosexuality, voting with a unanimous court to deny a lesbian mother custody of her children.[69] Employers in the state had used the law to fire employees known to be homosexual. Landlords used it to evict gay tenants. "It's held over us," said one gay Alabaman. "After today, it won't be as easy."[70]

In Missouri, one of the four states with a specifically antigay sodomy law, and where penalties for a first-time offense could be as high as a $1,000 fine and one year in jail, rallies celebrating the decision were held in Columbia, St. Louis, Kansas City, and Springfield.[71]

In Washington, D.C., a rally began at seven that evening in Dupont Circle, the focal point of the city's gay neighborhood. Bill Hohengarten and his partner were there for the celebration, but by now they were a little worse for the wear, since their champagne had begun flowing at noon.[72]

Joyous demonstrations occurred across the United States: in Atlanta, Boston, Charleston, Cleveland, Detroit, Miami, New Orleans, Oklahoma City, Philadelphia, Pittsburgh, Richmond, Salt Lake City, and Tucson, among others. In Los Angeles, five hundred people showed up for a celebration held at the West Hollywood auditorium.[73] These were followed by an especially raucous set of gay-pride celebrations that weekend.

In New York City, hundreds of people rallied in Sheridan Square, near the site of the Stonewall Inn in the heart of Greenwich Village.[74] Situated at the intersection of Seventh Avenue and West Fourth Street, it was one site of the draft riots against compulsory military service in July 1863 as well as the Stonewall rebellion in June 1969. On the night of the *Lawrence* decision, the denizens of local bars and restaurants were joined by more politically minded activists in a spontaneous celebration of liberty. The day's heat was intensified by the crowd and the passions of the moment.

Paul Smith had caught a flight for New York after the decision in order to meet with a client on another matter. He arrived in Sheridan Square just in time for the rally. It was an older crowd than usual for public protests, filled as it was with many who had been in the exact same place in June 1986 to protest the decision in *Bowers*. Many had lost friends and family in the AIDS epidemic. The crowd cheered when Smith was identified and briefly spoke. He was now a dragon slayer in their minds, a lawyer whose name would be etched in civil rights history, if not in marble. "It's a place that was very central to the movement," Smith said of Sheridan Square. That night "people had a real sense of history there." Afterward, the new gay knight partied late into the night with deliriously gay New Yorkers. He didn't pay for a single drink. Strangers handed him bottles of champagne. "I've never been so popular in the Chelsea bars," he recalled, hazily.[75]

IN SAN FRANCISCO, news of the ruling came before the workday started. As it had for more than five years, a large rainbow flag flew atop an eighty-foot pole at the corner of Castro and Market streets, ringed by the Victorian architecture common to the heart of the city's gay neighborhood. The design for the twenty-by-thirty-foot flag first emerged for the 1978 San Francisco pride parade, the summer before Harvey Milk's assassination. The flag was visible from large swaths of the city, fluttering twenty-four hours every day of the year (except for maintenance and repair, it was never lowered). To gay men and lesbians living in the city as well as those visiting from around the country and abroad, it was both a symbol and a reassurance, its appearance affirming that there was at least one place where they were accepted.

Now the rainbow flag's designer, the Kansas-born Gilbert Baker, had an idea. The banner should be lowered for this one day and be replaced by an American flag, as a way of proclaiming in effect, "Finally, we're Americans." He called the writer Armistead Maupin, a friend, who thought it was a brilliant idea. Baker also contacted a few activists, including Teddy Witherington, the city's pride director.[76] "We had been embraced by our country in a way that allowed us to express our patriotism without reservation," remembered the English-born Witherington. Gay men and lesbians love their country as much as anyone, he added, but showing it publicly had always been complicated by their "exclusion from full citizenship." Gay leaders in that famously fractious city, one that had been pronounced un-American by traditionalists in political campaigns and rhetoric, enthusiastically approved dipping the rainbow flag in honor of American ideals.[77]

At noon, Witherington and his friends began an impromptu ceremony, a growing crowd around them, fed by those entering and exiting from the nearby subway station. They filled the sidewalk around the flagpole, spilling into the street, crowding across the intersection, straining to see. Some held makeshift signs, proclaiming "Keep Your Laws Off Our Bodies" and "We Won!"

Baker carefully lowered the rainbow flag. A group of veterans in the American Legion's Alexander Hamilton Post, several of whom had been expelled from military service for being gay, saluted as Baker raised a gigantic American flag in its place.[78] A rousing cheer went up. Many of those present, including Baker, were in tears. The crowd sang the national anthem, led by the San Francisco Gay Men's Chorus. Jenny Pizer, a Lambda lawyer, told the assembled throng, "This is our Declaration of Independence. We now have the right to love and to make love. We have the right to be fabulous."[79]

The contrast was unmistakable: while antigay extremists had stomped on an American flag in Washington, D.C., gay men and lesbians honored it. San Francisco values were American values.

BACK IN TEXAS, where the sodomy fight began, demonstrations supporting the Supreme Court decision were held in Dallas, Austin, San Antonio, and Galveston. But the celebration was biggest and most heartfelt in Houston, the birthplace of the case 1,734 days earlier. The afternoon of the decision there, like the night of the original arrests, was anything but routine. From the towering steel-and-glass cathedrals of commerce in the city's downtown to the expansive suburban tracts, from the fetid bayous to the languid lanes lined with Texas live oaks, and on the freeways that crisscrossed all of it, few could have foreseen the transformation of two humble men into civil rights heroes. Few could have predicted that John Lawrence and Tyron Garner's arrests for the misdemeanor of "homosexual conduct"—an act they probably never committed with each other, and later denied ever happened—would commence a careful and calculated constitutional campaign. Then humiliated on a dank night, they were now feted under a roaring sun.

Mitchell Katine and other activists, coordinating with Lambda, called an early afternoon press conference.[80] They arrived with Lawrence and Garner, so long absent from the case, in tow. Lawrence carefully and dryly read a brief prepared statement to the Houston media:

I'm not a public speaker. We are very pleased with this ruling. We never chose to be public figures or to take on this fight. But we also never thought we could be arrested this way. We are glad not only that this ruling lets us get on with our lives but that it opens the door for gay people all across the country to be treated equally. We are grateful to everyone who has respected our privacy over the last few years even if the state of Texas did not respect it that night in 1998. And we thank everyone who saw how important this case was and fought for us. We share this victory with gay people in all fifty states who are better off today than they were yesterday, thanks to this ruling.

Garner stood by, mute. He had not been given anything to say. He and Lawrence smiled but looked overwhelmed, and barely acknowledged each other as Lambda's regional director, Lee Taft, entertained questions from the assembled media.[81]

Organizers cautioned reporters several times that Lawrence and Garner expected the press to "respect their privacy." They would not permit the press to ask them any questions. One journalist wanted to know why the men had been "shrouded in secrecy" and were not permitted to talk freely about the case. "Do you have to be perfect to win in the Supreme Court? Y'all didn't want the blemishes in their background to be out there?"

Taft brushed off the question, repeating the mantra that the men were not seeking publicity and wanted their privacy respected, but the reporters grew impatient. "Not to invade the dome of privacy, but can we get their ages?" queried another reporter, with obvious sarcasm. This was public information, but Taft would not even let them answer that question. He said they just wanted to return to "leading lives of normalcy."

"Will they be leading it together?" a third journalist persisted.

Taft ignored him, quickly closing the press conference. Lambda was not about to let any off-message information get into the news cycle that day. The monitoring of Lawrence and Garner would continue for the indefinite future.

Gay-rights advocates held a rally on the steps of Houston city hall at 5 p.m.[82] On short notice on a weekday, in the hottest part of the summer day, a crowd estimated at from one to three hundred people showed up.[83] Whatever the attendance, they were jubilant. When Katine arrived with Lawrence and Garner, a cheer went up. "A lot of people was waiting for us to come around and maybe say a few words," Garner recalled. "Everybody was happy that we was there."[84]

The crowd included almost all of the city's gay leaders. Former state representative Debra Danburg, who had for years sponsored bills to repeal the state's Homosexual Conduct law, was there. Linda Morales, who had lost her challenge to the Texas sodomy law in 1994 when the state supreme court decided she had taken her case to the wrong high court, was there. So was Sue Lovell, a lesbian activist and future city council member. Annise Parker was joined by her partner and their adopted children.

Lane Lewis, whose initial efforts had gotten the case into the hands of capable lawyers, appeared at the rally but was not asked to speak. He called himself a "significant insignificant" in that if he hadn't been "out in the community, then I would not have had the information and leads to put myself out to the Justice of the Peace courts."[85] A spitfire, he had been disconnected from the case once Lambda fully took charge. The case, as became clear, was managed with almost military discipline, according to a plan developed by strategists far from the initial skirmish in Lawrence's apartment.

When someone suggested they start the rally with "The Pledge of Allegiance," Lewis objected. "I turned around and said no!" Lewis recalled. "The Supreme Court never had the right or authority to take away my right to express love or sex through sodomy, so we shouldn't validate the system that leads to that." He appealed to the organizers, "Why are we all down on our knees thanking them for giving us something they should never have taken away?" The politicians and dignitaries present ignored him and began the rally with the pledge.[86] "Welcome to a free Houston!" shouted Katine, opening the rally.

Brian Chase, who had assisted on the *amicus* briefs, spoke on behalf of Lambda. Anticipating a positive outcome, Chase had drafted his speech the night before. "Seventeen years ago this week," he began,

every gay and lesbian person in America was told that he or she could be jailed for little more than being who they are. Seventeen years ago this week every gay and lesbian teenager was told that they were doomed to lives as criminals. Seventeen years ago the Supreme Court told every American suffering in the closet that he or she should keep living a lie or risk living as a criminal.

The movement veterans in the audience recalled the legal nightmare induced by *Bowers*. "That all changed today," Chase continued, to rising cheers.

Today every gay kid in America learned that he or she has a fighting chance to be treated like an equal citizen. Today everyone suffering in the closet heard loud and clear that our voices do matter and that we can all come out and live open, honest lives. Today is a great new day for all Americans who value freedom, liberty, and "the right most valued by civilized men, the right to be left alone."

He was quoting loosely from a famous opinion by Justice Louis Brandeis affirming the right to privacy.[87] The audience roared with delight.

Parker spoke, followed by Linda Morales. Both noted the absence of movement heroes like Gene Harrington, a gay law professor, and Patrick Wiseman, a heterosexual ACLU lawyer, who had fought the state sodomy law for decades before their deaths. (Others had noted the absence of Mort Schwab and Keith McGee, pioneering Houston gay leaders of the 1970s who had been lost to AIDS.) " 'Our country 'tis of thee,'" Morales concluded in her Latina accent, almost singing the words, " 'Sweet land of liberty!' "

Up next was Ray Hill, the gray-bearded defender of gay rights, porn stores, and prison inmates. In full preacher cadence, with the self-assurance of a father and a vigor nobody else could match, he captured the feelings of generations of gay Americans. "Well, children, it's been a long hunt," he began, in paternal fashion. "The last time we had this many people this close to city hall we ran Anita Bryant out of town." The audience laughed, recalling the crucial 1978 protest against the Miss America runner-up and orange-juice huckster turned antigay activist. Hill dispatched the false idea that getting rid of Section 21.06 was unimportant because it was almost never enforced.

Every time you went to apply for a job somebody thought, "You're a criminal when you go home and you can't have the job." And every time that you wanted to be a police officer, they said, "No, this lesbian violates Texas law when she goes home at night and she can't be a police officer." So we went through that on adoptions. We went through that with custody. We went through that in probate court. And we went through that with employment. So 21.06 was enforced *every day*, but not as a criminal statute.

After that rush of words, he paused, allowing the enormity of the state sodomy law to sink in one last time. He continued slowly for emphasis: "And *this day* is important to me. I'm an old man. I'm sixty-two years old. But you know, if I get lucky this afternoon it will be the first time in my life I have been intimate without violating a law in the state of Texas." The crowd burst out in laughter and applause.

With uncharacteristic brevity, Hill closed, reaching a crescendo and drawing inspiration from the sea of hopeful faces before him. "We have eliminated the criminalization of gay and lesbian intimate behavior," he proclaimed, carefully enunciating every word now, as the activists beamed and began applauding more loudly. "Coast to coast. Border to border. Slam that door. We can *never*, by this decision, go back!" This was greeted by an emotional and joyous effusion.

Garner and Lawrence, never given to public oratory, did not speak. After the rally they stood as the audience spontaneously lined up to thank them and ask for their autographs. Three days later they rode together in an open convertible at the head of the Houston gay pride parade, drawing ovations of gratitude from thousands of people lining the streets. That night as they toured the city's various gay bars, they heard someone shout, "My god, look who's here!" It was two officers from the Houston Police Department who rushed over to congratulate them.[88] There would be several more such congratulatory appearances over the next few months.

TO JOHN LAWRENCE, the result justified everything he had been through—from the arrest and being dragged down the apartment stairs to the court appearances and meetings with attorneys. "Why should a law be passed that only prosecutes certain people? Why build a law that only says, 'Because you're gay you can't do this. But because *you're* heterosexual, you can do the same thing'?"[89] A man who had previously never given much thought to gay rights had been thoroughly politicized by his experience.

Garner was less voluble about his role in history and about the larger meaning of it all. "I felt like a celebrity," he said, reliving the day of the decision. But he demurred when told he was considered a hero. "I'm not a hero. But I feel like we've done something good for a lot of people. I feel kind of proud of that." He hoped the decision would send a positive message to gay people. "Be who you are. And don't be afraid."[90]

There was, nevertheless, a long way to go, Garner believed. "We still have a lot of work to do as far as getting equal treatment and jobs and housing and employment."[91] For Garner, a man with few employment prospects of his own, equality could not stop the moment he left the bedroom. There was now a constitutional right to have sex, an important step forward. But in most states, including Garner's own Texas, a person could still be fired from a job or denied housing simply because he was gay.

Like Lawrence, Garner never worked for gay-rights groups, either before or after the decision. But unlike his copetitioner in the Supreme Court, few remember Garner or invoke his name.

It was, after all, *Lawrence v. Texas*.

EPILOGUE

Sweet Land of Liberty

⁓

J OHN LAWRENCE CONTINUED TO LIVE IN HOUSTON, ALTHOUGH HE
moved out of the Colorado Club Apartments, with its exotic dancers,
midnight pool parties, and flagrant sodomites, gay and straight. In
2006, he bought a house so that he could live with his partner, Jose Garcia. Jose's children from a former marriage occasionally visited, and
Lawrence did not think it appropriate to display the erotic James Dean
sketches that had so excited the interest of the sheriff's deputies. So he
put them away in a closet—relics of another time. Lawrence's journey
toward a domesticated liberty paralleled the one taken by many gay men
both before and after *Lawrence.*

Lawrence was sometimes asked to speak about the case. He obliged
the requests, usually with a minder there to make sure he didn't say
anything that might tarnish the legend. His private life was his, thanks
to his namesake case, but his public life was managed, thanks to those
who engineered it. For the most part he returned to a life of anonymous
normalcy. He died of heart-related illness on November 20, 2011, in his
home in Houston, and in the care of Jose.

Time was less kind to Garner. Mitchell Katine tried to get national
gay-rights groups to use him as a spokesperson for the cause. But after
Garner imbibed too much at a national black-tie dinner in the men's
honor in Washington, D.C. and accepted his gay-rights award with a
rambling speech, there were no takers. "It would've changed his life,"
speculated Katine, "but he didn't have the training or education."[1]

When I picked Garner up for our interview in June 2005, he was living with relatives in a low-income area of Houston. The home was a

fairly worn ranch with a brick façade. A barbecue pit, some old chairs, a bucket, and a few other things were strewn about the front yard. Neither Garner's white dress shirt nor his gray dress pants seemed to fit him. He smelled of cologne. When I took him back home at the end of the interview, at about two in the afternoon, he asked me to stop at a corner gas station and borrowed some money to buy a large malt liquor beer.

A little over a year later, on September 11, 2006, he died, three years after the opinion was rendered, six years after the death of Robert Eubanks, and not quite eight years after his arrest in John Lawrence's apartment. Despite his youth, he had been sick for months. His brother Darrell said that he died of complications from meningitis.[2] Others said it was tuberculosis. Lawrence, who didn't know his alleged paramour was ill, believed it was pneumonia.[3]

Unlike his arrest and Supreme Court case, Garner's death was received mostly with silence in the media, including the gay media. His family did not have enough money to bury him or cremate him. Calling Garner's contributions to the gay community "immense," Kevin Cathcart, executive director of Lambda Legal, appealed to that community for funds to defray disposal and funeral costs. Two weeks after his death, $200 had been raised. For weeks, the civil-rights hero's body lay in cold storage in the Harris County morgue. Finally, in mid-October, with only $25 more having been donated, Garner's brother released his body to the county for cremation (at no cost). The family wanted to place his remains in a modest metal urn, instead of a plastic bag, and run a proper obituary in the newspaper. But they needed $200 more for that and didn't have the money.[4] There was no memorial service for him in the gay community. There was no funeral, period.[5]

The background facts in *Lawrence v. Texas* do not make for an easily packaged story with idealized characters. Lawrence and Garner were not in a long-term committed relationship—if they were involved at all. This may help explain the decision of the men's lawyers to shield them so completely from media scrutiny. They were never "poster people," their lawyers informed us. They would not have been chosen to lead the charge against the Texas law.[6] The background did not make for very good public relations, but the deputies whose flagrant conduct gave us *Lawrence* didn't oblige public relations needs by enforcing the sodomy law against model citizens in the privacy of their well-appointed homes.

How could this jumble become the occasion for Justice Kennedy's musings about the "transcendent dimensions" of life, "the most intimate and personal choices a person may make," and "personal dignity," together with a lamentation on the way the law "demean[ed] their existence"?[7] One obvious answer is that, by design, the Supreme Court knew little about the facts of the case. And none of these background facts would have made any difference to the constitutional claim made by Lawrence and Garner. Even if the Court had known everything we now know, the men nevertheless would have been entitled to the liberty to make their own choices about their private sexual conduct.[8] American liberty includes the freedom to make choices the majority finds distasteful or even loathsome.

The deeper answer is that *Lawrence*, in all its emotional, social, and legal complexity, is a reflection of life itself. People do indeed lead complex lives. They fall in love, cheat, lie, drink. None of this makes them any less entitled, as Justice Kennedy put it, to "respect for their private lives."[9] If it were otherwise, there would be very few people—gay or straight—entitled to liberty.

AS IT TURNED OUT, the decision had an immediate effect in that it rendered unenforceable the sodomy laws of thirteen states. Four of them applied only to gay sex—Texas, Missouri, Oklahoma, and Kansas. Another nine applied to all adults but were widely understood mainly to target gay sex—Alabama, Florida, Idaho, Louisiana, Mississippi, North Carolina, South Carolina, Utah, and Virginia. If *Lawrence* did nothing more, this accomplishment by itself was considerable.

Considerable, but not quite complete. Almost a decade after *Lawrence* was decided, eighteen states—including Texas—still officially had sodomy laws on their books. Episodic and overzealous enforcement continued, as in 2009 when El Paso police instructed two men in a restaurrant to stop kissing because their act violated the state's "homosexual conduct" law. While any actual prosecution under such laws would be dismissed because of *Lawrence*, the laws themselves remained in place. Legislators stubbornly and proudly refused to repeal them. One Texas legislator said he was "hesitant to do any changing" of the law because it "better reflects the views of a lot of citizens." In Montana, lawmakers rejected a repeal effort, repeatedly linking homosexuality to bestiality and pedophilia, and warning that gay sex would drive up the cost of health care and spread HIV.[10]

But for gay America the decision meant much more than making specific sex statutes unenforceable. It didn't matter that most gay Americans, like most Americans, were unaware such laws existed. It made no difference that even those who knew they existed hardly expected to be arrested in their bedrooms. A sodomy law anywhere meant they were sodomites everywhere.

As long as *Lawrence* shielded them, never again would gay men and lesbians be presumptive criminals because of their sexual orientation. Never again, they hoped, would they be denied jobs because their lives were defined by membership in an outlaw class. Never again could a landlord refuse them shelter because they were unindicted lawbreakers. Never again would their children be taken from them solely because the sex of the person they loved made the parents misdemeanants or even felons.[11] Never again would their rights be dismissed by the highest tribunal in the land as, at best, facetious. Never again would their legal representatives have to argue around a precedent that attached a stigma to their very bodies. Never again would they wonder whether the words engraved on the pediment of the Supreme Court building, "Equal Justice Under Law," included them. The Constitution was now their constitution, too.

If *Lawrence* has an uncovered past, it still has an uncertain future. Before *Lawrence*, when it was possible for a state to criminalize the sexual lives of gay people, it was much easier to deny them a host of the other rights and privileges taken for granted by most Americans. Before *Lawrence*, it was logical to say the government could disfavor them in jobs where they might be regarded as role models, like police officers or teachers. It was possible to believe that they, like any class of criminals, should be watched around children, even their own, or should be altogether prohibited from adopting and raising kids. It was possible to make homosexual acts a crime and thus grounds for discharge under the military's own criminal law, even if the conduct took place off the base and involved a civilian partner. And if their sexual conduct could be made a crime, it was no stretch to declare that their relationships need not be formally recognized by the law, including in marriage. Indeed, it would have been exceedingly odd to say that, as a matter of constitutional law, the government was required to sanction same-sex marriage but was free to make the private sexual lives of those very spouses a crime.

As we have seen, the gay-rights lawyers who brought us *Lawrence* very carefully and deliberately avoided marriage—the "m" word. They knew that the United States Supreme Court, in a nation where no gay marriage had yet been recognized, would be unwilling to mandate it. In the *Lawrence* opinion itself, Justice Kennedy carefully reserved the question of marriage for another day.[12] But thanks in part to *Lawrence*, which did not so much clear the whole constitutional path as remove one huge roadblock, that day may yet come.

And even before that watershed, the end of constitutionally sanctioned sodomy laws allowed a blossoming conception of gays as part of—rather than apart from—America's sometimes dueling libertarian and moral values. *Lawrence* was a death knell for a worldview that had long since lost any connection to the actual lives of gay Americans and to the society in which they were thriving. Unwelcome in American society for the better part of 400 years, gay men and lesbians had moved in, earned their keep, and taken their seats at the dinner table. Even if a few hold-outs still doubted their propriety, *Lawrence* declared that they could legitimately call the place home.

So in the years to follow, the acceptance of homosexuals in civic life would grow. More jurisdictions banned antigay discrimination. Businesses, too, rejected discrimination against them. More openly gay politicians were elected. Movies and television were suffused with openly gay characters. States began recognizing same-sex relationships through domestic partnerships, civil unions, and even marriages. Just months after *Lawrence*, the Massachusetts Supreme Court, citing Justice Kennedy's decision, issued an opinion legalizing same-sex marriages. Within a decade same-sex marriages were recognized in six states and the District of Columbia.

Congress voted to repeal the "Don't Ask, Don't Tell" statute, allowing gays to serve openly in the most conservative institution in American society, at the very heart of the obligation of citizenship. *Lawrence* did not cause all of this change, but it ratified and intensified the underlying cultural shift that made it possible. It also furnished a constitutional basis for further changes to come.

The case was a strike of lightning in the lives of Tyron Garner and John Lawrence. It briefly illuminated them on a dark Texas landscape. And then it was gone, leaving a memory of the flash, a legacy of wreckage, and a transformed legal and cultural landscape. The storm passed to other frontiers.

Acknowledgments

THIS BOOK COULD NOT HAVE BEEN COMPLETED WITHOUT THE HELP of numerous people. For reading drafts of the book or individual chapters, I would like to thank Karl Barrett, Brian Bix, Don Dripps, Jeff Kahn, Heidi Kitrosser, Mae Kuykendall, Elizabeth Marquardt, Brett McDonnell, David McGowan, Miranda McGowan, Doug NeJaime, Martha Nussbaum, Mike Paulsen, Ann Rostow, Paul Rubin, Mike Tonry, and Bryan Vezey. Also of great assistance were participants in Jill Hasday's Public Law Workshop at the University of Minnesota Law School; participants in Mary Anne Case's Workshop on the Regulation of Family, Sex, and Gender at the University of Chicago Law School; and participants in the faculty workshop at SMU's Dedman School of Law.

I would also like to thank the University of Minnesota Law School, which helped with research and travel funds and provided the assistance of numerous staff members, including my secretaries Dee Gibbons, Lisa Sartwell, and the late Harriet Carlson. The law school also supplied terrific student research assistants who helped research and edit the book, including Brad Emmons, Joseph Gesley, Ryan Scott, Jennifer Singleton, and Eric Taubel.

A special thanks goes to Arthur Leonard, who offered invaluable guidance and suggestions as the book progressed. Art also got me in contact with my excellent and indefatigable editor at Norton, Bob Weil, who made the book sing where it only droned on. Norton added value to the book at every stage of production. I'm especially grateful to my copy editor, Trent Duffy, whose eagle eye for detail, encyclopedic knowledge of the subject matter, and close attention to tone and style made the book incalculably better.

All remaining errors in the book are, of course, my own.

Notes

Epigraph

1 According to both Lawrence and the lead arresting officer, these are the words Lawrence first spoke to police when they walked into his bedroom on September 17, 1998. Telephone interview with Joseph Quinn (August 9 and 31, 2003); interview with Joseph Quinn, Houston (June 20, 2005); interview with John Lawrence, Houston (June 14, 2005).

Introduction

1 Tex. Penal Code Ann. § 21.06(a) (Vernon 2003).
2 539 U.S. 558 (2003). The factual account given in this paragraph closely follows the Supreme Court's own description of the facts:

> In Houston, Texas, officers of the Harris County Police Department were dispatched to a private residence in response to a reported weapons disturbance. They entered an apartment where one of the petitioners, John Geddes Lawrence, resided. The right of the police to enter does not seem to have been questioned. The officers observed Lawrence and another man, Tyron Garner, engaging in a sexual act. The two petitioners were arrested, held in custody overnight, and charged and convicted before a Justice of the Peace.

Ibid., 562–63. The lower-court decisions, including the state intermediate appellate court panel and the *en banc* intermediate appellate court, offered very similar accounts. See, for example, *Lawrence v. State*, 41 S.W.3d 349 (Tex. App.—14th Dist. [Houston]) (2001) (*en banc*).
3 I occasionally call the Texas Homosexual Conduct law a "sodomy law," here and elsewhere in this book, fully aware that some will object to the term. Sodomy laws traditionally targeted both heterosexual and homosexual sex. The Texas law was a departure from this practice, singling out gay sex for the first time in 1973. I use the term, despite its technical deficiency, because it is so closely tied to homosexual sex in the public mind. "Sodomy" has a historical and popular antigay resonance that is lost in the clumsy modern phrase "homosexual conduct."
4 Early efforts to raise these issues, and to highlight the complexity of the background facts are Dale Carpenter, "The Unknown Past of *Lawrence v. Texas*," *Michigan Law Review* 102 (2004): 1464; and Berta E. Hernandez-Truyol, "Querying *Lawrence*," *Ohio State Law Journal* 65 (2004): 1151, 1235–40.
5 Compare *Jackson v. City and County of Denver*, 124 P.2d 240 (Colorado 1942), where the police arrested a couple for miscegenation, with obvious malice.

Chapter 1: *A Crime of Deep Malignity*

1 "Francis Higgeson's Journal . . . ," in *The Founding of Massachusetts* (Boston: Massachusetts Historical Society, 1930), 71 (entry of June 29, 1629). The General Court of the Massachusetts Bay Colony sent two members to a director of the Massachusetts Bay Company in England on September 29 to inform him of the crime: see Nathaniel B. Shurtleff, ed., *Records of the Governor and Company of the Massachusetts Bay Colony . . .* (Boston: William White, 1853–54), 1:52, 54 (courts of September 19 and 29, 1629). The punishment of hanging for sodomy is noted in Edwin Powers, *Crime and Punishment in Early Massachusetts: 1620–1692* (Boston: Beacon, 1966), 43. See also Jonathan Ned Katz, *Gay/Lesbian Almanac* (New York: Carroll & Graf, 1994): 73.

2 In canon law, sodomy was confused with "unnatural acts," a term with a different origin that applied even to procreative marital acts in disapproved positions or performed with contraceptive intent: Brief *Amicus Curiae* of Professors of History George Chauncey et al., *Lawrence v. Texas*, No. 02-102 (January 16, 2003), 5 (hereinafter, Historians' Brief).

3 William Blackstone, *Commentaries on the Laws of England* (1769), book 4, chapter 15.

4 Historians' Brief, 6.

5 The text of the Virginia law is available in William Strachey, *For the Colony in Virginea Britannia, Lavves Diuine, Morall and Martiall, &c.*, in *Tracts and Other Papers, Relating Principally to the Origin, Settlement, and Progress of the Colonies in North America*, comp. Peter Force (1844; repr., New York: Peter Smith, 1947), 9–10. See also Katz, *Gay/Lesbian Almanac*, 68.

6 William B. Rubenstein, ed., *Cases and Materials on Sexual Orientation and the Law*, 2nd ed. (St. Paul, Minn.: West, 1997), 81.

7 Ibid., 87. See the King James version of Leviticus 18:22 ("Thou shalt not lie with mankind, as with womankind: it is abomination") and Leviticus 20:13 ("If a man also lie with mankind, as he lieth with a woman, both of them have committed an abomination: they shall surely be put to death; their blood shall be upon them").

8 The text of the Maryland law is recorded in William Kilty, ed., *Report of All Such English Statutes as Existed at the Times of the First Emigration of the People of Maryland* (Annapolis, Md.: John Chandler, 1811), 161; see also Katz, *Gay/Lesbian Almanac*, 73.

9 The Massachusetts law is quoted in William. H. Whitmore, ed., *The Colonial Laws of Massachusetts* (Boston: Rockwell and Churchill, 1890), 55; and George L. Haskins, "The Capitall Lawes of New England," *Harvard Law School Bulletin* 7 (February 1976): 10–11. See also Katz, *Gay/Lesbian Almanac*, 76; in the Massachusetts bestiality law, the animal was also to be "slain, and buried" (ibid.).

10 Katz, *Gay/Lesbian Almanac*, 66–133.

11 William N. Eskridge Jr., *Gaylaw: Challenging the Apartheid of the Closet* (Cambridge, Mass.: Harvard University Press, 1999), 328–37. (The cited pages are in an appendix listing the dates of the first sodomy laws for each state, starting in 1610.)

12 Historians' Brief, 8.

13 Blackstone, *Commentaries on the Laws of England*, book IV, chapter 15.

14 Historians' Brief, 8; Eskridge, *Gaylaw*, 25. By 1900, the city prosecuted more than twice that number *every year*. Even accounting for population increases, that was a dramatic rise.

15 Eskridge, *Gaylaw*, 20–21.

16 Historians' Brief, 8–9.

17 Eskridge, *Gaylaw*, 27–34.

18 Ibid., 42.

19 Ibid., 34–37.

20 Ibid., 47–48.

21 Ibid., 60.

22 Historians' Brief, 15–17.

23 David K. Johnson, *The Lavender Scare: The Cold War Persecution of Gays and Lesbians in the Federal Government* (Chicago: University of Chicago Press, 2004): 26.

24 Eskridge, *Gaylaw*, 69.

25 Dale Carpenter, "Expressive Association and Antidiscrimination Law After *Dale*: A Tripartite Approach," *Minnesota Law Review* 85 (2001): 1515.

26 Eskridge, *Gaylaw*, 72–74.

27 George Chauncey, *Gay New York: Gender, Urban Culture, and the Making of the Gay Male World, 1890–1940* (New York: Basic Books, 1994), 137–41, 183–86, 197–98, 249–50.

28 Eskridge, *Gaylaw*, 78–80.

29 Ibid., 63–65.

30 Eskridge, *Gaylaw*, 75–76, 114.

31 The discussion in this section owes much to the excellent compendium of information about sodomy laws, sodomylaws.org, and especially to the rich discussion of the history of the Texas sodomy law by George Painter. "The Sensibilities of Our Forefathers (Texas)," Sodomylaws.org, http://www.sodomylaws.org/sensibilities/texas.htm.

32 L. 1859–60 Tex. Gen. Laws 97.

33 Joseph Chitty, *A Practical Treatise on the Criminal Law*, vol. 2 (1847), 49; Robert Desty, *A Compendium of American Criminal Law* (1882), 143; John Wilder May, *The Law of Crimes* (1881), 223.

34 The word "homosexual" was first used publicly in Germany in 1869 and was not used in the English language until the 1890s: Colin Spencer, *Homosexuality in History* (New York: Harcourt Brace, 1995), 10.

35 *Frazier v. State*, 39 Tex. 390 (1873); *Fennell v. State*, 32 Tex. 378 (1869); *State v. Campbell*, 29 Tex. 44 (1867). The Texas statute was stricter about clarity in criminal statutes than the U.S. Constitution was understood to be. The statutory language had a well-understood meaning derived from the common law—see *Wainwright v. Stone*, 414 U.S. 21 (1973).

36 Tex. Penal Code, art. 4 (1879); see also *Ex parte Bergen*, 14 Tex. App. 52, 56 (1883).

37 *Munoz v. State*, 281 S.W. 857 (Tex. Crim. App. 1926); *Mitchell v. State*, 95 S.W. 500 (Tex. Crim. App. 1906); *Prindle v. State*, 21 S.W. 360 (Tex. Crim. App. 1893).

38 *Harvey v. State*, 115 S.W. 1193 (Tex. Crim. App. 1909).

39 *Lewis v. State*, 35 S.W. 372 (Tex. Crim. App. 1896).

40 *Ex parte Copeland*, 91 S.W.2d 700, 702 (Tex. Crim. App. 1936).

41 Thirty-seven years later, in 1973, the state legislature would, however, "ignor[e] the moral sense of the people" by repealing the laws criminalizing seduction on promise of marriage, adultery, fornication, and heterosexual sodomy, but leaving homosexual sex criminal: 1973 Tex. Gen. Laws 917.

42 1943 Tex. Gen. Laws 194.

43 Painter, "The Sensibilities of Our Forefathers," n. 42.

44 1943 Tex. Gen. Laws 194, excerpted in Painter, "The Sensibilities of Our Forefathers," n. 42.

45 "Carnal copulation" was interpreted to mean "sexual intercourse," presumably anal or vaginal sex: *Furstonburg v. State*, 190 S.W.2d 362, 363 (Tex. Crim. App. 1945).

46 381 U.S. 479 (1965).

47 405 U.S. 438 (1972).

48 *Baker v. Wade*, 553 F. Supp. 1121, 1150 (N.D. Tex. 1982).

49 308 F. Supp. 729 (N.D. Tex. 1970).

50 1973 Tex. Gen. Laws 917.

51 Ibid., § 21.01.

52 Ibid., § 21.06(a). The law was further amended in 1981 to prohibit "the penetration of the genitals or the anus of another person with an object": Tex. Penal Code Ann. § 21.06 (Vernon Supp. 1982). On its face, the 1981 amendment appeared to criminalize pelvic or prostate examinations if the doctor and patient were of the same sex. Two years earlier, the state had criminalized the sale, or possession for sale, of dildos and artificial vaginas: 1979 Tex. Gen. Laws ch. 778, sec. 1, § 43.21(a)(7), and sec. 2, § 43.23(a).

53 In a challenge to Section 21.06, plaintiffs served Requests for Admissions on attorneys for the state, asking the state to admit the law prohibited same-sex—but not opposite-sex—conduct. The state's response contained what the court called "an unfortunate but Classic Typo," to wit: "Section 21.06 proscribes a *mole* engaging in 'deviate sexual intercourse' with another *mole* and likewise proscribes a female engaging in 'deviate sexual intercourse' with another female": *Baker v. Wade*, 553 F. Supp. at 1150, n. 6.

54 1973 Tex. Gen. Laws ch. 339, § 21.06(b); ibid., ch. 429, § 4.01(a)(3).

55 William Eskridge, *Dishonorable Passions: Sodomy Laws in America, 1861–2003* (New York: Viking, 2008), 303.

56 Rob Shivers, "Lone Star Solons Defeat Sodomy Reform," *The Advocate*, August 13, 1975, 5; James T. Sears, *Rebels, Rubyfruit, and Rhinestones* (New Brunswick, N.J.: Rutgers University Press, 2001), 217–18.

57 *Baker v. Wade*, 553 F. Supp. at 1151.

58 "Two Texas Men Challenge State's Ban on Gay Sex," Reuters, November 18, 1998; *Lesbian/Gay Law Notes*, May 1993. Also in 1993, the Texas legislature passed, and Governor Ann Richards signed, a bill broadening the state's sex-offender treatment law. Under the new version, anyone convicted of "a sex crime under the laws of a state or under federal law" was subject to sex-offender treatment: 1993 Tex. Gen. Laws ch. 590, sec. 1, § 1(4)(A). The "sex crime" of "homosexual conduct" would seem to be included.

59 Eric Berger, "Danburg Again Files Bill Seeking Sodomy Law's Removal," *Houston Chronicle*, January 20, 2001, 31.

60 Ibid. Representative Debra Danburg, a Democrat from Houston who had previously filed sodomy law repeal bills, insisted that *two* Republicans support her bill before it could be voted out of committee. One Republican on the committee apparently supported the repeal, but no others.

61 *Baker v. Wade*, 769 F.2d 289, 292 (5th Cir. 1985 [en banc]); *State v. Morales*, 869 S.W.2d 941 (Tex. 1994).

62 *Baker v. Wade*, 769 F.2d at 292.

63 *State v. Morales*, 869 S.W.2d at 948.

64 The state of Texas claimed in *Baker v. Wade*, 553 F. Supp. at 1146, that Section 21.06 had never been enforced against private activity between consenting adults. This, as we shall see, is simply not true.

65 *Medrano v. State*, No. 23,774, 1947 Tex. Crim. App. LEXIS 1369 at *1 (Tex. Crim. App. Nov. 5, 1947).

66 Cases involving a public or quasi-public space include: *Young v. State*, 263 S.W.2d 164 (Tex. Crim. App. 1953) and *Jones v. State*, 308 S.W.2d 48 (Tex. Crim. App. 1957), both of which involved parked cars; *Sinclair v. State*, 311 S.W.2d 824 (Tex. Crim. App. 1958), which involved a theater; and *Shipp v. State*, 342 S.W.2d 756 (Tex. Crim. App. 1961) and *Buchanan v. State*, 471 S.W.2d 401 (Tex. Crim. App. 1971), both of which involved public restrooms. Cases involving acts in a jail include: *Blankenship v. State*, 289 S.W.2d 240 (Tex. Crim. App. 1956), *Bue v. State*, 368 S.W.2d 774 (Tex. Crim. App. 1963), and *Bishoff v. State*, 531 S.W.2d 346 (Tex. Crim. App. 1976).

67 Cases involving alleged force or coercion include: *Gordzelik v. State*, 246 S.W.2d 638 (Tex. Crim. App. 1952), *Willard v. State*, 338 S.W.2d 472 (Tex. Crim. App. 1960), and *Pruett v. State*, 463 S.W.2d 191, 192 (Tex. Crim. App. 1970).

68 Cases involving a minor include: *Brown v. State*, 99 S.W. 1001 (Tex. Crim. App. 1907), *Holmes v. State*, 269 S.W. 95 (Tex. Crim. App. 1925), *Slusser v. State*, 232 S.W.2d 727 (Tex. Crim. App. 1950), *Pipkin v. State*, 230 S.W.2d 221 (Tex. Crim. App. 1950), *Sartin v. State*, 335 S.W.2d 762 (Tex. Crim. App. 1960), *Moats v. State*, 402 S.W.2d 921, 922 (Tex. Crim. App. 1966), and *Johnston v. State*, 418 S.W.2d 522 (Tex. Crim. App. 1967).

69 *Buchanan v. Batchelor*, 308 F. Supp. 729, 733 (N.D. Tex. 1970). In *State v. Morales*, 826 S.W.2d 201 (Tex. Ct. App. 1992), the court found no reported sodomy prosecutions at all since 1973 (ibid., 203).

70 Telephone interview with Ray Hill (August 6 and 7, 2003). In Supreme Court history, Hill is best known for *Houston v. Hill*, 482 U.S. 451 (1987), in which his conviction for violating a disturbing-the-peace ordinance was reversed as abridging his First Amendment rights to criticize a police officer in the process of making an arrest.

71 Eskridge, *Gaylaw*, 87.

72 Interview with Ira Jones, Houston (August 27, 2003).

73 Hill interview (2003). The facts about this arrest, which occurred in 1982 or 1983, come from this interview alone. To my knowledge, there is no official record of the arrest or of the subsequent proceedings.

74 See, for example, *Kyllo v. United States*, 533 U.S. 27, 33 (2001), and *Katz v. United States*, 389 U.S. 347, 361 (1967) (Harlan, J., concurring).

75 Hill interview (2003). I attempted to verify Hill's account by contacting the defense attorney he named, but the attorney did not respond to a request for an interview.

76 Ibid.

77 Nan Hunter used "specification" to describe the evolution of sodomy laws: Nan Hunter, "Life After *Hardwick*," *Harvard Civil Rights–Civil Liberties Law Review* 27 (1992): 531, 538.

78 *State v. Morales*, 826 S.W.2d at 202–03.

79 See Christopher R. Leslie, "Creating Criminals: The Injuries Inflicted by 'Unenforced' Sodomy Laws," *Harvard Civil Rights–Civil Liberties Law Review* 35 (2002), 103, for a discussion of the ways in which state sodomy laws burdened homosexuals.

80 *Darling v. State*, 47 S.W. 1005, 1005 (Tex. Crim. App. 1898), quoting the defendant's description of the prosecutor's argument, a description the court dismissed as "in no way verified as being true." The truncated factual description

does not reveal whether the defendant's victims were male, female, or both, but the description of Darling's behavior as "abominable and detestable" suggests at least some homosexual element.

Chapter 2: *The City and the Cause*

1   Bruce Remington, "Twelve Fighting Years: Homosexuals in Houston, 1969–1981" (master's thesis, University of Houston, 1983), 2 (on file with author).

2   Interview with Ray Hill, Houston (June 28, 2005).

3   George Rimmey, "When I Come Back, I'm Going to Be Gay" (unpublished autobiography, on file with author), 69.

4   James T. Sears, *Rebels, Rubyfruit, and Rhinestones* (New Brunswick, N.J.: Rutgers University Press, 2001), 53

5   Brief *Amicus Curiae* of Professors of History George Chauncey et al., *Lawrence v. Texas*, No. 02-102 (Supreme Court, January 16, 2003), 19 (hereinafter, Historians' Brief).

6   Hill interview (2005).

7   Historians' Brief, 19.

8   Rimmey, "When I Come Back," 122–23.

9   Ibid., 124.

10   Ibid., 123.

11   Ibid.

12   Ibid., 124.

13   Ibid., 126–27.

14   Interview with George Rimmey, Houston (April 9, 2007).

15   Sears, *Rebels, Rubyfruit, and Rhinestones*, 49.

16   Hill interview (2005).

17   Rimmey, "When I Come Back," 126.

18   Charles Gillis, "A Brief History of the Gay Community of Houston, Texas," *Gay Pride Week '80 Guide* (June 1980), 64 (pamphlet on file with author)

19   Sears, *Rebels, Rubyfruit, and Rhinestones*, 53–55. The Promethean Society was named for the Greek god Prometheus, who brought fire and light to mortals. "Now why you would name a gay organization after a mythological figure whose liver is torn out every day without a concern about hepatitis A, B, or C, is a mystery to me," commented Hill: Hill interview (2005).

20   Gillis, "A Brief History," 64.

21   Sears *Rebels, Rubyfruit, and Rhinestones*, 57–58; Hill interview (2005).

22   Charles Kaiser, *The Gay Metropolis: 1940–1996* (Boston: Houghton Mifflin, 1997), 197.

23   Ibid., 198–99.

24   Ibid., 201.

25   See generally Martin Duberman, *Stonewall* (New York: Dutton, 1993).

26   Gillis, "A Brief History," 64.

27   Sears, *Rebels, Rubyfruit, and Rhinestones*, 167.

28   Ibid.

29   Ibid., 172.

30   Gillis, "A Brief History," 65.

31   Thorne Dreyer and Al Reinart, "Montrose Lives!" *Texas Monthly*, April 1973; Sears, *Rebels, Rubyfruit, and Rhinestones*, 167–73.

32   Sears, *Rebels, Rubyfruit, and Rhinestones*, 167–73.

33 Gillis, "A Brief History," 68.
34 Hill interview (2005).
35 Gillis, "A Brief History," 65.
36 Jack Olsen, *The Man with the Candy* (New York: Simon & Schuster, 1975).
37 Sears, *Rebels, Rubyfruit, and Rhinestones*, 219; Hill interview (2005).
38 Sears, *Rebels, Rubyfruit, and Rhinestones*, 219.
39 Ibid., 220.
40 Hill interview (2005); Sears, *Rebels, Rubyfruit, and Rhinestones*, 221.
41 Anita Bryant, *The Anita Bryant Story: The Survival of Our Nation's Families and the Threat of Militant Homosexuality* (Old Tappan, N.J.: Revell, 1977), 145–48.
42 Hill interview (2005); Sears, *Rebels, Rubyfruit, and Rhinestones*, 268.
43 Hill interview (2005).
44 Sears, *Rebels, Rubyfruit, and Rhinestones*, 269.
45 Hill interview (2005).
46 Interview with Annise Parker, Houston (June 27, 2005).
47 Hill interview (2005).
48 Sears, *Rebels, Rubyfruit, and Rhinestones*, 284.
49 Hill interview (2005).
50 Sears, *Rebels, Rubyfruit, and Rhinestones*, 305.
51 "Gay Power in Macho Houston," *Newsweek*, August 10, 1981.
52 Mark Obbie, "Gay Bars Get Surprise Visitor," *Houston Post*, January 9, 1984, 1A.
53 Tom Kennedy, "Gays a Force to Be Reckoned With," *Houston Post*, January 12, 1984.
54 Parker interview (2005). According to Parker, the problem began to be addressed only when Whitmire was elected mayor and appointed the first commission to investigate citizen complaints against the police.
55 Ibid.
56 "Gay Rights Support Rebounds from 1985," *Houston Post*, March 1986.
57 "Much Ado About Very Little," *Texas Monthly*, September 1984, 124.
58 Minutes, "Meeting of concerned community activists to discuss referendum on jobs," July 11, 1984 (on file with author).
59 "Gay Quarantine Idea Draws Verbal Attack from George Greanias," *Houston Digest*, January 7, 1985, 2.
60 Jon Verboon, "Whitmire 'Crashes' Anti-gay Rights Event," *Houston Chronicle*, January 6, 1985.
61 "Future Gay Plans Worry CPA Chief," *Houston Digest*, January 7, 1985, 1.
62 Letter to voters from Judi Wilson (on file with author).
63 Letter to voters from Campaign for Houston, December 30, 1984 (on file with author) (emphasis in original). In fact, the documentary was not screened at the event because of legal disputes between the group and CBS: Leslie Loddeke and John Gravois, "Homosexual Rights Foe to Sue over Alleged Libel," *Houston Post*, January 9, 1985, 12A.
64 John Gravois, "Gay Vote Opponents Still Fighting over 'Real Issue,'" *Houston Post*, January 17, 1985, 1A.
65 Ed Falk, "Statement Before City Council," August 1984, 3 (on file with author).
66 John Gravois, "Mayor Slams Chamber on Gay Vote," *Houston Post*, December 20, 1984, 1A; Mike Yuen and John Gravois, "Protection for Gays Could Harm City, Louie Welch Says," *Houston Post*, January 4, 1985, 10A; Nene Foxhall, "Council, Chamber Deadlock on Gay Issue," *Houston Chronicle* December 20, 1984, 1.
67 John Gravois, "Ex-Rep. Jordan Makes Gay Rights Endorsement," *Houston Post*, January 16, 1985, 14A.

68 Nene Foxhall and Tom Moran, "Distortion Charges Fly at Gay Job Rights Forum," *Houston Chronicle*, January 16, 1985, 1.

69 Advertisement from Campaign for Houston, *Houston Post*, January 13, 1985, 7B.

70 "Doctors Form Anti-gay Group," *Houston Chronicle*, 1984.

71 Thomas J. Coleman Jr., "Gays May Face Tough Legal Sledding," *Houston Post*, March 8, 1985, 3B.

72 Rad Sallee, "Group of Pastors Joins Fight Against Gay Measures," *Houston Chronicle*, January 10, 1985, 22.

73 Jane Ely and Emily Grotta, "County GOP Urges 'No' Votes," *Houston Post*, January 15, 1985, 1A.

74 "Much Ado About Very Little," 126.

75 John Gravois, "Gay Rights Debate Flares on City Council; Vote Postponed," *Houston Post*, 1984.

76 Ibid.

77 John Gravois, "Ex-Rep Jordan Makes Gay Rights Endorsement," *Houston Post*, January 16, 1985, 14A.

78 Advertisement from Committee for Public Awareness, *The Informer and Texas Freeman*, January 19, 1985, 4 (emphasis in original).

79 Advertisement from Committee for Public Awareness, *Houston Chronicle* (on file with author).

80 Brochure paid for by Campaign for Houston (emphasis in original) (on file with author).

81 Brochure paid for by Texans for Moral Government (on file with author).

82 Brochure paid for by the Institute for the Scientific Investigation of Sexuality (on file with author).

83 John Gravois, "Both Sides Work to Boost Turnout," *Houston Post*, January 10, 1985, 1A.

84 Interview with John Lawrence, Houston (April 22, 2011).

85 "Pastors, Doctors, Lawyers Join Anti-gay Rights Forces," *Houston Digest*, January 14, 1985, 1. The political scientist quoted was the University of Houston's Kent Tedin.

86 George F. Barnhart, "Bitter Lessons in Houston Referendum," *Montrose Voice*, January 25, 1985, 3; "Gay Rights Support Rebounds from 1985," *Houston Post*. Only 27 percent supported gay rights. A year later, in 1986, the public was more nearly split, opposing gay equality 47 to 43 percent: ibid.

87 Robert Reinhold, "AIDS Remark Is at Issue in Houston Vote Today," *New York Times*, November 5, 1985. Days after the remark, T-shirts sprouted in the city bearing the slogan "Louie, Don't Shoot!": Parker interview.

88 Parker interview.

89 Ibid.

90 Ibid.

91 Ibid. Parker's conscious downplaying of her homosexuality, without denying it, is an example of what Yale law professor Kenji Yoshino has called "covering": Kenji Yoshino, *Covering: The Hidden Assault on Our Civil Rights* (New York: Random House, 2006).

92 John Aston, "Ten Years Later," *Outsmart*, July 2001 (available at http://www.outsmartmagazine.com/issue/i07-01/broussard.html).

93 Ibid.

94 Ibid.

95 Parker interview.

Chapter 3: *The Defendants and the Troublemakers*

1 Dana Calvo, "Private Lives amid a Very Public Decision," *Los Angeles Times,* July 1, 2003, E1. The lawyers representing Lawrence and Garner consistently shielded the men from public scrutiny. They declined media requests (and my request) for interviews until June 2005. Even then, my interviews with Lawrence and Garner were conducted at Mitchell Katine's office, with Katine present, objecting to questions occasionally and instructing Lawrence and Garner not to answer questions about whether they were having sex the night of the arrests, and directing the men not to speculate or stray off-topic while answering a question. It was a bit more like taking depositions than conducting interviews for historical purposes. Only in April 2011 was I able to interview Lawrence about his relationship with Garner and whether they were having sex. Even then, Katine was present for the interview.
2 Telephone interview with Lane Lewis (August 7 and 8, 2003). Lewis served as president of the Houston Gay and Lesbian Political Caucus.
3 Interview with Suzanne Goldberg, New York City (April 24, 2007).
4 Unless otherwise noted, this section is based on my first interview with John Lawrence, Houston (June 14, 2005).
5 Interview with apartment managers, Houston (June 20, 2005).
6 Interview with Joseph Quinn, Houston (June 20, 2005), interview with Donald Tipps, Houston (April 16, 2007).
7 Tipps interview.
8 Interview with John Lawrence, Houston (April 22, 2011).
9 Harris County Sheriff's Department, Inmate Processing—Warrant Pending—DIMS Worksheet, September 18, 1998, John Lawrence (on file with author). "DIMS" stands for Departmental Information Management System. See also R. A. Dyer, "Two Men Charged Under State's Sodomy Law," *Houston Chronicle* November 6, 1998, A1; this was the first newspaper story about the arrests.
10 Calvo, "Private Lives amid a Very Public Decision"; telephone interview with Ray Hill (August 6 and 7, 2003); Lewis interview.
11 Harris County Sheriff's Department, JIMS Booking Inquiry—LBKI, November 6, 1998, John Lawrence (on file with author). "JIMS" stands for Justice Information Management System.
12 Interview with David Jones, Houston (April 13, 2007).
13 Lewis interview.
14 Lawrence interview (2005).
15 Ibid.
16 Harris County Sheriff's Department, Inmate Processing—Warrant Pending—DIMS Worksheet, September 18, 1998, Tyron Garner (on file with author).
17 Everyone close to the case attests to this, including Garner himself. Hill interview (2003); Lewis interview; Goldberg interview; interview with Ruth Harlow, New York (April 25, 2007); Katine interview (2003).
18 Interview with Tyron Garner, Houston (June 28, 2005).
19 Goldberg interview.
20 These were my impressions of him during our afternoon-long interview and car ride together both before and after the interview.
21 Garner interview.
22 Ibid.; Lawrence interview (2005).
23 Garner interview; Lewis interview.

24 JIMS Booking Inquiry—LBKI, November 6, 1998, Tyron Garner (on file with author); Lisa Teachey, "Defendant in Sodomy Case Out of Jail After Assault Charges Dismissed," *Houston Chronicle*, November 25, 1998, A3; Bruce Nichols, "Men Whose Sodomy Case Led to Supreme Court Ruling Keep Low Profile," *Dallas Morning News*, June 26, 2003.

25 JIMS Booking Inquiry—LBKI, November 6, 1998, Tyron Garner (on file with author).

Chapter 4: *The Department and the Deputies*

1 For information about District 3, see http://www.hcso.hctx.net/Patrol/district3/default.asp (accessed May 22, 2007).

2 Interview with Donald Tipps, Houston (April 16, 2007).

3 Roma Khanna and Lise Olsen, "One in Three Police Shootings Involve Unarmed People," *Houston Chronicle*, July 25, 2004.

4 Ibid.

5 Ibid.

6 Sarah Fenske, "Black and White: Good 'Ol Boys Prosper at the Harris County Sheriff's Office. Many Blacks Don't," *Houston Press*, November 11, 2004.

7 Ibid.

8 Ibid.

9 Ibid.

10 Ibid.

11 Telephone interview with anonymous Harris County Sheriff's Office employee, (April 17, 2007). After a brief discussion over the telephone about the antigay atmosphere within the department, this source declined to comment further or sit for a longer interview, even with a guarantee of anonymity. The fear in her voice was palpable and she seemed almost to break down discussing the issue over the phone.

12 Interview with Nathan Broussard, Houston (June 20, 2005); interview with Sheryl Roppolo, Houston (June 20, 2005).

13 Tipps interview (2007).

14 The employment policy is available at http://www.hcso.hctx.net/employment.asp (accessed March 24, 2010).

15 Interview with Annise Parker, Houston (June 27, 2005). By contrast, Parker and Lane Lewis personally led gay-awareness training sessions for city of Houston police officers in the 1990s and 2000s.

16 Telephone interview with Lieutenant John Martin (April 18, 2007); Martin was then the public information officer for the department. When I asked whether he knew of any openly gay officers in the department he paused for about twenty seconds, then replied, "Uh . . . not that I would want to discuss in this context." He subsequently sent me an e-mail attaching the department's bias-based profiling policy, which specifically prohibits profiling on the basis of characteristics like race and sexual orientation: e-mail from John Martin to Dale Carpenter, April 18, 2007. As best I can tell, this was the only department policy that specifically mentioned sexual orientation.

17 Unless otherwise noted, the discussion of Quinn's life and career that follows is based on my interviews with Quinn, over the phone on August 9 and 31, in 2003, and in person on June 20, 2005.

18 Broussard interview. Nathan Broussard is no relation to Paul Broussard, the young gay banker murdered in 1991 (see chapter 2).

19 Ibid.
20 Interview with Mike Parrott, Houston (June 22, 2005).
21 Ibid.
22 Tipps interview (2007). See also Broussard interview.
23 Roppolo interview.
24 Unless otherwise noted, the material in this section is based on my interview with William Lilly, Houston (June 23, 2005).
25 Unless otherwise noted, the biographical and quoted material about Tipps come from my 2007 interview with him.
26 The quote is taken from the group's website http://www.boysandgirlscountry.org (accessed November 15, 2010).
27 Landry did not respond to repeated requests for an interview, so the biographical material about him is based on my interviews with Quinn, Lilly, and Tipps.

Chapter 5: *The Intrusion*

1 Interview with John Lawrence, Houston (April 22, 2011).
2 Interview with John Lawrence, Houston (June 14, 2005); interview with Tyron Garner, Houston (June 28, 2005). The account of what happened in Lawrence's apartment prior to the arrival of the police is based on these 2005 interviews, unless otherwise noted.
3 Telephone interview with Lane Lewis (August 7 and 8, 2003); Garner interview.
4 Lawrence interview (2005). Quinn indicated in his internal Offense Report that Eubanks claimed he had HIV. There is no independent confirmation that Eubanks was HIV-positive, had AIDS, or suffered from dementia.
5 Interview with Joseph Quinn, Houston (June 20, 2005).
6 Ibid.; interview with William Lilly, Houston (June 23, 2005); interview with Donald Tipps, Houston (April 16, 2007). The following material is based on my interviews with these deputies.
7 Lawrence interview (2005); Garner interview.
8 In our first interview in 2003, Quinn remembered Tipps and Landry going into the bedroom on the left. In our 2005 interview he said that he had cleared the bedroom by himself and then gone into the kitchen area. The 2003 account is more credible because it was closer in time to the events, is consistent with the other deputies' recollections, and makes more sense than a scenario in which Quinn is literally involved in everything going on in the apartment.
9 Detail Report for Harris County Law Enforcement, September 18, 1998, 5 (hereinafter cited as "Offense Report") (on file with author). Man #4 is not mentioned as a witness in the pair of Probable Cause Affidavits Quinn filed that night: Joseph Richard Quinn, Probable Cause Affidavits, September 17, 1998 (hereinafter "Quinn Affidavit [Lawrence]" and "Quinn Affidavit [Garner]") (both affidavits on file with author). Nor does his name appear in any of the other court documents I have obtained. No media account mentions him. I have not been successful in tracking down Pelayo-Velez or in identifying anyone else who might have been Man #4.
10 Quinn interview (2005).
11 Lawrence interview (2011).
12 Quinn interview (2005).
13 Ibid.; Lilly interview.
14 Quinn interview (2005); Lilly interview.

15 Quinn interview (2005). Tipps remembered the sequence differently: he said that Quinn alone entered the back bedroom and then, apparently seeing Lawrence and Garner, "hollered something"; only then, did Lilly go to the back bedroom to assist him (Tipps interview). However, Quinn and Lilly both say they entered the bedroom at the same time, and since they were closest to the actual event, their account is more reliable.

16 Quinn interview (2005).

17 Janice Law, *Sex Appealed: Was the U.S. Supreme Court Fooled?* (Austin: Eakin Press 2005), 18. Law's book, filled with conspiracy theories, is generally not a reliable guide to the events.

18 Lilly interview.

19 Quinn interview (2005).

20 Lilly interview.

21 Quinn interview (2005).

22 Ibid.

23 In our first interview, in 2003, Quinn claimed that Tipps and/or Landry helped him push Lawrence away from Garner. In our second interview, in 2005, Quinn said that he alone disentangled them. The second version is more consistent with the stories told by the other deputies, none of whom remembered Lawrence being pushed away from Garner, much less doing so personally.

24 Quinn interview (2005); Lilly interview; Tipps interview (2007).

25 Quinn interview (2005).

26 Offense Report, 5. The intake worksheets for both Lawrence and Garner indicate that they had been using alcohol, but not drugs; they do not indicate whether they were intoxicated: Harris County Sheriff's Department, Inmate Processing—Warrant Pending—DIMS Worksheet, September 18, 1998, John Lawrence; Harris County Sheriff's Department, Inmate Processing—Warrant Pending—DIMS Worksheet, September 18, 1998, Tyron Garner (both on file with author).

27 Quinn interview (2005); Lilly interview; Tipps interview (2007).

28 Quinn interview (2005).

29 Not all of the attorneys were silent about this issue or about communications between the defendants and lawyers. David Jones, who attended the very first meeting between the lawyers and the men, and who assisted in the defense early in the case, said that Lawrence and Garner never told him whether they were or were not having sex when the police entered the apartment. "They just didn't want to go into it," he said. Nevertheless, Jones believed they were having sex: interview with David Jones, Houston (April 13, 2007). Lawrence contradicted Jones, saying that he informed the lawyers that he and Garner were not having sex: Lawrence interview (2011).

30 Lawrence interview (2005); Garner interview. Mitchell Katine, the Houston attorney who first took on the matter, was present during the interviews of Lawrence and Garner in 2005, as well as during the interview of Lawrence in 2011. As noted in the text, Lambda attorneys, along with Katine, cited a need to protect the men's privacy, which, they argued, was the basis for the whole lawsuit. This seemed pretextual, given that the men's sexual privacy had already been invaded by the police and a denial of the officers' allegations could not further erode it.

   Lambda attorneys may actually have been concerned that their own ethics as lawyers would be questioned because they let the case proceed on what they suspected to be a false factual basis. Yet defense attorneys are perfectly justified to let officers' factual allegations go unchallenged if they fear police perjury might be believed by a jury or judge.

The other rationale for keeping Garner and Lawrence mute on the issue might have been a concern for the legacy of *Lawrence v. Texas* itself. Of course, the Supreme Court is not going to overrule the decision based on disputed statements made by one side years after the events. The concern about revealing the truth, or at least what the defendants said is the truth, is more amorphous than that. As it stands, the official public record of the case states that the police invaded the private space of a bedroom and arrested two adults for having sex. Most of the public, even if they are unsympathetic to homosexuals or to gay-rights causes, opposes such intrusions. Admitting that the sex never occurred complicates the otherwise straightforward story behind *Lawrence*. It might also fuel the theories of antigay commentators who believe the whole case was built on a lie and who think gays will advance the "gay agenda" by any means necessary. On this view, revealing the truth might tarnish the case, not in a narrow legal sense but in a broader cultural and political one. For reasons given in chapter 8, my own view is that, if indeed sheriff's deputies made up a story about two men having sex as a justification to arrest them for, in part, underlying homophobic and other invidious reasons, then *Lawrence* raises even more profound and deeper concerns about antigay legislation like the Texas Homosexual Conduct law. (Ruth Harlow agrees: interview with Ruth Harlow, New York [April 25, 2007].) At any rate, the aim of this book is to tell the story of *Lawrence v. Texas* as accurately as it can be told, wherever that truth might lead.

31 Lawrence interview (2011).
32 Ibid.
33 Ibid.
34 Garner interview.
35 Ibid.
36 Ibid.
37 Ibid.
38 Ibid.
39 Lawrence interview (2005).
40 Lewis interview.
41 Lane Lewis, handwritten notes (on file with author); Lewis interview.
42 Telephone interview with Ray Hill (August 6 and 7, 2003).

Chapter 6: *Uncivil Disobedience*

1 Telephone interview with Joseph Quinn (August 9 and 31, 2003); telephone interview with Donald Tipps (August 15, 2003).
2 Interview with John Lawrence, Houston (April 22, 2011).
3 Quinn interview (2003); interview with John Lawrence, Houston (June 14, 2005).
4 Interview with Tyron Garner, Houston (June 28, 2005).
5 Quinn interview (2003); interview with William Lilly, Houston (June 23, 2005).
6 Lawrence interview (2011).
7 Ibid.
8 Quinn interview (2003) and interview with Joseph Quinn, Houston (June 20, 2005); Lilly interview: Tipps denied making any such jokes at the scene: Tipps interview (2007).

9 Garner interview.

10 Lawrence interview (2005); Garner interview. In his first interview, Quinn recalled that Lawrence had in fact been led into the living room handcuffed and naked: Quinn interview (2003); he changed that account in the second interview: Quinn interview (2005). The second account is consistent with what Lilly and Tipps remember about the sequence.

11 Garner interview.

12 Quinn interview (2005); Tipps interview (2007); Lawrence interview (2005).

13 Quinn interview (2005).

14 Adams retired in 2002. On September 12, 2003, I interviewed him by telephone about the case. I have not included his account of what happened because it is so radically different from the other deputies' that I do not regard it as credible. For example, he told me that when the deputies first walked into the apartment Lawrence and Garner were having sex on the living room couch. No other deputy claimed that was the case. Also, Adams had no firsthand knowledge of what was happening in the apartment when the deputies first arrived. Adams, by all accounts other than his own, arrived only after the other deputies had conducted an initial search of the apartment and had secured Lawrence, Garner, and Man #4. Interestingly, Adams's recollection that Lawrence and Garner were in the living room area—not the bedroom—when police arrived is consistent with Lawrence's own account. Lawrence interview (2011).

15 Garner interview.

16 Quinn interview (2005); Lilly interview; Tipps interview (2007).

17 Tipps interview (2007); see also Quinn interview (2005) and Lawrence interview (2005). Lawrence later publicly described the deputies' actions as "sort of Gestapo": Steve Brewer, "Texas Men Post Bonds, Challenge State's Sodomy Law," New York Times News Service, November 20, 1998.

18 Quinn interview (2005).

19 Lawrence interview (2005).

20 Quinn interview (2005).

21 Ibid.; Lilly interview.

22 Janice Law, *Sex Appealed: Was the U.S. Supreme Court Fooled?* (Austin: Eakins Press, 2005), 18.

23 Tipps interview (2007).

24 Quinn interviews (2003 and 2005); Lilly interview; Tipps interview (2007).

25 The intake worksheets for Lawrence and Garner indicate Kay Lynn Williford was the "intake D.A." However, this is probably a mistake. Williford was not on duty until later that night and fielded only a subsequent administrative question about the arrests. It is her answer to this subsequent call that probably resulted in her name appearing as the intake D.A. on the worksheet: telephone interview with Kay Lynn Williford (August 27, 2003).

26 Jones was the assistant D.A. who in 1980 had advised officers they could not arrest gay men under the Homosexual Conduct law simply for having a party in a private home. See chapter 2.

27 Telephone interview with Ira Jones, Houston (August 27, 2003).

28 Lawrence and Garner concur that they probably would have let the matter go: Lawrence interview (2005); Garner interview.

29 Quinn interview (2003). Quinn's concern for the men's lives recalls the concern expressed by the lead officer of the raiding party at the Stonewall Inn bar in 1969, the event that sparked a riot and the modern phase of the gay civil rights move-

ment. Describing how tense the situation became, he said, "You have no idea how close we came to killing somebody": Charles Kaiser, *The Gay Metropolis: 1946– 1996* (Boston: Houghton Mifflin, 1997), 197.

30 Quinn interviews.
31 Tipps interview (2007).
32 Lilly interview; Quinn interviews.
33 Tipps interview (2007).
34 Lilly interview.
35 Ibid.
36 Quinn interview (2003).
37 Interview with Jeri Brock, Houston (June 20, 2005).
38 Quinn interview (2005); Lilly interview; Tipps interview (2007).
39 Lawrence interview (2005); Garner interview.
40 Ibid.
41 Quinn interview (2003). One author claims that Deputy Landry told her Lawrence spit at him during the arrest: Law, *Sex Appealed,* 23. It is very unlikely that any such thing occurred, and none of the three deputies I interviewed recalled any spitting incident: Quinn interviews; Lilly interview; Tipps interview (2007). Lawrence denied that he spat at anyone: Lawrence interview (2005).
42 Lawrence interview (2005); Garner interview.
43 These were of course references to the statutory number assigned to the Texas Homosexual Conduct law, Section 21.06 of the state criminal code.
44 Quinn Affidavit (Lawrence).
45 Quinn Affidavit (Garner).
46 Ibid.
47 Offense Report, 5–6. The original punctuation and the format in all capital letters have been preserved, but personal identifying information has been deleted. Quinn is the sole author of this report. "ADA" in the sixth paragraph is a reference to "assistant district attorney." "IPC" in the next-to-last paragraph is a reference to "internal processing center." Offense Report, 5–6. The reference to "Williford" is probably erroneous. See n. 25.
48 Quinn interviews: Tipps interview (2007).

Chapter 7: *A Probable Explanation for an Improbable Case*

1 Interview with Joseph Quinn, Houston (June 20, 2005).
2 Telephone interview with William Delmore (August 27, 2003).
3 Steve Brewer, "Texas Men Post Bonds, Challenge State's Sodomy Law," New York Times News Service, November 20, 1998.
4 See, for example, Joseph Farrah, "How Staged Sex Crime Fooled Supreme Court; Landmark Sodomy Case Faked from Start, Shrouded in Murder Mystery, Says Judge," WoldNetDaily.com, October 24, 2005 (available at http://www.wnd.com/ news/article.asp?ARTICLE_ID=46984) (accessed May 30, 2010).
5 Interview with William Delmore, Houston (June 30, 2005).
6 Delmore interview (2003).
7 *State v. Morales* 869 S.W.2d 941, 943 (Tex. 1994).
8 See *Morales*, 869 S.W.2d at 947–48.
9 Cases like this, said Ray Hill, "strike like lightning" in the lives of ordinary citizens: interview with Ray Hill, Houston (June 28 2005).
10 One self-published book alleging a grand conspiracy in the case has already

appeared: Janice Law, *Sex Appealed: Was the U.S. Supreme Court Fooled?* (Austin: Eakins Press, 2005). The book speculates, among other things, that Man #4 may have been the Latino partner of Mitchell Katine, choreographing Lawrence and Garner's sex acts while on the phone with Katine when police entered the apartment. Katine's partner, Walter Avila, denies any involvement in the case; he did not even meet Katine until a year after the arrests, something Law did not bother to ask: interview with Walter Avila, Houston (April 14, 2007). Law also suggests that gay-rights attorneys, including Katine, may have been involved in killing Robert Eubanks in 2000 as a way to keep him from exposing the alleged setup. There is no basis for believing such a conspiratorial charge. Law was a judge in the Harris County system in 1998, and was almost assigned to handle the *Lawrence* case. She was defeated in the GOP primary in her reelection bid.

11 *Griswold v. Connecticut*, 381 U.S. 479 (1965). See also David Garrow, *Liberty and Sexuality* (New York: Macmillan, 1994); Dale Carpenter, "Revisiting *Griswold*: An Exploration of Its Political, Social, and Legal Origins" (senior history essay, Yale College, 1989) (on file with author).

12 Quinn interview (2005).

13 Delmore agreed that this undercuts the test-case theory: Delmore interview (2005).

14 Hill interview (2005); Lewis interview; interview with William Lilly, Houston (June 23, 2005); interview with Mike Parrott, Houston (June 23, 2005); Quinn interview (2005); interview with Donald Tipps, Houston (April 16, 2007). See also Lou Chibbaro Jr., "Taking Credit for *Lawrence vs. Texas* Decision," *Washington Blade*, July 18, 2003. This *Washington Blade* story credits unnamed sources for the claim. A lawyer for Lawrence and Garner claimed that the motive for the false report was a "personality conflict between the caller and the people in the apartment." The jealousy motive for the false report is supported by the fact that Garner was later arrested for a Class C misdemeanor assault on Eubanks: Delmore interview (2005).

15 Lilly interview.

16 Tipps interview (2007).

17 "Umbrella Man" is the pseudonym given by conspiracy theorists for a person believed to have been a second shooter in the 1963 assassination of John F. Kennedy. In some pictures of the grassy knoll near the route of Kennedy's motorcade, taken at the time of the assassination, a blurry shadow in the trees is alleged to be an unknown man who appears to be standing under an umbrella.

18 Delmore interview (2005).

19 Interview with Annise Parker, Houston (June 27, 2005).

20 Ibid.

21 Interview with Ruth Harlow, New York (April 25, 2007).

22 None of these details about the incident appear in the Investigative Narrative of the Offense Report.

23 Lilly interview; Tipps interview (2007).

24 Telephone interview with Sheryl Roppolo (August 11, 2003).

25 Delmore interview (2003).

26 Interview with Judge Sherman Ross, Houston (April 17, 2007).

27 Deputy Donnie Tipps and Sergeant Ken Adams offer this as a possibility: telephone interview with Tipps (August 15, 2003); telephone interview with Adams (September 12, 2003).

28 Offense Report.

29 Tipps also offers this as a possibility: Tipps interview (2003).

30 Tipps interview (2003).

31 Roger Roots, "Are Cops Constitutional?," *Seton Hall Constitutional Law Journal* 11 (2001): 685, 718; Stanley Z. Fisher, "'Just the Facts, Ma'am: Lying and the Omission of Exculpatory Evidence in Police Reports," *New England Law Review* 28 (1993–94): 1, 9–17.

32 Christopher Slobogin, "Testilying: Police Perjury and What to Do About It," *University of Colorado Law Review* 67 (1996): 1037, 1044.

33 Morgan Cloud, "The Dirty Little Secret," *Emory Law Journal* 43 (1994): 1311 ("Police perjury is the dirty little secret of our criminal justice system"); Donald A. Dripps, "Police, Plus Perjury, Equals Polygraphy," *Journal of Criminal Law and Criminology* 86 (1996): 693; Myron W. Orfield Jr., "Deterrence, Perjury, and the Heater Factor: An Exclusionary Rule in the Chicago Criminal Courts," *University of Colorado Law Review* 63 (1992): 75.

34 See, for example, William N. Eskridge Jr., *Gaylaw: Challenging the Apartheid of the Closet* (Cambridge, Mass.: Harvard University Press, 1999), 87. Especially in the context of law enforcement operations to entrap homosexuals for violating public lewdness laws, "police officers often misrepresent the facts of their enticement rackets, in which they frequently invite propositions, then fabricate critical details, including offers of compensation": Evan Wolfson and Robert S. Mower, "When the Police Are in Our Bedrooms, Shouldn't the Courts Go In After Them? An Update on the Fight Against 'Sodomy' Laws," *Fordham Urban Law Journal* 21 (1994): 1006.

35 Jordan Blair Woods, "Don't Tap, Don't Stare, and Keep Your Hands to Yourself! Critiquing the Legality of Gay Sting Operations," *Journal of Gender, Race and Justice* 12 (2008–09): 545, 553.

36 Matt Lum, "Where Is the Outrage?" *The Texas Triangle*, August 2, 2001, quoted in Woods, "Don't Tap, Don't Stare," 553 n. 60.

37 Woods, "Don't Tap, Don't Stare," 553 n. 61.

38 Amnesty International, "Stonewalled: Police Abuse and Misconduct Against Lesbian, Gay, Bisexual and Transgender People in the U.S.," 2005, available at http://www.amnestyusa.org/outfront/stonewalled/report.pdf (accessed June 17, 2010).

39 Delmore interview (2005). There is, in fact, no evidence that whatever Lawrence and Garner were doing was nonconsensual, commercial, or in public view. In its Supreme Court brief, the State pointed to this gap in the evidentiary record as a reason to dismiss the appeal: Respondent's Brief, *Lawrence v. Texas*, 123 S. Ct. 2472 (2003) (No. 02-102). The Supreme Court was uninterested in these arguments, and not a single Justice asked a question about them or referred to the circumstance in the opinions in the case.

40 Eskridge, *Gaylaw*, 87 (noting disproportionate guilty pleas in sodomy cases).

41 Quinn interview (2005).

42 Tipps interview (2007).

43 Quinn interview (2005); Tipps interview (2007); Lilly interview.

44 The deputies may have suffered a moment of what the scholar Eve Kosofsky Sedgwick has termed "homosexual panic," one's fear of one's own potential for homosexual desire: Eve Kosofsky Sedgwick, *Epistemology of the Closet* (Berkeley: University of California Press, 1990).

45 Eskridge, *Gaylaw*, 209 (explaining the narcissistic and obsessional qualities of homophobia).

46 James D. Woods, *The Corporate Closet* (New York: Free Press, 1993), 65 (emphasis added).

47 Martin Duberman, *Stonewall* (New York: Dutton, 1993).

48 Lewis interview.

49 Hill interview (2005). See also chapter 4 for a discussions of the department's record of poor race relations.

50 Hill interview (2003).

51 Lambda attorney Ruth Harlow speculated that an interracial pair may have seemed an easier mark to the police: Harlow interview.

52 See, for example, Ron Fournier, "Bush, Kerry Put Value in Beliefs of Voters," *Houston Chronicle*, July 14, 2004, 10 (noting that the religious right has pursued ballot measures to ban gay marriage in swing states, partly to drive a wedge between white Democrats and black Democrats, who are "more socially conservative than most people realize").

53 In Lilly's account, Garner was performing fellatio on Lawrence: Lilly interview.

Chapter 8: *The Homosexual Status Law*

1 *Tennessee v. Garner*, 471 U.S. 1, 7 (1985).

2 Interview with Ira Jones, Houston (August 27, 2003) (discussing an earlier case where deputies had busted up a party in a private home).

3 Telephone interview with William Delmore (August 27, 2003).

4 See Cass Sunstein, "What Did *Lawrence* Hold? Autonomy, Desuetude, Sexuality, and Marriage," *Supreme Court Review* 2003 (2003): 27, 27–28.

5 *Romer v. Evans*, 517 U.S. 620 (1996) (holding animus impermissible as a basis for legislation under the Equal Protection Clause).

6 *Lawrence v. Texas*, 539 U.S. 558, 567 (2003).

7 Model Penal Code § 213.2 cmt. 2 (1962, Comments Revised 1980).

8 William N. Eskridge Jr., *Gaylaw: Challenging the Apartheid of the Closet* (Cambridge, Mass.: Harvard University Press, 1999).

9 *Lawrence*, 539 U.S. at 575. The Court's argument here is reminiscent of Kendall Thomas, "Beyond the Privacy Principle," *Columbia Law Review* 92 (1992): 1431.

10 Interview with John Lawrence, Houston (April 22, 2011).

Chapter 9: *From the Jail to the Bar*

1 Unless otherwise noted, the following account of the initial arraignment is taken from my 2005 interviews with John Lawrence and Tyron Garner.

2 Lawrence and Garner did not recall where Eubanks was taken that night, but it's likely he was also taken to the Harris County jail.

3 Telephone interview with Richard Carper (August 25, 2003). Carper, the supervisor of clerks in the Justice of the Peace courts for Harris County, was present at Lawrence and Garner's arraignment.

4 Interview with John Lawrence, Houston (April 22, 2011).

5 Judgment, *State v. Lawrence* (November 20, 1998) (Case No. CR31C1000002) (hereinafter cited as "Lawrence Judgment"); Judgment, *State v. Garner* (November 20, 1998) (Case No. CR31C1000003) (hereinafter "*Garner* Judgment") (both on file with author).

6 Lawrence Hearing Form, *State v. Lawrence* (September 18, 1998) (Case No. CR31C1000002); Garner Hearing Form, *State v. Garner* (September 18, 1998) (Case No. CR31C1000003) (both on file with author).

7 Interview with Ray Hill, Houston (June 28, 2005). The justice of the peace's

administrator confirmed this very easily could have been the outcome: interview with Sheryl Roppolo, Houston (June 20, 2005).

8 Lawrence interview (2011).

9 Ibid.

10 Interview with Nathan Broussard, Houston (June 20, 2005). Unless otherwise noted, the quotations and other information that follow regarding Broussard and Mark Walker are taken from my interview with Nathan Broussard.

11 When I first called Broussard to ask him about the case in August 2003, he declined to be interviewed and was clearly upset that I had called him. Two years later, after Walker had died, he agreed to be interviewed.

12 Roppolo interview (2005); interview with Mike Parrott (June 22, 2005).

13 Broussard interview.

14 Telephone interview with Lane Lewis (August 7 and 8, 2003).

15 Declaration of Allan Bérubé in Support of Memorandum of Points and Authorities in Support of Ex Parte Application for Leave to Intervene, at 4, *State ex rel. Agnost v. Owen* (Cal. App. Dep't Super. Ct. 1984) (No. 830-321).

16 John D'Emilio, *Sexual Politics, Sexual Communities: The Making of a Homosexual Minority in the United States, 1940–1970* (Chicago: University of Chicago Press, 1983), 186–92.

17 Ibid.

18 Eskridge, *Gaylaw*, 405 n. 98 (collecting sources on the role of gay bars in Buffalo, Detroit, Chicago, Denver, Philadelphia, San Francisco, New Orleans, Richmond, and Washington).

19 Lewis interview.

20 Lawrence interview (2005).

21 The following account of the initial conversation between Lawrence and Lewis comes from my interview with Lewis and from Lewis's handwritten notes on the faxed arrest report. Lewis notes (on file with author).

22 Mitchell Katine, the men's local lawyer, concurs that Lawrence was initially angry about being cited and about the way he was treated: interview with Mitchell Katine, Houston (June 17, 2005). "Had they simply been given a ticket it wouldn't have generated the same feelings of anger," said Katine. This anger may explain their ultimate decision to challenge the law.

23 If that's what Lawrence told Lewis in the telephone conversation, it is inconsistent with Lawrence's later insistence that he was sitting on the living room sofa, but consistent with his denial that the men were having sex. Lawrence interview (2011).

24 Lewis interview.

25 Lawrence interview (2011).

Chapter 10: *From the Gay Bar to the Bar*

1 Telephone interview with Lane Lewis (August 7 and 8, 2003).

2 Interview with Ray Hill, Houston (June 28, 2005).

3 Interview with Annise Parker, Houston (June 27, 2005).

4 Hill interview (2005). Far from being a Republican, Hill claims to have gone to Cuba in the late 1950s to support Fidel Castro's rebels. "We got down there and discovered that they were using live ammunition in that revolution," he says. "And that cooled our revolutionary spirit severely." This story is entertaining but unverified.

5 482 U.S. 451 (1987).

6 Hill interview (2005).

7 Parker interview.

8 Ibid.

9 Katine interview (2005).

10 According to Katine, the date on his copy of the fax is October 1 at 3:37 a.m., so it is possible that this conversation did not occur until that date, which would have been just four days before the scheduled appearance in the Justice of the Peace court: Katine interview (2005). I am dubious that the call to Katine came that late—a full two weeks after the arrests. The copy of the fax Katine now possesses may not be the original one he received; or the date and time stamp may be in error. Additionally, Katine is certain that he asked Lewis to fax the report during their first phone call. Lewis would not have waited until 3:37 a.m. to do so and did not send the fax before they actually spoke to each other. Finally, based on the recollections of others in the case, sometime early in the week of September 21 seems more likely for the first call to Katine.

11 Hill interview (2005).

12 Interview with David Jones, Houston (April 13, 2007); Katine interview (2005).

13 D. Jones interview.

14 Katine interview (2005).

15 Ibid.

16 Interview with Suzanne Goldberg, New York City (April 24, 2007).

17 517 U.S. 620 (1996).

18 The Arkansas litigation was filed in January 1998, eight months before the arrests in *Lawrence*. It resulted in a victory for Lambda Legal in 2002 when the state supreme court held that the state's same-sex sodomy law violated the right to privacy and equality guaranteed by the state constitution: *Jegley v. Picado*, 80 S.W.3d 382 (Ark. 2002). However, the legal victory was limited to Arkansas, leaving other sodomy laws, like the one in Texas, in place. "While Arkansans have been freed of that state's unconstitutional sodomy law, gay and lesbian Texans still carry the yoke of the Texas 'Homosexual Conduct Law,'" Ruth Harlow, legal director for Lambda, said at the time. "We are asking the U.S. Supreme Court to strike that law down once and for all": "Another Lambda Legal Victory—Arkansas Supreme Court's Decision Strikes Down State's Sodomy Law," press release, July 9, 2009 (available at http://www.lambdalegal.org/news/pr/ny_20020709_another-lambda-victory-ar-supreme-court-strikes-sodomy-law.html) (accessed February 1, 2011).

19 478 U.S. 186 (1986).

20 Goldberg thought that it was probably the week of September 21: Goldberg interview.

21 Ibid. When I asked Goldberg whether Katine had told her that there was some question about whether the men were actually having sex, she invoked the attorney-client privilege and declined to answer. By the time I interviewed her in 2007, Garner had died and she noted that it was now impossible to get his permission to waive the privilege and discuss the matter. Goldberg was forthcoming with me about everything else in this case.

22 Ibid.

23 Interview with Ruth Harlow, New York City (April 25, 2007).

24 Ibid. Harlow drafted an *amicus* brief for the American Bar Association in *Romer*. It was the first time the ABA had submitted a brief in a gay-rights case.

25 The Equal Protection Clause of the Fourteenth Amendment states, "[N]or shall

any state . . . deny to any person within its jurisdiction the equal protection of the laws": U.S. Const., Amend. XIV.

26 Harlow interview.

27 Ibid.

28 Ibid.

29 Dohrn stepped down as legal director of Lambda in 2000 and was replaced by Harlow. Cathcart remains the group's executive director, a position he has held since 1992.

30 Interview with John Lawrence, Houston (June 14, 2005).

31 Ibid.

32 Katine interview (2005).

33 Interview with John Lawrence (April 22, 2011).

34 D. Jones interview; Katine interview (2005).

35 D. Jones interview; Katine interview (2005).

36 D. Jones interview.

37 Katine interview (2005); D. Jones interview.

38 Lawrence interview (2005).

39 D. Jones interview.

40 Ibid.

41 Lewis interview.

42 Ibid.

43 Lawrence interview (2005).

44 Interview with Tyron Garner, Houston (June 28, 2005).

45 Ibid.

46 Lewis interview.

47 Ibid.

48 Lawrence interview (2011).

49 Harlow interview.

50 Lawrence interview (2005).

Chapter 11: *Into the Texas Courts*

1 Letter from David A. Jones to Judge Parrott, October 13, 1998 (on file with author).

2 Unless otherwise noted, the following discussion regarding the JP courts is based on my interviews in Houston with Sheryl Roppolo (June 20, 2005) and Mike Parrott (June 22, 2005).

3 Parrott interview.

4 R. A. Dyer, "Two Men Charged Under State's Sodomy Law," *Houston Chronicle*, November 5, 1998, 1.

5 769 F.2d 289 (1985).

6 Interview with William Delmore, Houston (June 30, 2005).

7 Dyer, "Two Men Charged."

8 Bruce Nichols, "Houston Case May Test Sodomy Law," *Dallas Morning News*, November 7, 1998.

9 Delmore interview (2005).

10 Ibid.

11 Nichols, "Houston Case May Test Sodomy Law."

12 See, for example, "Texas Case Could Kill Sodomy Law," *Chicago Tribune*, November 6, 1998; "Nation in Brief—Texans Vow Court Challenge of Sodomy Law," *The Atlanta Journal-Constitution*, November 7, 1998, A4.

13 See, for example, letter to Sheryl Roppolo from Robert L. Arnold, news reporter for AM 740 KTRH, November 16, 1998 (requesting "any and all public information . . . regarding the two men charged with the Class-C Misdemeanor of 'Homosexual Conduct'") (on file with author).

14 Interview with Suzanne Goldberg, New York City (April 24, 2007).

15 Interview with John Lawrence, Houston (June 14, 2005); interview with Tyron Garner, Houston (June 28, 2005).

16 Goldberg interview.

17 Parrott interview (2005).

18 Interview with David Jones, Houston (April 13, 2007). Lawrence had previously been in front of Parrott for a traffic violation, but the ticket was dismissed when the officer failed to show up: Lawrence interview (2005).

19 Goldberg interview.

20 Delmore interview (2005). Ligon later became the D.A. for a neighboring county. His office did not respond to a request for an interview about *Lawrence*.

21 Parrott interview (2005).

22 D. Jones interview.

23 Ibid. Whether this was actually the case under state law is a bit uncertain. Texas law appears to allow the court of appeals to hear a criminal appeal if the fine exceeds \$100 *or* the sole issue is the constitutionality of the law: Tex. Crim Code, Art 4.03 (Vernon's Ann.). Out of caution, however, it made sense for the defendants to ask for a larger fine. A few dollars was not worth the risk of losing a once-in-a-generation case.

24 Parrott interview (2005).

25 Reuters reported that the deputies "burst" into the bedroom: Andrew Kelly, "Two Texas Men Challenge State's Ban on Gay Sex," Reuters, November 18, 1998.

26 Telephone interview with Mike Parrott (August 6, 2003).

27 Steve Brewer, "Texas Men Post Bonds, Challenge State's Sodomy Laws," New York Times News Service, November 20, 1998.

28 Ibid.

29 Ibid.; Terri Langford, "No Contest Plea in Texas Sodomy Case," Associated Press, November 20, 1998 (on file with author).

30 Interview with Mitchell Katine, Houston (April 22, 2011).

31 Langford, "No Contest Plea in Texas Sodomy Case."

32 Paul Duggan, "Texas Sodomy Arrest Opens Legal Battle for Gay Activists," *Washington Post*, November 29, 1998.

33 *Powell v. State*, 510 S.E.2d 18 (Ga. 1998).

34 Lisa Teachey, "Defendant in Sodomy Case Out of Jail After Assault Charges Dismissed," *Houston Chronicle*, November 25, 1998, A23. The Montagu Hotel, built in 1911, was destroyed in 2008. Interested readers can watch a YouTube video of the demolition and read guest reminiscences of the "hanky panky" that went on there at http://www.glasssteelandstone.com/BuildingDetail/2144.php (accessed June 11, 2010).

35 Teachey, "Defendant in Sodomy Case Out of Jail," A22.

36 Ibid., A23.

Chapter 12: *The Constitutional Case Takes Shape*

1 Interview with Judge Sherman Ross, Houston (April 17, 2007). Ross dismissed Law's speculation, advanced in her conspiratorial, self-published book, that her

removal from the Lawrence case may have been engineered by Chow and Ross to advance the sodomy challenge. "It's all supposition and cloak and dagger and this and that and it's all nonsense": ibid. Law served four years as a county criminal court judge but was defeated in the Republican primary when she ran for reelection in 2002. Her brief reign on the county criminal court was, to say the least, controversial: see, for example, George Flynn, "Law and Disorder," *Houston Press*, September 2, 1999. Law was ranked "unqualified" to be a judge by a large margin in a poll of Houston attorneys: Margaret Downing, "HBA Releases Bar Poll, Bad News for Former Judge Janice Law and Others," *Houston Press*, February 18, 2010.

2   Interview with Angela Beavers, Houston (April 17, 2007).

3   In 1999 her partner gave birth to a child, whom Beavers legally adopted through a judge in San Antonio willing to allow same-sex couple adoptions (most judges in Texas will not allow a same-sex adoption, even though there is no explicit state law against it): ibid.

4   Interview with David Jones, Houston (April 13, 2007). Beavers acknowledged that she advised the defense team about the court's procedures, what papers to file, and so on, but she denied that her sexual orientation was relevant in any way to her prosecution of the case: Beavers interview.

5   Beavers interview. Beavers insisted that her feelings in opposition to the state Homosexual Conduct law were not what determined her decision to follow the case into Ross's court: ibid. Jones, while not suggesting that Beavers did anything wrong, observed that there "was just something in her face that told me this mattered to her as much as it did to anybody else"; she "was there to help, but you weren't going to get much out of her mouth that could come back to haunt her": D. Jones interview.

6   Beavers interview.

7   D. Jones interview. It is doubtful that, under Texas criminal procedure, a fine could be so low that it would prevent a constitutional challenge to a conviction.

8   D. Jones interview; Beavers interview.

9   D. Jones interview.

10   Ibid.

11   The D.A.'s office defends the constitutionality of state laws "unless the unconstitutionality of the statute is just obvious on its face": interview with William Delmore, Houston (June 30, 2005).

12   On this point, Bill Delmore disagreed. A prosecution might be dropped, for example, because the cost of flying in a witness from a long distance in a misdemeanor case would seem wasteful: ibid. Witness transportation costs would not have been a factor in the Lawrence and Garner case.

13   Interview with Suzanne Goldberg, New York City (April 24, 2007).

14   Filing a motion to quash was an idea advanced by Neil McCabe, then a professor at South Texas College of Law, as a necessary means to preserve the defendants' constitutional arguments in the Supreme Court. Transcription of Proceeding, 46 *South Texas Law Review* 323, 329 (2004) (remarks of Mitchell Katine). Katine says that McCabe provided much-needed advice on the procedural aspects of the case in the lower levels of the Texas courts: interview with Mitchell Katine, Houston (June 17, 2005).

15   Defendant's Motion to Quash Complaint/Information Under Texas Penal Code 21.06 (*State of Texas vs. Tyron Garner*) (on file with author); Defendant's Motion to Quash Complaint/Information Under Texas Penal Code 21.06 (*State of Texas vs. John Lawrence*) (on file with author) (hereinafter "Motions to Quash").

16 Motions to Quash, pp. 2–4.
17 Texas Constitution, Art. I, sec. 3.
18 Ibid., sec. 3a.
19 Motions to Quash, p. 2.
20 Ibid., p. 3 (citing *United States v. Virginia*, 518 U.S. 515, 533 [1996], which held that the Virginia Military Institute's exclusion of women was unconstitutional).
21 517 U.S. 620 (1996).
22 Motions to Quash, p. 3.
23 Ibid., p. 4.
24 Ibid., p. 5.
25 478 U.S. 186 (1986).
26 Beavers interview.
27 Ross interview.
28 Ibid.
29 Ibid.
30 Ibid.
31 Goldberg interview.
32 Except where noted, the description of the hearing is taken from the official transcript of the hearing before Judge Ross on December 22, 1998 (on file with author).
33 Beavers interview.
34 Ross says that a member of the media later asked him whether there was any significance to his "respectfully" denying the defendants' constitutional objections. There was no significance, but the fact that such a question would even be asked shows how carefully the media were by now following the case: Ross interview.
35 Criminal Court transcript (emphasis added).
36 Goldberg interview.
37 For some reason, Goldberg's interjection did not make it into the official transcript of the hearing. Only Beavers's self-correction is reflected in it.
38 D. Jones interview.
39 Misdemeanor Plea of Guilty/Nolo Contendere (Defendant Has Attorney), *State of Texas v. Tyron Garner* (Cause No. 9848531); Misdemeanor Plea of Guilty/Nolo Contendere (Defendant Has Attorney), *State of Texas v. John Lawrence* (Cause No. 9848530) (both on file with author).
40 Katine interview (2005).

Chapter 13: *The Politics of Law*

1 Defendant's Motion to Consolidate, *John Geddes Lawrence v. State of Texas* (Case No. 14-99-00109-CR) (March 18, 1999) (on file with author).
2 Brief of Appellants, *John Geddes Lawrence and Tyron Garner v. State of Texas* (Case Nos. 14-99-00109-CR and 14-99-00111-CR) (April 16, 1999) (on file with author) (hereinafter cited as "Appellants' Brief").
3 Ibid., p. 3.
4 Ibid., p. 4.
5 Ibid., p. 10 n. 6.
6 Ibid., 7, 9–10 (citing *Loving v. Virginia*, 388 U.S. 1 [1967]).
7 Andrew Koppelman, "Why Discrimination Against Lesbians and Gay Men Is Sex Discrimination," *New York University Law Review* 69 (1994), 197.

8 An exception was *Baehr v. Lewin*, 910 P.2d 112 (Hawaii 1996), holding that the restriction of marriage to opposite-sex couples was "sex discrimination" under the state constitution.

9 See ibid.

10 Texas Constitution, Article I, sec. 3a.

11 Appellants' Brief, p. 17.

12 Ibid.

13 Ibid., pp. 19–23.

14 Ibid., p. 24.

15 Ibid., p. 23.

16 Ibid., p. 25.

17 Unless otherwise indicated, the material in this section is based on my interview with William Delmore, Houston (June 30, 2005).

18 William N. Eskridge Jr., *Gaylaw: Challenging the Apartheid of the Closet* (Cambridge, Mass.: Harvard University Press, 1999), 220.

19 State's Appellate Brief, *John Geddes Lawrence and Tyron Garner v. The State of Texas* (Case Nos. 14-99-00109-CR and 14-99-00111-CR) (June 16, 1999), pp. 17–18 (on file with author) (hereinafter "State's Appellate Brief").

20 Ibid., pp. 13–16.

21 Delmore interview (2005).

22 State's Appellate Brief, pp. 14–15.

23 Delmore interview (2005).

24 Ibid.

25 State's Appellate Brief, p. 23.

26 Ibid., p. 6.

27 Ibid., pp. 15, 24.

28 Interview with Suzanne Goldberg, New York City (April 24, 2007).

29 Reply Brief of Appellants John Geddes Lawrence and Tyron Garner, *John Geddes Lawrence and Tyron Garner v. State of Texas* at 10–11 (Case No. 14-99-00111-CR) (July 16, 1999), pp. 10–11 (on file with author). Laws dealing with incest and drug use are also justified by the harm such activities do to the person himself or to others; the state made no harm-based claim about the state sodomy law: ibid., p. 11 n. 8.

30 Ibid., p. 9.

31 Letter from Mary Jane Gay (court clerk) to Mitchell Katine and William J. Delmore III, October 6, 1999 (on file with author).

32 Biographical information on John S. Anderson is available at http://www.14thcoa.courts.state.tx.us/court/justice_janderson.asp (accessed April 18, 2010).

33 Biographical information on J. Harvey Hudson is available at http://www.14thcoa.courts.state.tx.us/court/justice_jhudson.asp (accessed May 25, 2010).

34 Unless otherwise indicated, the material in this section is based on my interview with Judge Paul Clarence Murphy, Houston (May 15, 2007).

35 Goldberg interview. Goldberg went on leave to take care of her and her partner's child. She left Lambda in 2000 to begin teaching law. This brought her active participation in *Lawrence* to an end, but she did write an *amicus* brief for pro-gay-rights religious groups when the case reached the Supreme Court.

36 Interview with Ruth Harlow, New York City (April 25, 2007).

37 Ibid.

38 Ibid.

39 Delmore interview (2005).

40 Harlow interview. However, Delmore does not admit that he had any sympathy for the defendants: Delmore interview (2005).

41 Harlow interview.

42 Nathan Koppel, "Anti-Sodomy Law Challenged," *Law News Network*, November 9, 1999 (available at http://www.glapn.org/sodomylaws/usa/texas/txnews35.htm) (accessed June 11, 2010).

43 Delmore interview (2005).

44 Delmore interview (2005).

45 Steve Brewer, "Conduct Law Unfair to Gays, Attorney Says," *Houston Chronicle*, November 4, 1999.

46 *Baker v. Vermont*, 744 A.2d 864 (Vt. 1999).

47 Bruce Nichols, "Men Whose Sodomy Case Led to Supreme Court Ruling Keep Low Profile," *Dallas Morning News*, June 26, 2003.

48 Murphy interview.

49 Ibid.

50 *Lawrence v. Texas* (Case No. 14-99-00111-CR) (Tex. App.—Houston 14th), June 8, 1999, p. 5 (available at http://www.14thcoa.courts.state.tx.us/case/opinions/060800/990109f.pdf) (reversed by 41 S.W.3d 349 [Tex. App.—Houston 14th, 1999 (*en banc*)]).

51 Ibid., p. 7.

52 Ibid., p. 8, n. 8.

53 Ibid.

54 Ibid.

55 Ibid., p. 3 (Hudson dissenting).

56 Ibid., pp. 5–6.

57 Ibid., pp. 8–9.

58 Ibid., p. 9.

59 Ibid., p. 10.

60 Ibid., pp. 3, 7, n. 13.

61 Harlow interview.

62 *Republican Party of Texas v. Dietz*, 940 S.W.2d 86, 89 (Tex. 1997). I should disclose here that at the time I was state president of the group, the Log Cabin Republicans of Texas.

63 Quoted in Kevin Drum, "The New Model Republican Party," *Washington Monthly*, October 2003.

64 Alan Bernstein, "Texas Republicans Target One of Their Own," *Houston Chronicle*, July 3, 2000.

65 Murphy interview.

66 State's Brief in Support of Its Motion for Rehearing *En Banc*, *John Geddes Lawrence and Tyron Garner v. State of Texas* (August 23, 2000) (Case Nos. 14-99-00109-CR and 14-99-00111-CR) (on file with author).

67 Ibid., p. 3.

68 Ibid., p. 4.

69 Interview with Tyron Garner, Houston (April 28, 2005).

70 Ibid.

71 A copy of the Eubanks autopsy report is on file with the author.

72 Murphy interview.

73 "Race, Justice, and Texas," *Newsweek*, February 25, 2008.

74 Murphy interview.

75 *Lawrence v. Texas*, 41 S.W.3d 349 (Tex. App.—14th Dist. [Houston]), 2001 (*en banc*).

76   Ibid. at 356.
77   Ibid.
78   Ibid. at 376 (Anderson dissenting).
79   Ibid. at 384 (Anderson dissenting) (quoting Tex. Code Jud. Conduct, Canon 3[B] [5]).
80   Murphy interview.
81   Telephone interview with Frank Harmon (April 12, 2007).
82   *Lawrence v. Texas*, 41 S.W.3d at 363 (Yates concurring) (quoting Tex. Code Jud. Conduct, Canon 3[B][2]).
83   Ibid.
84   Ibid.
85   Ibid. at 364.
86   Wendy K. Mohon, "Sodomy Case Goes to Highest Texas Court," *Houston Voice*, April 13, 2001.
87   Armando Villafranca, "Legislature Likely to Take Up Sodomy Law Again," *Houston Chronicle*, April 19, 2001.
88   *State v. Morales*, 869 S.W.2d 941 (Tex. 1994).
89   478 U.S. 194 (1986).
90   Harlow interview.
91   Delmore interview (2005).

Chapter 14: *The Constitutional Mainstream*

1   Interview with Tyron Garner, Houston (June 28, 2005).
2   Interview with John Lawrence, Houston (April 22, 2011).
3   Bruce Nichols, "Men Whose Sodomy Case Led to Supreme Court Ruling Keep Low Profile," *Dallas Morning News*, June 26, 2003.
4   Interview with John Lawrence, Houston (June 14, 2005).
5   Interview with Ruth Harlow, New York City (April 25, 2007).
6   Tony Mauro, "Justices Asked to Reconsider *Bowers v. Hardwick*," *Fulton County Daily Report*, November 27, 2002 (available at http://www.glapn.org/sodomy laws/lawrence/lwnews011.htm) (accessed May 17, 2010).
7   521 U.S. 702 (1997).
8   Interview with William Hohengarten, Washington, D.C. (May 16, 2007).
9   Harlow interview.
10   This was a theme developed to great effect in Lambda's cert petition and in its briefs. The attorneys drew heavily on an article by Christopher Leslie, "Creating Criminals: The Injuries Inflicted by 'Unenforced' Sodomy Laws," *Harvard Civil Rights–Civil Liberties Law Review* 35 (2000): 103–82.
11   Telephone interview with Lindsay Harrison (May 5, 2010).
12   *Jegley v. Picado*, 80 S.W.3d 332 (Ark. 2002).
13   Harlow interview.
14   Petition for Writ of Certiorari, John Geddes Lawrence and Tyron Garner, Petitioners (July 16, 2002), p. i (hereinafter cited as "Cert Pet.").
15   Harlow interview; Hohengarten interview.
16   Harlow interview.
17   Cert Pet., p. 18.
18   Ibid., p. 19.
19   Harlow interview; Hohengarten interview; interview with Paul Smith, New York City (April 23, 2007).

20 Harlow interview; Hohengarten interview; Smith interview.

21 Harlow interview; interview with Suzanne Goldberg, New York City (April 24, 2007).

22 Harlow interview; Hohengarten interview; Smith interview.

23 Harlow interview.

24 Cert Pet., p. 22 n. 22.

25 Ibid., pp. 21–22.

26 Harlow interview; Hohengarten interview.

27 Hohengarten interview.

28 Cert Pet., p. 22.

29 Ibid., pp. 2, 3.

30 Ibid., p. 3 n. 1.

31 Ibid., p. 5.

32 Ibid., pp. 23–24.

33 Ibid., p. 27.

34 Ibid., p. 28.

35 Hohengarten interview; Harlow interview.

36 Cert Pet., p. 28, citing the Mychal Judge Police and Fire Chaplains Public Safety Officers' Benefit Act of 2002, Pub. L. No. 107-196, 116 Stat. 719 (June 24, 2002).

37 Ibid., pp. 28–29.

38 Ibid., p. 30.

39 Hohengarten interview.

40 Hohengarten remembered that Bill Rubenstein, his mentor, proposed an *amicus* brief that would delve into such subcommunities: ibid.

41 Harlow interview.

42 Interview with William Delmore, Houston (June 30, 2005).

43 Ibid.

44 Gromer Jeffers Jr., "Kirk, Cornyn Differ on Issues Facing Gays; Rivals Split on What Federal Law Should Cover," *Dallas Morning News*, September 14, 2002.

45 Delmore interview (2005).

46 Ibid.

47 The antigay Pro-Family Law Center had made exactly such claims in an *amicus* brief filed in August 2002, urging the Court not to hear the case.

48 Respondent's Brief in Opposition to Certiorari, *John Geddes Lawrence and Tyron Garner v. State of Texas* (No. 02-102) (October 21, 2002), pp. 4–5.

49 Ibid., p. 12.

50 Ibid., pp. 12–20.

51 Ibid., p. 20.

52 Patty Reinert, "Court May Review Texas Sodomy Law," *Houston Chronicle*, November 3, 2002.

53 Reply Brief of Petitioners (on petition for certiorari), *John Geddes Lawrence and Tyron Garner v. State of Texas* (No. 02-102) November 5, 2002.

54 Linda Greenhouse, *Becoming Justice Blackmun: Harry Blackmun's Supreme Court Journey* (New York: Henry Holt, 2006), 150.

55 Indeed, five Justices *did* initially vote to strike down sodomy laws, but Justice Lewis Powell changed his mind and voted to uphold them: Joyce Murdoch and Deb Price, *Courting Justice: Gay Men and Lesbians v. the Supreme Court* (New York: Basic Books, 2002) 313–14. In 1990, Powell said he regretted his vote. "I think I probably made a mistake in that one," he said during a lecture at New York University Law School: ibid., 339.

56 Order granting certiorari, *Lawrence v. Texas*, Case No. 02-102.

57 Smith interview.

58 Hohengarten interview.

59 Ibid.

60 Harlow interview.

61 Smith interview. In its opinion in *Lawrence*, the Court mentioned "relationship" or "relationships" 11 times; "intimate" or "intimacy," 10 times; and "private" or "privacy," 28 times. Other than in its quotations from the Texas statute and Deputy Quinn's affidavit, it made no mention of anal sex.

62 Katherine Franke, "The Domesticated Liberty of *Lawrence v. Texas*," *Columbia Law Review* 104 (2004): 1399.

63 Smith interview.

64 Hohengarten interview; Harlow interview; Brief of Petitioners (Merits), *Lawrence v. Texas*, No. 02-102, January 16, 2003 (hereinafter "Pet. Brief on Merits").

65 Harlow interview.

66 Pet. Brief on Merits, p. 9.

67 Harlow interview.

68 381 U.S. 479 (1965). *Griswold* has a familial resemblance to *Lawrence* in more ways than one. Like *Lawrence*, it upheld claims to privacy in the home regarding decisions about sex. More important, the anticontraceptives law struck down in *Griswold* was not enforced against private use in the home. Instead, it was used to shut down family-planning clinics that gave advice and dispensed contraceptives to women who could not afford private doctors: David Garrow, *Liberty and Sexuality* (New York: Macmillan, 1994); Dale Carpenter, "Revisiting *Griswold*: An Exploration of Its Political, Social, and Legal Origins" (senior history essay, Yale College, 1989). In *Lawrence*, there was similarly little enforcement against private activity. The law was more a symbolic statement and its practical effect was in the public realm insofar as it was used to justify broad discrimination against gay men and lesbians.

69 405 U.S. 438 (1972).

70 505 U.S. 833 (1992).

71 Pet. Brief on Merits, p. 26.

72 Harlow interview.

73 Ibid.

74 Smith interview. One of the *amici* supporting Texas, the Center for Marriage Law, suggested that desuetude would "seem more fitting than a constitutional argument" because sodomy laws are rarely enforced: *Amicus* Brief of Center for Marriage Law in Support of Respondent, *Lawrence v. Texas*, No. 02-102 (February 18, 2003), 27.

75 Pet. Brief on Merits, p. 32, n. 24.

76 Hohengarten interview.

77 Smith interview.

78 Pet. Brief on Merits, p. 50.

79 Telephone interview with Susan Sommer (May 13, 2010).

80 Telephone interview with Brian Chase (June 4, 2010).

81 Sommer interview.

82 Harlow interview.

83 530 U.S. 640 (2000).

84 Harlow interview. I was a coauthor of the *amicus* brief by the Republican Unity Coalition. The main author of this brief was Erik Jaffe, a former clerk for Justice Clarence Thomas.

85   Alan Simpson, "Lawrence v. Texas," *Wall Street Journal*, March 26, 2003.

86   Letter from Gerald R. Ford to Charles Francis, March 6, 2003 (available at http:// www.glapn.org/sodomylaws/lawrence/RUCfordLTR.jpg (accessed June 13, 2010).

87   Harlow interview.

88   In addition to Jenner & Block itself, the law firms backing the petitioners included Covington and Burling; Wilmer, Cutler and Pickering; O'Melveny and Myers; White and Case; Debevoise and Plimpton; Irell and Manella; Simpson Thatcher and Barlett; and Baker Botts (a major Houston-based firm).

89   Delmore interview (2005).

90   Brief of Respondent (Merits), *Lawrence v. Texas*, No. 02-102, February 18, 2003, p. 4, (hereinafter "Resp. Brief on Merits").

91   Ibid., p. 6.

92   Ibid., p. 13.

93   Ibid., pp. 6–7.

94   Ibid., p. 14.

95   Ibid., p. 22.

96   Ibid., p. 40 n. 27.

97   Resp. Brief on Merits, p. 48 n. 31.

98   Smith interview.

99   Dale Carpenter, "How the Law Accepted Gays," *New York Times*, April 29, 2011, A27.

100 See, for instance, Brief in Support of Respondent on Behalf of *Amici Curiae* Texas Physicians Resource Council, et al., *Lawrence v. Texas*, No. 02-102 (February 18, 2003), 28 n. 39.

101 Ibid., p. 11.

102 Brief of the States of Alabama, South Carolina, and Utah as *Amici Curiae* in Support of Respondent, *Lawrence v. Texas*, No. 02-102 (February 18, 2003), 17.

103 Brief of Liberty Counsel as *Amicus Curiae* in Support of Respondent, *Lawrence v. Texas*, No. 02-102 (February 18, 2003), 11.

104 Ibid., p. 15.

105 Brief of Liberty Counsel as *Amicus Curiae*, *Lawrence v. Texas*, 18–20.

106 The full text of this "manifesto" is available at http://www.feastofhateandfear .com/archives/homosexual.html (accessed December 11, 2011).

107 Jim Burroway, "The Watchmen in Riga, Part 3: The 'Secrets' of Homosexuality," *Box Turtle Bulletin*, December 3, 2007 (available at http://www.boxturtlebulletin .com/2007/12/03/1057) (accessed December 11, 2011).

108 Brief of *Amici Curiae* Pro-Family Law Center, Traditional Values Coalition, Traditional Values Education and Legal Institute, and James Hartline, in Support of Respondents, *Lawrence v. Texas*, No. 02-102 (February 18, 2003), 15.

109 See, for instance, Brief *Amicus Curiae* of United Families International in Support of Respondent, *Lawrence v. Texas*, No. 02-102 (February 13, 2003), 14: "Neither petitioners nor their *amici* have provided the Court with any principled basis on which it could distinguish sodomy from adultery, incest [between adult relatives], group sex or even prostitution, all of which may be committed in the privacy of the home."

110 Motion for Leave to File Brief *Amicus Curiae* and Brief *Amicus Curiae* of the Center for Law and Justice International Supporting Respondent, *Lawrence v. Texas*, No. 02-102 (February 18, 2003), 16.

111 Ibid., p. 17.

112 Brief of *Amici Curiae* Pro-Family Law Center, Traditional Values Coalition, et al., *Lawrence v. Texas*, 3.

113 Ibid., p. 2.

114 *Amicus* Brief of the American Center for Law and Justice, *Lawrence v. Texas*, 19.

115 Brief *Amicus Curiae* of the Family Research Council, Inc., and Focus on the Family in Support of Respondent, *Lawrence v. Texas*, No. 02-102 (Feb. 18, 2003), 17.

116 Brief of *Amici Curiae* Pro-Family Law Center, Traditional Values Coalition, et al., *Lawrence v. Texas*, 29.

117 Sommer interview.

118 Hohengarten interview.

119 Delmore interview (2005).

120 Brief of Petitioners (Merits), *Lawrence v. Texas*, No. 02-102 (March 10, 2003), 10 (hereinafter "Pet. Reply Brief").

121 Ibid., n. 10. See also ibid., p. 19.

122 Ibid., pp. 15–16.

123 See Brief of the American Public Health Association, National Mental Health Association, American Orthopsychiatric Association, AIDS Action, National Alliance of State and Territorial AIDS Directors, Association of Nurses in AIDS Care, National Minority AIDS Council, and the Whitman-Walker Clinic as *Amici Curiae* in Support of Petitioners, *Lawrence v. Texas*, No. 02-102 (January 16, 2003), 14–15.

124 Pet. Reply Brief, pp. 16–19.

Chapter 15: *Mismatch at the Supreme Court*

1 Laurence Tribe, *American Constitutional Law*, 3rd ed. (New York: Foundation Press, 1999). Citing time constraints, Professor Tribe declined to be interviewed for this book.

2 William Eskridge, *Dishonorable Passions: Sodomy Laws in America, 1861–2003* (New York: Viking, 2008), 242.

3 Joyce Murdoch and Deb Price, *Courting Justice: Gay Men and Lesbians v. the Supreme Court* (2001; repr., New York: Basic Books, 2002), 294.

4 Quoted in ibid., 302.

5 Ibid., 303.

6 Interview with William Hohengarten, Washington, D.C. (May 16, 2007).

7 Interview with Ruth Harlow, New York City (April 25, 2007); Hohengarten interview.

8 Hohengarten interview.

9 Harlow interview.

10 Interview with Paul Smith, New York City (April 23, 2007).

11 Harlow interview.

12 Smith interview.

13 Murdoch and Price, *Courting Justice*, 339–40; Anand Agneshwar, "Ex-Justice Says He May Have Been Wrong," *National Law Journal* (November 5, 1990), 3; John C. Jeffries Jr., *Justice Lewis F. Powell* (New York: Scribner, 1994), 530.

14 Murdoch and Price, *Courting Justice*, 342.

15 Smith interview.

16 Ibid.; Harlow interview; Hohengarten interview; telephone interview with Susan Sommer (May 13, 2010).

17 Smith interview.

18 The material in this section is based on my interview in Houston with William Delmore (June 30, 2005). Through a spokesperson at the Harris County D.A.'s office, Rosenthal declined to be interviewed for this book.

19 Harlow interview; interview with John Lawrence, Houston (June 14, 2005). Tyron Garner did not attend the oral arguments at the Supreme Court, although neither Harlow nor Lawrence could recall why; in our interview, Garner wasn't exactly sure either, but thought he probably stayed in Texas to nurse his dying parents: interview with Tyron Garner, Houston (June 28, 2005).

20 Interview with Mitchell Katine, Houston (June 17, 2005).

21 Telephone interview with Lindsay Harrison (May 5, 2010). Except where noted, the following discussion about the scene in front of the Court draws on my interview with Harrison.

22 Edward Walsh, "Justices Hear Challenge to Texas Sodomy Law," *Washington Post*, March 27, 2003.

23 Telephone interview with Bob Summersgill (June 4, 2010). Summersgill was the president of the Gay and Lesbian Activists Alliance, a Washington, D.C., gay-rights group, in 2003. He arrived at five o'clock that morning, so he had no chance to get a seat for the argument.

24 In an appearance on *Fox News Sunday* on March 6, 2011, Marge Phelps recounted her group's protest in front of Supreme Court on the morning of the oral argument in *Lawrence v. Texas*. The actual greeting, uttered by the Court's marshal every time the Justices enter the Court, is: "The Honorable, the Chief Justice, and the Associate Justices of the Supreme Court of the United States. Oyez oyez oyez. All persons having business before the Honorable, the Supreme Court of the United States, are admonished to draw near and give their attention, for the Court is now sitting. God save the United States and this honorable Court." Available at http://www.oyez.org/tour/courtroom/marshal_detail/ (accessed March 6, 2011).

25 Summersgill interview; Bob Summersgill, personal account of the oral argument (available at http://www.glapn.org/sodomylaws/lawrence/lwnews160.htm) (accessed on May 23, 2010). I have found no independent press account of the encounter between the students and antigay protesters. By itself, this is not surprising. Most reporters were there to cover the oral argument itself, not the crowd outside, and either were inside the press box of the courtroom or had not yet arrived.

26 E-mail from Bob Summersgill to Dale Carpenter, May 24, 2010; Summersgill interview. Lambda's Susan Sommer heard a similar version of this event: Sommer interview. Summersgill observed that the confrontation sent the perfect message: "If you're antigay, you're anti-American."

27 Smith interview.

28 The case was *Overton v. Bazetta*, 539 U.S. 126 (2003).

29 Katine interview (2005).

30 Smith interview.

31 Sommer interview.

32 Lawrence interview (2005).

33 Smith interview.

34 Interview with John Lawrence, Houston (April 22, 2011).

35 I was present at the oral argument, seated next to RUC chairman Charles Francis and Erik Jaffe, my coauthor on the RUC brief. Jaffe arranged for us to get reserved seats through Justice Thomas, for whom he had clerked in the 1996–97 term. Some of the descriptions and impressions of the oral argument that follow are based on my own recollection of the event.

36 The quotes from the oral argument are drawn from the official transcript, available

at http://www.supremecourt.gov/oral_arguments/argument_transcripts/02-102 .pdf (accessed May 24, 2010). Interested readers may listen to an audio recording of the oral argument, synchronized with the transcript, at http://www.oyez.org/ cases/2000-2009/2002/2002_02_102/argument (accessed May 24, 2010).

37 Harlow interview. Smith was unsure whether Scalia intended a bawdy reference, but also thought it was probably a Freudian slip: Smith interview. For what it's worth, I also thought the double meaning was unintentional. Scalia betrayed no hint of mischief or humor when asking the question.

38 *Barnes v. Glen Theatre, Inc.*, 501 U.S. 560, 574 (1991) (Scalia, J., concurring).

39 Harrison interview.

40 Smith interview.

41 Delmore interview (2005).

42 Smith interview.

43 Harlow interview; Smith interview.

44 Smith interview.

45 Ibid.

46 Ibid.

47 Ibid.

48 One prominent criticism of the autonomy arguments for gay rights in *Bowers* was that they asked only for a grudging tolerance, not full appreciation of the normative good of gay relationships: Michael Sandel, "Moral Argument and Liberal Toleration: Abortion and Homosexuality," *California Law Review* 77 (1989): 521–38.

49 Smith interview.

50 Ibid.

51 Harlow interview.

52 Smith interview. The *amicus* briefs, especially the one filed by gay civil rights groups, highlighted the dramatic changes toward equality in American law post-*Bowers*.

53 Delmore interview (2005).

54 Smith interview.

55 Ibid.

56 Eskridge, *Dishonorable Passions*, 324.

57 Katine interview (2005).

58 William N. Eskridge Jr., *Gaylaw: Challenging the Apartheid of the Closet* (Cambridge, Mass.: Harvard University Press, 1999), 149; Murdoch and Price, *Courting Justice*, 344 (*Bowers* was announced at the same time as "Bowers's ex-mistress was revealing his sodomous exploits").

59 Mike Tolson, "Rosenthal's Ex-Secretary Quits Rather than Switch Jobs," *Houston Chronicle*, March 27, 2008. Rosenthal admitted having an affair with his secretary in the 1980s, after numerous amorous e-mails sent to her were divulged in late 2007.

60 Here Rosenthal was apparently referring to the *amici* supporting Texas.

61 Hohengarten interview.

62 Delmore interview (2005).

63 Smith interview.

64 Linda Greenhouse, "Supreme Court Seems Set to Reverse a Sodomy Law," *New York Times*, March 27, 2003.

65 Lawrence interview (2005).

66 Smith interview.

67 Ibid.
68 Ibid.
69 Murdoch and Price, *Courting Justice*, 302.
70 Eskridge, *Dishonorable Passions*, 242.
71 Carolyn Lockhead, "Landmark Gay Ruling May Put Bush in Bind," *San Francisco Chronicle*, June 15, 2003.
72 Harlow interview.
73 Smith interview.
74 "Seven in Ten Adult Americans Support U.S. Supreme Court Overturning Same-Sex Sodomy Laws" (results of online poll by Witeck-Combs Communications and Harris Interactive) (available at http://www.harrisinteractive.com/news/all newsbydate.asp?NewsID=616) (accessed May 27, 2010).

Chapter 16: *Respect for Their Private Lives*

1 Some of what follows is based on the standard Supreme Court protocol available at the website for the United States courts, available at http://www.uscourts.gov/ EducationalResources/ConstitutionResources/SeparationOfPowers/USSupreme CourtProcedures.aspx (accessed June 3, 2010).
2 Anonymous Supreme Court insider interview.
3 Jeffrey Toobin, *The Nine: Inside the Secret World of the Court* (New York: Doubleday, 2007), 189.
4 Interview with William Hohengarten, Washington, D.C. (May 16, 2007).
5 539 U.S. 306 (2003).
6 539 U.S. 244 (2003).
7 Cecilia M. Vega, "Gays Await Rights Ruling from Supreme Court," *Santa Rosa Press-Democrat*, June 6, 2003.
8 Interview with Ruth Harlow, New York City (April 25, 2007).
9 Hohengarten interview.
10 A transcript and accompanying audio recording can be found at the website Oyez, http://www.oyez.org/cases/2000-2009/2002/2002_02_102/opinion (accessed May 24, 2010).
11 Hohengarten interview.
12 Telephone interview with Susan Sommer (May 13, 2010).
13 Interview with Mitchell Katine, Houston (June 17, 2005).
14 Interview with John Lawrence, Houston (June 14, 2005).
15 Interview with Tyron Garner, Houston (June 28, 2005).
16 Toobin, *The Nine*, 189.
17 Harlow interview.
18 Hohengarten interview.
19 432 U.S. 678 (1977) (striking down a state law forbidding the distribution of contraceptives to minors under sixteen).
20 *Lawrence v. Texas*, 539 U.S. 558, 579 (2003) (O'Connor, J., concurring).
21 Toobin, *The Nine*, 190; Linda Greenhouse, "Justices, 6–3, Legalize Gay Sexual Conduct in Sweeping Reversal of Court's '86 Ruling," *New York Times*, June 27, 2003.
22 347 U.S. 483 (1954).
23 163 U.S. 537 (1896).
24 Indeed, the Court suggested in *Brown* that *Plessy* might have been *right* in its particular time and place, noting that circumstances in American public education

and in the psychological understanding of the effect of segregation had changed considerably in the intervening fifty-eight years.

25 *Lawrence*, 539 U.S. at 567.

26 Ibid.

27 "'Our obligation is to define the liberty of all, not to mandate our own moral code.'" Quoting *Planned Parenthood of Southeastern Pa. v. Casey*, 505 U.S. 833, 850 (1992).

28 *Lawrence*, 539 U.S. at 578–79.

29 Harlow interview.

30 *Lawrence*, 539 U.S. at 558, 605–6 (Thomas, J., dissenting).

31 Interview with Paul Smith, New York City (April 23, 2007).

32 Greenhouse, "Justices, 6–3, Legalize Gay Sexual Conduct."

33 Lawrence interview (2005).

34 Katine interview (2005).

35 Garner interview.

36 Harlow interview.

37 Greenhouse, "Justices, 6–3, Legalize Gay Sexual Conduct."

38 "Quotes on Gay Sex Ban Ruling," Associated Press, June 26, 2003 (available at http://www.glapn.org/sodomylaws/lawrence/lwnews189.htm) (accessed May 30, 2010).

39 Brian Rogers and Peggy O'Hare, "Rosenthal Cites Prescription Drugs in Decision to Quit DA Post," *Houston Chronicle*, February 16, 2008; Mike Tolson "Rosenthal's Ex-Secretary Quits Rather than Switch Jobs," *Houston Chronicle*, March 27, 2008. In our interview in Houston in 2005, almost three years before the affair was revealed, Delmore called Rosenthal "a very private person": Delmore interview.

40 Dean E. Murphy, "Gays Celebrate, and Plan Campaign for Broader Rights," *New York Times*, June 27, 2003.

41 Delmore interview (2005).

42 Murphy, "Gays Celebrate."

43 Interview with Joseph Quinn, Houston (June 20, 2005).

44 Telephone interview with Joseph Quinn (August 9 and 31, 2003).

45 Interview with William Lilly, Houston (June 23, 2005).

46 Telephone interview with Donald Tipps (August 15, 2003). This distinction between homosexual acts and gays as people—captured by the phrase "love the sinner, hate the sin"—is a classic formulation of the opposition to gay equality.

47 Interview with Nathan Broussard, Houston (June 20, 2005).

48 Interview with Mike Parrott, Houston (June 22, 2005); interview with Sheryl Roppolo, Houston (June 20, 2005).

49 Telephone interview with Mike Parrott (August 6, 2003).

50 Interview with Angela Beavers, Houston (April 17, 2007).

51 Interview with Judge Sherman Ross, Houston (April 17, 2007).

52 Interview with Judge Paul Clarence Murphy, Houston (May 15, 2007).

53 Interview with Annise Parker, Houston (June 27, 2005).

54 Neil A. Lewis, "Conservatives Furious over Court's Direction," *New York Times*, June 27, 2003.

55 William Eskridge, *Dishonorable Passions: Sodomy Laws in America, 1861–2003* (New York: Viking, 2008), 327. Eskridge reports that this impromptu prayer meeting occurred but gives no source, and I have been unable to verify it independently.

56 United States Conference of Catholic Bishops "Conference President Criticizes Supreme Court Decision," press release, June 27, 2003 (available at http://www .glapn.org/sodomylaws/lawrence/lwnews090.htm) (accessed May 30, 2010).

57 Eskridge, *Dishonorable Passions*, 327–28.

58 Lola Alapo, "Local Reaction Mixed on Gay Sex Ruling," *Knoxville News Sentinel*, June 27, 2003.

59 Quoted in Lewis, "Conservatives Furious over Court's Direction."

60 Eskridge, *Dishonorable Passions*, 330.

61 Cait Purinton, "Court Invalidates Kansas Law; Reaction Mixed," *Topeka Capital-Journal*, June 26, 2003.

62 "Conservative Arkansas Governor Supports Sodomy Ruling," *The Advocate*, July 4, 2003.

63 Lawrence interview (2005).

64 Dale Carpenter, "Gov. Bush, Sodomy Law Defender," *Independent Gay Forum*, September 13, 1999 (available at http://www.indegayforum.org/news/show/26683. html) (accessed May 30, 2010).

65 Greenhouse, "Justices, 6–3, Legalize Gay Sexual Conduct."

66 Beth Shapiro, "Supreme Court Ruling Celebrated from Stonewall to Golden Gate," 365Gay.com, June 27, 2003 (available at http://www.glapn.org/sodomy laws/lawrence/lwnews133.htm) (accessed May 30, 2010).

67 Amy Jenniges, "Sodom and Seattle: Supreme Court Sodomy Ruling Reactivates Gay Activists," *The Stranger*, June 26–July 1, 2003 (available at http://www.the stranger.com/current/city2.html) (accessed May 30, 2010).

68 Gary D. Robertson, "N.C. Gay Rights Groups Applaud Supreme Court's Sodomy Ruling," *Charlotte Observer*, June 26, 2003.

69 *Ex Parte H.H.*, 2002 Ala. Lexis 44 (February 15, 2002) (Moore concurring).

70 Jay Reeves, "Alabama Gay Group Praises Court Ruling on Sodomy Law," Associated Press, June 26, 2003 (available at http://www.glapn.org/sodomylaws/law rence/lwnews123.htm) (accessed May 30, 2010).

71 Missouri's Anti-Sodomy Law Similar to Texas Case," KOLR10-TV (Springfield, MO), June 26, 2003 (available at http://www.glapn.org/sodomylaws/lawrence/ lwnews186.htm) (accessed May 30, 2010).

72 Hohengarten interview.

73 Telephone interview with Jon W. Davidson (June 15, 2010).

74 Shapiro, "Supreme Court Ruling Celebrated."

75 Smith interview.

76 Telephone interview with Gilbert Baker (June 16, 2010).

77 Telephone interview with Teddy Witherington (June 4, 2010).

78 Ibid.; Tom Musbach, "Ruling Sparks Revelry, Political Jockeying," Gay.com/Planet Out.com Network, June 26, 2003 (available at http://www.glapn.org/sodomy laws/lawrence/lwnews050.htm) (accessed May 30, 2010); Shapiro, "Supreme Court Ruling Celebrated."

79 Murphy, "Gays Celebrate"; Matthew S. Bajko, "SF Gays Overjoyed at Sodomy Ruling," *Bay Area Reporter*, July 3, 2003.

80 Oral recording of post-*Lawrence* press conference, Houston, June 26, 2003 (recording on file with author). The account of the press conference that follows is drawn from this recording.

81 Bruce Nichols, "Men Whose Sodomy Case Led to Supreme Court Ruling Keep Low Profile," *Dallas Morning News*, June 27, 2003.

82 Oral recording of post-*Lawrence* rally, Houston, June 26, 2003 (recording on file

with author). Unless otherwise noted, the account of the rally that follows is drawn from this recording.

83 Parker interview; Katine interview (2005).

84 Garner interview.

85 Telephone interview with Lane Lewis (August 7 and 8, 2003).

86 Ibid.

87 *Olmstead v. United States*, 277 U.S. 438, 478 (1928). See also Louis Brandeis and Samuel D. Warren, "The Right to Privacy," *Harvard Law Review* 4 (1890), 193.

88 Interview with John Lawrence, Houston (April 22, 2011).

89 Lawrence interview (2005).

90 Garner interview.

91 Ibid.

Epilogue: *Sweet Land of Liberty*

1 Interview with Mitchell Katine, Houston (April 22, 2011).

2 Douglas Martin, "Tyron Garner, 39, Plaintiff in Gay Sodomy Case," *New York Times*, September 14, 2006.

3 Interview with John Lawrence, Houston (April 22, 2011).

4 E-mail exchange between author and Mitchell Katine (September 27, 2006, and October 18, 2006) (on file with author).

5 Katine interview (2011).

6 Interview with Mitchell Katine, Houston (June 17, 2005).

7 *Lawrence*, 539 U.S. 558 at (respectively) 562, 574 (quoting *Planned Parenthood v. Casey*, 505 U.S. 833, 851 [1992]), 578 (2003).

8 Laurence Tribe, "*Lawrence v. Texas*: The 'Fundamental Right' That Dare Not Speak Its Name," *Harvard Law Review* 117 (2004): 1893, 1904–05.

9 *Lawrence*, 539 U.S. at 578.

10 Carlos Maza, "State Sodomy Laws Continue to Target LGBT Americans," *Equality Matters*, August 8, 2011 (available at http://equalitymatters.org/print/blog/201108080012) (accessed October 20, 2011).

11 Courts in some states continue to view a parent's homosexuality as a negative factor in child-custody and visitation decisions.

12 Ibid., at 567.

Bibliography

BOOKS

Blackstone, William, *Commentaries on the Laws of England*. 1769.

Bryant, Anita. *The Anita Bryant Story: The Survival of Our Nation's Families and the Threat of Militant Homosexuality*. Old Tappan, N.J.: Revell, 1977.

Chauncey, George. *Gay New York: Gender, Urban Culture, and the Making of the Gay Male World, 1890–1940*. New York: Basic Books, 1994.

Chitty, Joseph. *A Practical Treatise on the Criminal Law*. Vol. 2. 1847.

D'Emilio, John. "Gay Politics and Community in San Francisco Since World War II." In *Hidden from History: Reclaiming the Gay and Lesbian Past*, edited by Martin Bauml Duberman, Martha Vicinus, and George Chauncey Jr., 456–73. New York: Meridian, 1990.

———. *Sexual Politics, Sexual Communities: The Making of a Homosexual Minority in the United States, 1940–1970*. Chicago: University of Chicago Press, 1983.

Desty, Robert. *A Compendium of American Criminal Law*. 1882.

Duberman, Martin. *Stonewall*. New York: Dutton, 1993.

Eskridge, William. *Dishonorable Passions: Sodomy Laws in America, 1861–2003*. New York: Viking, 2008.

———. *Gaylaw: Challenging the Apartheid of the Closet*. Cambridge, Mass.: Harvard University Press, 1999.

Garrow, David. *Liberty and Sexuality*. New York: Macmillan, 1994.

Greenhouse, Linda. *Becoming Justice Blackmun: Harry Blackmun's Supreme Court Journey*. New York: Henry Holt, 2006.

Higgeson, Francis. "Francis Higgeson's Journal (entry of June 29, 1629)." In *The Founding of Massachusetts*. Boston: Massachusetts Historical Society, 1930.

Jeffries, John C., Jr. *Justice Lewis F. Powell*. New York: Scribner, 1994.

Johnson, David K. *The Lavender Scare: The Cold War Persecution of Gays and Lesbians in the Federal Government*. Chicago: University of Chicago Press, 2004.

Kaiser, Charles. *The Gay Metropolis: 1940–96*. Boston: Houghton Mifflin, 1997.

Katz, Jonathan Ned. *Gay/Lesbian Almanac*. New York: Carroll & Graf, 1994.

Kilty, William, ed. *Report of All Such English Statutes as Existed at the Times of the First Emigration of the People of Maryland*. Annapolis, Md.: John Chandler, 1811.

Law, Janice. *Sex Appealed: Was the U.S. Supreme Court Fooled?* Austin: Eakin Press, 2005.

May, John Wilder. *The Law of Crimes*. 1881.

Murdoch, Joyce, and Deb Price. *Courting Justice: Gay Men and Lesbians v. the Supreme Court*. 2001. Reprint, New York: Basic Books, 2002.

Olsen, Jack. *The Man with the Candy*. New York: Simon & Schuster, 1975.

Powers, Edwin. *Crime and Punishment in Early Massachusetts: 1620–1692*. Boston: Beacon, 1966.

Rubenstein, William B., ed. *Cases and Materials on Sexual Orientation and the Law*, 2d ed. St. Paul, Minn.: West, 1997.

Sears, James T. *Rebels, Rubyfruit, and Rhinestones*. New Brunswick, N.J.: Rutgers University Press, 2001.

Sedgwick, Eve Kosofsky. *Epistemology of the Closet*. Berkeley: University of California Press, 1990.

Shurtleff, Nathaniel B., ed. *Records of the Governor and Company of the Massachusetts Bay Colony. . . .* Vol. I. Boston: William White, 1853–54.

Spencer, Colin. *Homosexuality in History*. New York: Harcourt Brace, 1995.

Strachey, William. *For the Colony in Virginea Britannia, Lavves Diuine, Morall and Martiall, &c.* In *Tracts and Other Papers, Relating Principally to the Origin, Settlement, and Progress of the Colonies in North America.* Compiled by Peter Force. 1844. Reprint, New York: Peter Smith, 1947.

Toobin, Jeffrey. *The Nine: Inside the Secret World of the Court*. New York: Doubleday, 2007.

Tribe, Laurence. *American Constitutional Law*, 3d ed. New York: Foundation Press, 1999.

Whitmore, William H., ed. *The Colonial Laws of Massachusetts*. Boston: Rockwell and Churchill, 1890.

Woods, James D. *The Corporate Closet*. New York: Free Press, 1993.

Yoshino, Kenji. *Covering: The Hidden Assault on Our Civil Rights*. New York: Random House, 2006.

ARTICLES AND ESSAYS

Agneshwar, Anand. "Ex-Justice Says He May Have Been Wrong." *National Law Journal* 3 (November 5, 1990).

Amnesty International. "Stonewalled: Police Abuse and Misconduct Against Lesbian, Gay, Bisexual and Transgender People in the U.S." 2005. http://www.amnestyusa .org/outfront/stonewalled/report.pdf.

Carpenter, Dale. "Expressive Association and Antidiscrimination Law After *Dale*: A Tripartite Approach." *Minnesota Law Review* 85 (2001): 1515–90.

———. "Revisiting *Griswold*: An Exploration of Its Political, Social, and Legal Origins." Senior history essay, Yale College, 1989 (on file with author).

———. "The Unknown Past of *Lawrence v. Texas*." *Michigan Law Review* 102 (2004): 1464–1527.

Cloud, Morgan. "The Dirty Little Secret." *Emory Law Journal* 43 (1994): 1311–50.

Dripps, Donald A. "Police, Plus Perjury, Equals Polygraphy." *Journal of Criminal Law and Criminology* 86 (1996): 693–716.

Fisher, Stanley Z. "'Just the Facts, Ma'am': Lying and the Omission of Exculpatory Evidence in Police Reports." *New England Law Review* 28 (1993–94): 1–62.

Franke, Katherine. "The Domesticated Liberty of *Lawrence v. Texas*." *Columbia Law Review* 104 (2004): 1399–1426.

Haskins, George L. "The Capitall Lawes of New England." *Harvard Law School Bulletin* 7 (1976): 10–11.

Hernandez-Truyol, Berta E. "Querying *Lawrence*." *Ohio State Law Journal* 65 (2004): 1151–1264.

Hunter, Nan. "Life After *Hardwick*." *Harvard Civil Rights–Civil Liberties Law Review* 27 (1992): 531–54.

Koppelman, Andrew. "Why Discrimination Against Lesbians and Gay Men Is Sex Discrimination." *New York University Law Review* 69 (1994): 197–287.

"*Lawrence v. Texas* Symposium: Introduction and Panel Discussion; Transcription of Proceedings, February 13, 2004." *South Texas Law Review* 46 (2004): 323–51.

Leslie, Christopher R. "Creating Criminals: The Injuries Inflicted by 'Unenforced' Sodomy Laws." *Harvard Civil Rights–Civil Liberties Law Review* 35 (2000): 103–82.

Orfield, Myron W., Jr. "Deterrence, Perjury, and the Heater Factor: An Exclusionary Rule in the Chicago Criminal Courts." *University of Colorado Law Review* 63 (1992): 75–162.

Painter, George. "The Sensibilities of Our Forefathers (Texas)." Sodomylaws.org, http://www.sodomylaws.org/sensibilities/texas.htm.

Roots, Roger. "Are Cops Constitutional?" *Seton Hall Constitutional Law Journal* 11 (2001): 685–758.

Sandel, Michael. "Moral Argument and Liberal Toleration: Abortion and Homosexuality." *California Law Review* 77 (1989): 521–38.

Slobogin, Christopher. "Testifying: Police Perjury and What to Do About It." *University of Colorado Law Review* 67 (1996): 1037–60.

Sunstein, Cass. "What Did *Lawrence* Hold? Autonomy, Desuetude, Sexuality, and Marriage." *Supreme Court Review* 2003 (2003): 27–74.

Thomas, Kendall. "Beyond the Privacy Principle." *Columbia Law Review* 92 (1992): 1431–1516.

Tribe, Laurence. "*Lawrence v. Texas*: The 'Fundamental Right' That Dare Not Speak Its Name." *Harvard Law Review* 117 (2004): 1893–1956.

Wolfson, Evan, and Robert S. Mower. "When the Police Are in Our Bedrooms, Shouldn't the Courts Go In After Them? An Update on the Fight Against 'Sodomy' Laws." *Fordham Urban Law Journal* 21 (1994): 997–1056.

Woods, Jordan Blair. "Don't Tap, Don't Stare, and Keep Your Hands to Yourself! Critiquing the Legality of Gay Sting Operations." *Journal of Gender, Race and Justice* 12 (2008–09): 545–78.

Index

About the Author

Raised in Corpus Christi, Texas, Dale Carpenter first began researching the *Lawrence v. Texas* decision in 2003 and published an article in the *Michigan Law Review* on the background of the case in 2004. The Earl R. Larson Professor of Civil Rights and Civil Liberties Law at the University of Minnesota, he teaches and writes in the areas of constitutional law, the First Amendment, and sexual orientation and the law. In 1989, he received his BA degree in history, magna cum laude, from Yale College. In 1992, he earned his JD, with honors, from the University of Chicago Law School. At the University of Chicago he was editor-in-chief of the law review. He received a prize for excellence in legal scholarship and the John M. Olin Foundation Scholarship for Law & Economics. Professor Carpenter clerked for the Honorable Edith H. Jones of the United States Court of Appeals for the Fifth Circuit from 1992 to 1993. After his clerkship, he practiced from 1993 to 1999 at Vinson & Elkins, a law firm in Houston, where he was active in gay civil rights work. Moving to San Francisco, he then worked for Howard, Rice, Nemerovski, Canady, Falk & Rabkin from 1999 to 2000.

Carpenter joined the faculty of the University of Minnesota Law School in 2000 and is a member of the state bars of Texas and California. He is a frequent television, radio, and print commentator, with his work appearing in the *New York Times*, the *Chicago Sun*, the Minneapolis *Star Tribune*, the *Houston Chronicle*, and other publications. He also writes for the legal blog *The Volokh Conspiracy*.

Professor Carpenter coauthored an *amicus* brief in support of the petitioners in *Lawrence v. Texas*.